Battle Hymn

REVELATIONS OF THE SINISTER PLAN FOR A NEW WORLD ORDER

John Scura

Dane Phillips

Black Rose Writing

www.blackrosewriting.com

The final approval for this literary material is granted by the author.

Second printing

All characters appearing in this work are real. This work is meant to inform, in a journalistic style and representation.

ISBN: 978-1-61296-043-2

PUBLISHED BY BLACK ROSE WRITING

www.blackrosewriting.com

Printed in the United States of America

Battle Hymn is printed in Times New Roman

To Ed and Margo

Also

To all of the Children, Survivors & those who have suffered
The Phillips Family & Friends
The Body of Christ, Calvary Chapel & the Lord's House
Keith Green & Family
Presidents Jackson, Lincoln & Kennedy
Rep. Louis T. McFadden
Ty & Renee — The Ziegel & Kline Families
Brooke Army Medical Center
Gary Caradori & Family
Army Navy Academy & Penn Military Institute
Delta Sigs — The Brothers & Sisters

Special thanks to:

Elisa Weeks — A truly beautiful and courageous lady
Dr. A. True Ott — My brother in truth & spirit
Ted Gunderson, Sen. John DeCamp, Ron Patton & Sen. Loran Schmit
Ginger Tafoya, Grant Dunmire, Bob Dempsey & Ginny Deering

September 11, 2001 — We shall never forget

America — Our patriots are coming to take this country back

The Black Robe Regiment — It's time to stand up and speak out

TABLE OF CONTENTS

TABLE OF CONTENTS CONT...

TABLE OF CONTENTS CONT...

Battle Hymn

REVELATIONS OF THE SINISTER PLAN

FOR A NEW WORLD ORDER

PRELUDE

What you are about to read may frighten you. It should enrage you. It may even sicken you. No matter how you react, the facts, evidence and expert opinions offered in the following pages will stay with you and perhaps alter your outlook forever.

The purpose of this book is quite simple: to offer evidence of a centuries-old plan for total world domination by a few elites — a plan that, at this writing, is very nearly realized. To the uninitiated, this may sound like paranoia. I wish I could agree.

When Dane Phillips approached me with an offer to write this book six months ago, I insisted on doing my own independent research. Dane already had created the websites BattleHymn.com and BBNWorld-News.com, which cover the same subject and most of its many aspects. Dane purchased the domain names at personal expense in order to create a brand for what had become a personal passion. His site has a fundamentalist Christian slant, which I felt was effective with those people who already believed the material offered, but would not appeal to those of us who are not involved in the conservative Christian movement. I wanted to take a different, but parallel course.

Dane and I have been friends since our college days at Loyola University in Los Angeles. We lived in the same fraternity house on the beach in Playa Del Rey, shared the usual youthful adventures, and remained as friends throughout the years that followed. This foundation produced a strong trust, and allowed me to work without interference in creating a secular, sober, journalistic offering of the subject matter. I thank Dane for that trust and consideration.

When I first undertook this project, I was a skeptic. I even used the term "lunatic fringe" to describe the people who saw conspiracies in wars, revolutions, plagues and the 9/11 attacks. For this reason, I deliberately avoid using the word conspiracy in the body of this work, because I believe that we have been conditioned by our media to discount any arguments that suggest such a thing. Decades of criticism and ridicule by the mainstream newspapers, magazines and TV news have marginalized even the best reportage on any matter that contradicts the orthodox and official view of things.

But the journalist's job is to gather evidence and go where it leads,

1

no matter how disturbing or bizarre the endpoint of that journey may become. Like a trial lawyer preparing a case, a journalist must collect facts in documents, eyewitness testimony, visual and audio recordings, expert opinion and various other channels to create a convincing argument. I hope I have done that.

The journey you are about to begin will take you through myriad aspects related to the plans and deeds that are intended to create a New World Order of one government, one justice system and one religion — all under the complete control of an unelected elite. This small cabal of powerful men will rule from the shadows through selected agents, posing as political leaders, who will do their bidding. They will have the ability to control populations through propaganda, fear, and if necessary, force, owing to their empire over the press, the police, the politicians, the judges and the military. You will learn how far along they are in completing this control.

This book contains nine sections, each dealing with different aspects of the story. The principals who currently work toward these goals are introduced immediately. In many cases, they state their intentions clearly in their own words. Certainly they have revealed their intentions in their deeds. If anything should be garnered from this first section, it is the fact that their scheme for control is generational, going back to at least the 18th century.

The second section, "Confederacies of Dunces" (with apologies to the late John Kennedy Toole), refers not to the men at the apex of the modern secret societies, but to those men and women who make up the outer echelon of groups like the Council on Foreign Relations, the Trilateral Commission and the Bilderberg Group. These well-meaning people unwittingly do the work of those few at the top of each group's carefully crafted pyramid in an aged system designed for manipulation. The underlings, proud to have been invited to join such elite organizations, eagerly work to promote policies friendly to the master plan as political advisors, military personnel, intelligence agents, religious leaders and corporate leaders.

The older secret societies and their mandates appear in the third section, where the reader will learn that what is taking place now was set in motion long ago. How these protocols have taken hold in America is the subject of the following section, and it truly is a "trail of tears." The struggle to establish a privately owned central bank in the United States extends from Alexander Hamilton to Woodrow Wilson, when the European interests finally succeeded in saddling Americans with the Federal Reserve System. This entity is the sacred cow of the international bankers, and anyone who threatens it, including US presidents, is ruthlessly eliminated, as you will learn in the disturbing conclusion of this section.

Most of us do not realize the degree of control our democratic system has gathered over Americans in the last half century. This is the topic of the next section, a look at how the oligarchs steadily have added the entire US media, science, politics, the economy and our children's education to their list of holdings. All that remains in the way of total control is to tag every individual electronically, and you will learn that legislation for this already is written.

What do the elite plan to do with this control? Their dark plans are the subject of the next section, which reveals programs already underway that are so ruthless and so cruel as to stagger credibility. The average mind rebels against such charges, but the evidence of words and deeds is impossible to ignore.

Underscoring the complete lack of compassion for humanity among the elite, I've offered a detailed history of how wars and revolutions have been instigated and managed with the intent to create national debt and gather great riches. Many millions have died or have been permanently maimed in all the wars involving America, from the Revolution to Iraq. This is meaningless to those who believe the end always justifies the means, and their end has been realized through battle — the theft of the world's physical and monetary wealth at the expense of populations they look upon as mere livestock.

The extent of their ruthlessness reveals itself in the events of September 11, 2001. I ask the reader, in the words of Thomas Huxley, to sit down before facts as a child, as I had to do in researching this awful chapter of American history. The episode of 9/11 is still fraught with emotion, and I already have received sharp reactions from people for simply looking into what happened that day. My purpose is not to form an opinion or draw conclusions in this section of the book. I simply have gathered evidence and offer it for the readers to decide for themselves whether this tragedy was a premeditated giant step toward realizing globalist goals.

I deliberately saved the section titled "Through the Looking Glass" for the book's end, partially because its "Alice in Wonderland" aspect would be incredible unless all the more credible information on this subject has been previously digested. The stories may seem like science fiction. Unfortunately they are quite true and, like the rest of the information in this book, are documented and available online to all those who wish to see for themselves.

The only nebulous tales are those of the mind control victims, whose claims easily can be credited to delusion since all of them suffer from Multiple Personality Disorder. Indeed, this has been the almost universal initial opinion of therapists who have worked with them, until it became clear that these victims — never having met — tell the same stories.

I chose to use the information I received from one of these victims as both the first and last chapters of this book. It was not for the sake of sensationalism (though her testimony certainly is sensational), but because she is the only mind control victim to have solid corroboration of her story from witnesses.

I hope the reader will not be annoyed that I have constructed this book like a symphony. "The Battle Hymn of the Republic" was, after all, a musical piece. I believe it also was a prayer, applicable to the revelations that follow, for if there is a recurring theme in this book, it is the ruthlessness of the persons attempting to enact their New World Order.

The following material is liberally littered with the bodies of those courageous patriotic men and women who were murdered or who died in suspicious circumstances because they posed a threat. Their deaths prove the ruthlessness of the globalist planners.

Battle Hymn co-author, Dane Phillips, came close to death when a front tire on his truck inexplicably exploded on a freeway in September 2010, as he drove home from a private summit he had organized in Ogden, Utah, which exposed government-sponsored child trafficking in the United States. This experience only deepened Dane's resolve, commitment to activism and never back down attitude to accomplish the extraordinary – to awaken a sleeping nation.

The first step before action is knowledge. I hope that the material in this book will provide at least a bit of that knowledge, enough to fire curiosity and a hunger for more knowledge. Perhaps this will spur action before it is too late. If not, I fear the world that our children and grandchildren inherit from us will have passed into a new Dark Age.

John Scura
Los Angeles, California
November 2010

Battle Hymn

OVERTURE - *ARIETTA*

"The individual is handicapped by coming face to face with a conspiracy so monstrous he cannot believe it exists. The American mind simply has not come to the realization of the evil which has been introduced to our midst."

—J. Edgar Hoover, from the *Elks Magazine*, August 1956

The Honey Trap

She has come to Las Vegas to kill. It has nothing to do with gambling. Her killing will not be at the dice or blackjack tables. It will be in a suite in one of the posh hotel-casinos on the Strip.

She feels eyes following her as she enters the casino. Those eyes do not suspect her mission. They are filled with lust and longing. They scan her from top to toe, beginning with her blonde hair and her milk-white complexion, which contrast so exquisitely with her form-fitting black dress, black stockings and black shoes. She pays no attention to the stares. Instead, her eyes scan the area for her contact.

It is 1980, a time when organized crime still maintains a stranglehold on Las Vegas, before the big corporations moved in. The city is in the midst of a great wave that seems to have no end, setting new all-time revenue records. It is the era portrayed in the Martin Scorsese film, *Casino,* an era of untold riches and spectacular homes. It also is an era of drug trafficking and murder.

She is 18, just one of many persons living inside her sleek body. She has no knowledge of the others sharing that form in the black dress. They have no knowledge of her, or of each other. They are compartmentalized individuals, each with specific tasks and talents. It was planned that way by her programmers. They have systematically created her since early childhood, first shattering her psyche into fragments through intense trauma — psychological, emotional, physical and drug-induced. The programmers conditioned these dissociated personality fragments into separate individuals — children, women, animals — to be skilled at certain assignments, to obey orders, and to forget everything when the job is done.

Now she is a collection of human robots, each taking turns coming to the surface. They are brought forth as needed through pre-programmed triggers. She has no ability to resist them. On this day, she is one of several personalities who are skilled at murder.

She has no memory of the killings. She does not know how many lives she's taken. She only knows that she has murdered, through flashing scenes that would invade her mind years later. They show male and female victims. Not all of them are adults.

Her character on this day is an apparent innocent, although she has tremendous sexual energy. She is the fantasy of many men, a honey trap. She is known to herself only as The Kill Alter. This one is a psychopath.

Walking through a narrow part of the casino, she glances to the right at several blackjack tables. Beyond them is a row of black and silver pay phones partitioned by faux wood against the wall. A man stands near one of them, a phone in his left ear. He is facing her. He's dressed in dark clothes and wears sunglasses.

She looks closely at him and feels a rush of sexual energy. She has a connection to him. She's glad he's there. He is her handler.

His eyes find her. She knows this, even though he wears sunglasses. Her eyes turn away after the initial glance. She is not supposed to look at him. But she feels his eyes following her.

She strides to the last of five poker tables on the right, where an older man in a gray suit stands. His hair also is gray and he wears no tie. He is her target.

There are three empty chairs. She knows that she is supposed to sit in the chair closest to the target. When she does this, she spins her chair to face him. He turns toward her. They lock eyes. She crosses her legs, takes his hand and places it on her hosed thigh. He leans in toward her and says, "Place a bet on it." It is a trigger phrase that brings forth another alternate personality. This one is purely sexual. The Kill Alter no longer is conscious. She sees none of what happens next.

The target leads this new personality upstairs to his hotel room. She ties him naked to the bed, fulfilling his request for a sadomasochistic performance involving asphyxia. They begin to have sex. A new personality emerges in her. She knows this one as Alter 14, a woman with unusual physical strength. This alter is filled with rage and skilled at killing with her bare hands.

She tells him she intends to kill him at his moment of orgasm. The target enjoys this new twist. He is aroused. Alter 14 sees what she believes is a snake, within inches of her face, about to strike and kill her. She reacts as she has been trained. Her right hand strikes snakelike at her target's throat. She crushes his windpipe. The target is dead.

The young woman leaves the scene. She walks out of the hotel-casino in her original personality, not knowing who she just killed, or how or why.

Although this tale sounds like a spy novel, it is a true story according to the woman in question. Now 48 years old, she identifies herself only as "Liz," for obvious reasons. She is a diagnosed sufferer of Multiple Personality Disorder (MPD), or, to use the newer clinical term, Dissociative Identity Disorder (DID). She has been in therapy and deprogramming for years, constantly reclaiming memories of what her alternate personalities have seen and done.

We are tempted, after hearing her stories, to believe she is delusional. Her claims are too incredible to accept. But as the reader will learn in the last section of this book, the details of her experiences in trauma programming and conditioning mirror those of so many other alleged mind control victims — nearly all of whom never have met — and so these claims must be taken seriously.

This is the conclusion reached by many therapists specializing in patients such as Liz. And in her special case, there is strong corroboration from an intended target she could not kill. Their tale will be told in the final chapter of this book.

But what has this to do with the plan to create a New World Order? We trust that by the time you finish reading the material offered in the subsequent pages, you will be able to answer that question quite definitely on your own.

FIRST MOVEMENT - *DIVERTIMENTO*
THE PUPPET MASTERS

"The Rockefeller file is not fiction. It is compact, powerful and frightening...The drive of the Rockefellers and their allies is to create a one-world government combining super capitalism and communism under the same tent, all under their control...Do I mean conspiracy? Yes I do. I am convinced there is such a plot, international in its scope, generations old in planning, and incredibly evil in intent."

—Congressman Larry McDonald, 1975. In 1981 McDonald called for a comprehensive congressional investigation of the Council on Foreign Relations and the Trilateral Commission. On September 1, 1983, McDonald died aboard Korean Airlines Flight 007 when it was shot down by a Soviet interceptor after accidentally straying over the Sakhalin Islands.

The Manipulators

"Some of the biggest men in the United States, in the field of commerce and manufacture, are afraid of somebody, are afraid of something. They know there is a power somewhere so organized, so subtle, so watchful, so interlocked, so complete, so pervasive that they had better not speak above their breath when they speak in condemnation of it."

—Woodrow Wilson

The term "New World Order" first appeared in print in 1919 with the publication of Samuel Zane Batten's book, *The New World Order.* Batten cloaked his theories in Christian religious concepts while calling for a system with social control over all people and all resources around the globe. The book promotes a World Federation and a World Parliament, with a global police force sending criminals to an international court. On the street level, this new order would enforce the disappearance of class distinction "and the solidarity of all interests in the economic process… Every person must do some useful work."

Batten also wrote of creating an "international mind with a world consciousness and a world patriotism." This would involve "the destruction of every arbitrary power that can separately and of its single choice disturb the peace of the world."

H.G. Wells took up the torch of manipulating populations with his book, *The New World Order,* in which he predicted: "Countless people, from maharajahs to millionaires and from pukkha sahibs to pretty ladies, will hate the new world order, be rendered unhappy by frustration of their passions and ambitions through its advent and will die protesting against it. When we attempt to estimate its promise we have to bear in mind the distress of a generation or so of malcontents, many of them quite gallant and graceful-looking people."

Decades after Wells, in 2000, the billionaire founder of Sun Microsystems, Bill Joy, revealed this plan was still in motion and took it to its logical conclusion. He said there is a "cancerous consensus" among the technocratic elite that humanity will be completely enslaved by the year 2030. At worst, he said mass extermination of everyone but the elite would take place by then.

Many of the members of this technocratic elite are in the Trans Humans or Post Humanist Movement. Most don't realize that Trans Humanism was founded by eugenicist Julian Huxley, who designed it to progress into tyranny. Leading Trans Humanist Ray Kurzweil has said that technological advancements will allow those who can afford them to live forever. He then admits that most people will not be able to keep pace with the new master race. This, of course, has always been the intention of the elitist family bloodlines portrayed in this section.

The Rockefellers

If character and morality can be traced in genetic bloodlines, then one need look no further than the father of John D. Rockefeller. William Rockefeller sold cancer "cures" from a medicine wagon. John's daddy, known as "Big Bill" to friends, taught his boy to leap into his arms from a high chair. After young John became confident in this feat, his father held out his arms one day, but pulled them in when the child jumped. After hitting the ground, little John heard his father say, "Never trust anyone completely, not even me."

This story comes from Nelson Rockefeller, and it gives insight to why his grandfather became the richest and most despised man in America.

John D. Rockefeller began his career as a commodities broker in Cleveland, Ohio, where he became interested in the potential of the petroleum industry there. In 1863, he partnered with other brokers to build a refinery. Seven years later, he incorporated the Standard Oil Company of Ohio. Rockefeller immediately set out to form a monopoly in the oil refinery business with help from the National City Bank of Cleveland, a bank allegedly belonging to the European Rothschilds, according to a congressional hearing.

In his quest for monopoly, Rockefeller was ruthless. If he could not merge or buy out competition, he cut prices until they had to sell. "Competition is a sin," he was quoted as saying. His deals with the railroads allowed him to achieve a stranglehold on oil transportation as well. In just a decade, Rockefeller owned or controlled about 95 percent of all the oil produced in the US.

Rockefeller's deeds finally caught up with him in 1902, when Ida Tarbell, daughter of an oil producer who was forced out of business by his harsh strategies, wrote a series of articles published in *McClure's Magazine* entitled "The History of Standard Oil Company." Tarbell's years of research into Rockefeller's business practices led to court and government investigations.

At first, it appeared that the Standard Oil monopoly had been shattered, but Rockefeller had planned for such a problem 20 years earlier when he created the Standard Oil Trust. This entity was a collection of almost undecipherable legal structures that defied investigation. Seeing the trust for what it was, the Ohio Supreme Court in 1892 ordered it dissolved, but Rockefeller dodged the ruling by moving the Standard Oil headquarters to New York. By 1899, he'd transferred his entire operation and renamed it the Standard Oil Company of New Jersey.

Rockefeller ran afoul of the US government again in 1906 after being charged with violating the Sherman Anti-Trust Act. The legal maneuverings ended in 1911, when the US Supreme Court ruled that "Seven men and a corporate machine have conspired against their fellow citizens. For the safety of the Republic we now decree that this dangerous conspiracy must be ended by November 15th."

Rockefeller juggled his oil empire to mimic the diversity demanded by the Supreme Court. Standard Oil of New York merged with the Vacuum Oil Company, forming Socony-Vacuum. In 1966, this company became Mobil Oil. The Standard Oil companies of Kansas, Nebraska and Indiana merged into another entity which would morph into the Amoco Corporation in 1985. Other mergers, which seemingly dissolved the Standard Oil monopoly, were simply shams that resulted in the creation of the Chevron Corporation, Atlantic Richfield and Pennzoil, to name a few. Finally, Standard Oil of New Jersey became Exxon in 1972.

The "breakup" of Standard Oil made Rockefeller even wealthier, because he owned about 25 percent of the 33 newly created companies. In 1917, the magnate began transferring his fortune and control of his companies to his only son, John D. Rockefeller Jr. In five years, the handover was complete and the younger Rockefeller continued his father's business practices, which crystallized in his anti-union dealings. But he had to change his position somewhat following the 1914 Ludlow Massacre of 40 strikers at the Rockefeller-owned Fuel and Iron Company by the Colorado militia. Rockefeller Jr. responded by creating a number of philanthropic organizations to ease the public's impression of the family. By World War II, he'd created the USO to entertain soldiers overseas, and after the war, he donated land in Manhattan for the construction of the United Nations building.

Rockefeller Jr. sired six children, five of them sons — John III, Nelson, Laurance, Winthrop and David. The eldest son chaired the Rockefeller Foundation, which donated substantial funds to various international agencies like the Population Council, which dealt with overpopulation and family planning. This was the continuation of the family's three generations of interest in promoting eugenics, the attempt to inject science into maintaining and improving desirable human characteristics through genetics and population control. John III died in 1978, but his son, John Davison Rockefeller, continued the family's success, entering politics to become governor of West Virginia.

Nelson Rockefeller had a much brighter political career, which began when President Franklin Roosevelt and Secretary of Defense James Forrestal appointed him as coordinator of inter-American affairs. This was an intelligence position, but it led to his appointment as assistant secretary of state for Latin American affairs in 1944. His mission was to monopolize the raw materials of the region for the US, and exclude the Europeans. It was a bold-faced money grab in which Rockefeller and his staff took over Britain's most valuable Latin American holdings.

In this activity, Rockefeller had to deal with many of the German expatriates who enjoyed most-favored status in South America, despite the fact that America was at war with Germany at the time. By war's end, Rockefeller had enormous influence with the governments of Latin America as well as a history of working with the Germans. This was an enormous bargaining chip when the United Nations was established, and future Israeli Prime Minister David Ben-Gurion knew how to turn it to his advantage. He wanted the UN to pass a resolution that partitioned Palestine and created an Israeli state. As Rockefeller could deliver the Latin American votes, Ben-Gurion simply used blackmail to make sure he did just that.

Rockefeller thus far had been able to squelch stories about his cooperation with the Nazis in South America, as well as his family's prewar and wartime relations with them. But the Jewish faction confronted Rockefeller with a dossier full of embarrassing information, according to John Loftus and Mark Aarons in their book, *The Secret War against the Jews.* The authors wrote, "They had his Swiss bank records with the Nazis, his signature on correspondence setting up the German Cartel in South America, transcripts of his conversations with Nazi agents during the war, and, finally, evidence of his complicity in helping Allen Dulles smuggle Nazi war criminals and money from the Vatican to Argentina."

Loftus and Aarons based this on classified CIA and NATO files to which they had access. They also interviewed a member of the Jewish faction who was present at the Rockefeller ambush, and who gave this account:

"Rockefeller skimmed through the dossier and coolly began to bargain. In return for the votes of the Latin American bloc, he wanted guarantees that the Jews would keep their mouths shut about the flow of Nazi money and fugitives to South America. There would be no Zionist Nazi-hunting unit, no testimony at Nuremberg about the bankers or anyone else, not a single leak to the press about where the Nazis were living in South America or which Nazis were working for Dulles. The subject of Nazis was closed. Period. Forever. The choice was simple, Rockefeller explained, 'You can have vengeance, or you can have a country, but you cannot have both.'"

The bargain was consummated on November 29, 1947, when the UN General Assembly approved a resolution recommending the partition of Palestine, much to the shock of the Arab nations. And to this day, Israel holds this same trump card over the US leadership, assuring nearly total support for Israel.

Nelson recovered nicely from this episode and went on to serve four terms as New York governor. Prior to that he was undersecretary of the Department of Health, Education and Welfare (HEW), which gave him the opportunity to initiate social programs.

Nelson Rockefeller failed three times to be nominated as the Republican presidential candidate in 1960, '64 and '68. He finally gained the White House as Gerald Ford's vice president in 1974, following the resignation of Richard Nixon due to the Watergate scandal.

In 1979, Nelson Rockefeller died at age 70 in suspicious circumstances that involved a young female staff assistant named Megan Marshak. The official coroner's report states that Rockefeller died of a heart attack during sexual intercourse. Instead of calling for an ambulance when Rockefeller collapsed, Marshak phoned a female friend who came to the scene. It was the friend and not Marshak who called for the ambulance about one hour after Rockefeller's heart attack. The medical report quotes the ambulance attendants' claim that Rockefeller was still alive when they took him to the hospital and that he died en route. This indicates that he possibly could have been saved if Marshak had called for help immediately. Marshak received $50,000 and the deed to a New York townhouse in Nelson Rockefeller's will.

Nelson's brother Laurance Spellman Rockefeller did not burn quite so brightly. He became a successful venture capitalist, co-owning Eastern

Airlines with World War I flying ace Eddie Rickenbacker. Under his solid business direction, the airline became one of the largest in the world. He also invested in McDonnell-Douglas Aircraft. His philanthropic activities centered on the environment and wildlife protection.

The fourth son, Winthrop, was somewhat of a family black sheep. He dropped out of Yale in 1934 and worked as a simple oil field hand. During World War II, he was an ordinary combat infantryman, earning a Bronze Star and a Purple Heart for his bravery. In the few years immediately following the war, Winthrop became a New York café society playboy, but in 1953 he gave that up and moved to Arkansas, where three years hence he was voted "Arkansas Man of the Year." He became governor of that state in 1967. Only six years later, Winthrop died of cancer.

If not the most famous of the Rockefeller boys, David certainly has become the most powerful. He attended the London School of Economics, which was funded by the family's Rockefeller Foundation, and by the Carnegie United Kingdom Trust Fund. In the London school, David was influenced by the teachings of Harold Laski of Britain's Socialist Party. During the war, he worked for the Office of Strategic Services (OSS) in North Africa and France. It was at this point that he developed high level intelligence contacts.

David Rockefeller achieved the chairmanship of the Rockefeller Institute's board of trustees in 1948, and also joined the staff of the Chase National Bank of New York. This bank's history can be traced all the way back to the Bank of Manhattan Company, which was established by Alexander Hamilton in 1799. Rockefeller was very instrumental in the merger that took place which created the Chase Manhattan Bank in 1955. By 1969, the bank was part of the larger Chase Manhattan Corp., with David acting as board chairman and CEO.

As early as 1941, David Rockefeller had joined the Council on Foreign Relations (CFR), and in 1950 he was elected vice president of the group. Over the years, the CFR has received steady donations from the Rockefeller Brothers Fund. This Fund also made considerable contributions to a wide variety of groups, including the Trilateral Commission. In the Fund's 1997 report, Rockefeller's niece, Abby O'Neill — chairperson of the Fund at that time — wrote that the Fund had, "a refocused One World strategy, with an explicitly global perspective and an emphasis on the convergence of national and international frameworks."

David Rockefeller has not been reticent to air his globalist views. He wrote in his memoir, "Some even believe we are part of a secret cabal working against the best interests of the United States, characterizing my family and me as 'internationalists' and of conspiring with others around the world to build a more integrated global political and economic structure — one world, if you will. If that's the charge, I stand guilty and I am proud of it."

The extent of his influence among world leaders became apparent during the 1976 official state visit of Australian President Malcolm Fraser, who conferred with Rockefeller before meeting President Gerald Ford. Author Ralph Epperson wrote, "This is truly incredible, because David Rockefeller has neither been elected nor appointed to any governmental position where he could officially represent the United States government."

In the proceeding pages it will become obvious how David Rockefeller has wielded this unusual influence on American politicians and events.

The Morgans

The term "robber baron" has been applied to John Pierpont Morgan so often that it qualifies as his occupation. This man created a banking empire that continues to wield awesome power over political and business decision made in America to this day.

Morgan's family tree is well rooted in the Eastern establishment. His great grandfather helped to found Yale University. His grandfather was a pro-British preacher who wielded considerable influence. His father, Junius Spencer Morgan, became connected to the British Rothschilds when he traveled to England as a financier. There, he partnered with another American named George Peabody, who arranged his entree to the Rothschild circle, and formed Peabody, Morgan & Co. Junius accumulated great wealth during the American Civil War by obtaining loans for the federal government.

John Pierpont Morgan was born in 1837, and by the time he was 27, he and his father took charge of the business following Peabody's retirement, renaming the firm Morgan and Company. It was at this point that J.P. Morgan became close to the Rothschilds, to the point of being an occasional guest in their mansion. It was the beginning of a lifelong business relationship that many authors claim made Morgan the *de facto* American agent of the Rothschild banking empire. According to author Eustace Mullins, "The Rothschilds preferred to operate anonymously in the United States behind the façade of J.P. Morgan and Company." One of the reasons probably had to do with the rise of anti-Semitism in the US in the late 19th century, and Morgan, a Protestant capitalist who could trace his family's roots in the US to before the American Revolution, was a fine fit.

Prior to joining his father in business, Morgan traveled to Germany where he studied at the University of Gottingen, a center for anti-establishment activities and secret societies that led to the expulsion of the "Gottingen Seven," which included the Grimm brothers and Karl Marx.

Morgan was back in America at the start of the Civil War, where he sold 5,000 rifles at $22 each to the commander of the St. Louis federal army garrison. But when the rifles arrived, the commander refused to pay, saying they were defective and obsolete. Morgan sued the army and the court awarded him $109,912, but a subsequent congressional investigating committee ruled that Morgan had defrauded the government by supplying "thoroughly unserviceable, obsolete and dangerous" rifles. What's more, the committee learned that Morgan had purchased the rifles for $3.50 apiece from a Morgan employee at the New York arsenal. Based on the St. Louis commander's initial agreement to buy, Morgan used this promise as collateral to borrow the money that paid for the rifles. In other words, Morgan had sold the army its own guns at a 500 percent profit without taking any personal financial risk.

Apparently the Washington politicians didn't heed this warning, because by the 1870s Morgan was the principal source of US government financing as head of J.P. Morgan and Company. According to the *New Encyclopedia Britannica,* "Because of his links to the Peabody firm, Morgan had intimate and highly useful connections with the London financial world, and during the 1870s he was thereby able to provide the rapidly growing industrial corporations of the United States with much-needed capital from British bankers." The Rothschilds certainly were among those bankers.

Riding this wave of growth, the Morgan firm became one of the most powerful banking establishments in the world, second only to that of the Rothschilds. And when his father died in a carriage accident in 1890, Morgan inherited the entire family business. He immediately stepped up his reorganization of the largest American railroads so that by 1902 he'd become the dominant man in rail transportation.

Morgan now was so powerful that he could manipulate the entire economy of the US. Many believe he helped to cause the bank panic of 1893, only to turn around and bail out the government's monetary reserves with $62 million in Rothschild gold. Also in this decade, Morgan oversaw the merger of Edison General Electric and the Thompson-Houston Electric Company to form General Electric, soon to become the dominant force in America's electrical equipment manufacturing. Morgan then handled the merger of several steel firms into the United States Steel Corp., and later melded several agricultural equipment manufacturers into the International Harvester Company.

Much like John D. Rockefeller, Morgan's empire was diversified while stamping out competition. Morgan achieved a stranglehold on American commercial and economic life. And while he and Rockefeller were competitors, they joined forces in creating the Federal Reserve Bank, which will be covered in detail in a subsequent chapter.

Following J.P. Morgan's death, his son, Pierpont Jr., oversaw the steady increase in the Morgan empire fortune. The young man had spent eight years working in the company's London office, where he forged strong ties to Britain's bankers, including the Rothschild bank.

By the end of the First World War, Morgan had underwritten more than $1 billion in Allied bonds through more than 2,000 banks. The firm's Rothschild connections allowed it to be the only banker purchasing supplies for both the British and French governments.

The Morgans benefited greatly from their business relations with the true Puppet Masters of the Western World, the Rothschild bankers of Europe.

The Rothschilds

Mayer Amschel Bauer was born in Frankfurt, Germany, on February 23, 1744. The son of a man who had to surreptitiously sell his stock in trade, fine silk cloth, due to the widespread anti-Semitism in that region, Mayer studied to become a rabbi. But the death of both parents forced him to leave rabbinical school and Mayer found work as an apprentice at a banking house. He was quick on the uptake and eventually rose to the position of court financial agent to William IX, Hesse-Kassel's royal administrator. He cemented his bonds to William by aping his employer's interest in Freemasonry, as William was a prominent member of that secretive society. Mayer also ingratiated himself by finding ancient coins and selling them to William at knock-down prices.

Mayer's influential client list grew with the addition of the Thurn und Taxis family, which administered a courier service throughout the Holy Roman Empire. While in their employ, Mayer learned that advance information gained through the couriers can lead to wise investments and great profits. He also learned how vital it was to guard this information, seeing how the Thurn und Taxis family wrote all of its correspondences in a code called *Judendeutsch,* which was German written in Hebrew characters.

Mayer set a pattern that his family would follow strictly — doing business with the reigning houses of Germany and later, Europe. It paid off when Britain needed troops to fight rebellious colonists in America. The British government paid William IX a large amount of money to provide Hessian soldiers for this duty, and he gave this money to Mayer to make investments for him. According to many accounts, Mayer used it instead to establish his son Nathan as head of the London branch of the family banking business. He repaid William in time, but this money established the Rothschild fortune, providing Nathan with cash and prestige.

According to Rothschild biographer Niall Ferguson, Nathan's entree to British royalty came as a result of his father purchasing the outstanding debts of George, then Prince Regent and soon to become King George IV, and his brothers. Ferguson added that the Rothschild influence continued through all subsequent generations of British royalty, down to Queen Victoria's husband, Prince Albert, and his son. England's politicians also were involved with the Rothschilds, including John Russell, William Gladstone, Benjamin Disraeli, Arthur Balfour and Randolph Churchill, father of Winston.

According to Nathan's own boasts, it took him just 17 years in England to increase the original 20,000 pounds his father gave him to 50,000,000 pounds, which would be equal to many billions of dollars in today's currency. By 1815, Nathan had become the principal financier for the British government and the Bank of England. Later, the Rothschilds took control of the Bank of England through an extraordinary gambit that will be detailed shortly.

Mayer Bauer had changed his name to Rothschild, which means "red shield," around the time that Nathan arrived in London in 1804. It was taken from the red shield emblem on the home of his ancestors, who lived in the Jewish ghetto section of Frankfurt. The name change almost definitely was intended to fend off the anti-Semitism then raging in Germany. The Rothschilds also used non-Jewish agents for the same purpose.

But the Rothschilds certainly were unashamed of their Jewish heritage, as evidenced by the family's devout observance of Jewish traditions. The Rothschilds donated large amounts of money over the years to Jewish causes, and may well have been instrumental in establishing the state of Israel. But they did not take offense when J.P. Morgan made several anti-Semitic remarks in public, as they probably knew that he was camouflaging his deep and profitable connections to them. There was a similar connection between the Rothschilds and the Rockefellers.

Mayer's other sons followed Nathan's lead, establishing themselves and the Rothschild business interests in several European nations. Jakob, the youngest son, who preferred to be called James, entered the Paris banking business in 1811, while Salomon established himself in Vienna and Karl in Naples. A tremendous, and rather secret, banking empire was built under the noses of European royalty and political power brokers, with their frequent cooperation. In a short time, the Rothschilds exerted an extraordinary influence on European policies and history. This influence bled into the United States, although much more covertly.

The Rothschilds quickly learned how to work both ends of a situation for their own profit. A perfect early example is that of Napoleon

Bonaparte, who refused to take loans from the Rothschilds and established his own Bank of France. This worked until Napoleon's defeat at Leipzig, which resulted in his exile to the island of Elba in the Mediterranean. But when he returned to France in 1815, he had no choice but to borrow five million pounds from Nathan Rothschild in order to raise and pay a new army to fight the British and Prussian forces under Wellington and Blucher.

Nathan took the opportunity to smuggle large sums of gold to Wellington, equipping his army and helping him to score the final defeat of Bonaparte at Waterloo. News of this victory was carried to London by Rothschild couriers, arriving a full day ahead of Wellington's own announcement. Nathan used this intelligence to his advantage, feigning disappointment and ordering the sale of his stocks. Investors, assuming this meant Wellington had been defeated, sold their stocks and plunged the market. Then Nathan ordered his agents to buy up a large portion of Britain's debt for much less than its true value. "It was the best business I have ever done," boasted Nathan later. This would lead to Rothschild dominance of the Bank of England.

The power and fantastic riches acquired by the Rothschilds allowed them to receive titles of nobility from indebted royal families and governments during the 19th century. The title "de" became part of the family name of the French Rothschilds in 1816. The Austrian branch in 1882 became barons and Nathaniel Rothschild, grandson of Nathan, became a British baron in 1885.

With banks in nearly all the Western nations, the Rothschilds increased their wealth by financing Cecil Rhodes in his quest to monopolize the diamond and gold mines of South Africa. In America, the Rothschilds financed the Harrimans and Vanderbilts in their railroad holdings, and Andrew Carnegie's steel industry. The family's control of J.P. Morgan became obvious when Morgan died and his will revealed that he owned only 19 percent of the Morgan companies. The Rothschilds were the majority owners of those firms, basically casting Morgan in the role of their employee.

In modern times, the Rothschilds have managed to keep a low profile in the popular media, perhaps because they have some financial control of certain mainstream broadcast and print outlets. The family name appeared unhappily on the media radar in 1996 when chairman of the clan's empire, Amshel Rothschild, allegedly committed suicide. Reportedly uncomfortable with his role in the banking concern after being forced into the family business by his father, Lord Victor Rothschild, Amshel didn't manage well. The family firm lost $9 million in the year before Amshel's death, according to reporter Sally Bedell Smith. Amshel's lifeless body was discovered in his Paris hotel room, apparently having hung himself by his terrycloth robe belt from a towel rack that was just five feet above the marble floor. Quipped a reporter, "Hanging himself could not have been easy for a man six feet one."

Amshel left no suicide note, and the police report bypassed the usual channels and went straight to the French minister of the interior, in deference to the supposedly publicity-shy family. Hardly a word of this suspicious suicide appeared in the mainstream media, despite the prominence and power wielded by this man. This could be another clear sign of how much control the Rothschilds exercise over the news we receive.

The international scope of the family empire continues to grow. Rothschild influence over the Nomura banking house of Japan began with the relationship between that bank's founder, Tsunao Okumura and Baron Edmond de Rothschild, who continues to be called "the father of modern Israel."

Today, the most visible member of this banking family is David de Rothschild, who is known worldwide for his "Live Earth" environmental program. Hailed as the "new global religion," Live Earth combines the hip (rock concerts) with the fallacious notion that humanity is solely responsible for global warming. Ignoring the scientific facts that the sun is the single greatest influence on rising global temperatures (as well as on temperatures in the entire solar system, which are also rising) and that the much richer plant life on earth in the distant past required much greater levels of carbon dioxide, the movement is pushing for population reduction and a worldwide carbon tax. Rothschild admitted in an interview with journalist Alex Jones that there is a lot of money to be made in the global warming arena, seemingly the new family interest.

But the basic credo of the Rothchilds has remained the same. The family patriarch, Mayer Rothschild, stated it clearly: "Permit me to control the money of a nation, and I care not who makes its laws."

The Rothschild Invasion of America

In 1837, America had no central bank, no national debt and no inflation, owing to the policies of President Andrew Jackson. This made the young nation a sore point and an inviting target to international bankers who wished to find profits in the New World. For this purpose, Amshel Rothschild dispatched a representative named August Schoenberg to America, his arrival coinciding with the retirement of the irksome Jackson. Schoenberg changed his name to August Belmont and set to buying American government bonds with no clear source of personal capital. Eventually he opened what would become one of America's largest banking houses, August Belmont & Company.

Belmont took advantage of the US-Mexico War, which began in 1846, by purchasing more bonds. This gave the Rothschilds investments in a wide variety of American businesses — railroads, banks, gold, industry, cotton and tobacco. With some of the profits, Belmont made generous contributions to the Democratic Party, which led to his appointment as US Representative to The Hague between 1853 and 1857. He cemented his social position by marrying the daughter of Commodore Matthew Perry, and later became president of the American Jockey Club, owing to his role in bringing thoroughbred racing to the US. Belmont Park in New York still bears his assumed name.

Prior to this, in 1849, Alphonse Rothschild arrived in New York to see about opening a permanent family banking house there. Alphonse was duly impressed with America as "the cradle of a new civilization," but he was overruled by James and Lionel Rothschild in opening a family bank. The Rothschilds continued doing business through intermediaries like Belmont and later the Morgans, Harrimans, Carnegies and Vanderbilts, garnering profits, increasing investments and awaiting an opportunity to make a bold move.

That opportunity arrived in 1861 with the opening shots of the American Civil War, to be detailed in a subsequent chapter.

SECOND MOVEMENT – *ARPEGGIO*
CONFEDERACIES OF DUNCES

"In a time of deceit, telling the truth is a revolutionary act."

—George Orwell

The Council on Foreign Relations

During World War I, President Woodrow Wilson's advisor, Colonel Edward Mandell House, gathered together many wealthy and powerful men to create a plan for the postwar world. Meeting in New York in 1917, they called the gathering "The Inquiry" and tabled what would become the basis of Wilson's Fourteen Points. Many of the points that Wilson would give to Europe's leaders were surprisingly globalist, including the call for removing all economic barriers between nations and forming a "general association of nations." These globalist points were heavily influenced by House, an admitted Marxist.

When Germany asked for an armistice in 1918, the fighting stopped and the following year, Wilson ventured to the Paris Peace Conference with many members of "The Inquiry" in tow, including House and bankers Paul Warburg and Bernard Baruch. The European leaders agreed to the American peace plan, including the formation of a League of Nations. It was Wilson's finest hour. Unfortunately, it was just that. The League covenant had to be ratified by the US Congress, which voted against it. There would be no American participation, which doomed the League of Nations.

House didn't give up his dream, meeting in the Majestic Hotel in Paris on May 30, 1919, with other British and American peace delegates. Their meeting resulted in the creation of an "Institute of International Affairs" to be headquartered in the US and England. The goal of this organization was to promote a one-world government to the people of both nations. The British branch came to be called the Royal Institute of International Affairs (RIIF) while the American version was incorporated as the Council on Foreign Relations (CFR) on July 21, 1921. This title came from a previous New York dinner club gathering of bankers and attorneys to discuss international trade and finance. The new version of the CFR would be far more secretive, even writing into Article II of its bylaws that any person revealing information gleaned from CFR meetings would be excised from membership.

The press treated the CFR as a club of East Coast liberal elitists, most of whom lived in New York or Washington DC. Membership was by invitation, originally only 1,600 strong, but today estimates put the CFR roster at between 3,000 and 4,000, including leaders in finance, academics, communications and commerce. In order to be invited for membership, one has to be proposed by a member, seconded by another member, approved by the membership committee, screened and finally approved by the board of directors. The current Council headquarters is a four story mansion, the Harold Pratt House, on the corner of 68th Street and Park Avenue in New York City.

The media usually portrays the CFR as an open forum. The Council does print its annual report for public consumption, listing all members. The public can subscribe to the CFR publication, *Foreign Affairs,* as well as surf its website, which explains the group's structure. What the press doesn't report is that about 90 percent of CFR members also have joined the Bilderberg Group and/or the Trilateral Commission, and the shocking amount of influence all three groups exercise over American government and policy.

Despite the kid glove treatment by the press, the CFR had early political opponents who tried to sound a warning about its intentions. New York Mayor John Hylan said in a March 26, 1922 speech, "The real menace of our republic is the invisible government, which, like a giant octopus, sprawls its slimy length over our city, state and nation. At the head is a small group of banking houses generally referred to as 'international bankers.' This little coterie of international bankers virtually runs our government for their own selfish ends."

Since its inception, the CFR has broadened its membership to include some women and African American leaders, and has branched out to a wide number of cities across the US. Among its original members were "Colonel" House, John Foster Dulles, Christian Herter (both future secretaries of state), Allen Dulles (future head of the CIA), Secretary of State Elihu Root and newspaper columnist Walter Lippmann. The first CFR president, John W. Davis, was J.P. Morgan's attorney, and the first vice president, Paul Cravath, also represented Morgan. To complete the Morgan influence, one of his business partners, Russell Leffingwell, became the first CFR chairman.

Not surprisingly, Morgan supplied funding for the CFR, along with John D. Rockefeller, Jacob Schiff, Bernard Baruch and Paul Warburg. These contributors have been replaced in modern times by corporations like Xerox, Texaco, General Motors, the Rockefeller Brothers Fund, the Ford Foundation and the Andrew W. Mellon Foundation, to name just a few.

The CFR over the decades has produced a stunning list of presidents and presidential candidates, often running against each other to insure that a Council member would gain the White House. In the 1952 and 1956 presidential elections, both Dwight Eisenhower and Adlai Stevenson had CFR memberships. The same situation occurred in 1960 when CFR members John Kennedy and Richard Nixon vied for office. The 1968 election pitted Nixon against CFR member Hubert Humphrey. Four years later, Nixon defeated George McGovern, a CFR member. The 1976 election pitted CFR members Gerald Ford and Jimmy Carter against each other. The 1980 election saw Carter defeated by Ronald Reagan, who was not a CFR member but whose running mate, George Bush, was. Even the third party candidate that year, John Anderson, was with the CFR. In his first term, Reagan's administration featured an incredible 313 CFR members.

In 1984, Reagan's challenger was CFR member Walter Mondale. When George Bush finally gained the White House in 1988, he defeated CFR member Michael Dukakis. Four years later, CFR and Bilderberg group member Bill Clinton defeated Bush, and populated his administration with nearly 100 Council members. Clinton gained reelection in 1996 against CFR member Robert Dole. The 2000 election pitted CFR member Al Gore against George W. Bush, who was not a Council member but who staffed his administration with CFR habitués like Dick Cheney, Condoleeza Rice, Paul Wolfowitz, Lewis Libby and Colin Powell. Bush defeated CFR member John Kerry in the next election, and in 2008, CFR member John McCain lost to Barack Obama. Although Obama was not a Council member, the top levels of his administration are filled with CFR, Bilderberg and Trilateral Commission members, which will be detailed in a subsequent chapter.

Since 1952, only the Lyndon Johnson-Barry Goldwater contest in 1964 featured two candidates who were not CFR members. Shock waves went through the Council when Goldwater defeated Nelson Rockefeller, the CFR candidate, for the Republican Party nomination. A whirlwind press campaign soon attacked Goldwater, portraying him as a mentally unstable radical who would drop nuclear bombs on Hanoi and abolish Social Security, ushering Johnson into another term by a landslide vote.

It is difficult to digest the success the CFR has had in placing one of its members in the nation's highest office. With the exception of Lyndon Johnson, between 1928 and 1981, every American president has been a

Council member. Johnson more than made up for this by adding 387 CFR members to the upper echelons of his administration. And the CFR has been almost completely successful in getting its members named secretaries of defense. Since the National Security Act of 1947 established that post, 14 CFR members have been appointed secretary of defense. In addition, since 1940 every secretary of state except Hillary Clinton and James Byrnes has been a member of the CFR or its offshoot Trilateral Commission. And over the last eight decades, virtually every high level US national security and foreign policy advisor has been a Council member. Readers can see the awesome list of names for these and other important US government posts in Daniel Estulin's book, *The True Story of the Bilderberg Group.*

In its mission statements, the CFR professes to be a think tank of prominent men who wish to serve the nation with ideas for a better and safer world. A number of researchers claim, however, that it is a secret cabal of powerful men bent on world domination through international business practices, and that these men have manipulated governments and wars for nearly a century.

One such accusation came from a former CFR member, Admiral Chester Ward, who was judge advocate general of the US Navy. According to Ward, the single objective of the CFR is "to bring about the surrender of the sovereignty and national independence of the United States." He went on to claim that the members seek a world banking monopoly over whichever power emerges with control of a global government. Admiral Ward detailed CFR methods in the book he co-authored with Phyllis Schlafly in 1975, *Kissinger on the Couch*, saying, "Once the ruling members of the CFR have decided that the US government should adopt a particular policy, the very substantial research facilities of CFR are put to work to develop arguments, intellectual and emotional, to support the new policy, and to confound and discredit, intellectually and emotionally, any opposition."

Rockefeller family biographer Alvin Moscow went further: "In fact, it is difficult to point to a single major policy in US foreign affairs that has been established since [President] Wilson which was diametrically opposed to then current thinking in the Council on Foreign Relations."

The noted economist, John Kenneth Galbraith, resigned from the CFR in 1970, complaining about the dinner meetings where its members were briefed on policy by US government officials. "Why should businessmen be briefed by government officials on information not available to the public," asked Galbraith, "especially since it can be financially advantageous?"

Senator Barry Goldwater was much more vociferous in his disapproval of the CFR and its claim that members strove for a future with less war, less poverty and more efficient use of the world's resources. Goldwater warned, "This would inevitably be accompanied by a loss in personal freedom of choice and re-establishment of restraints that provoked the American Revolution." Of the regular change in US administrations, he pointed out, "There has been a great turnover in personnel, but no change in policy. Example: During the Nixon years, Henry Kissinger, a council [CFR] member and Nelson Rockefeller protégé, was in charge of foreign policy. When Jimmy Carter was elected, Kissinger was replaced by Zbigniew Brzezinski, a council [CFR] member and a David Rockefeller protégé."

Another senator, Jesse Helms, cautioned, "In the globalist point of view, nation-states and national boundaries do not count for anything. Political philosophies and political principals seem to become simply relative. Indeed, even constitutions are irrelevant to the exercise of power. Liberty and tyranny are viewed as neither necessarily good nor evil, and certainly not a component of policy...All that matters to this club is the maximization of profits resulting from the practice of what can be described as finance capitalism, a system which rests upon the twin pillars of debt and monopoly. This isn't real capitalism. It is the road to economic concentration and to political slavery."

Even the loyal members of the CFR openly admit their globalist plans for ending US sovereignty. In the 50th anniversary issue of the Council's quarterly publication, *Foreign Affairs,* then US Ambassador to Great Britain and Yale University President Kingman Brewster wrote, "Our national purpose should be to abolish American nationality and to take some risks in order to invite others to pool their sovereignty with ours." In the April 1974 issue of that same publication, former Deputy Assistant Secretary of State Richard Gardner wrote, "An end run around national sovereignty, eroding it piece by piece, will accomplish much more than the old fashioned assault."

John F. Kennedy relied on CFR member Walt Rostow to advise him on the Vietnam War. That Rostow was an avowed believer in ending national sovereignty is clearly stated in his book, *The United States in the World Arena,* where he wrote "It is a legitimate American national objective to see removed from all nations — including the United States

— the right to use substantial military force to pursue their own interests. Since this right is the root of national sovereignty, it is therefore an American interest to see an end to nationhood as it has been historically defined."

Not surprisingly, Rostow's father was a Marxist revolutionary in Russia and two of his aunts had joined the Communist Party. What a man with Rostow's background was doing in such a high advisory position in the Kennedy White House is mysterious, as he had been rejected by the Eisenhower administration for employment in the State Department, and dropped from a contract by the CIA. Apparently Rostow's CFR connections were sufficient to get Kennedy to fire his State Department head of security, Otto Otepka, in order to hire him. Rostow's "Blueprint for the Peace Race," calling for the replacement of all national armies by a UN military force, is available online today in "Department of State Publication 7277," after being "unavailable" for decades due to its sensitive nature.

Bowing to Rostow's suggestion of a unilateral American disarmament, Kennedy in 1961 signed Public Law #87-297, calling for the elimination of US national forces and further declaring that "no one may possess a firearm or lethal weapon except police or military personnel." During the following administrations, this law has been updated 18 times and is still active and "in transition," according to ex-President George W. Bush and Admiral William Crowe. Its companion document, Publication 7277, released in 1962, describes a two-phase operation reducing the US armed forces to 2.1 million while those of China and the Soviet Union do the same. One half of our armed forces were to be merged with China and Russia's.

The second phase required the remaining half of our forces to be placed under the command of the UN Security Council and by agreement would always be headed by a Russian. The world's smaller nations were to put all of their armed forces under the same UN umbrella, achieving a situation in which "no state [nation] would have the military power to challenge the progressively strengthened UN Peace Force...." Congress still appropriates funds to support this program, even though it is clear its final passage would give policing powers in America to foreign troops.

The Council makes policies like these more palatable to the public through an intricate process of studies published by various think tanks, often tax funded. Sociologist Hadley Cantril, a respected public opinion researcher during and after the 1940s, wrote in his book *The Human*

Dimension, "Psycho-political operations are propaganda campaigns designed to create perpetual tensions and to manipulate different groups of people to accept the particular climate of opinion the CFR seeks to achieve in the world."

Among the CFR-associated, tax-funded think tanks is the Tavistock Foundation, which runs a $6 billion per year operation in the US. Under its direct control are 10 major institutions containing about 400 subsidiaries and 3,000 other study groups and think tanks that initiate programs intended to control public opinion. John Coleman in *Conspirators' Heirarchy* flatly states, "Tavistock and like-minded American foundations have a single goal in mind — to break down the psychological strength of the individual and render him helpless to oppose the dictators of the World Order."

Tavistock originated in London as the Institute of Human Relations in 1921, when the Marquess of Tavistock donated a building to the organization to study the effects of shell shock on British soldiers after World War I. Its purpose, according to retired US Air Force Colonel Byron Weeks, "was to establish the breaking point of men under stress, under the direction of the British Army Bureau of Psychological Warfare...."

Tavistock opened its doors in America armed with a variety of psychological gambits designed to shape public opinion. "This opinion is formulated by the dominant Council on Foreign Relations members," wrote author and Florida State Emeritus Professor of Political Science Thomas Dye, "who belong to an inner circle called the 'Special Group' that plan and coordinate the psycho-political operations used to manipulate the American public, and through a vast governmental undercover infrastructure called the 'Secret Team' that include the legislative, executive and judicial branches of government, such as the secretary of state, the secretary of defense, the secretary of the treasury and the director of the CIA; those who control television, radio and newspaper corporations; who head the largest law firms; who run the largest and most prestigious universities and think tanks; who direct the largest private foundations and who direct the largest public corporations."

Tax-free foundations are the preferred CFR means of funding favorable policy-making processes, and Dye claimed that nearly 40 percent of all foundation assets come under the aegis of just 10 or 11 CFR-controlled foundations. The Rand National Defense Research

Institute is an exception, as it is federally funded, but its executive vice president is CFR member Michael Rich, who has held that second highest position in the organization since 1993. One of the key tasks that Rand handles, aside from national security and population control, concerns studying strategies to manipulate and misinform large segments of a population.

Dye points out that by remaining hidden from the other CFR members, the "Secret Team" and the "Special Group" protect themselves from possible prosecution. These elite members only need to deny participating in any operation, which is identical to the operation of the Bilderberg group.

A case when this system didn't work was the Iran-Contra affair in which the CFR Special Group within the Reagan administration urged the president to disregard the arms embargo on Iran, selling that nation munitions and using the money to fund the anti-Marxist Contra guerillas in Nicaragua. This Special Group included CFR members George H.W. Bush, Donald Regan, Elliot Abrams, John Poindexter, Caspar Weinberger, William Casey, Robert Gates of the CIA and Robert McFarlane. When news of the scheme leaked out, a scandal ensued and the members of the Special Group faced charges. But six years later, when Bush was finishing his term of office, he pardoned Weinberger, McFarlane, Abrams and three CIA chiefs.

Elements of the CIA have been a willing tool for the CFR over the decades. The marriage between the CFR and the CIA, many of whose top level administrators were or are Council members, was obvious as early as 1968 during a discussion group in which CIA Director of Plans Richard Bissell called for more discretion during the interplay between the Agency and the Council. Addressing situations in which CFR-dominated corporations act as covers for CIA operations, Bissell said, "If the Agency is to be effective, it will have to make use of private institutions on an expanding scale, though those relations which have been 'blown' cannot be resurrected. We need to operate under deeper cover, with increased attention to the use of 'cutouts' [intermediaries]. The CIA's interface with the rest of the world needs to be better protected."

The intelligence game understandably requires seemingly innocent business covers to achieve goals. Every major intelligence outfit in the world uses the same system. But the interrelationship between an enormous secret spy organization that has repeatedly toppled governments and instigated wars, and a collection of power brokers who wish to see American sovereignty and its Constitution destroyed, is deeply disturbing.

The CFR is imbedded in our government's high cabinet positions today, and holding these positions allows members to control the government entities that protect the oligarchs' property and investments worldwide. And when an appointee takes office, he generally hires other CFR members to join his staff.

Witness the career of Henry Kissinger. In 1955 he was just another academic who attended a meeting hosted by Nelson Rockefeller, one of President Eisenhower's foreign affairs assistants at that time. A friendship blossomed between the two, which led to Kissinger being brought into the fold with David Rockefeller and other CFR members. These connections provided funds that allowed Kissinger to work with officials of the State Department, the CIA, the Atomic Energy Commission and all three military branches. His access to them led to his best-selling book, *Nuclear Weapons and Foreign Policy,* which stated his opinion that a nuclear war could be winnable.

When Kissinger joined the Nixon Administration as secretary of state, it followed a presidential campaign between Nixon and Hubert Humphrey that was rendered absolutely meaningless, according to Gary Allen in his momentous best-selling book, *None Dare Call it Conspiracy.* Allen stated: "There really was not a dime's worth of difference. Voters were given the choice between CFR world government advocate Nixon and CFR world government advocate Humphrey. Only the rhetoric was changed to fool the public."

The influx of CFR members in high government positions has remained high with each successive administration. The Clinton administration contained nearly 100 CFR members, according to published reports, including ambassadorships to Great Britain, Australia, Russia, France, Italy, India, South Africa, Chile, Spain, Syria, Poland and the Philippines.

To protect against scrutiny into the awesome influence it has on national policy, the CFR created an offshoot organization.

The Trilateral Commission

The Trilateral Commission is deliberately more open to scrutiny. It publishes its membership and its position papers, but its inner workings are secret. George Bush Sr. was a Trilateralist, and a CFR member. The administrations of Presidents Jimmy Carter and Bill Clinton were filled with Trilateral members.

Former CFR chairman David Rockefeller helped to create the Trilateral Commission in the early 1970s. It was meant to deflect unwanted press attention that the CFR was receiving. The concept of the Trilateral Commission, however, came from Zbigniew Brzezinski, who headed the Russian Studies Department at Columbia University at that time. Brzezinski wanted to create greater cooperation between the trilateral regions of Europe, North America and Asia. In 1970, Brzezinski had published his book, *Between Two Ages: America's Role in the Technetronic Era,* and wrote, "National sovereignty is no longer a viable concept." He predicted a merging of nations into a single entity, funded by a global taxation system.

His plan for a commission of trilateral nations was presented in 1972 at a Bilderberg meeting in tiny Knokke-Heist, Belgium. There were worries among the international financiers over then-President Richard Nixon's policies and the rising price of OPEC oil. The Trilateral Commission began gathering members at the Rockefeller estate in Pocantico Hills, New York on July 23, 1972. Present at the meeting were Brzezinski, Rockefeller, Karl Carstens, McGeorge Bundy, Max Kohnstamm, Robert Bowie, C. Fred Bergsten, Rene Foch, Henry Owen, Guido Colonna di Paliano, Francois Duchene, Kiichi Miyazawa, Tadashi Yamamoto and Saburo Ikita.

The Trilateral Commission officially began on July 1, 1973, Rockefeller holding the chairman position, and Brzezinski taking North American director duties. Georgia Governor Jimmy Carter and Congressman John Anderson were among the North American members, while European founding members included *Economist* editor Alistair Burnet, Fiat Motors president Giovanni Agnelli, and Raymond Barre, then vice president of the Commission of European Communities. The

Trilateral Commission set up headquarters in New York, Tokyo and Paris, with an Executive Committee that today numbers about 350 members who meet more than once a year in one of the three headquarters.

In its first 18 months of existence, the Commission published six position papers called *The Triangle Papers* presenting its agenda and measuring public reaction. The reaction of Gary Allen in *The Rockefeller File* was not what members wanted to hear: "If *The Triangle Papers* are any indication, we can look for four major thrusts toward world economic controls." Allen believed the first would rearrange the world monetary system. The second would loot US resources to continue fomenting radicalism in the Third World. The third thrust would increase trade with communist nations, and the fourth would use the 1973 energy crisis to achieve more control.

Nearly four decades later, all of Allen's predictions have come true.

Thrust One: The European Union and the North American Free Trade Agreement (NAFTA) that is to lead to a North American Union, have come into being. An Asian monetary union currently is being arranged.

Thrust Two: The US and Western nations have provided financial aid in the billions to Third World nations, creating debt and agreements that allow a plundering of the emerging nations' natural resources.

Thrust Three: The US trade exchange with the Soviet Union and China exploded with billions of dollars in American technology going to the communist countries.

Thrust Four: The Western globalists have profited from several energy crises, each one enriching them further while providing greater control of the world's oil reserves. Today, the concept of an energy crisis has been morphed into a "global warming" crisis, intended to increase control over governments and individuals.

The effects of accomplishing these 1973 goals have been dramatic. Economist Doug Henwood, contributing editor of *The Nation,* pointed out that "each member of the Triad has gathered under itself a handful of poor nations to act as sweatshops, plantations and mines: the US has Latin America; the EC, Eastern and Southern Europe and Africa; and Japan, Southeast Asia. In a few cases, two Triad members share a country — Taiwan and Singapore are split between Japan and the US; Argentina between the US and the EC; Malaysia between the EC and Japan; and India is shared by all three."

The Trilateral Commission continues to grow, and in the last few years has added members from such emerging Asian economies as Malaysia, Indonesia, the Philippines and Thailand, along with representatives of the established capitalist countries of Australia, New Zealand, Singapore and South Korea. Other new Trilateral members come from Kuwait, Jordan, Morocco, Argentina and the Ukraine. The Commission will include economies from the entire world, excepting equatorial Africa and the Indian sub-continent, making it a global force in policymaking. A cross-section of the membership today reveals that the largest number of representatives comes from global corporations.

The Trilateral Commission is not government funded. It operates on donations made by tax-exempt foundations like the Rockefeller Brothers Fund and the Ford Foundation, in addition to corporate funding from Exxon, General Motors, Texas Instruments and Wells Fargo.

The Commission's newsletters and reports are issued publicly and contain little that is controversial, although Harvard professor of political science, Samuel Huntington, did make a case that America needed to modify its democracy to allow leaders with "special talents" to operate freely during times of emergency, overriding "the claims of democracy." Three years after Huntington wrote those opinions, President Jimmy Carter appointed him as coordinator of security planning for the National Security Council. While in this position, Huntington prepared Presidential Review Memorandum 32, which resulted in the 1979 presidential order establishing the Federal Emergency Management Agency (FEMA). The mandate for FEMA is that in an emergency, it has the power to take totalitarian control of government functions. It does not answer to the president during these situations, but only to the National Security Council.

Many other Trilateral Commission members became appointees in the Carter administration, which led to accusations by certain members of the press of having formed a shadow government. Laurie Strand wrote in the *People's Almanac #3,* "The Trilateral Commission's tentacles have reached so far afield in the political and economic sphere that it has been described by some as a cabal of powerful men out to control the world by creating a super-national community dominated by the multinational corporations."

Carter administration Trilaterals included Andrew Young, Elliot Richardson, Warren Christopher, Richard Cooper and Richard Holbrooke. Prominent Republicans also were members, including Henry

Kissinger, George H.W. Bush, John Danforth and Caspar Weinberger. Perhaps most disturbing, Carter appointed Trilateral member Paul Volcker to take charge of the Federal Reserve Bank. Volcker also had membership in the Council on Foreign Relations and the Bilderberg group. His replacement during the Reagan administration was Alan Greenspan, also a member of all three groups.

The influence of these Rockefeller-run entities on US policy was not lost on Senator Barry Goldwater, who wrote, "What the Trilaterals truly intend is the creation of a worldwide economic power superior to the political government of the nation-states involved. As managers and creators of the system, they will rule the world."

In his 1979 book, *With No Apologies,* Goldwater wrote that Rockefeller's Trilateral Commission "is intended to be the vehicle for multinational consolidation of the commercial and banking interests by seizing control of the political government of the United States."

An early example of Trilateral influence on policy was the manner in which Brzezinski dealt with Iran after the Shah was deposed. Former ambassador to Iran William Sullivan complained, "By November 1978, Brzezinski began to make his own policy and establish his own embassy in Iran."

Concern over the commission's influence on policy spurred the American Legion to pass Resolution 773 in 1980, calling for a congressional investigation of the Trilaterals and of the Council on Foreign Relations. The following year, the Veterans of Foreign Wars (VFW) adopted a similar resolution, and Congressman Larry McDonald introduced these resolutions in the House. But there was no congressional investigation and McDonald, who was national chairman of the John Birch Society, subsequently died in the Soviet shoot-down of Korean Airlines Flight 007 on September 1, 1983.

During the 1980 Republican primaries race, which pitted Ronald Reagan against George H.W. Bush, Reagan criticized Bush for his membership in the Trilateral Commission and the CFR, promising that Bush would have no place in his government. But during the Republican Convention, pressure mounted on Reagan to choose Gerald Ford as his running mate. Faced with the possibility of a divided presidency, Reagan advanced Bush as his vice presidential choice. Following the victory of this ticket, Reagan's 59-member transition team included 28 CFR members, 10 Trilaterals and 10 Bilderberger group members. His appointees to the top cabinet posts included CFR members Alexander

Haig as secretary of state, Caspar Weinberger as secretary of defense, and Donald Regan as secretary of the treasury. Also, Reagan's chief of staff, James Baker, came from a family long connected with the Rockefeller oil interests.

Only weeks into his administration, an assassin shot Reagan. It was another "lone nut gunman," John W. Hinckley, whose brother had scheduled dinner with Bush's son Neil the night of the assassination attempt. Also, Hinckley's father was a Texas oil man and a longtime friend of George H.W. Bush. If John Hinckley's aim had been just a quarter inch higher, he would have killed Reagan and propelled Bush into the presidency just weeks into the new administration.

The disturbing influence wielded by the CFR and the Trilateral Commission on US policy becomes much more sinister due to the close connection these organizations enjoy with a non-American dominated group of international oligarchs and royals: the Bilderbergers.

The Bilderberg Group

In June 2010, the Dolce Hotel in Sitges, one of the most exclusive resorts in Spain, hosted a collection of powerful international bankers, politicians, intellectuals and businessmen. About 200 of them meet annually at different venues to hash out current world economic and political problems. On that year's agenda was the fear that the economically troubled nations of Portugal, Ireland, Greece, Italy and Spain might be tempted to exit the European Union, which would collapse the euro. This was a nightmare to the group of men and women that met in Sitges. Also, the presence of Donald Rumsfeld, former Bush administration defense secretary, raised dark possibilities that an attack upon Iran would be discussed.

Among the elder statesmen in the gathering were David Rockefeller, now 96, and 88-year-old Henry Kissinger, but sightings of Queen Beatrix of the Netherlands and Queen Sofia of Spain also were made. The term "sightings" is appropriate, because the Dolce emptied itself of all guests prior to the arrival of this group, and the hotel grounds were cordoned off by Spanish police as well as private security. The presence of Spain's tax-supported police irked bystanders, who rightly pointed out that this small cadre of elitist foreigners received protection from their prying eyes at their own expense.

Just two days prior to the start of the meetings, the police in Barcelona struck in protest of a coming pay cut, and yet the Catalan police who cover Sitges admitted its presence at the Dolce would cost 600,000 Euros for the four-day event. A longtime follower of these meetings, Jim Tucker, pointed out that all expenses incurred by host nations of these meetings are reimbursed by the group, which simply made local police an army for hire.

To make matters worse, the police began taking away digital cameras from the citizens who were standing on public property quite legally, and in some instances, deleted photos. In spite of this, the journalists who have covered these meetings noticed a sea change among the police in 2010. There was much less harassment and much more comradeship with the prying public. It also was easier than ever to talk hotel staffers into rummaging through trash cans or memorizing overheard conversations and pass the information along. Some theorized that the popularity of Dan Brown's books revealing the Illuminati agenda had opened a lot of eyes to this ultra-secretive group of elites, known as the Bilderbergers. But who exactly are these guys?

The Bilderberg group is a collection of powerful men and women — many from European royal families — who meet secretly each year to discuss current events and issues. Some researchers claim that these meetings are intended to manufacture and manipulate world events.

Radical watchdog groups like the Liberty Lobby have gone so far as to charge the Bilderbergers with conspiring to create a world government, run by an unelected elite, that would supplant national sovereignty and constitutional rights. The Lobby's founder, Willis Carto wrote of the Bilderberg members, "Their loyalty is only to their money, wherever it may be and derived from whatever source. These capitalists are the greatest advocates of free trade and are implacable enemies of national sovereignty. They are far more dangerous to the nation than the communists ever were."

A large number of the Bilderberg membership also belongs to the Trilateral Commission and the CFR. The group has no official name. It has acquired the name of the place where the public first noticed it in 1954, the Bilderberg Hotel in Oosterbeek, Holland. The group had its initial meeting on US soil three years later on Saint Simons Island, near Jekyll Island, Georgia, the birth site of the Federal Reserve Bank in 1913.

The initial meeting in Oosterbeek, which took place during the first year of the Eisenhower administration, featured significant participation by wealthy and influential Americans. It is known that the CIA played an important role in this.

The official creation of the Bilderberg group took place in the early 1950s, and included two European foreign ministers, Prince Bernhard of Holland and Dr. Joseph Hieronim Retinger, a Polish socialist who is regarded as the father of the organization. Retinger was brought to the US by Averill Harriman when he was America's ambassador to England. Harriman, a CFR member, introduced him to Nelson and David Rockefeller, John Foster Dulles and other prominent CFR members.

The American Committee on a United Europe had previously been formed by Retinger along with Allen Dulles and George Franklin, both of whom were in the CFR. Retinger would continue his Bilderberg activities until his death in 1960. He also played an active role in the Polish government-in-exile during World War II. He was in London on September 1, 1939, when Germany began the war by invading Poland. Once the Polish government gathered itself in London, Retinger became the most important advisor to the exiled Polish prime minister, General Wladislaw Sikorski.

Retinger's exploits were not limited to the boardroom. In 1944, at the age of 56, he became the oldest man ever to parachute into hostile territory when he jumped into his occupied homeland as part of Operation Salamander. Dressed in a British army uniform with false identity papers, he ran afoul of suspicious members of the Polish Home Army, who ordered him liquidated. An assassin posing as a nurse, Izabela Horodecka, was ordered to poison him, but she gave him only one half of the required dose. The poison did not kill him, but Retinger was paralyzed for months before finally regaining his health in London.

At this time, Retinger began working with Prince Bernhard during meetings with other exiled ministers. Among the items they discussed was a postwar European Union. This was on the agenda at the May 1948 Congress of Europe, held at The Hague and attended by Winston Churchill, then-current British Prime Minister Anthony Eden, West German Chancellor Konrad Adenauer and Bertrand Russell. Although the meeting was organized by Retinger, Churchill presided over the 800 political representatives and discussed plans for a European Union.

Two months later, Retinger traveled with Churchill and former Belgian Prime Minister Paul-Henri Spaak to the US and raised money for the EU program. A direct result was the establishment of the American Committee on a United Europe on March 29, 1949, chaired by former OSS Director William Donovan. Allen Dulles, soon-to-become CIA Director, was the vice chairman. Clearly there was a powerful US intelligence connection to the plan for creating the EU.

The prominence of Prince Bernhard in the Bilderberg meetings is compelling, owing to the fact that Bernhard was a Nazi, an officer in the Reiter SS Corps in the early 1930s, and a board member of Farben Bilder, a Paris-based subsidiary of the chemical mega-firm I.G. Farben. His association with Farben Bilder has caused some to believe this, and not the Bilderberg Hotel, is the source of the group's name. This is supported by the fact that Heinrich Himmler had organized a Bilderberg-similar collection of powerful business oligarchs into a "Circle of Friends" with the aid of Farben executives.

Bernhard's wife was Princess Juliana of the Netherlands, which allowed him to become a major shareholder in Dutch Shell Oil, joining the firm's other major shareholder, Lord Victor Rothschild of England. Bernhard and his family moved to London on orders from Queen Wilhelmina after the German invasion of the Netherlands in May 1940. Against the orders of Wilhelmina, who also fled to Britain, Bernhard slipped back into his native country to set up a resistance movement. Failing this, he escaped a second time to Britain in a patrol boat, and remained there until the war ended. He was quite influential during the conflict, acting as the chief liaison officer between the Dutch and British military. He also organized the War Weapons Fund, collecting money from overseas Dutch companies to purchase warplanes for the Royal Air Force (RAF). Bernhard even joined the fighting as an RAF pilot.

Bernhard agreed with Retinger and others at a Paris meeting in 1952 that Europe had to involve the US more deeply in its affairs. With this goal in mind, Retinger went to America and met with David Rockefeller, Averill Harriman and current CIA Director General Walter Bedell Smith. The result was a Europe-focused American group, chaired by Burroughs Corporation President John Coleman.

It was at this time that Retinger and Rothschild convinced Bernhard to form the Bilderberg group, which he chaired until 1976. Bernhard may have revealed the Bilderberg agenda when he stated, "Here comes our greatest difficulty, for the governments of the free nations are elected by the people, and if they do something the people don't like they are thrown out. It is difficult to reeducate the people who have been brought up on nationalism to the idea of relinquishing part of their sovereignty to a supranational body."

Bernhard and the other Bilderberg members proceeded with their plan to combine Europe into a free-trade conglomerate that would make it impossible for developing nations in Africa and Asia to adopt trade restrictions. "From sheer necessity these people will have to join in free trade," Bernhard said.

One of the first successes of this program came immediately after the war with the creation of the European Coal and Steel Community (ECSC) under the Schuman Plan. It combined French and German steel and coal resources within a supranational authority, which some historians believe was the incipient beginning of the EU. The scheme was brokered by Jean Monnet, a lifelong socialist whose resume included the post of deputy secretary-general of the League of Nations.

Monnet met Retinger in this capacity.

During World War II, Monnet served British interests in the US as a member of the British Supply Council, arranging war materiel purchases. Following the war, Monnet became the key figure in the Committee for European Economic Cooperation (CEEC) as its vice chairman. With the help of Washington attorney George Ball, who would join the Bilderberg group later, Monnet succeeded in getting the US aid needed to breathe life into the CEEC. For this and other achievements, John F. Kennedy credited Monnet with doing more in 20 years to unite Europe than 1,000 years of conquerors.

Into the 1950s, Monnet continued to pursue his goal, founding the Action Committee for a United States of Europe, which led directly to the 1957 Treaty of Rome that created the European Common Market. According to George McGhee, a Bilderberg member and former US ambassador to West Germany, the Treaty of Rome was "nurtured at Bilderberg meetings." This is supported by the fact that the movement was almost completely funded by the Marshall Plan, the CIA and Bilderberg-related organizations like the Rockefeller, Ford and Carnegie Foundations.

Monnet didn't live to see his dream, the formation of the EU, realized. On January 1, 1999, the euro became the common currency of every Western European nation except Great Britain. A European Central Bank was created to handle monetary policy, issuing euro notes and coins on January 1, 2002, and pre-existing national currencies were removed from circulation two months later.

The formation of NATO after World War II was a major coup for the globalist Bilderbergers, because not only did it blend the military power of many nations into a single force, it created an operations base for subverting recalcitrant governments. Chief among those was the French government of Charles de Gaulle, who recognized the Bilderberg Plan to eliminate national sovereignty and combine nations into an Anglo-American dominated whole. Chief among the problems was de Gaulle's refusal to allow France to join NATO and to eliminate his country's nuclear deterrent, despite its vital importance in countering the Soviet nuclear threat. Within de Gaulle's government, Prime Minister Georges Pompidou and Ministers Antoine Pinay and Guy Mollet actively opposed their leader's policy. All three were associated with the Bilderbergers.

Another frustration to the group's plans involved British nationalism, causing its politicians to hesitate in joining the European

Common Market and later the European Union. This hesitance continued for decades, extending to Britain's failure to embrace the euro at first. Sources privy to the inner workings of the 1998 Bilderberg conference at the Turnburry Hotel in Scotland claimed that Prime Minister Tony Blair was lectured like a schoolboy for his inability to put his nation on the new currency.

Prince Bernhard's reign atop the Bilderberg group ended in 1976 with the revelation that he had accepted bribes of more than $1 million from Lockheed Aircraft when he was inspector general of the Dutch armed forces. The investigation indicated that he solicited the bribes in exchange for influencing the purchase of fighter planes by the Dutch government. Along with his Bilderberg position, Bernhard relinquished his public offices and military titles. He died in 2004, but his daughter, Queen Beatrix of the Netherlands, is a regular attendee of Bilderberg conferences.

Since Bernhard, the Bilderberg chairmen have been marked by their high political positions and their connections to world banking empires like that of the Rothschilds. For instance, Lord Peter Carrington chaired the Bilderbergers in the 1990s after having been a British cabinet minister, the secretary-general of NATO, the president of the Royal Institute of International Affairs (the British arm of the CFR) and an associate of the Rothschilds on both a business and personal level. The current steering committee president, Etienne Davignon, achieved a high post in the Belgian government before attaining the vice presidency of the European Commission, the executive body of the EU. Davignon also chaired the Rothschild-connected bank, *Societe Generale de Belgique,* for more than a decade.

Based on the names of power brokers, both American and foreign, who have attended Bilderberg meetings over the years, some researchers have tabbed the group as an unofficial international version of the CFR. The recognizable American attendees included Dean Rusk, McGeorge Bundy, Dean Acheson, Zbigniew Brzezinski, J. Robert Oppenheimer, Robert McNamara, Jacob Javits and Henry Ford II. European attendees included Giscard d'Estaing, Helmut Schmidt, Georges-Jean Pompidou and Baron Edmond de Rothschild.

Former British intelligence officer Dr. John Coleman claimed that the Bilderbergers are a creation of MI-6, the equivalent of the CIA in the UK. And upon seeing the many members and attendees who have known connections with the CIA, it is likely that the group is at least partially sponsored by that agency.

Jim Tucker, a journalist who has investigated the Bilderbergers for many years, said, "The Bilderberg agenda is much the same as that of its brother group, The Trilateral Commission....David Rockefeller founded the Trilaterals but shares power in the older Bilderberg group with the Rothschilds of Britain and Europe."

Today the Bilderberg meetings continue to be held annually. They are marked by the strictest security. Arrests have been made of reporters foolish enough to approach the meetings. In 1998, reporter Campbell Thomas of the *Scottish Daily* was handcuffed by security officers and held for eight hours because he walked past the cordon protecting a Bilderberg meeting at the Turnberry Hotel near Glasgow.

Despite the secrecy of its meetings, minutes from the very first Bilderberg gathering were leaked. Included was this statement: "Insufficient attention has so far been paid to long-term planning, and to evolving an international order which would look beyond the present day crisis [the Cold War]. When the time is ripe our present concepts of world affairs should be extended to the whole world."

The influence exercised by the Bilderbergers over media coverage is awesome. Take the case of reporter C. Gordon Tether, who wrote in the London *Financial Times* in 1975, "If the Bilderberg group is not a conspiracy of some sort, it is conducted in such a way as to give a remarkably good imitation of one." A year later, Tether's editor, Max Henry Fisher, a member of the Trilateral Commission, fired him.

In June 2001, *American Free Press* Midwest Bureau Chief Christopher Bollyn traveled to the Hotel Stenungsbaden in Gothenburg, Sweden, where that year's annual Bilderberg meeting took place. On the first day of the meetings, Bollyn took photos from a private property adjacent to the hotel, having received permission from the property's owner. Swedish police seized him anyway, drove him six miles into a wilderness area and left him there.

Journalist Daniel Estulin has been dogging the Bilderbergers for nearly two decades. The son of a Russian dissident who was jailed and tortured by the KGB, his family was expelled from the Soviet Union in 1980. Estulin claims he receives valuable information from former KGB agents, owing to the fact that his grandfather was a colonel in that intelligence organization. He also admits to having "conscientious objectors" inside the Bilderberg Group who smuggle information to him.

One of Estulin's Russian sources is a former KGB agent he calls

"Vladimir." During a surreptitious meeting at a restaurant, Vladimir showed him a number of documents, including the orchestrated removal of Philippine President Ferdinand Marcos by the Trilateral Commission. Other documents included minutes of meetings where the JFK assassination was discussed, and minutes from the Club of Rome 1980 meeting in Washington DC, in which attendees endorsed a radical global genocide plan called the Global 2000 Report. Details of this incredible Malthusian scheme are in a subsequent chapter of this book.

One of Estulin's "conscientious objector" sources inside the Bilderberg meetings tape recorded a Henry Kissinger speech given on May 21, 1992 at the Evian, France, conference. Kissinger's words speak for themselves: "Today, Americans would be outraged if UN troops entered Los Angeles to restore order. Tomorrow they will be grateful. This is especially true if they were told there was an outside threat from beyond, *whether real or promulgated*, that threatened our very existence. It is then that all people of the world will plead with world leaders to deliver them from this evil. The one thing every man fears is the unknown. When presented with this scenario, *individual rights will be willingly relinquished* for the guarantee of their well-being granted to them by their world government." (Emphasis added).

Some of Estulin's insiders have been attending Bilderberg meetings for decades. One of them reported a conversation he overheard in the late 1970s between Kissinger and Canadian Prime Minister Pierre Trudeau, in which Kissinger said, "Jimmy Carter is not the President of the United States. The Trilateral Commission is the President of the United States. I represent the Trilateral Commission."

Estulin claims his revelations of the Bilderberg secret agenda have made him the target of threats and even possible attempts on his life. During the 1996 Bilderberg meetings in Toronto, Canada, Estulin met with one of his moles who handed him notes he'd scribbled from the various speeches. The pair left the hotel room where they met and went to the elevator. When the elevator door opened and Estulin moved to enter, his mole grabbed him. There was no elevator, just an empty shaft with an 80-foot drop. A hotel security guard later explained that someone had manually stopped the elevator, which could be accomplished only in an emergency.

Estulin believes the Bilderberg meetings follow the protocol established during the Versailles peace conference of 1919, in which participants may use information from various speeches, but are prohibited from identifying the speakers or their affiliations, and from identifying any other participant.

The price tag for the annual four-day Bilderberg conferences is staggering. Bilderberg participants have estimated that the 2003 meeting held in the Trianon Palace in Versailles cost 10 million euros, according to Estulin. One of the palace's staff members told Estulin that David Rockefeller ran up a 14,000 euro telephone bill in three days.

Currently, the Bilderberg conferences feature about 80 regular members who have been attending for many years. Added to this number are those invitees who report on subjects within their own expertise, but may be ignorant of the group's globalist agenda.

Paul Wolfowitz was photographed in 2005 at a Bilderberg meeting. He'd just been appointed to head the World Bank. Wolfowitz reportedly attended previous meetings while serving as deputy secretary of defense, a violation of the Logan Act, which stipulates that it is a federal offense for any member of the federal or state government to meet with members of a foreign government without the express authority and authorization of the president or Congress. This is why the names of American politicians who attend the Bilderberg meetings are not included on the list of attendees. However, leaks from sources inside the conference have provided an impressive list of Logan Act violators: CIA Director Allen Dulles, Senator William Fulbright, Governor Nelson Rockefeller, Defense Secretary Robert McNamara, US Ambassador to the USSR George Kennan, Governor John D. Rockefeller IV, Secretary of State Cyrus Vance, National Security Advisor Zbigniew Brzezinski, Secretary of State Alexander Haig and Secretary of State Henry Kissinger.

The Bilderberg dominance among the advisors to US administrations began with the Kennedy presidency, whose State Department virtually was staffed by what *Life* magazine publisher C.D. Jackson called "Bilderberg alumni." Among the alumni were Secretary of State Dean Rusk, Undersecretary of State George Ball, and advisors Walter Rostow, George McGhee, Arthur Dean, McGeorge Bundy and Paul Nitze.

There have been many accusations that the Bilderberg group has become "kingmakers." An early example of this occurred in 1975 when, for the first time, the group invited a female to attend the annual meeting. She was only a back bench conservative member of British Parliament at the time, and a grocer's daughter. Four years later, Margaret Thatcher became prime minister of England. But by 1987, Thatcher's resistance to placing Britain in the EU had become obnoxious to the Bilderberg agenda. A challenge to her leadership of the Conservative Party caused Thatcher to resign in 1990.

A similar fate befell President George H.W. Bush when, in its 1990 meeting at Glen Cove, New York, the Bilderbergers allegedly decided that debts owed to international banks required the US to raise taxes. Bush's campaign of "Read my lips, no new taxes" fell on deaf ears within the group. Bush then signed one of the largest tax increases in American history and was defeated in the 1992 election after serving just one term.

Tony Blair attended the 1993 Bilderberg conference and gained leadership of his party the following year. In 1997, Blair became Britain's prime minister.

Romano Prodi, who served as president of Europe from 1999 to 2005 before becoming prime minister of Italy in 2006, attended the 1998 Bilderberg conference.

Jimmy Carter qualifies as another Bilderberg/CFR/Trilateral creation. In the fall of 1973, David Rockefeller had dinner in London with Carter to sound him out on important issues. He was impressed with the Georgia governor's track record in leading the state's trade missions overseas. Rockefeller invited Carter to join the Trilateral Commission and according to a *London Times* account, he believed Carter "could project an image of a Southern Governor that could be used to fool many voters by appearing 'conservative' or 'moderate,' while in fact favoring the most left-wing of agendas. The idea was to court both White and Black voters who could be delivered by the Democratic Party's big urban political machines."

According to Gary Allen's harsh appraisal of Carter's character in his 1976 book, *Jimmy Carter, Jimmy Carter,* the globalists saw in him a willing and controllable player. "Carter's overwhelming ambition and corruptibility made him vulnerable," wrote Allen. "It included conniving with his own personal banker, Bert Lance, to funnel back depositors' money into Carter's peanut business and into the bank accounts of Lance associates and family members to finance Carter's campaign, while waiting for federal matching funds. The illegalities involved were enough to send the whole gang to jail. And the key to exposure was in the hands of David Rockefeller and his fellow banking insiders."

In a campaign scenario that would be repeated with the emergences of Clinton and Obama in their respective primary campaigns, Carter went from five percent support among Democrats to the clear choice of his party and rode the wave into the White House.

"To accomplish this purpose," wrote Barry Goldwater, "they mobilized the money power of the Wall Street bankers, the intellectual influence of the academic community — which is subservient to the wealth of the great tax-free foundations — and the media controllers represented in the membership of the CFR and the Trilateral."

The man who replaced George Bush in the White House, Bill Clinton, had attended and addressed the 1991 Bilderberg meeting. According to Estulin, prior to announcing his candidacy in 1992, Clinton was sent by the Bilderbergers to Moscow to bury the KGB files that existed on his student era anti-Vietnam War activities. Estulin also claims that during this junket, Clinton promised then-Russian President Boris Yeltsin that if he won the election, Russian warships would be given refueling and other privileges in all US naval bases.

When Clinton took office in January 1993, he urged Congress to ratify the Bilderberg-backed North American Free Trade Agreement (NAFTA) that had been signed by Bush, Mexican President Carlos Salinas de Gortari and Canadian Prime Minister Brian Mulroney in December 1992. It is not difficult to believe the claims that Bush had been urged to sign this agreement by the Bilderbergers, because it would eliminate trade barriers among the three nations. There was significant opposition to the treaty in all three nations. American labor unions warned of a dramatic loss of American jobs when domestic firms would relocate to countries with lower wage scales. Others claimed the agreement would lead to a flood of illegal immigrants pouring into the US from Mexico. But Clinton succeeded in convincing Congress to ratify NAFTA. Its immediate result was the loss of four million American jobs and, in time, a quadrupling of illegal immigrants from Mexico.

NAFTA, in fact, was a prime reason for the boom in illegal immigration, according to *Washintgon Post* writer Harold Meyerson. Taking information from economist Jeff Faux in 2006, Meyerson wrote, "Mexico had been home to a poor agrarian sector for generations, which the Mexican government helped sustain through price supports on corn and beans, but NAFTA had put those farmers in direct competition with incomparably more efficient US agribusinesses. It proved to be no contest: From 1993 through 2002, at least two million Mexican farmers were driven off their land."

Mexican industry fared no better. In 1975, Mexican wages amounted to 23 percent of US wages. By 2002, after ratification of NAFTA, that figure had shrunk to 12 percent. Yet George W. Bush embraced NAFTA as a great success, an example why all national impediments to trade should be removed.

Clinton continued to promote the Bilderberg agenda when he addressed the Asia-Pacific Economic Community (APEC) meeting in Seattle, Washington, saying, "The Asia-Pacific region should be a united one, not divided." Like NAFTA, the critics of APEC charged the agreement with destroying national economies and handing control of trade to a small group of oligarchs.

Clinton also had an active hand in creating what some historians refer to as a new kind of war when he ordered US armed forces to lead NATO in its attack on Serbia in 1999. This so-called Kosovo war was celebrated by Bilderberg participants at their May 1999 conference in the Caesar Park Hotel in Sintra, Portugal, as the first "post-nationalist war." They believed it solidified the EU by changing foreign policy toward universal aims rather than national interests.

In 2004, a little-known senator from North Carolina attended the Bilderberg meeting and spoke glowingly about NAFTA in his speech during the conference's second day. His name was John Edwards. Various sources inside the meeting told Daniel Estulin that the speech had so impressed the membership, Henry Kissinger phoned then presidential candidate John Kerry immediately and said, "We have found your vice president." Edwards apparently was being groomed as a presidential candidate for the 2008 race until he disgraced himself with an extramarital affair while his wife was terminally ill. Currently he is under indictment for using campaign money to support his mistress and the child he sired with her.

The list of Bilderberg meeting attendees immediately moving into high political positions is not limited to heads of state. George Robertson, who became NATO secretary general in 1999, attended the previous year's Bilderberg meeting. Other NATO secretaries general who belonged to the Bilderberg group included Joseph Luns (1971-84), Lord Carrington (1984-88), Manfred Woerner (1988-94), Willy Claes (1994-95), Javier Solana (1995-99), and Jaap G. de Hoop Scheffer (2004).

Politicians willing to promote the Bilderberg gospel are abundant, reducing them almost to puppets. The group's goals have been set in stone, and perhaps never more clearly than in a presentation made at the

1968 Bilderberg conference by former diplomat and cabinet member George Wildman Ball, called "Internationalization of Business." Author Peter Beaudry summed up the talk in his book *Synarchy Movement of Empire*: "Ball presented an outline of the advantages of a new colonial world economic order based on the concept of a world company, and described some of the obstacles that needed to be eliminated for its success. According to Ball, the first and most important thing that had to be eliminated was the archaic political structure of the nation state....For Ball, the very structure of the nation state, and the idea of the commonwealth, or of a general welfare of a people, represented the main obstacle against any attempt of freely looting the planet, especially the weak and poor nations of the world, and represented the most important impediment to the creation of a neo-colonial world empire."

That the Bilderbergers affect the lives of every American was never clearer than during 1973 energy crisis and its associated inflation. Supposedly caused by the OPEC oil embargo levied against the US for its support of Israel in the Yom Kippur War of that year, the shortage wreaked havoc across America. Lines of cars extended for up to half a mile from literally every gas station, sometimes creating hours-long waits to get to the pump. There were violent incidents, including shootings. But Daniel Estulin believes the cause of the shortage was Bilderberg-inspired and much more sinister.

"At a meeting in Saltsjobaden, Sweden, in 1973," he wrote, "the Bilderbergers agreed to increase the price of oil to $12 a barrel, a 350 percent jump meant to create economic chaos in the United States and Western Europe, in order to prop up the oil corporations' sagging fortunes. The perceived oil shortage formed part of the backdrop of the staged Arab-Israeli war, and provided a cover for the formal endorsement of major price agreements negotiated prior to the outbreak of war."

Author and former MI-6 agent Dr. John Coleman also implicates the Bilderberg group in the assassination of former Italian Prime Minister Aldo Moro in 1978. Moro, leader of the Christian Democrat Party, opposed the zero population growth plans of the globalists. For this reason, Coleman wrote in *Conspirators' Heirarchy*, Moro "was murdered by assassins controlled by P2 Masonry with the object of bringing Italy into line with Club of Rome and Bilderberg orders to de-industrialize the country and considerably reduce its population....Moro's plans to stabilize Italy, through full employment and industrial and political peace, would have strengthened Catholic opposition to Communism and made the destabilization of the Middle East — a prime goal — that much harder."

A left-wing terrorist group called the Red Brigades was blamed for kidnapping and incarcerating Moro in broad daylight and shooting him weeks after killing all of his bodyguards. But years later, Moro's friend Gorrado Guerzoni dropped a bombshell in a Rome courtroom by testifying that Moro was "threatened by an agent of the Royal Institute for International Affairs [RIIA] while he [the threatening party] was still Secretary of State."

Coleman points out that several members of the Red Brigades at their trial "testified that they knew of high level US involvement in the plot to kill Moro." The widow of Moro testified in June and July 1982 that serious threats against his life had been made by "a high ranking United States political figure." Her recollection of the threat was identical to what Guerzoni had recalled: "Either you stop your political line or you will pay dearly for it."

The trial judge recalled Guerzoni and asked him to identify the person who made the threat. Guerzoni testified that it was Henry Kissinger. To the author's knowledge, not a single American television news program broadcast this information.

Coleman also connects the Bilderbergers to Watergate, specifically through member Katherine Graham, who was publisher of the *Washington Post* between 1963 and 1993. Graham was the daughter of Wall Street entrepreneur Eugene Meyer, who was implicated but never convicted of embezzling massive funds from the World War I Liberty Bonds drive, and wound up as a governor of the Federal Reserve. Meyer also became president of the World Bank. In 1933, he bought the *Washington Post* cheaply in a bankruptcy sale.

Daughter Katherine married Phillip Graham, an attorney, who became publisher of his father-in-law's newspaper. In 1963, Graham died, either by suicide or murder. Coleman's book accuses his wife of murdering him so she could take control of the paper. Interestingly, no libel suit resulted from the bold accusation.

When the Watergate break-in became news, it began a long and almost unbroken series of *Washington Post* "exclusives," which were repeated by an obedient electronic media. Coleman and other authors provide evidence that these news items were handed to Graham's paper by CIA agents, some of whom actually were involved in the original break-in. The reason why the CIA and the Bilderbergers wanted Nixon out of office, according to Coleman, was because he vehemently opposed the General Agreement on Tariffs and Trade (GATT). This was an important legislative step in the Bilderberg strategy for "post industrial zero growth," the de-industrializing of the US and the reduction of America's armed forces following the end of the Vietnam War.

Playing a dark background role at this time was, once again, Henry Kissinger. As Nixon's National Security Advisor, Kissinger also had charge of a small Bilderberg-arranged group that included Alexander Haig, James Schlesinger and *Pentagon Papers* whistle blower Daniel Ellsberg. They worked alongside Noam Chomsky of the Institute of Policy Studies (IPS), a creation of Britain's Round Table which received its agenda from the Tavistock Institute. Together, beginning in the 1960s, they helped to create the "New Left," an apparent grass roots movement, to promote unrest and violence. It was a repetition of the old game in which a frightening, violent element is created in order to justify more stringent policies to combat it, including Constitutional violations.

When Nixon publicly declared his opposition to GATT, David Rockefeller became infuriated, according to Estulin. He added that Rockefeller also "was enraged with Nixon's New Economic Policy (NEP) of 1971, which tried to impose government management over the most basic elements of the market through wage and price controls and increased tariffs. For 90 days, Nixon succeeded in freezing wages and prices to check inflation."

Rockefeller attempted to pull Nixon back on to his own liberal internationalist course during a private meeting on international currency and trade, but his views were dismissed as "not especially innovative."

Rockefeller apparently went to Plan B. Shortly after Kissinger became national security advisor, he and his Bilderberg-arranged group put in motion the RIIA Watergate plan to oust the president. In April 1974, Nixon had to abolish the NEP system. Four months later, he resigned amidst a blizzard of Watergate-related criminal evidence. Ironically, the shamed Nixon was proved right just 20 years after his resignation when European Parliament member and billionaire Sir James Goldsmith testified to the US Senate that GATT would erode American sovereignty.

The reach of Bilderberg influence even has extended into the American educational system. During the annual meeting at Bad Ragaz, Switzerland, in 1970, the group hatched a plan that became reality in the "Goals 2000" program under President George H.W. Bush to rearrange the American public school system. The stated goal of the new educational approach was "subordination of national ambitions to the idea of the international community...." The ultimate aim was to teach American children to consider themselves "world citizens."

There is no question that US policy often is set down in secret Bilderberg meetings. One example, US government refusal to allow domestic firms to accept lucrative contracts to build nuclear power plants in Third World nations, has been sold in the media as prevention of nuclear proliferation. But according to former MI-6 agent and author John Coleman, the real reason is that both the US and the Bilderbergers know that nuclear power would provide cheap and abundant energy, which would bring "Third World countries out of their backward state....Third World countries would gradually become independent of US foreign aid, which keeps them in servitude, and begin to assert their sovereignty."

But not all American policy has been Bilderberg-friendly. Serious friction still exists over the US invasion of Iraq in 2003. According to *Asia Times* reporter Pepe Escobar, "American imperial adventures are usually rehearsed at Bilderberg meetings. Europe's elite were opposed to an American invasion of Iraq since the 2002 Bilderberg meeting in Chantilly, Virginia...Europe's elite, according to those close to Bilderberg, are suspicious that the United States does not need or even want a stable, legitimate central government in Iraq. When that happens, there will be no reason for the United States to remain in the country. Europe's elite see the United States...establishing a long-term military presence and getting the oil flowing again under American control."

One surprising admission which followed the most recent Bilderberg meeting in Sitges, Spain, came from former NATO Secretary General Willy Claes during an interview on Belgian radio. Claes, fresh from the meetings at the Hotel Dolce, said to host Koen Fillet that Bilderberg does indeed decide global policies for the coming year.

The "surprise" element affected only those who wished to believe the tale that the Bilderbergers are simply a think tank that provides advice.

The Institute for International Affairs

The CFR was created in 1919 as the American branch of Europe's Institute for International Affairs. The British branch was formed about the same time as the Royal Institute for International Relations (RIIA) by the estate of Cecil Rhodes under the guidance of Boer War veteran Lionel Curtis. Its purpose: expand British world influence. The creation of the American version sought to marry the interests of the two nations' upper classes in policymaking.

The inspiration for both organizations can be traced to the Round Table group of Cecil Rhodes. Aside from founding the Rhodes Scholarship, Rhodes' fortune went to this secret society after his death, with instructions to preserve and expand the British Empire.

Rhodes was born in 1853, immersed throughout his youth in religious training by his vicar father. In 1879, he traveled to South Africa to work with his brother on a cotton farm, but soon the brothers became enamored of diamond prospecting. Rhodes split time between this and his studies at Oxford University in England, where he began his relationship with John Ruskin, the professor who became his mentor. Ruskin, too, was deeply religious in his early life before he fell under the influence of esoteric spiritualist Helena Blavatsky and became an atheist. The concept of secret societies became his new religion.

It has been written that Ruskin read Plato's *Republic* daily, smitten by its description of the ideal social structure based on centralized leadership of a ruling class. He once wrote, "My continual aim has been to show the eternal superiority of some men to others, sometimes even of one man to all others."

Psychologists would have a field day studying the complex Ruskin, whose sexual problems resulted in the annulment of a six-year marriage that he never consummated. His lone sexual release was through masturbation, reportedly fantasizing about underage girls.

And yet, Cecil Rhodes was enamored with the teachings of this man, despite the fact that Rhodes mixed with Britain's most influential people — Lord Randolph Churchill, Arthur Conan Doyle, Oscar Wilde and Rudyard Kipling — as a fellow Freemason.

Rhodes returned to South Africa, where he established his diamond company, de Beers, and by the early 1890s, the firm owned 90 percent of all diamond production worldwide. In the mid-1890s, he created the Diamond Syndicate and also moved into South Africa's burgeoning gold mining business. He did all of this with financial aid from the Rothschild banks, a business relationship that continues to this day with de Beers.

According to author John Coleman, the Rothschild money also aided in the creation of Rhodes' Round Table group, which was actually a collection of groups in the Freemason mold. An inner membership, called the Circle of Initiates, was steeped in secrecy while the outer circle lived up to its title, Association of Helpers. Among the inner circle members were Lord Victor Rothschild and Sir Alfred Milner, British high commissioner of South Africa. Milner is blamed by many historians for instigating of the Boer War, which gave Britain control of South Africa's rich resources.

Backed by the tremendous wealth from the Rhodes diamond and gold mines, the Round Table established groups in a wide array of nations, influencing financial policies and even politics in each place. It became an early version of the multi-national corporations of today with myriad companies, banks, foundations and educational institutions. Its purpose has continued to be the perpetuation of British rule throughout the world, including — as written in Rhodes' will — "the ultimate recovery of the United States of America."

When Rhodes succumbed to a heart attack in 1902, control of the Round Tables fell to Milner, Rothschild and other bankers who, after World War I, expanded the groups even further and created the RIIA as a cover organization. The new groups included the Institute for Advanced Study (IAS) at Princeton University, whose members — Robert Oppenheimer, Albert Einstein and Niels Bohr — became major contributors to the atom bomb project.

The new IAS joined yet another university-based secret society already fully functional in America.

Skull and Bones

In 1832 at Yale University, General William Russell and Alphonso Taft (father of US President William Howard Taft and himself once the US attorney general) founded the secret order of Skull and Bones. The order's insignia, the familiar pirate emblem of a skull with crossed bones above the number "322," may very well have been derived from the original emblem of the Knights Templar.

According to one report, Russell took the idea for the order from a secret German society and founded it as an American extension. There is no solid evidence as to which secret German group influenced Russell, but it is possible that the Illuminati of Bavaria was the source, especially since it also used the skull and crossbones emblem. In addition, various Masonic iconography, German slogans and the Order's initiation room are identical to Masonic lodges associated with the Illuminati.

According to Anthony Sutton in his book, *America's Secret Establishment,* the members of Skull and Bones "know it as The Order. Others have known it for more than 150 years as Chapter 322 of a German secret society....It was also known as the Brotherhood of Death."

Authors Webster Griffin Tarpley and Anton Chaitkin went so far as to claim the Skull and Bones is a "story of opium and Empire, and a bitter struggle for political control over the new US republic." The "opium" reference points to the fact that General Russell's cousin, Samuel Russell, helped to instigate Britain's Opium Wars in China. It also supports a rumor that the original purpose of the society was drug smuggling.

The Order of Skull and Bones officially became incorporated as the Russell Trust in 1856 and meets annually at secluded Deer Island in the St. Lawrence River between New York and Canada. Only 15 new members are invited to join each year following their junior year at Yale University. As with other secret groups, new members must begin at the lowest rung and work their way up to full membership, known as the Patriarch level.

Obviously, invitations to join depend greatly on family heritage, as only a handful of families make up the core of Skull and Bones. Among them are the Rockefellers, Harrimans, Bushes and Paynes. Some of the oldest family membership names are known to have created their fortunes originally in the slave trade.

Having achieved permanent membership, a young man's career success is practically assured, owing to the nepotism of the group. Skull and Bones also helps members in times of trouble, as evidenced by the potential scandal that involved George H.W. Bush with the Bank of Credit and Commerce International (BCCI) criminal activities in the 1980s. Bush, a Skull and Bones member, was bailed out by the failure of a senate investigation to prove anything substantial against him. This investigation was chaired by Senator John Kerry, himself a Skull and Bones member. According to Jack Blum, a special counsel on Kerry's committee, "A high level cover-up of everything concerning BCCI was set into place after Customs stumbled across their money-laundering operation in Miami, and it's still in place."

Skull and Bones has produced an inordinate number of men in powerful positions ranging from politics to publishing. As US presidents, CIA officials, publishers, and CEOs, the Skull and Bones inner circle has influenced the history of America for more than a century. Some researchers have maintained that the Order is a means to joining the CFR, the Trilateral Commission and the Bilderberg group.

Headquartered in a nearly windowless Greco-Egyptian building called The Tomb on High Street in the middle of the Yale campus, little is known of the rituals and ceremonies performed by Skull and Bones members inside. However, *New York Observer* reporter Ron Rosenbaum accompanied a group of Yale students who managed to videotape part of the group's initiation ceremony, which took place in the courtyard of The Tomb. It was impossible to see or videotape the indoor portion of the ceremony.

During the outdoor ceremony, the camera captures rituals that imitate human sacrifice. There is a lot of hysterical screaming by the senior student members wearing hooded robes as the 15 "neophytes" are inducted. Their chants include, "The devil equals death, and death equals death." The "neophytes" are forced to kiss a skull at one point.

New members are assigned secret names, by which they are called for the rest of their lives. The name "Long Devil," goes to the tallest member. A member who achieves athletic prowess often earns the name "Boaz," which is short for Beelzebub. Publisher Henry Luce earned the name "Baal." The names "Gog" and "Magog" go to incoming members with the least and most sexual experience.

Among the most pervasive rumors about Skull and Bones is that initiates must masturbate in a coffin while recounting their sexual exploits to members. Allegedly, they are rewarded for the humiliation with a gift of $15,000. Bonesmen who have been sworn to secrecy during these initiations have not denied the rumors when questioned by journalists.

Once initiated, they become "brothers under the skin." They have their meals together in The Tomb, drinking non-alcoholic beverages out of skull-shaped mugs.

One rumor had it that the skull of the Native American hero Geronimo decorates one of The Tomb's walls, stolen in 1917 by Prescott Bush, father and grandfather of two presidents. Under pressure from Apache tribal chairman Ned Anderson in the 1980s, the society had to offer the skull for inspection. It didn't match Anderson's records of Geronimo, and so was returned to The Tomb.

The number 322 refers to the year in which the Greek orator, Demosthenes, died in 322 BC, according to the more sober accounts of the group's traditions. The society maintains that Demosthenes made what amounts to a Second Coming upon its inception in 1832. But there have also been claims that the number 322 was the combination to Skull and Bones member Averill Harriman's briefcase containing top secret dispatches between the US and Great Britain during World War II.

The living membership is between 500 and 800 at any given time. Nearly every one of them is or has been in highly influential positions in politics, finance and business. Skull and Bones clearly is more than just another foolish college fraternity. And it draws its organizational structure as well as its insistence on secrecy — like all of the other groups described in this section — from much older societies.

THIRD MOVEMENT – *DIMINUENDO*
SECRETIVE SOCIETIES

"The very word secrecy is repugnant in a free and open society, and we are a people inherently and historically opposed to secret societies, the secret oaths and secret proceedings. We decided long ago that the dangers of excessive and unwarranted concealment of pertinent facts far outweighed the dangers which are cited to justify it."

—John Fitzgerald Kennedy, in his inaugural speech, 1961

The Illuminati

According to *The New Encyclopedia Britannica,* "the Illuminati, [is] a rationalist secret society organized by [Adam] Weishaupt [a professor at Ingolstadt University]. Its goal was to rival and replace the Catholic sense of community in 18th century France."

The term, Illuminati, means "holders of the light," indicating the group's fealty to Lucifer, the Lord of the Light.

Three years prior to the forming of the Illuminati, Pope Clement XIV banned the Jesuit order. Adam Weishaupt, who had spent years studying to become a Jesuit, broke with the Church, but he retained his Jesuit teachings. He also came under the influence at this time of a mysterious man known to history simply as Kolmer. Sources indicate that Kolmer had lived in the Near East for many years, becoming versed in esoteric knowledge from Persia and Egypt. The doctrine he preached to Weishaupt was a throwback to the Gnostic school, which the Church called heretical Manichaeism, and which coined the word "Illuminated" some time before the 3rd century.

Weishaupt's goal was to combine Kolmer's knowledge with other occult systems, forming a new "Illuminated" order that denied formal religions. When adherents gathered, Weishaupt organized a hierarchy in a pyramid structure similar to the way the Jesuits and Freemasons were organized. A series of levels, "degrees," placed the most important, dedicated and talented persons at the top.

Secrecy was vital, as the Church continued to torture and burn heretics through the Inquisition. Weishaupt even used a code name, Spartacus, among his fellow members.

The Bavarian Illuminati officially came into being on May 1, 1776, under the guidance of Weishaupt. Note that this date remains sacred into modern times as May Day, the traditional communist International Workers' Day. Weishaupt formed the group with help from Prince William of Hesse, according to some claims. You will recall that William at that time employed Mayer Amschel Bauer (Rothschild). This has led to speculation that Rothschild was the prime mover in convincing Weishaupt to create the Illuminati.

Evidence for this lies in copies of a speech Rothschild made during a meeting he'd arranged with 12 wealthy Europeans in Frankfurt am Main, Germany, as early as 1773. The 30-year-old Rothschild proposed a plan to gain control of most of the world's riches and resources, thereby controlling the world's population. Details of this 25-step plan are available in the Epilogue of this book.

During the meeting, Rothschild discussed the shortcomings of the English Revolution, how it had not been fast or ruthless enough in eliminating reactionaries. He urged that a future revolution would require a reign of terror to cow the masses.

Former Canadian naval commander William Guy Carr in his book, *Pawns in the Game,* summed up the achievements of these powerful European bankers in the previous decades: "By means of intrigue carried out on an international scale, they had increased the national debt steadily by loaning the money to fight the wars and rebellions they had fomented since 1694."

Rothschild promised his audience that the financial gain they enjoyed from those years would be insignificant compared to the riches and power to be obtained from a French revolution. He proposed a new plan which, according to Carr, "would be backed by all the power that could be purchased with their pooled resources....By clever manipulation of their combined wealth it would be possible to create such adverse economic conditions that the masses would be reduced to a state bordering on starvation by unemployment. By use of cleverly conceived propaganda, it would be easy to place the blame for the adverse economic conditions on the King, his Court, the Nobles, the Church, Industrialists, and the employers of labor."

Weishaupt revised the Rothschild plan slightly in 1784, had it written in a document titled *Einige Original-Scripten,* and sent a copy of it by courier to other members of his Illuminati in Paris. But en route, the courier, named Lanze, died from a lightning strike while passing through Ratisbon, and Bavarian police discovered the documents on his body. They forwarded them to higher Bavarian authorities, who immediately raided Weishaupt's new Lodges of the Grand Orient and the homes of his associates, like the castle of Baron Bassus-in-Sandersdorf. The additional evidence gained in the raids convinced authorities that the Illuminati was a satanic secret organization dedicated to fomenting war and overthrowing governments through violent revolution. Monarchies and religions were to be replaced, according to the plan, by a one-world government and religion, under Illuminati control.

An 18th century professor from Edinburgh University, John Robison, provided another peek into the secretive Illuminati plans. As secretary of the Royal Society of Edinburgh, Robison accepted an invitation to join the Illuminati, and was disturbed by what he learned. He gathered this information into a book, ponderously titled, *Proofs of a Conspiracy Against All the Religions and Governments of Europe Carried on in the Secret Meetings of the Free Masons, Illuminati and Reading Societies.* In it, Robison quoted some of Weishaupt's letters to fellow members. One reads: "The great strength of our Order lies in its concealment. Let it never appear in any place in its own name, and another occupation. None is fitter than the three lower degrees of Freemasonry; the public is accustomed to it, expect little from it, and therefore takes little notice of it. Next to this, the form of a learned or literary society is best suited to our purpose...By establishing reading societies and subscription libraries...we may turn the public mind which way we will. In like manner we must try to obtain an influence in...all offices which have any effect, either in forming, or in managing, or even in directing the mind of man."

Robison also revealed that Weishaupt instructed his higher degree members to conceal their true intentions from their own initiates so they might be led toward goals unknown to them. In Weishaupt's words, "I have two immediately below me into whom I breathe my whole spirit, and each of these two has again two others, and so on. In this way I can set a thousand men in motion and on fire in the simplest manner, and in this way one must impart orders and operate on politics."

Weishaupt often used the phrase, "the end justifies the means," and added, "The Order will rule the world. Every member therefore becomes a ruler."

Weishaupt also was a Freemason, having joined Munich's Lodge Theodore of Good Counsel, which included among its members Honore Gabriel Riqueti, known as the French revolutionary, Mirabeau.

Aside from its natural hostility toward the Catholic Church, the Illuminati also opposed the governments which supported that religion. "Man is not bad except as he is made so by arbitrary morality," wrote Weishaupt. "He is bad because religion, the state, and bad examples pervert him. When at last reason becomes the religion of men, then will the problem be solved."

The Bavarian government saw the Illuminati as a threat for obvious reasons, and in 1785 outlawed the group, causing its members to flee to other lands. New and more secret Illuminati orders appeared in France, Italy, Britain and America. But Weishaupt remained at the apex of his pyramid organization, wholly anonymous to all but a few of his underlings.

Although the Bavarian government tried to warn other national leaders of the danger posed by this Order, members of the Illuminati managed to infiltrate the French Freemasons. In a few short years, the political agenda of the Bavarian Illuminati had become that of the French Masonic lodges. In a way, the Illuminati had become a secret society within another secret society.

These secret societies helped to instigate the French Revolution under the guidance and leadership of the Duke of Orleans. The Duke was grandmaster of French Masonry until he resigned after the revolution was underway, and after the Jacobin Club — radicals who were at the heart of the revolutionary movement — was founded by Freemasons.

France was close to bankruptcy following its tremendous financial and military support of the successful revolution in America. The rich court of Louis XVI and his wife Marie Antoinette at Versailles contrasted sharply with the squalor and starvation of nearby Parisians. Food was already scarce when the Duke of Orleans reportedly pushed the situation toward the crisis point by purchasing all of the French grain in the harvest of 1789 and either sold it abroad or hid it. His contemporary, Galart de Montjoie, literally placed the whole blame for the revolution upon Orleans, but warned that he "was moved by that invisible hand which seems to have created all the events of our revolution in order to lead us to a goal that we do not see at present."

The French Freemasons had by this time become thoroughly infiltrated by the Bavarian Illuminati, according to Guiseppe Balsamo, who gained historic fame as Count Cagliostro in the court of Louis XVI. "By March 1789," wrote Balsamo, "the 266 lodges controlled by the Grand Orient [Lodge of Freemasons] were all 'illuminized' without knowing it, for the Freemasons in general were not told the name of the sect that brought them these mysteries, and only a very small number were initiated into the secret."

These "illuminized" Freemasons became part of the National Constituent Assembly, and formed a group they called the Society of the Friends of the Constitution. When the National Assembly moved to Paris, this group held its meetings in a hall leased from the Jacobin convent of the Dominican order. Radically pro-revolution and anti-aristocracy, they came to be known as the Jacobin Club.

The great names of the French Revolution are a collection of men that were initiated into the "third degree" of Illuminized Freemasonry: Orleans, Lafayette, Marat, Danton, Robespierre, Mirabeau and Demoulins, to name a few. Mirabeau, who delivered "The Oath of the Tennis Court" that led to the storming of the Bastille, held political and social views that were identical to those of Adam Weishaupt. Mirabeau wrote of his desire to create complete anarchy, adding that while the public should be promised power, it should be withheld from them. His views toward the Catholic clergy called for its complete destruction.

There were about 2,000 Masonic Lodges in France by 1789, so it should not surprise that the 605-member Estates General, which was called to solve the nation's financial problems, consisted of 447 Freemasons. And when the Freemason-populated National Assembly issued its Declaration of the Rights of Man, this proclamation was filled with the Masonic tenets of liberty, equality, the right to resist oppression and the inviolability of private property. King Louis refused to approve this declaration, and a Paris mob forced him to move from Versailles to virtual house arrest in his royal Parisian palace. He had to sit by while the National Assembly made new laws, nationalizing all Church property to pay the country's debt.

After a failed attempt to escape the country, the king was captured and placed under guard, eventually meeting his end at the guillotine. The French Revolution had consumed its monarchy. Soon it would consume itself.

But the Illuminati sect which had instigated the uprising and guided its terror not only survived, but flourished. In the wars that would follow for the next quarter century, international bankers, especially the Rothschilds, enriched themselves through interest-laden government loans. In the end, the Rothschilds would have control of the Bank of England and a number of continental national banks. They would be the undisputed masters of European finance, and thereby masters of Europe itself.

Mayer Amschel Bauer's 1773 plan had come to fruition.

The Secret Masonic Agenda

Simply stated, Freemasonry has been the vehicle for passing the secret doctrines and mysteries of the ancients through the ages to the present day. The higher degrees of Freemasonry reportedly receive this information, which contains the hidden knowledge of ancient Egypt and the teachings of Pythagoras. How this information has been used is why religions and governments have been hostile to Freemasonry through the centuries.

The Masons have a Latin slogan, *Ordo ab Chao,* which means "Order out of Chaos." Some believe this seemingly innocent phrase actually refers to the Hegelian statement that "crisis leads to opportunity." It follows that a secret society with this agenda would create chaos or crisis whenever possible in order to further its plans.

One excellent example of this in recent history is the P2 Masonic Lodge of Italy. It continued well into the 20th century after its founding in 1877 as *Propaganda Masonica Due.* Licio Gelli headed P2 beginning in 1966, and increased its membership from just 14 to nearly 1,000. One of the new members, Mino Picorelli, was a journalist who blew the whistle on CIA funding of P2, and he paid for it with his life, shot in the mouth.

Besides heading P2, Gelli was the business partner of convicted Nazi war criminal Klaus Barbie, financially backed fascist Argentine dictator Juan Peron, and according to an Italian court indictment, ran a secret structure that had "the incredible capacity to control a state's institutions to the point of becoming a state-within-a-state."

Gelli mixed with American Presidents Ronald Reagan (he was a guest at the 1980 inauguration) and George H.W. Bush. The extent of his P2 plot came to light in 1981, when Italian police turned up a list of his Masonic co-conspirators, including three Italian cabinet ministers, 40 members of Parliament, 43 generals, eight admirals, numerous industrialists, bankers, journalists, diplomats and the police chiefs of four cities.

His plan was displayed in a document titled "The Strategy of Tension," which laid out means of creating a rash of leftist terrorism in order to move the Italian people toward desiring an authoritarian government. The plan was a spinoff of an American operation created by James Jesus Angleton shortly after World War II, called "Gladio." Italy was in danger of succumbing to communist rule at the time, so Gladio called for alliances between the Mafia and Vatican officials to create what would appear to be leftist terrorism.

"False flag" bombings killed innocent civilians throughout Europe. The bombs were made and planted by NATO operatives, but the blame was placed on Marxist terrorists. These astonishing charges were proved in Italian courts by documents and corroborated by Italy's President Francesco Cossiga, who admitted that he actually founded the Italian Gladio operation.

Investigators directly connected P2 with the bombing of the Bologna train station in 1980, which killed 85 people. There even was some evidence that P2 had a hand in the Pan Am Flight 103 bombing over Lockerbie, Scotland, in 1988. The airline's insurance investigators reported that on board was a team of researchers en route to Washington to report CIA drug smuggling and gun running in the Middle East, financed by P2.

Author Jonathan Vankin wrote of allegations made by the Italian media that P2 was partially funded through a Panamanian company, Amitalia, and that the 1989 invasion of Panama ordered by President Bush was partially intended to destroy records of Amitalia that linked him, the CIA and P2 to the Pan Am crash.

Henry Kissinger also became implicated in the P2 trials, as mentioned in a previous section of this book. While looking into the kidnap-murder of former Italian Prime Minister Aldo Moro in 1978, Moro's widow and one of his close associates testified that Kissinger had warned Moro to change his stabilizing policies in Italy "or you will pay dearly for it." Moro's murder had been blamed on the leftist terrorist group the Red Brigades.

An article in the London *Independent* echoed this evidence and suggested Moro's murder may have been arranged by the CIA with P2 members inside the Italian government.

The P2 scandal spread to consume the Vatican. P2 Lodge members Roberto Calvi and Michele Sindona engineered several shady financial deals with the Vatican Bank, which was then under the directorship of Bishop Paul Marcinkus, an American. Charges of money laundering for the Mafia and questionable investments in Calvi's *Banco Ambrosiano* implicated the Vatican and began a series of suspicious deaths.

Calvi, who fled to London, turned up at the end of a rope, hanging beneath Blackfriars Bridge. Enemies hanged by rope above water are a repeated feature in Freemason-suspected assassinations, which will be addressed again in the final chapter of this book. Just hours before Calvi's body was discovered, his secretary and P2 Lodge bookkeeper Graziella Corocher "fell" from the fourth floor of the *Ambrosiano* bank.

In 1979, an estate liquidator named Giorgio Ambrosoli was shot and killed soon after he discovered evidence of crimes committed by P2 Lodge member Michele Sindona. Seven years later, Sindona was convicted of arranging this murder. Two days after receiving his life sentence, Sindona was found dead in his cell from cyanide poisoning.

Bishop Paul Marcinkus returned to the US, where an attempt to extradite him to New York for trial by prosecutor Frank Hogan was blocked by the White House. He died at age 84 in Arizona, refusing to the last to discuss the scandal.

Gelli escaped his Italian indictments and went into hiding. The most recent reports have him living comfortably in a large villa near Arezzo, Italy, aged 91.

This sad episode is merely a recent example of the war between the Catholic Church and Freemasonry. Mystery schools began to suffer suppression in the 6th century, which is when they went underground into secret societies. Pope Clement XII condemned Freemasonry outright in 1738, charging that the organization is pagan and promised excommunication to any Catholic who joined it.

Over the centuries, charges of Satanism have been leveled at the higher degrees of Freemasonry. Modern authors like Ralph Epperson concluded that the secret god of the Masons is Lucifer, and that its basic plan is the utter destruction of Christianity.

The Luciferian aspect of the cult has been mentioned by Masonic writers, too. W.L. Wilmshurst, a Mason author of several books that attempt to explain the organization, wrote, "Christian and Masonic doctrine are identical in intention though different in method. The one says *'Via Crucis'* [through the Cross]; the other *'Via Lucis'* [through Lucifer, or Light]; yet the two ways are but one way."

At one stroke, Wilmshurst seems to connect the Freemasons with the Albigensians, the name the Church branded upon the Cathars that flourished in southern France between the 11th and 13th centuries. This sect held a dualistic view of creation, in which two separate deities — one good which ruled the heavens, the other evil, ruling the earth — are in a constant struggle for the soul of mankind. As the Cathars taught that the Christian, Hebrew and Muslim deities are the evil god, it was only a matter of time before they were brutally exterminated in the Church-mandated Albigensian Crusade that began in 1209.

A chilling revelation of the upper degrees of Masonry has been offered by Leo Lyon Zagami, who had achieved the 33rd Masonic degree, a high membership post in P2, and a place on the Masonic Executive Committee of Monte Carlo. Zagami rose to such prominence among the Italian Illuminati that he was groomed to succeed Licio Gelli as the Illuminati "king."

Zagami's alleged aristocratic Illuminati bloodline — he claims to be a descendant of Giuseppe Balsamo, known to history as Cagliostro, the Illuminati Grand Master — meant that he was deeply involved with the Order since childhood. His mother was of the Lyon family, the same bloodline as the mother of England's Queen Elizabeth. His father is of the diGregorio family, keepers of the Sicilian Knights of Malta, the high-ranking echelon within Freemasonry.

But after many years of participation in the cult's rituals, which according to Zagami were satanic and involved mind control, black magic, torture and death, he broke with the Illuminati and fled to Norway, his current residence. Claiming that he's received death threats, Zagami has been exposing the dark practices of the various Illuminati lodges in order to make himself known and perhaps more difficult to eliminate. He's accepted interviews on various broadcast programs, made videos posted on sites such as YouTube, and opened a website called "Illuminati Confessions."

Zagami admits that "most of the Masons on the lower levels are misled, and the ones who start seeing the real light are thrown out of the organization…because they pose a threat." He adds that those among the upper levels of the Illuminati perform a satanic ritual called the "Eleventh Degree," evoking the demon Choronzon which only can be accomplished through anal intercourse. According to Zagami, this ritual was devised by the famed British satanist, Aleister Crowley, and is at the root of at least some of the pedophilia scandals currently plaguing the Vatican and the Catholic Church in America.

One of the surprises in Zagami's revelations involves his claim that the Sicilian Mafia, Freemasonry and the Vatican are closely tied together in Italy. "The members of these lodges were high level Vatican clergy, high level Mafiosi from all the main Sicilian Mafia families, and many politicians," wrote Zagami. "Mafia and Freemasonry in Trapani and Palermo have ruled the scene for a long time…Powerful Mafiosi Natale L'Ala was an *Iside-2* [Isis-2] and [the] politician Canino, [a] member of the Scontrino circle, openly admitted that their lodges were full of Catholic bishops and government ministers. But it was Mafia boss Stefano Bontate, a creation of the Jesuits, that rebelled and founded his own Grand Lodge…known as the powerful Lodge of the 300…."

Zagami claims that a Vatican Illuminati exists, made up mostly of Jesuits with a New World Order agenda for a single world government and a single world Luciferian religion. He named Bishop Marcinkus among the members of his P2 lodge in Monte Carlo.

Zagami also maintains that Vatican Illuminati were known as "brothers of the ear," meaning they do the bidding of the lodge Grand Master only after receiving verbal requests, with nothing in writing that might implicate them. Though this flies in the face of the supposed death struggle taking place between Freemasonry and the Catholic Church, it does fit into the Hegelian dialectic philosophy of the Illuminati to combine thesis and antithesis for synthesis.

The Jesuit connection to the Illuminati extends centuries into the past, according to Zagami, who claims that his ancestor Cagliostro always brought along a Jesuit priest in his travels. The priest, according to Zagami, would precede Cagliostro to a place, gather information on various people including secrets he gained during confessions, and report it to his cohort so he could impress the populace with his "so-called magical powers of prediction."

It's important to note that the Jesuit order, which was under a Vatican ban at this time, constantly schemed to regain its position in the Church. Zagami maintains the Jesuits were "involved in the black arts and they were themselves actually atheists at heart." He added that most modern Illuminati Satanists are atheists who "don't even believe in Satan, they just believe in nothing…."

Today the "main base" for Jesuit-Freemason synergy is in Livorno, according to Zagami, who claims its choice has to do with its large Jewish community. He says the city's port is the entry point for illegal arms deals brokered by the US and recently, China. The connection also extends to an organization called Cesnur, headed by Massimo Introvigne and sponsored by the Jesuits, which researches and infiltrates new religious groups.

Introvigne, supposedly a conservative Catholic, also is a member of

Draconis, a notorious meeting place for Satanists, according to Zagami. Introvigne had connections to Alberto Moscato, a former ranking member of the *Guardia di Finanza,* which investigated Internet fraud and pedophile rings. But Moscato, who has disappeared, was a heroin addict, Grand Master of the Satanic Illuminati *Ordo Templi Orientis Caliphate,* and had connections to the satanic Anton LaVey church, according to Zagami.

There also is a close connection between the Illuminati and various intelligence services like the CIA, MI-6 and even the Mossad. In a radio interview on the GCN Network, Zagami said, "When you actually work within the frame of the Illuminati, you end up also working with the intelligence [organizations]. There is like an interconnection down the line, because we work with some of the same things. For example, one of the main specialties of the Illuminati is mind control."

He went on to say further connections involved striving toward a New World Order "known in Italy as *Unita Mundiale.* One World, without frontiers, one single currency...." He claims the Jesuits have been cooperating with Zionists, specifically the Rothschilds, toward this end.

Since blowing the whistle on Illuminati practices, however, Zagami shifted his stance radically during a two-month Tour of Hope in the US, claiming to be the Grand Master of European and US Illuminati, representing the "good side" of the order.

The Masons refer to their "good" God of the heavens as the Great Architect of the Universe, and their teachings also hint of powerful nonhuman "gods" that were present on Earth in the remote past, bringing civilization to humanity. This concept can be traced to the translated writings of the Sumerians, the oldest civilization known to modern archeology.

The Rosicrucian Order shares many aspects with the Freemasons, so many in fact that some authors claim Freemasonry emerged from this secret brotherhood whose teachings are said to be ancient. Its proper title, Order of the Rosy Cross, has been traced to 1188 when it was founded by a Templar Knight (the same military entity that would later change Freemasonry to its current state) named Jean de Gisors. The presence of Rosicrucian philosophy among the higher degrees of European Freemasonry became apparent in the mid-18th century.

About a century prior to that, books published under the name of Christian Rosencreutz, the last name meaning "rosy cross," presented a tale of travel through the Holy Land collecting esoteric knowledge. The book also contained many symbolic references to the Knights Templar, which resulted in its condemnation by the Catholic Church, accusing the Rosicrucians of being Satanists guilty of child sacrifices. Defenders of the Rosicrucians claim that the Order simply represented scientific rationalism which inevitably collided with Church dogma. In either case, the hostility of the Christian religions forced the Rosicrucian Order underground.

That Francis Bacon was a Rosicrucian in addition to being a Freemason indicates the overlapping relationship between the two orders. By the late 18th century, the Masonic and Rosicrucian Orders had fundamentally merged.

Writers like Dr. Henry Makow, creator of the game "Scruples," Australian political scientist Dr. Michael Salla, and former *Forbes* magazine bureau chief Benjamin Fulford believe there is an intense struggle today between the Western Illuminati and the secret societies inside China and Japan. Much of the conflict is fueled by the New World Order agenda of depopulation, which would mostly affect the densely populated nations like China and India. According to Salla, these huge populations are the reason why new energy technologies, already in existence, have been suppressed.

Salla wrote: "Cheap inexpensive energy that could be produced in-house would rapidly transform major population centers like China and India, which currently struggle to feed and provide jobs for all citizens, into flourishing financial powerhouses where its citizenry's full productive capabilities are utilized. Such a development would transform the way global financial structures are dominated from capital intensive industries in US/Europe to energy/intellectual intensive industries in China/India...That would not only lead to a great erosion of Illuminati power and prestige due to its current control of global financial institutions, but would also lead to a diffusion of technological capacities that would significantly erode US hegemony in that area."

Salla, who is convinced that there are multiple extraterrestrial races visiting the Earth and who has written of the political implications regarding the extraterrestrial presence, believes a secret reverse engineering program on alien technology currently is dominated by the US military-industrial complex. He claims the Illuminati are "providing significant financial resources and global networks to ensure that the US gets the lion's share of extraterrestrial technologies recovered world wide."

Former *Forbes* magazine Bureau Chief Benjamin Fulford claims that, should the New World Order depopulation program begin, the Western Illuminati will be targeted for death by the secret Chinese Green and Red Societies that boast 100,000 assassins and 1.8 million Asian gangsters.

"The Illuminati, with the exception of Japan, is very much a white man's game," Fulford said, warning Asia that the Illuminati plans to reduce Asia's population to 500 million with race-specific biological weapons. Fulford, who lives in Japan, claims to have been in contact with the Chinese secret societies and says he provided them with a list of 10,000 people associated with the groups Bilderberg, CFR, and Skull and Bones.

He also claims that Japan has been controlled by the Western Illuminati since the end of World War II, and in that time Americans have murdered more than 200 Japanese politicians and influential citizens, including former Prime Ministers Tanaka, Takeshita, Ohira and Obuchi. Although all died from apparent strokes, Fulford's sources say these were induced by a special drug.

Fulford also claims that the agenda for the New World Order changed with the debacle of the Iraq War, going from a US-dominated one-world government to one led by the EU. "To do this, they will sabotage the US economy," he predicted in 2005. With the American economic calamity that began late in 2008, Fulford seems to have been correct.

"However, there is a big schism in the secret government," Fulford wrote. "Jay Rockefeller and Philip Rothschild support one faction, the global warming faction. Opposing them is the war on terrorism faction, supported by David Rockefeller and the J.P. Morgan descendants (Bush, Harriman, Walker, etc.). The warming people want to sell 500 nuclear power plants to China and a similar amount to the rest of the world. The terrorism guys want to keep US dominance by maintaining control over oil."

There have been other enormous setbacks suffered recently by the Illuminati. When Vladimir Putin came to power in Russia, he arrested or forced the exile of Illuminati members like Nieslev, Bereshovsky and Khordokovsky, and according to Fulford, "He basically kicked the Rockefellers and Rothschilds out of Russia. I have good Russian sources and I am confident that Putin is a nationalist who is fighting the

Illuminati with all his might."

Past setbacks included India, where the Illuminati was forced to leave when Mahatma Ghandi took power, after centuries of dominance through the East India Company. Mao Tse Tung kicked the Illuminati out of China in the 1960s, which nearly caused nuclear war with then Illuminati-dominated Russia.

Fulford claims the Illuminati currently is attempting to create a financial crisis in China which would allow them into the Chinese financial system, but he predicts they will fail in this venture.

Many of these far-reaching plans of the Western Illuminati are formulated, according to some researchers, in the seemingly relaxed atmosphere of a California camp ground that caters to the most powerful men in North America.

The Bohemian Grove

The Bohemian Club was founded in 1872, with its members seeking a remote place in Northern California that was removed from what they considered the backwardness of the West Coast. Its membership has included every Republican president since Calvin Coolidge.

The associated Bohemian Grove is located near the town of Monte Rio, north of San Francisco, and consists of 2,700 acres of redwood wilderness. The annual gatherings, which begin on Bastille Day, July 14 and last three weeks, always have involved what Bohemian members call "druid rituals." All of the campgrounds, the Mandalay Camp, the Wolf Camp, the Hill Billies' Camp to name a few of the 119 sites, are decorated with wooden or stone owl sculptures.

Each annual gathering begins with the "Cremation of Care" ceremony, an elaborate ritual in which participants burn an effigy of "Dull Care" at the Grove's 40-foot-tall, owl-shaped lakeside altar. Dressed in a hooded robe similar to those used in the Skull and Bones initiation and in Masonic ceremonies, a "high priest" chants against this "arch enemy of beauty," according to an excerpt from the ceremony text.

"Dull Care," represented by another robed person, responds to the burning by reminding the gathering, "When again ye turn your feet toward the marketplace, am I not waiting for you as of old?" The priest responds, "We know thou waitest for us when this our sylvan holiday shall end," but concludes, "Our fellowship has banned thee for a space, and thy malevolence that would pursue us here has lost its power beneath these friendly trees."

The ceremony was surreptitiously videotaped from a distance during the July 2000 conclave by a film crew under the direction of journalists Mike Hanson and Alex Jones and is available online at various sites like YouTube. It reveals groups of men in hooded robes gathered around the owl altar in torchlight, apparently participating in a mock sacrifice. The sight would be strange enough in itself, but it becomes truly bizarre when the participants are revealed.

The Bohemian Grove has become a meeting place for the elite of the world. Membership is highly coveted, and it is not rare for men to wait 10 to 15 years before being approved after a member recommends them. Currently there are more than 2,500 members.

Over the years, membership has included Presidents William Howard Taft, Herbert Hoover, Dwight Eisenhower, Ronald Reagan, Richard Nixon, Bill Clinton, George H.W. Bush and his son George W. Bush. Many of the highest ranking persons in the federal government are Bohemian Club members, including the men who have controlled the Federal Reserve Bank since its inception in 1913. Alan Greenspan was photographed leaving the Bohemian Grove just a month before his appointment as Chairman of the Federal Reserve. Of course, Henry Kissinger and David Rockefeller also are members, completing the list of the usual suspects.

The membership also includes celebrities and foreign notables. One of the foreign leaders, Helmut Schmidt, former Chancellor of Germany, wrote about the club in his memoir, *Men and Powers: A Political Retrospective.* In it he revealed that he met many of the future power brokers and influential politicians of America at the Bohemian Grove, and was able to gauge US policy long before it was implemented thanks to these meetings.

Schmidt described the grounds in detail: "The encampment in the grove is not a large common camp; the two thousand or so men who spend the weekend together live in five or six dozen small camps, almost entirely concealed by trees and bushes, scattered along the hillside. Some of the camps consist of log cabins, others of wooden huts, still others are made up of tents; there are electric light and running water."

Schmidt also wrote of the presence in the Grove of "professional intellectual politicians who never run for office but offer their services to the elected politicians and the candidates — *at times even force them on them* — as expert advisers and executive officers." (Emphasis added).

The suspicion that national policy is made here has caused the creation by Mary Moore of the Bohemian Grove Action Network (BGAN), an organization that has monitored and exposed the annual lakeside talks for many years. On its fact sheet, the network claims Grove members "drink heavily from morning through the night, [and] bask in their freedom to urinate on the redwoods, and perform pagan rituals."

The Nation columnist Andrew Cockburn supported the BGAN assertion that drunkenness is rife during the three-week retreats. He described the scene as "hundreds of near-dead white men sitting by a lake listening to Henry Kissinger, plus many other near-dead white men in adjacent landscapes in a state of intoxication so advanced that many of them have fallen insensible among the ferns, gin fizz glasses gripped firmly till the last."

Press coverage inside the Bohemian Grove gatherings is almost non-existent, and for good reason. Many members of the club own powerful media outlets like Time Warner, which spiked a story by the San Francisco bureau chief of its *People* magazine, Dirk Mathison, in 1991. Mathison had infiltrated the Grove three times in July 1991 before being recognized by a Time Warner executive who was attending the retreat and who escorted him to the gate. Mathison and his managing editor, Landon Jones, believed he had enough for a large story in *People* anyway, and scheduled it to appear in the magazine's August 5, 1991 issue. It never made it to press, and Landon issued the lame excuse that he'd killed the story because Mathison hadn't been in the Grove long enough. Mathison carefully commented that his editors' spiking of the story "had more to do with their bosses, not mine."

On December 31, 1991, less than six months after his Bohemian adventure, Mathison lost his job when Time Warner shut down his San Francisco bureau in an alleged cost-cutting measure.

Another enterprising reporter had better luck. In 1989, Philip Weiss of *Spy* magazine not only managed to infiltrate the Grove posing as a member, but brought along a tape recorder and camera (violating a Grove rule) and stayed for the entire three-week session. Weiss provided the most detailed descriptions of life among the redwoods and the oligarchs, who he concluded were emotionally arrested in pre-adolescence due to their crass misogynistic jokes and their penchant for pissing outdoors.

Weiss described a typical day: "The traditional 7:00 a.m. gin fizzes served in bed by camp valets set the pace. Throughout the skeet-shooting, the domino-playing and the museum talks, right up through the 'afterglows' that follow each evening's entertainment, everyone is perpetually numbed and loose, but a clubbish decorum prevails just the same. No one throws up. Now and then, though, a Bohemian sits down in the ferns and passes out."

Aside from Weiss, the only other truly successful infiltration of the Grove took place in 1974 when San Francisco writer John van der Zee posed as a waiter and wrote a book about what he saw, titled *The Greatest Men's Party on Earth*.

Stories from inside the Grove rarely make it to print because so many media moguls have been members or guests. These include former Times-Mirror CEO Franklin Murphy, William Randolph Hearst Jr., Jack Howard and Charles Scripps of the Scripps-Howard newspaper chain, and former CNN president Tom Howard. Louis Boccardi spoke at one of the lakeside talks when he was president of Associated Press, and the late Walter Cronkite was a member of the same Grove lodge that housed George H.W. Bush. In fact, Cronkite's voice has served as the voice of the Owl of Bohemia during the rituals.

These media members and guests have agreed never to report what takes place during the Grove gatherings, which is why National Public Radio did not air a surreptitiously recorded Kissinger "lakeside talk" it had obtained in 1982, and why the story by *Time* magazine reporter Bob Buderi, who had successfully penetrated the Grove as a waiter, was spiked that same year.

Still, some information continues to trickle out into the open. The BGAN reported that in 1981, the secretary of defense in the new Reagan administration, Caspar Weinberger, delivered a sermon in the Grove titled "Rearming America." The US embarked on a massive rearmament program immediately afterward, indicating that the concern of the BGAN over creating policy in the Grove is not unwarranted.

Lakeside talks similar to Weinberger's occur twice daily during the gatherings in the Grove every summer. Over the years, these talks have consistently predicted policies and events. On July 22, 1991, former Nixon administration Secretary of Defense Elliot Richardson's talk was titled "Defining a New World Order." Supreme Court Justice Antonin Scalia spoke of "Church, State and the Constitution" on July 25, 1997. Henry Kissinger on July 29, 2000, titled his talk, "Do We Need a Foreign Policy?"

The BGAN fact sheet claims that the Manhattan Project, which built the first American atomic weapons, "was conceived at the Grove in 1942." Berkeley physicist Ernest Lawrence developed the cyclotron, vital to uranium enrichment, in the 1930s. He and his protégé, Berkeley physicist Luis Alvarez, sought and received funding through the Bohemians after attending a Grove gathering in 1942. At this meeting, considered the first of what eventually became the Manhattan Project, they chose the site where plutonium would be weaponized for nuclear bombs, which eventually came to be known as the Lawrence Livermore Labs. This information is corroborated in the Bohemian Grove Museum

Committee's own publication, *Walking Bohemians Home,* which identified the Club House Chalet in the Grove as "the site of the meeting which conceived the Manhattan Project, resulting in the atom bomb."

In 1974, University of California, Santa Cruz Professor G. William Domhoff published *The Bohemian Grove and Other Retreats: A Study in Ruling Class Cohesiveness,* which revealed that the powerful elite in the US are able to communicate freely and in secret through organizations like the Bohemian Club. Domhoff concluded there is no doubt deals are made at the Grove, affecting the future of nations.

This is precisely the reason why protesters gather outside the Grove's entrance every year. The BGAN fact sheet explains: "This close-knit group determines whether prices rise or fall by their control of the banking system, money supply and markets, and they make money whichever way the markets fluctuate. They determine what our rights are, and which laws have effect, by appointing judges. They decide who our highest officials shall be by consensus among themselves, and then sell candidates to us via the media, which they own."

Touted as an innocent gathering of men — the Bohemian Club is restricted to males only and women were not permitted to work there until a 1987 Supreme Court ruling — the Grove received some unwanted publicity in 1993 when Clinton advisor David Gergen quit and aired his reasons in the press. Gergen stated to the *Washington Times* that he left the group because he "would not run around naked." He cited the ritualistic chantings which required members to strip naked. Gergen also resigned from 17 other interest groups, including the Trilateral Commission, the Bilderbergers and the CFR.

In the July 22, 2004 edition of the *New York Post,* the Grove received another black eye when it was reported that a gay porn star who uses the stage name Chad Savage worked there as a valet. Savage, who earned a decent living performing in films such as *How the West Was Hung,* almost certainly was not there to collect small wages (tips are forbidden in the Grove) as a valet.

Rumors of rampant homosexuality have dogged the Bohemian Grove for decades, and the resort was named as the site of a gay child pornographic snuff video shot during the 1980s. The accusation was made by a victim, Paul Bonacci, who was a child at the time the alleged killing took place. Although there is no reason to assume the incident occurred during a Bohemian conclave, it is disturbing that the men responsible had access to the exclusive property. Bonacci's astonishing tale will be detailed in a subsequent book.

Homosexuality in the Grove also has been noted by the BGAN, which claims in its fact sheet that an estimated 20 percent of the members "engage in homosexual activity, but few of them support gay rights or AIDS research. They watch and participate in plays and comedy shows in which women are portrayed by male actors. Although women are not allowed in the Grove, members often leave at night to enjoy the company of the many prostitutes who come from around the world for this event...Employees of the Grove have said that no verbal description can accurately portray the bizarre behavior of the Grove's inhabitants."

Spy magazine reporter Weiss saw it firsthand. "Even 100-year-old Grove annals have a homoerotic quality," he wrote, "with references to 'slender young Bohemians, clad in economical bathing suits.' Nudity was more common then. Today AIDS has put a damper on the Grove's River Road pickup scene, which Herb Caen used to write about in his *San Francisco Chronicle* gossip column. Just the same, a man on his own often gets invited back to camps by gay Bohemians."

Weiss also noted that the atmosphere during the "Cremation of Care" ritual has "vaguely homosexual undertones...as they do much of the ritualized life in the Grove. The main priest wore a pink-and-green satin costume, while a hamadryad appeared before a redwood in a gold spangled bodysuit dripping with rhinestones. They spoke of 'fairy unguents' that would free men to pursue warm fellowship...."

When Richard Nixon's voluminous taped conversation transcripts from the Oval Office were declassified in October 1999, one recording caught the president saying, "The Bohemian Grove, which I attend from time to time...is the most faggy goddamned thing you could ever imagine with that San Francisco crowd."

A young man who worked at the Grove in 2004 and 2005 came to journalist Alex Jones with insider information on this issue. Preferring to remain anonymous under the name "Kyle," he claimed that he constantly was approached by "old men" with propositions for sexual favors. These "old men" are the movers and shakers of America and the world. Kyle also spoke of an annual festivity at the Grove, known as Gypsy Jazz, where one year the all-male audience booed when the performer announced that the composer of the previous tune liked women.

Kyle proved that he did indeed work in the Grove by producing photos he'd taken with a concealed pen camera. He said the site has an elite section, the Mandalay Camp, which is off limits to all but certain

Bohemian Club members. According to him, Secret Service and private security agents patrol the perimeter and refuse to allow anyone within 100 yards of that campground. The compound is located on a hilltop, accessible only by a cable car.

Former Mandalay residents have included IBM director S.D. Betchel; Leonard Firestone, director of Firestone Corp.; ex-President Gerald Ford; former Secretary of State George Schultz; and Najeeb Halaby and Phillip Hawley, co-directors of the Bank of America, to name just a few. Mandalay "guests" have included Kissinger and CIA Director William Casey.

As Grove members like to boast that global policy is made there, Mandalay apparently is the campfire capstone of the New World Order pyramid.

FOURTH MOVEMENT – *ARS ANTIQUA*
THE TRAIL OF TEARS

"When a government is dependent upon bankers for money, they and not the leaders of the government control the situation, since the hand that gives is above the hand that takes. Money has no motherland. Financiers are without patriotism and without decency. Their sole object is to gain."

—Napoleon Bonaparte, 1815

Central Banks in America

The first central bank in the US was created in 1781. Prior to that, the settlers of the New World used Colonial Scrip, issued by the various colonies in proportion to the demands of trade and industry. It allowed products to pass easily from producers to consumers, and also enabled the colonies to control the purchasing power of their money without having to pay interest on its creation.

The Currency Act of 1764 put an end to this. British Parliament passed the bill at the urging of the Bank of England. Benjamin Franklin claimed that this, as much as any other factor, caused the American Revolution, because the bill created an economic depression and boosted unemployment. America had its first taste of debt-encumbered money.

After the Revolution established the American republic, Alexander Hamilton and the Federalists pushed for a central bank overseen by a wealthy elite class. Hamilton's opponents referred to him as a tool of the international bankers. Chief among Hamilton's accusers was Thomas Jefferson, who knew from his service in France that a central bank could quickly come to dominate a nation's government. "Banking establishments are more dangerous than standing armies," he said. Years later he wrote to John Taylor in 1816 that "the principle of spending money to be paid by posterity under the name of funding is but swindling futurity on a large scale…The issuing power should be taken from the banks and restored to the people, to whom it properly belongs."

Jefferson even felt that a central bank would violate the US Constitution, quoting from it that "all powers not delegated to the United States by the Constitution, nor prohibited by it to the States or to the People," are unconstitutional. He saw that the basic role of any central bank, setting interest rates and controlling the money supply (creating inflation or deflation) was in the hands of a few unelected individuals, totally beyond control or approval by the populace.

Hamilton and the Federalists won the day, however, and the Bank of North America was created by Robert Morris in 1781. It was modeled after the Bank of England, creating a partnership between the government and the banking interests. It practiced "fractional reserve banking," lending money it did not possess at interest. The bank's charter required private investors to put up $400,000 in capital, but Morris was unable to raise this sum, so he deposited gold lent to the US by France and then re-lent this money to himself and to friends to be invested in Bank of North America shares. Few Americans saw the irony of creating a system in their new republic that they had fought a revolutionary war to avoid.

The fledgling US government granted the new central bank a monopoly over the national currency. Under this arrangement, American currency plummeted in value. The experiment lasted only four years. Congress refused to renew the Bank of North America charter following widespread fraudulent practices and a ruinous inflation.

Leading the anti-central bank faction in Congress was William Findley, who said, "The institution, having no principle but that of avarice, will never be varied in its object...to engross all the wealth, power and influence of the state."

A former proponent of the central bank, Gouverneur Morris, radically changed his position after witnessing the inflation, and said, "The rich will strive to establish their dominion and enslave the rest. They always did. They always will....They will have the same effect here as elsewhere, if we do not, by government, keep them in their proper spheres."

In 1791, Hamilton led another attempt, establishing the First Bank of the United States, again overcoming strong opposition from Jefferson. Modeled once more on the Bank of England, 20 percent of this new bank's capital was obtained through the federal government and the rest pledged by private investors. Among these investors were foreign bankers like the Rothschild family. In 1790, Amschel Rothschild had announced from his bank in Frankfurt, Germany, "Let me issue and control a nation's money and I care not who writes the laws."

Hamilton's persistence in establishing a central bank in America reveals him as a tool of the international bankers like the Rothschilds. One of Hamilton's first positions after graduating from law school in 1782 was aide to Robert Morris, then head of the Bank of North America. Morris may have hired the young firebrand based on a letter Hamilton wrote to him the previous year, which said, "A national debt, if it is not excessive, will be to us a national blessing."

The First Bank of the United States soon proved to be very much like its predecessor, creating inflation by using fractional reserve notes. It held a monopoly on printing US currency despite the fact that more than 80 percent of its stock was privately held. As with the previous American bank and the Bank of England, these stockholders never paid the full amount for their shares. The government put up $2 million in cash, allowing the bank to lend its charter investors enough money to cover the remaining $8 million needed to capitalize the bank. Like its predecessor, the names of the investors in the First Bank of the United States never were revealed, but historians are confident the Rothschilds were principal among them.

During its first five years of existence, the bank loaned $8.2 million to the US government, and in this same period, prices rose by 72 percent. Thomas Jefferson, witnessing this sad state of affairs, wrote, "I wish it were possible to obtain a single amendment to our Constitution, taking from the federal government their power of borrowing."

After 20 years of suffering by average citizens, the bank's charter came up for renewal in 1811. The Pennsylvania and Virginia legislatures passed resolutions that asked Congress to deny renewal. The press launched a campaign against the bank, calling it "a viper" and "a great swindle." Representative P.B. Porter said in Congress that if the charter was renewed, it will have "planted in the bosom of this Constitution a viper, which one day or another will sting the liberties of this country to the heart."

The charter renewal was defeated by a single vote in the House and was deadlocked in the Senate. Vice President George Clinton cast the tie-breaking vote there and the bank's charter was not renewed.

The power brokers in the Bank of England decided to intervene. After the US government ignored the dire warning of Nathan Rothschild that, "Either the application of the charter is granted, or the United States will find itself involved in a most disastrous war," the banker went into action. He pressured Parliament and the Crown to "Teach those impudent Americans a lesson. Bring them back to colonial status."

Within five months of the charter vote, Britain created hostilities with the United States in what came to be known as the War of 1812. That it was an expensive undertaking for the young nation which drained its treasury was no accident. The strategy of the bankers in England was to sink America into such a state of financial debt that the national credit standing would be destroyed and the nation would have to renew the central bank charter.

It worked. The War of 1812 drained American finances for two years before it ended with a treaty that had changed absolutely nothing except damaging the new nation's financial status. In 1816, Congress issued a new 20-year charter to the Second Bank of the United States. The new charter was identical to that of the previous one, in that the US Treasury paid its 20 percent of the shares in cash at the outset. This money was loaned by the bank to private investors who used the borrowed money to buy the remaining 80 percent of the shares. Although the stockholders' identities remained secret, at least one third of the shares definitely were sold to foreign investors. Some authors claim that by 1816, the Rothschilds owned the controlling interest in the Bank of England and also owned a significant stake in the Second Bank of the United States.

In 1828, the bankers heavily funded the candidate opposing Andrew Jackson, knowing that he was a staunch enemy of a central bank. Despite this, Jackson won the presidency and, being from Tennessee, was the first non-Eastern establishment elitist to hold that office. Since the bank charter would not expire until 1836, which would be at the end of a second term in office should Jackson survive, he had to settle for eliminating the bankers' representatives from government service during his first term. He was brutal in this undertaking, firing 2,000 of the 11,000 federal government employees.

When Jackson's first term approached its end, the bankers became proactive by asking Congress to pass a charter renewal bill four years early. Congress complied, but Jackson vetoed the bill, adding, "It is not our own citizens only who are to receive the bounty of our government. More than eight millions of the stock of this bank are held by foreigners….Is there no danger to our liberty and independence in a bank that, in its nature, has so little to bind it to our country? Controlling our currency, receiving our public monies and holding thousands of our citizens in dependence…would be more formidable and dangerous than a military power of the enemy." Congress attempted to override Jackson's veto, but failed.

In the1832 presidential campaign, Jackson went on the road for the first time in American history to bring his message directly to the people. His campaign slogan was crystal clear: "Jackson, and no bank." Senator Henry Clay was the opposition's candidate, and he received more than $3 million in campaign finances from the bankers in exchange for his position to renew the bank's charter. Despite this, Jackson defeated Clay by a landslide. But he warned, "The hydra of corruption is only scotched, not dead."

One of his first acts after reelection was to instruct his treasury secretary to begin removing government deposits from the Second Bank and place them in state banks. He refused and Jackson fired him and replaced him with William Duane, who also refused to follow his president's instructions. Jackson fired him too, and replaced him with Roger Taney, who later would sit on the Supreme Court. Taney obeyed orders and began removing government funds from the Second Bank in October 1833.

The president of the Second Bank, Nicholas Biddle, maneuvered the Senate into rejecting Taney's nomination, and threatened to create a depression by making money scarce if his bank's charter was not renewed. The banker boldly threatened, "Nothing but widespread suffering will produce any effect on Congress....Our only safety is in pursuing a steady course of firm restriction, and I have no doubt that such a course will ultimately lead to restoration of the currency and the re-charter of the bank." In an arrogant slap at Jackson, Biddle added, "This worthy president thinks that because he has scalped Indians and imprisoned judges, he is to have his way with the Bank. He is mistaken."

According to author Eustace Mullins, Biddle was an agent of Jacob Rothschild in Paris.

Biddle was as good as his word. His bank called in old loans while refusing to extend new ones, thus tightening money and leading directly to a financial panic and a depression. Biddle attempted to place the blame for this on Jackson's withdrawal of federal funds from the bank.

Businesses went bankrupt. Unemployment jumped while wages fell. The press followed Biddle's lead in blaming Jackson for the chaos, and Congress convened what has come to be known as "the Panic Session" in which the Senate passed a resolution officially censuring Jackson.

This was the first time in American history that a president was censured by Congress, but this only sharpened Jackson's fighting spirit against the central bank. He received help from Biddle, whose open boasts about having created the depression finally circulated among the politicians and the people.

In April 1834, the House of Representatives voted against re-chartering the Second Bank. In addition, lawmakers voted to create a special committee to investigate whether Biddle's bank had caused the crash. Officials armed with subpoenas to inspect the books of the bank and the correspondence between Biddle and various Congressmen were met with a blanket refusal. Biddle also refused to testify before the committee.

On the heels of Biddle's failed attempt to blackmail the government into renewing the bank charter, Jackson wrote, "The bold effort the present bank had made to control the Government, the distress it had wantonly produced...are but a premonition of the fate that awaits the American people should they be deluded into a perpetuation of this institution, or the establishment of another like it."

Jackson had a natural prejudice against paper money, and believed the central bank not only was unconstitutional, but incompetent in establishing a sound and uniform currency. Jackson also suspected the bankers of improper interference in the political process.

Long before winning re-election, Jackson issued sharp criticism at Biddle in his December 1829 message to Congress, saying "the rich and powerful too often bend the acts of government to their selfish purposes." He called the idea of a central bank "a curse to a republic, inasmuch as it is calculated to raise around the administration a moneyed aristocracy dangerous to the liberties of the nation." It was the first time in American history that a presidential veto rested on economic, political and social grounds, well beyond the customary constitutional reasons for past vetoes.

Jackson's position not only began what has become known in history as the "Bank War," it led to the first of a long line of "lone nut gunmen" seeking to assassinate American presidents. In 1835, Richard Lawrence, a mentally ill painter, stalked Jackson with two pistols he'd recently purchased. For several weeks before the assassination attempt, Lawrence was seen in a paint shop talking and laughing to himself.

On January 30, when Jackson attended the funeral of South Carolina Congressman Warren Davis, Lawrence positioned himself near a pillar. As Jackson passed, Lawrence aimed a pistol at the president's back. It misfired. Lawrence aimed his second pistol quickly and it also misfired. The would-be assassin was subdued by those present, including Congressman Davy Crockett, while Jackson struck him several times with his cane.

In his trial, Lawrence received a verdict of not guilty by reason of insanity, despite the efforts of prosecutor Francis Scott Key, creator of the American national anthem. During the trial, it came out that Lawrence believed the American government owed him a large sum of money but that Jackson was withholding it.

Despite the verdict, many people, including Jackson, believed that Lawrence had been supported and directed to assassinate the president. Jackson had many political enemies in America, but the fact that Lawrence had come from England was not lost on him, especially after Lawrence ranted in court that he was "in touch with the powers in Europe."

Just six months later, on July 4, 1835, Jackson received a letter threatening his life. It was addressed as "You damned old scoundrel," and demanded that Jackson pardon two prisoners named DeRuiz and DeSoto, who had received death sentences for piracy. The letter threatened, "I will cut your throat whilst you are sleeping." It was signed by Junius Brutus Booth, a famous Shakespearean actor, and for 175 years historians presumed the letter to be a fake. But in 2009, researchers working for the *History Detectives* television show proved that Booth actually had written the letter, based on his known whereabouts (which matched the envelope's return address), Booth's handwriting, and later apologies by Booth to his theater director for writing letters he shouldn't have to "authorities of the country."

It should not be overlooked that Junius Brutus Booth was born in England. More interestingly, he sired three sons who also entered the theater. One of them was John Wilkes Booth, who would murder President Abraham Lincoln.

Jackson remained true to his convictions by refusing to extend the central bank charter in 1836, calling the bank a "den of vipers." At the end of his term, the national debt had been entirely paid and the government was running on a surplus that allowed the next president, Martin Van Buren, to distribute funds to the states. Biddle was arrested and charged with fraud. Although acquitted, he fought civil suits to the end of his life.

The post-Jackson banking arrangement continued into the next century, despite numerous attempts to resuscitate a central bank. These attempts occurred in what historians call the "Bank Panics" of 1873, 1893 and 1907. All of the crises were deliberately created by bankers when they retracted loans and refused to renew old ones.

"A study of the panics of 1873, 1893 and 1907 indicates that these panics were the result of the international bankers' operations in London," wrote Eustace Mullins. Authors Gary Allen and Larry Abraham explained this process in their book, *None Dare Call It Conspiracy:*

"In order to show the hinterlands that they were going to need a central banking system, the international bankers created a series of panics as a demonstration of their power, a warning of what would happen unless the rest of the bankers got into line. The man in charge of conducting these lessons was J. Pierpont Morgan, American-born but educated in England and Germany. Morgan is referred to by many, including Congressman Louis McFadden (a banker who for 10 years headed the House Banking and Currency Committee), as the top American agent of the English Rothschilds."

In 1872, the Bank of England gave 100,000 pounds to an agent named Ernest Seyd with instructions to bribe US congressmen to vote for the demonetization of silver. As silver was plentiful in the US, the bankers would have trouble controlling it, so they opted to remove it from the money supply. Within a year, Congress passed the Coinage Act of 1873, abruptly ending silver minting.

In an incredible show of arrogance, Representative Samuel Hooper, who introduced the bill in the House, admitted that an agent of the Bank of England drafted it. A year later, this agent, Seyd, wrote, "I went to America in the winter of 1872-73 authorized to secure, if I could, the passage of a bill demonetizing silver. It was in the interest of those I represented, the governors of the Bank of England, to have it done. By 1873, gold coins were the only form of coin money."

The economic situation continued to worsen and by 1876, with one-third of America's work force unemployed, Congress created the United States Silver Commission, whose study blamed the monetary contraction on the national bankers. When Congress still refused to act, riots swept the nation.

Disregarding the unrest, the bankers urged their members to do everything possible to avoid the return to the interest-free "greenback" currency so popular and successful under the Lincoln administration. The policy dictated at a meeting of the American Bankers Association (ABA), calling for the banks to subvert both the Congress and the press, is public knowledge today in a letter from ABA Secretary James Buell:

"It is advisable to do all in your power to sustain such prominent daily and weekly newspapers, especially the agricultural and religious press, as will oppose the greenback issue of paper money and that you will also withhold patronage from all applicants who are not willing to oppose the government issue of money....To repeal the Act creating bank notes, or to restore to circulation the government issue of money will be to provide the people with money and will therefore seriously affect our individual profits as bankers and lenders. See your Congressman at once and engage him to support our interests, that we may control legislation."

The scheme didn't completely work, and in 1878, Congress passed the Sherman Law, which allowed a limited number of silver dollars to be minted. This placed small amounts of money back into circulation, and at the same time, the bankers became more liberal about making loans, ending the post-Civil War Depression.

But when James Garfield reached the White House several years later, the bankers learned they faced an implacable enemy. Garfield showed his distrust by saying, "Whosoever controls the volume of money in any country is absolute master of all industry and commerce....And when you realize that the entire system is very easily controlled, one way or another, by a few powerful men at the top, you will not have to be told how periods of inflation and depression originate."

Within a few weeks of making this pronunciation, Garfield was assassinated. It was another "lone-nut gunman" named Charles Guiteau who had fancied himself an influential political figure.

Shortly after Garfield's inauguration, Guiteau traveled to Washington expecting to be rewarded with an ambassadorship to Paris for a speech he wrote but never made. He lived like an indigent and when it was clear he never would receive a position in the new administration, he decided he'd been commanded to kill the ungrateful Garfield.

Guiteau purchased a large caliber, ivory-handled pistol with borrowed money and stalked the president. He chose the ivory model because he felt it would look good when it became a museum piece. He even tried to visit the District of Columbia jail to check out the facilities where he thought he would be incarcerated.

On July 2, 1881, Guiteau shot Garfield as he was boarding a train for a vacation. During his trial, Guiteau pleaded not guilty because Garfield's death was the will of God. During the trial he sang and was so confident of acquittal that he announced plans to run for the presidency in the 1884 election. He even dictated his autobiography to be serialized in the New York *Herald,* closing the piece with a personal ad for a lady under age 30.

The jury found Guiteau guilty despite his apparent mental illness and he was hanged. Garfield lingered for 11 weeks after the shooting before he died. The roadblock against banking interests had been removed by a madman.

Bankers launched a series of economic booms and troughs in the ensuing years, enabling them to buy up businesses and farms at a fraction of their worth. In 1891, the ABA signaled its plan to take down the American economy once again in a memo, now available in the Congressional Record. It stated: "On Sept. 1st, 1894, we will not renew our loans under any consideration. On Sept. 1st, we will demand our money. We will foreclose and become mortgagees in possession. We can take two-thirds of the farms west of the Mississippi and thousands of them east of the Mississippi at our own price....Then the farmers will become tenants, as in England."

This was a naked plot to create a national depression. It succeeded, and countless Americans suffered.

The return of silver minting had become the central issue in the presidential campaign of 1896. William Jennings Bryan, then only 36 years old, gave a stirring speech which won him the Democratic nomination, saying, "We will answer their demand for a gold standard by saying to them, 'You shall not press down upon the brow of labor this crown of thorns. You shall not crucify mankind upon a cross of gold.'"

Bryan's Republican opponent, William McKinley, favored the gold standard and naturally was well financed by the banking interests. The bankers also put out a tale through the press that if Bryan were elected, all factories would close and their workers would starve. The lie found willing listeners and McKinley won the presidency.

But McKinley didn't stay the international bankers' course. During his first administration, he expanded the number of US national banks to protect domestic interests from credit starvation. These banks would be stumbling blocks to the creation of any central bank in the US. He also ran afoul of foreign banking interests by supporting protective tariffs.

In addition, Britain and the Bank of England were deeply concerned over the expansion of American power in Latin America, as evidenced by the expulsion of Spain from its last Western bastion, Cuba, in the Spanish-American War of 1898. The success in this war propelled McKinley to a second term in 1900, but only months after his inauguration, on September 6, 1901, he was killed by yet another lone-nut assassin.

This killer, named Leon Czolgosz, was an unemployed factory worker who had become enamored of anarchism and actually spoke briefly with one of the movement's leaders, Emma Goldman, before the assassination. Goldman had been involved in an 1892 murder attempt with her lover, anarchist writer Alexander Berkman, on the life of industrialist Henry Clay Frick. Having been born in what is now Kaunas, Lithuania, Goldman had European ties and her anti-American activities certainly were viewed as advantageous to foreign interests.

However, Goldman never was connected to the McKinley assassination, despite being arrested and grilled by police. She stubbornly refused to condemn Czolgosz for killing the president, calling him a "supersensitive being," and compared him to Marcus Junius Brutus in the murder of Julius Caesar.

When Czolgosz shot McKinley with a pistol camouflaged in a white handkerchief while the president shook people's hands at an exposition in Buffalo, New York, he put Vice President Theodore Roosevelt into the Oval Office. Roosevelt quickly reversed course on the McKinley policy by arranging an alliance with Great Britain, which had been unthinkable to that point due to the long history of English hostility and interference in American affairs. Roosevelt would also create a new federal police force, the FBI, and increase the financial power of the J.P. Morgan interests, despite his claims of "trust busting."

Once again, the bullets of a mentally ill nonentity had changed policy in favor of the international bankers.

By the beginning of the 20th century, Morgan had already engineered several bank panics. How this was accomplished is clear in the statements that Senator Robert Owen made before a congressional committee. Owen testified that the bank he owned received what came to be called the "Panic Circular of 1893" from the National Bankers' Association. According to Owen, it said, "You will at once retire one-third of your circulation and call in one-half of your loans."

Morgan's role in the Panic of 1907 was to spread rumors that the Knickerbocker Bank and the Trust Company of America were insolvent, according to historian Frederick Lewis Allen. Oakleighe Thorne, president of the Trust Company of America, testified before a congressional committee that his bank had experienced only acceptable withdrawals, that he at no time applied for aid, and that it was the Morgan rumor which caused the run on his bank. This testimony, along with other evidence, indicated that Morgan initiated the panic that wiped out rival banks and strengthened the hegemony of the Morgan banks.

After achieving this, Morgan ended the panic. According to

Frederick Lewis Allen, "The lesson of the Panic of 1907 was clear, though not for some six years was it destined to be embodied in legislation: the United States gravely needed a central banking system."

After the Panic of 1907, Congress created the National Monetary System, intended to reform the US banking system. Senate Republican Leader Nelson Aldrich of Rhode Island chaired the commission and also created two other commissions, one to investigate the European banking systems and the other to study their American counterpart. Aldrich was closely tied to America's richest banking families. His daughter married John D. Rockefeller Jr.

Upon establishing his position in the National Monetary System, Aldrich spent two years in Europe, consulting with the central bankers of England, France and Germany. This junket cost American taxpayers an astronomical (at the time) $300,000. After reviewing the German banking model, Aldrich decided that a central bank was superior to the government-issued bond system currently in play.

The Aldrich plan received stout opposition in Congress, some politicians openly accusing the senator of being controlled by wealthy bankers like J.P. Morgan. But Aldrich was not dissuaded, and on November 22, 1910, he boarded his private rail car with the nation's most wealthy and powerful men, and rode in secrecy to an isle that would become infamous in American lore.

Jekyll Island

Jekyll Island is one of the "Golden Isles of Georgia," known for its beautiful beaches and serene ambiance. In 1910 the isle had already become a posh resort for the rich — the Morgans, the Rockefellers, the Vanderbilts — who gathered at the private Jekyll Island Club. It was here that Aldrich and a number of executives representing the banks of J.P. Morgan; Rockefeller; and Kuhn, Loeb & Co., met to plan how to establish a new American central bank.

Among the executives present were Frank Vanderlip, president of the National City Bank of New York; Henry Davison, senior partner of J.P. Morgan & Co.; and Colonel Edward House, who would go on to be advisor to President Woodrow Wilson and who founded the Council on Foreign Relations.

Also present was Paul Warburg, a German banker with Kuhn, Loeb & Co., who ran the meetings and guided the planning for what would become the Federal Reserve Act. Warburg was receiving an incredible annual salary of $500,000 from Kuhn, Loeb & Co. to lobby for the establishment of a privately owned central bank in the US.

Jacob Schiff, Warburg's business partner, was grandson of the man who shared the Greenshield House in Frankfurt with the Rothschild family. Schiff at this time was financing a plot with $20 million to overthrow Czar Nicholas II of Russia.

This troika of European banking families, the Warburgs, Rothschilds and Schiffs, were connected through marriages, much the same as marriages had connected their American counterparts, the Morgans, Rockefellers and Aldriches.

The meetings were so secretive that only first names were used, and the servants who normally worked at the Jekyll Island Club were replaced by new people who knew none of the participants. These banking families hatched a plan to ram a central banking act through Congress.

That the creation of this act and the Federal Reserve Bank was an outright plot perpetrated by these men on Jekyll Island is clearly proved in Frank Vanderlip's 1935 autobiography, *From Farmboy to Financier.* In it, Vanderlip flatly states: "I was as furtive as any conspirator. Discovery, we knew, simply must not happen, or else all our time and effort would have been wasted. If it were to be exposed that our particular group had got together and written a banking bill, that bill would have no chance whatever of passage by Congress. I do not feel it is any exaggeration to speak of our secret expedition to Jekyll Island as the occasion of the actual conception of what eventually became the Federal Reserve System."

The public remained ignorant of this plot at Jekyll Island for six years, until it was reported in the press by Bertie Charles Forbes. By this time, it was too late. The Federal Reserve Act had been passed three years previously.

The "Aldrich Plan" called for a private bank that would be free of government oversight and influence. It also called for a National Reserve Association to replace the National Monetary Commission. Despite support from many Republicans and of course, from Wall Street, the plan was violently attacked for seeking to allow wealthy men to control the National Reserve Association.

Conservative Democrats led by William Jennings Bryan called for a decentralized reserve system. "Big financiers are back of the Aldrich currency scheme," said Bryan, who was running for the presidency at that time. He added that if the bill passed, it would put big bank interests "in complete control of everything through the control of our national finances."

Several Republicans such as Representative Charles Lindbergh Sr., also spoke out against the bill. "The Aldrich Plan is the Wall Street Plan," Lindbergh said. "It means another panic, if necessary, to intimidate the people. Aldrich, paid by the government to represent the people, proposes a plan for the trusts instead....I have alleged that there is a money trust. The Aldrich Plan is a scheme plainly in the interest of the trust."

The Aldrich team countered by appointing Paul Warburg to head a committee intended to convince voters to support the Aldrich Plan. Offices popped up in 45 states, printing and distributing propaganda about the desirability of a central bank. Letter writing campaigns to congressmen were organized to give a grassroots impression that the people wanted the plan approved.

The New York banks created a $5 million "Educational Fund" to pay respected university professors for endorsing the central bank.

Woodrow Wilson, then a professor at Princeton, was one of the early recipients, and Wall Street financier Bernard Baruch was charged with his "education."

After the 1912 election brought Woodrow Wilson into the White House and gave the Democrats a majority in both houses of Congress, the Aldrich Plan became known as the Federal Reserve Act. Its passage enabled a privately owned central bank to overcome the rash of non-national banks that had flourished in America during the first decade of the 20th century, accounting for 43 percent of all deposits. Aldrich gloated, "Before passage of this Act, the New York bankers could only dominate the reserves of New York. Now we are able to dominate the bank reserves of the entire country."

The election of Wilson has an interesting aspect. It was engineered by campaign contributors connected to J.P. Morgan. Wilson was running against Republican incumbent William Howard Taft, and early polls indicated that he would lose the election. Taft had clearly stated that he would oppose the banking bill, so investors convinced Theodore Roosevelt to enter the election in a new Progressive Party, funded by the Morgan executives.

Roosevelt's presence robbed votes from Taft; and Wilson, who already had promised to sign the Federal Reserve Act, was narrowly elected. Congressman Lindbergh did not cease his attempts to quash the new Glass-Owen Bill, however, addressing the House with a stark warning:

"This is the Aldrich bill in disguise. The worst legislative crime of the ages is perpetrated by this banking bill. The banks have been granted the special privilege of distributing the money, and they charge as much as they wish. This is the strangest, most dangerous advantage ever placed in the hands of a special privilege class by any government that ever existed. The system is private. There should be no legal tender other than that issued by the government. The people are the government. Therefore, the government should, as the Constitution provides, regulate the value of money."

Wilson signed the bill anyway, but when he sent it for ratification in Congress, a number of Democrats demanded that this "Money Trust" be eradicated before major currency reforms began. Robert Henry of Texas led the charge, warning that regional banks would need to operate without the same government protections that large banks would enjoy.

Attorney Alfred Crozier of Ohio testified before Congress, "The bill grants just what Wall Street and the big banks for 25 years have been striving for, private instead of public control of currency. It does this as completely as the Aldrich Bill. Both measures rob the government and the people of all effective control over the public's money, and vest in the banks exclusively the dangerous power to make money among the people scarce or plenty."

The outburst nearly succeeded in killing the banking bill, but Wilson promised to add antitrust legislation safeguards after the bill was passed, and the opposition backed down.

The Federal Reserve Act became law on December 23, 1913. Being that it was just two days before Christmas, many Congressmen were not present for the final vote, having gone home. We attempted to verify the claim that there were only three senators present for this vote by requesting from the Library of Congress information on Senate Bill HR 7837, 63rd Congress, 2nd Session, specifically the House and Senate yea and nay votes. After searching, the US Senate archivist learned to his surprise that the record of this vote is missing. Later, another archivist found the record, indicating a good number of congressmen voted to pass the bill, contradicting the complaints of many senators of that time that they had been misled into going home for vacation with the assurance the bill would come to a vote long after the holiday ended.

Frank Vanderlip, who later would boast so proudly of the Jekyll Island plot and its success in his autobiography, also admitted that even though the bill did not contain the Aldrich name, it contained all the essential points of the Aldrich Plan.

Upon its passage, Congressman Charles Lindbergh Sr. glumly stated: "From now on, depressions will be scientifically created....The invisible government by the monetary power will be legalized. The people may not know it immediately, but the day of reckoning is only a few years removed....The worst legislative crime of the ages is perpetrated by this bill."

Even Woodrow Wilson regretted his role in signing the Federal Reserve Act. Near the end of his term of office, he said, "I am a most unhappy man. I have unwittingly ruined my country. A great industrial nation is now controlled by its system of credit. We are no longer a government by free opinion, no longer a government by conviction and the vote of the majority, but a government by the opinion and duress of a small group of dominant men."

Congressman Louis McFadden was much more blunt: "A world

banking system was being set up here...a super-state controlled by international bankers...acting together to enslave the world for their own pleasure. The Fed has usurped the government."

The immediate outcome of the new Federal Reserve Bank was to vastly increase the American money supply. Between 1914 and 1919, the money supply doubled. Then in 1920, the Fed called in loans and created a panic similar to the Morgan-manipulated crisis of 1907. Runs on the banks and bankruptcies occurred all over the nation, causing numerous small banks to collapse and thereby increasing the Federal Reserve's banking monopoly.

Wilson's successor in the White House, Warren G. Harding, was no friend to the international central bankers. During his first months in office in 1921, Harding accused the Federal Reserve during a Congressional inquiry of being a private banking monopoly and added, "The Federal Reserve Bank is an institution owned by the stockholding member banks. The government has not a dollar's worth of stock in it."

Harding died mysteriously during his first term in 1923. Poisoning was rumored, but never proved as his wife refused to permit an autopsy. While it certainly is possible Harding died of natural causes — he was a party animal who drank and smoked heavily and whose only exercise was the occasional golf game and the much more frequent love trysts — there is reason to suspect foul play.

For all of his dissipation, Harding, a stout farm boy, was vital to the end of his life. Members of his administration were utterly corrupt and the scandal threatened to spread to Harding, who made a new will shortly before his death, following several suspicious suicides among his disgraced cabinet members. After he died, there were persistent rumors that he'd been poisoned to silence him about the graft, despite the official report that he had succumbed to a stroke.

Whatever the reason, another president had died in office to the benefit of the central bankers. The way was clear for the Federal Reserve Bank to keep operating.

The Federal Reserve System

Quite simply, the purpose of any bank is to create debt. Depositors' money is loaned at interest back to them, which means the bank makes profits from money that does not belong to it. This system applies to individuals and to nations alike, creating indebtedness that gives bankers enormous power and influence over policy. This power and influence certainly has been used to manipulate world events, creating inflations, depressions and even wars.

The means of printing and lending money created from nothing today is a four-step process. First, the Federal Open Market Committee approves the purchase of US Bonds — essentially federal IOUs to be paid with interest at maturity — on the open market. Next, the Federal Reserve purchases these bonds from whoever sells them on the open market. The third step involves the Fed paying for bonds with electronic credits which appear in the seller's bank account. These credits are based on no monetary value. They simply are concocted by the Fed.

In the final step, banks use these valueless deposits as reserves, against which they can lend money to new borrowers equaling as much as 10 times the amount of their reserves, with interest. This has put into the hands of a few men the centralized control over America's national money supply.

Today, the Federal Reserve System is composed of 12 Federal Reserve banks serving different portions of the country. The banks are dominated by the New York Federal Reserve Bank, but all of the banks are run by a board of governors individually confirmed by the Senate from a list prepared by the bankers themselves.

This board of governors is an independent agency. It receives no funding from Congress, and the service terms of its seven members may be longer than many presidential and congressional terms. Its only responsibility to the federal government is to make an annual report on operations to the speaker of the House of Representatives. Aside from that, the board is independent of government in making monetary policy and also independently regulates the operation of the Federal Reserve Banks.

In short, the Board regulates the entire US banking system, independently of the federal government. All of its meetings are secret, and transcripts of these meetings rarely are released in less than five years.

No member of Congress, nor the president himself, knows exactly who owns the Federal Reserve banks. Due to a provision in the Federal Reserve Act, its "Class A" stockholders are not to be revealed.

But R.E. McMaster, who publishes a financial newsletter called *The Reaper,* claims he has learned the identities of these principal stockholders through sources in Switzerland and Saudi Arabia. Among the roughly 300 stockholders in the Federal Reserve Bank of New York, the Class A members represent the Rothschild Banks of London and Berlin; the Warburg Banks of Hamburg and Amsterdam; the Lehman Brothers Bank of New York; Kuhn, Loeb & Co. of New York; the Chase Bank of New York; Goldman, Sachs of New York; the Lazard Brothers Banks of Paris; and the Israel Moses Self Banks of Italy.

In many cases, the stockholders are related, either by blood or marriage. They represent less than 12 international banking establishments with only four of these based in the US. All the rest are Europe-based, the Rothschild banks being the most powerful and rumored to own 53 percent of the Federal Reserve stock. Each year, the Class A stockholders receive billions of dollars from US taxpayers whose income tax goes specifically toward paying the interest on Fed loans to the government.

That the Fed is still under control of the same entities that conspired to create it is clearly demonstrated by Eustace Mullins in his book, *The Secrets of the Federal Reserve.* Mullins supplied charts that connected the Federal Reserve Bank to the families of the Rothschilds, Morgans, Rockefellers, Warburgs, and several others, virtually identical to the McMaster list. Most disturbing are the connections to foreign bankers, as well as the elitist nature of the ownership.

"An examination of the major stockholders of the New York City banks shows clearly that a few families, related by blood, marriage or business interests, still control the New York City banks, which, in turn, hold the controlling stock of the Federal Reserve Bank of New York," Mullins wrote.

President Franklin Roosevelt understood this in 1933 during his first year in the White House when he said, "The real truth of the matter is that a financial element in the large centers has owned the government since the days of Andrew Jackson." Nearly half a century earlier, future British Prime Minister Benjamin Disraeli said, "The world is governed by very different personages from what is imagined by those who are not behind the scenes."

Every move the Fed makes is closely monitored by financial experts all over the world, because of its awesome effect on the world's economy. "The attention is warranted, since even the slightest interest rate tick can roil markets and create or destroy millions of jobs," wrote Kim Clark of *U.S. News & World Report.*

Senator Ron Paul has stated that the Federal Reserve System is illegal, adding "what we have given to this so-called agency is the authority to counterfeit money." This ability to print money which has no real backing has led to a constant state of inflation in which the true value of the dollar has shrunk to less than a nickel compared to its 1933 value.

The 2008-2009 "bailouts" of troubled banks by the Bush and Obama administrations clearly demonstrate how taxpayers are liable for the losses of private banks. This always has been the goal of the men behind the Federal Reserve, going back to its first proponents. Paul Warburg's statement that the government can be called upon to assume financial obligation should the reserve banks fail is simply admitting that Federal Reserve notes are privately issued money to be supported by taxpayer dollars should those banks that issue it show losses.

The means by which such losses are covered is our national income tax, instigated by the same men behind the bank's creation. President Wilson pushed legislation for the graduated income tax, to be enforced by the Federal Reserve System through a newly created Internal Revenue Service that would collect it.

The income tax is, by its very nature as a direct and un-apportioned tax, unconstitutional. The creation of this tax came with the 16th Amendment, but this amendment never was ratified by the required three-quarters of the states. The bankers convinced Secretary of State Philander Knox in 1913 to lie about the ratification, and as recently as 2003 it has been recognized in courts as an illegal amendment.

US District Court Judge James Fox ruled that anyone examining the 16th Amendment carefully "would find that a sufficient number of states never ratified that amendment." Two years later, Federal Judge Emmet Sullivan ruled the government is not required to answer its citizens' questions regarding the legality of federal income tax, even though this violates the 1st Amendment.

One of the first acts Ronald Reagan performed when he entered the White House was to hire Peter Grace to form a blue ribbon panel, known as the Grace Committee, to study the money flow of federal tax dollars in hopes of cutting waste. The panel's report stated, "100 percent of what is collected [through federal income tax] is absorbed solely by the federal debt [to the Federal Reserve Bank]….All individual income tax revenues are gone before one nickel is spent on the services that taxpayers expect from government."

In other words, the Grace Committee said that all of America's billions of dollars in annual income tax pays the interest the Federal Reserve Bank charges the US government to print money. Not a cent goes toward services to the citizenry.

Author G. Edward Griffin found that "the main purpose of the income tax is not to raise revenue, but to redistribute wealth and to control society." Revenues for education come mainly from state and local property taxes. Gasoline tax pays for much of the highway maintenance and improvement. Corporate income tax covers the costs of the American military.

Taxing corporations is legal and constitutional. Taxing the wages of individual citizens is not. The Supreme Court repeatedly upheld this opinion, that the US government has no right to impose a third form of taxation that is neither direct nor apportioned, as early as 1894.

Following the "passage" of the 16th Amendment, the Supreme Court continued to maintain this opinion in cases like Stanton vs. Baltic Mining, Stratton Independence vs. Hobart, Southern Pacific vs. Lowe, Burnett vs. Harmel, Doyle vs. Mitchell, and several other decisions.

The tax levels under the Obama Administration were to have risen to the point where Americans work more than four months out of the year just to pay their federal income tax. Not a penny of this revenue goes to government programs, which are financed by more loans from this same privately owned central bank. This means the money Americans earn during more than four months of every year goes directly into the pockets of international bankers.

Banking is quite simply a scam. President James Madison knew this when he called bankers "moneychangers," harkening back to the Biblical term. It's important to note that the only time Jesus used force during his ministry was when he drove the moneychangers from the Jerusalem temple. These early form bankers collected a temple tax which could only be paid in a coin called the "half shekel of the sanctuary," a half ounce of silver. This allowed them to monopolize the market on this coin and they raised its price to whatever the market would bear, earning themselves enormous profits. The forceful response to the moneychangers by Jesus was a reaction to their violation of the temple's sanctity.

Even before the time of Jesus, Roman emperors struggled against the control of the moneychangers. Two emperors were assassinated because they limited the practice of charging interest on loans, which they called usury, and put a cap on the amount of land an individual could own.

Julius Caesar wrested the power to coin money from these early bankers in 48 B.C. Minting coins instead created a much larger supply of money that allowed Caesar to build lasting public works projects. This made him intensely popular with the common people and anathema to the moneychangers.

Caesar was assassinated in 44 B.C., after proclaiming himself emperor and reducing the power of the senators who aligned themselves with the moneychangers. Subsequent emperors allowed the moneychangers to regain the right to mint coins. Eventually the Roman money supply shrank to 10 percent of what it had been under Caesar. This cruelly affected the common people, who lost land and homes.

The Middle Ages saw the advent of the goldsmith, a man who kept the gold of others in a safe vault and issued paper notes as receipts based on the value of the gold he stored for the depositor. The convenience of using paper money instead of carrying around heavy gold coins became popular and widespread.

But since few depositors ever demanded their gold, the goldsmiths began cheating by printing more money than the value of the gold in their possession. They lent this worthless money and collected interest, giving birth to the modern system of "fractional reserve banking." The deception worked, because borrowers were unaware of the scheme. This system continues today with every bank, which is allowed to lend 10 times more money than actually exists in its vault. By this means, banks make not just eight percent interest per year on their loans, but 80 percent.

When the negative effects of this scheme inevitably resulted in poverty and hardship, the Church and monarchies of the late Middle Ages passed laws making usury illegal with harsh punishments for the guilty. However, these entities had to compromise their positions when it became apparent that lending money had a cost to the lender in terms of risk, so lenders were allowed to impose charges.

Along the way, the lenders learned that they could manipulate monetary value by swinging between periods of high loan activity and low activity. This system has since been termed "rowing the economy." When money was easier to borrow, this expanded the amount of money in circulation. People made more loans and expanded their businesses.

Then the moneychangers made loans more difficult to get, forcing borrowers who could not repay their previous loans by making new loans into bankruptcy. These borrowers had to sell their assets to the lenders at a fraction of their worth. To this day, this manipulation continues to bankrupt businesses and enrich the bankers under the harmless-sounding modern term for it, "the business cycle."

When Britain's King Henry VIII relaxed the laws against usury in the early 16th century, the bankers made gold and silver coins plentiful for a few decades. As Queen Mary took the throne of England, she again tightened the usury laws and the moneychangers began hoarding their coins, removing them from circulation and damaging the British economy.

Queen Elizabeth I sought to right the situation by issuing gold and silver coins from the public treasury, effectively wresting control of the money supply from the bankers. This situation remained in place until Oliver Cromwell, financed by the bankers, overthrew King Charles and allowed the moneychangers to reconsolidate their financial stranglehold.

The result was half a century of wars which drained Britain's treasury. Enriched by war loans, the bankers purchased a square mile of property in the middle of London and established a financial center which remains in place to this day. When the Stuart King James II became obnoxious to Britain's bankers, they pooled their resources with the bankers of Amsterdam and financed the king's overthrow by William of Orange.

But the continuous wars had left England in financial ruin by the end of the 17th century. It became necessary to borrow money from the bankers, who set a condition that they must be allowed to create a central bank with the right to print money. This new entity, the Bank of England, became the world's first privately owned central bank in 1694.

The bankers immediately sold shares in their new corporation, amounting to 750,000 pounds, and lent to the government at interest several times more than they had in reserve. The British government secured this debt through direct taxation of the people. In short, the creation of the Bank of England authorized it to counterfeit paper money for profit from the populace.

The bankers printed money based on nothing, and soon this inflation caused prices to double. Loans were granted for the most preposterous reasons, one of which was a program to drain the Red Sea and regain the gold lost by the Egyptians when they were inundated in pursuit of the Israelites.

This system of thievery has served as the basic model for the central banks which exist today in every major nation. These privately owned corporations have complete control over national economies, creating a plutocracy of the rich.

In 2010, this plutocracy became stronger after the Federal Reserve Bank overcame a congressional challenge that would have stripped it of its supervisory oversight of banks and forced it to submit to a congressional audit of its interest rate decisions. Instead, Congress passed a law that gives the Fed more power, making it the primary regulator for large financial firms.

It was the first major boost in the Fed's influence since the inflationary spiral of the 1970s, when the bank received mandates both to promote price stability and also maximum sustainable employment. The new legislation created a Financial Stability Council, and allows the Fed to decide when it should vote on breaking up large firms if, in the opinion of its stockholders, they threaten the financial stability of the entire system.

The Federal Reserve is one of many central banks with an identical ultimate agenda — the creation of a one-world currency. In October 2010, the Institute of International Finance, representing 420 of the world's largest banks and finance houses, issued a new call for a one-world currency, ostensibly to prevent a currency war. The group's managing director, Charles Dallara, called for a return to the G-20 commitment to use the International Monetary Fund (IMF) to replace the US dollar with a new one-world currency as the standard for foreign exchange reserves. Such an occurrence would increase the already powerful control that central banks have on the world's currencies to a virtual stranglehold.

Many Americans still do not comprehend the way that banks work against them. Most do not know that, for instance, the vice chairman of the Federal Reserve could not answer Congressman Alan Grayson's question about what happened to the $1.2 trillion that the US government put out through that bank for buying distressed mortgage bonds in 2008. It remains unknown who received that huge sum, although Walter Burien of the Comprehensive Annual Financial Report (CAFR) believes the money bailed out the government's own investments to keep it in the black.

This sad fact underscores the stark comment of Henry Ford, who quipped, "It is well enough that the people of the nation do not understand our banking and monetary system, for if they did, I believe there would be a revolution before tomorrow morning."

Phase Two: Market Manipulation

Once the bankers had their privately owned central bank in place in 1913, they began to use it to manipulate the American economy. According to authors Allen and Abraham, "Using a central bank to alternate periods of inflation and deflation, and thus whipsawing the public for vast profits, had been worked out by the international bankers to an exact science. Having built the Federal Reserve as a tool to consolidate and control wealth, the international bankers were now ready to make a major killing. Between 1923 and 1929, the Federal Reserve expanded the money supply by 62 percent. Much of this new money was used to bid the stock market up to dizzying heights."

This created a boom in loans to the public and to banks. A new type of loan, the margin loan, emerged in the stock market. This allowed investors to pay only 10 percent of a stock's price to gain full control of the stock, the remaining 90 percent being lent to the broker. But margin loans could be called in at any time and had to be paid within 24 hours. These margin calls typically resulted in the investor selling the stock.

In 1928, the House Hearings on Stabilization of the Purchasing Power of the Dollar discovered that the Federal Reserve Board was working with the executives of the European central banks. The Committee also revealed the shocking plan to engineer a major crash, first formulated in meetings in 1927. More such meetings took place in Washington DC on February 6, 1929, when Montagu Norman, governor of the Bank of England, conferred with treasury secretary Andrew Mellon. Norman, who did business with J.P. Morgan, once boasted, "I hold the hegemony of the world."

During the summer of 1929, John D. Rockefeller, J.P. Morgan, Bernard Baruch and other insiders quietly sold their stock holdings, putting all of their assets in cash or gold, and left the market. Shortly afterward, the Federal Reserve Board raised its discount rate. Wrote Allen and Abraham, "The balloon, which had been inflated constantly for nearly seven years, was about to be exploded. On October 24, the feathers hit the fan."

What happened next was the historic Wall Street Crash of 1929, clearly caused deliberately by the central banks of Europe and America. On that "Black Thursday," Bernard Baruch brought Winston Churchill to the visitors' gallery of the New York Stock Exchange during the frenzied stock selling period to witness the panic taking place on the floor. Churchill was duly impressed with the control that Baruch and other business giants wielded.

In his book, *The United States' Unresolved Monetary and Political Problems,* William Bryan describes the specifics of how this control was accomplished: "When everything was ready, the New York financiers started calling 24-hour broker call [margin] loans. This meant that the stockbrokers and the customers had to dump their stock on the market in order to pay the loans. This naturally collapsed the stock market and brought a banking collapse all over the country, because the banks not owned by the oligarchy were heavily involved in broker call claims at this time, and bank runs soon exhausted their coin and currency and they had to close. The Federal Reserve System would not come to their aid, although they were instructed under the law to maintain an elastic currency."

Congressman Louis McFadden saw the crash as a means by which the European bankers could regain the vast amounts of gold they had sent to America to finance the armies of England and France during World War I. McFadden bluntly stated, "I think it can hardly be disputed that the statesmen and financiers of Europe are ready to take almost any means to reacquire rapidly the gold stock which Europe lost to America as the result of World War I."

The outcome of the crash was disastrous to investors, brokers and bankers alike. Within a year, $40 billion in wealth had been lost. But for those who were in on this financial manipulation, it was a different story. They had sold so that when the crash bottomed out, the insiders could buy back stock at a 90 percent discount from their former high water marks.

Allen and Abraham stated flatly: "To think that the scientifically engineered Crash of '29 was an accident or the result of stupidity defies all logic. The international bankers who promoted the inflationary policies and pushed the propaganda which pumped up the stock market represented too many generations of accumulated expertise to have blundered into 'the Great Depression.'"

This view was supported in the 1930s by Congressman Louis McFadden, then chairman of the House Banking and Currency

Committee: "It [the Great Depression] was not accidental. It was a carefully contrived occurrence. The international bankers sought to bring about a condition of despair here so that they might emerge as rulers of us all."

The Federal Reserve Bank exacerbated the crisis by reducing the money supply and this as much as anything fueled the Great Depression. If the Fed had quickly lowered interest rates, it would have stimulated the economy, but instead it further contracted the money supply by 33 percent between 1929 and 1933.

Milton Friedman, a Nobel Prize-winning economist, directly blamed the Federal Reserve for the Great Depression during a 1996 interview on National Public Radio. He also saw the Federal Reserve at the root of two other economic downturns between World War I and World War II.

He stated plainly that "at least a third of the price rise during and just after World War I is attributable to the establishment of the Federal Reserve System...and that the severity of each of the major contractions — 1920-21, 1929-33 and 1937-38 — is directly attributable to acts of commission and omission by the Reserve authorities....Any system which gives so much power and so much discretion to a few men, [so] that mistakes, excusable or not, can have such far-reaching effects, is a bad system. It is a bad system to believers in freedom, just because it gives a few men such power without any effective check by the body politic. This is the political argument against an independent central bank."

The billions of dollars in lost wealth during the Depression were not really lost, however. The wealth was redistributed among those insiders who sold their stock holdings just prior to the crash and purchased gold. In addition, American dollars were being spent overseas on projects like the financial reconstruction of Germany, which continued into the Hitler chancellorship. The Federal Reserve Board spent more than $30 billion in US money on German aid during the first years of the Depression.

McFadden tried to strike back by introducing a resolution to file charges against the Federal Reserve board members. The charges included various criminal acts and even made accusations of treason.

Board chairman Eugene Meyer resigned with the 1933 inauguration of Franklin Roosevelt. That same year, McFadden introduced House Resolution 158, which included articles of impeachment against the treasury secretary, two assistant treasury secretaries and the Federal Reserve Board.

In his speech to Congress in 1934, McFadden said, "Mr. Chairman, we have in this country one of the most corrupt institutions the world has ever known. I refer to the Federal Reserve Board and the Federal Reserve Banks...This evil institution has impoverished and ruined the people of these United States, has bankrupted itself and has practically bankrupted our government. It has done this through the defects of the law under which it operates, through the maladministration of the law by the Fed and through the corrupt practices of the moneyed vultures who control it."

This proved to be his final political act, as McFadden was defeated in his bid for reelection in 1934 by a mere 561 votes. McFadden remained in the public eye, however, continuing his campaign against the Fed, and survived two attempts on his life.

The first, according to *Pelley's Weekly,* "came in the form of two revolver shots fired at him from ambush as he was alighting from a cab in front of one of the Capital hotels. Fortunately both shots missed him, the bullets burying themselves in the structure of the cab."

The second attempt occurred during a Washington political banquet, when McFadden became violently ill. A physician friend saved his life with a stomach pump and later pronounced the incident to be a poisoning. A third apparent attempt occurred on October 3, 1936 when McFadden died suddenly following a New York banquet. The official explanation was "intestinal flu."

The manipulation of America's financial health continues today. During the latest American economic recession, which began in 2008, the Obama administration has blamed the US banks for all of the problems and is punishing them by making potentially lucrative business prospects off-limits. The foreign bankers have taken advantage of this situation, literally assuming the role of brokers for US bailout money.

Since domestic banks received bailout money, they are not allowed to compete for these promising contracts. This has led to unprecedented foreign bank spending on lobbying and political campaigns in the US. Their lobbyists monitor and influence the Wall Street reform legislation in Congress.

In 2009, the foreign bank trade group, the Institute of International Bankers, spent $810,000 in lobbying fees, nearly doubling the total it spent just the year before. Deutsche Bank spent nearly $1 million in lobbying fees in 2009 and indications are that figure is much higher in 2010. This fee helped win the German bank the right to auction the stock options of 11 American banks on behalf of the Treasury Department, netting a commission of more than $40 million.

Barclay's of Britain jumped on the gravy train in 2009 by spending nearly $3 million on lobbyists with such firms as the Rich Feuer Group. The bank then was selected by the Federal Deposit Insurance Corporation (FDIC) to sell partial interests in companies that had received nearly $6 million in loans from a pair of failed American banks. The commission Barclay's received is not known at this time.

The foreign bankers literally are "picking the bones" of domestic big banks, according to Rochdale Securities financial analyst Dick Bove. This will allow foreign banks to increase the share of American debt they sell. The foreign banks already account for nearly two-thirds of the 18 banks that deal with the US debt.

And this is not even the worst of it, as the reader is about to learn.

Fort Knox: The Great Gold Robbery

The Federal Reserve decided in 1933 to take the American economy off the gold standard. To accomplish this, the bankers would need to collect all of the nation's gold.

Franklin Roosevelt in his first months in office willingly complied with the bankers' demands by creating an executive order requiring all Americans to deliver their gold coins, bullion and gold certificates to a Federal Reserve Bank branch or agency. Under the Gold Reserve Act of 1934, failure to obey the order would result in possible prison terms of up to 10 years.

This amounted to a coercive confiscation of the coinage that most Americans used. The coins were withdrawn from circulation and stored in the form of bullion.

Those who obeyed the Act, also known as the Thomas Amendment, received the standard current rate of exchange, $20.66 per gold ounce, in paper money issued by the Federal Reserve. In exchange the Fed received gold certificates from the US Treasury.

In 1935, after most of the nation's gold was in federal hands, Roosevelt artificially boosted its price to $35 per ounce, creating a profit to the Federal Reserve Bank of $3 billion. It should be noted that the Roosevelt family had been in the New York banking business since the 18th century and that his uncle Frederick was an original member of the Federal Reserve Board.

As the value of gold increased, the value of the US dollar automatically decreased. This has continued steadily, until the modern US dollar has a purchasing power of less than a nickel compared to its 1933 value, while gold has ballooned to more than $1,500 an ounce.

Gold continued to be a commodity in the 1930s, but only foreign agents were permitted to sell gold at the new $35 price. This allowed the men who sold stock and bought gold before the 1929 crash to ship their gold to London and then sell it back to the US government at a profit of nearly $15 per ounce.

At the close of World War II, Fort Knox contained more than 700 million ounces of gold, which amounted to 70 percent of the world's gold supply. This was verified in the last physical audit of the Fort Knox gold in 1953. How much of that gold remains is a mystery, despite the federal law, Title 31 of the US Code, mandating an annual physical audit of the Fort Knox bullion. The US Treasury Department consistently has refused to conduct audits since 1953, when President Dwight Eisenhower ordered one.

Unofficial estimates of the US gold supply list a 52 percent drop in the amount of gold bullion owned by the Treasury Department due to foreign financial aid and debts between 1958 and 1968. Of the remaining amount, $12 billion was to be reserved to back the paper money then in circulation. This was based on a law requiring that US paper money be backed by 25 percent of its value in the gold reserve.

But this 1945 law was repealed in 1968, which caused a dip of more than one half of America's gold reserves, from 653.1 million troy ounces to 311.2 million ounces in just that year. The Treasury Department cited sales to foreign banking institutions as well as to domestic businesses as the reason for losing 341.9 million troy ounces of its gold supply.

By November 1981 sources claimed the US gold supply had dropped to 264.1 million ounces, and no one knew where it went. Senator Jesse Helms suspected that the OPEC nations had taken huge sums in gold from the US Treasury. Others looked toward the World Bank.

Financial researcher George F. Smith claims that one of his sources discovered counterfeit $5,000 and $10,000 Federal Reserve Notes were used to steal American gold reserves. "Illegal to own," Smith wrote, "these notes are actually checks which are used to transfer ownership of large amounts of gold without actually moving the gold itself." Smith's source claims he traced these bills through their serial numbers, which appear on the public record.

"It has been reported that 40 percent of the world's gold is five levels below street level in a sub-basement of the New York Federal Reserve Bank, behind a 90-ton revolving door," Smith claims. "Some of it is American-owned, but most is owned by the central banks of other countries. It is stored in separate cubicles, and from time to time is moved from one cubicle to another to satisfy international transactions."

Over the decades, the US gold supply in Fort Knox had been sold to European bankers at the standard fee of $35 per ounce, and by 1971 all the US gold had been secretly removed, according to several researchers. If true, this was at the same time it was illegal for Americans to buy their own gold from Fort Knox.

Details of this theft were revealed in the press in 1974, along with charges that the Rockefeller family manipulated the Federal Reserve into selling US gold at low prices to anonymous European speculators. The source of the story, Louise Auchincloss Boyer, longtime secretary to Nelson Rockefeller, mysteriously fell to her death from her New York apartment three days after the story broke.

In the opinions of some researchers, once all of America's gold returned to England, President Nixon repealed the Roosevelt Gold Reserve Act of 1934, finally allowing US citizens to buy gold. This skyrocketed the price of gold which rose to $880 per ounce just nine years after the Nixon repeal, and as mentioned previously, has breached $1,500 per ounce in 2011.

In 1981, newly elected President Ronald Reagan formed the Gold Commission to study the feasibility of putting America back on the gold standard. The following year, the commission shocked the administration with news that the US Treasury owned no gold at all, and that all the gold formerly held in Fort Knox currently was being held by the privately owned Federal Reserve Bank as collateral against America's national debt.

Former Texas Governor John Connally told the *New York Times* in 1981, "It's still the same problem we had in 1971: We don't have sufficient gold to back up the dollar."

Taking America off the gold standard meant that paper money printed by the Federal Reserve was essentially valueless. Even Alan Greenspan, a member of the banking elite, admitted in *Gold and Economic Freedom*: "In the absence of the gold standard, there is no way to protect savings from confiscation through inflation." Greenspan changed his tune when he became chairman of the Federal Reserve.

The Federal Reserve Bank lists gold on its balance sheet, claiming it is held for the US Treasury. This has raised suspicions that the Federal Reserve is, indeed, using the gold supply of the American people as collateral for the money it prints and the interest it charges for that service. According to Representative Ron Paul, Congress has refused to initiate an oversight into this matter.

In 2001, following the 9/11 attacks, and in 2008, in the wake of the Fanny & Freddie mortgage imbroglio, the markets again crashed. Although direct proof of these crashes having been manipulated by central bankers is still to be found, it certainly is valid to believe that if these men could do it once, they can do it again. Today's money markets are much easier to manipulate, being based on electronic transfers, and it's been demonstrated clearly how insiders who can control inflation and deflation of money are able to make tremendous profits from causing disastrous panics and crashes.

There is only one solution, stated clearly by Josiah Stamp, former Director of the Bank of England:

"The bankers own the earth. Take it away from them, but leave them the power to create money, and with the flick of a pen they will create enough money to buy it back again. However, take away from them the power to create money, and all the great fortunes like mine will disappear and they ought to disappear, for this would be a happier and better world to live in. But if you wish to remain the slaves of bankers and pay the cost of your own slavery, let them continue to create money."

End of the Trail:
George H.W., JFK, and John-John

The dark power that the central bankers have over even presidents is clear in a single historic fact. Only two American presidents ever tried to circumvent the central bankers by issuing interest-free money directly through the US Treasury Department. Abraham Lincoln did so during the Civil War when he issued "greenbacks." John F. Kennedy on June 4, 1963 signed Executive Order 11110, giving the US Treasury power to issue silver certificates against the silver in its possession, which brought $4.3 billion worth of new notes into circulation without paying interest.

Both of these presidents were murdered publicly during their terms.

Reams of material have been written about Kennedy's murder, amounting to a cottage industry. Without rehashing the myriad theories and suspects involved, there is one very interesting aspect that hasn't been widely discussed: the curious story of the "Gemstone File."

It was revealed to the author by Dr. A. True Ott, currently a nationally known expert in health and wellness with a Ph.D. in nutrition, and host of a weekly Internet radio talk show. Ott also is listed on the websites of the Sierra Club and the NRDC for his activism, following a sparkling career in finance, a separate career in broadcasting as host of a nationally syndicated Republic radio program, and as a high ranking member of the Mormon Church.

The tale begins when a powerful Las Vegas businessman named Christiansen hired Ott, a financial agent working for the firm of Hugh Wallace Pinnock at that time, to formulate a plan for him.

"He had a lot of property on the [Las Vegas] Strip," Ott told the author. "This was back in 1985. He was a very important figure in the Mormon Church and later one of its leaders. We primarily did estate plans for wealthy Mormons. We did charitable donations, trust structure, investment portfolios, stocks and bonds, life insurance. He had to change his will, obviously, and I had to get a copy of his will for my files. I thought it was eccentric that in the will he listed a bunch of things that seemed paranoid. Like, if he died from a gunshot wound, or a car accident, or a sudden heart attack, a specific file would need to go to a law firm on Wilshire Boulevard [in Beverly Hills, California]. It was a sealed manila envelope. I was given a copy of that file and his attorney was given a copy."

Ott kept the file in his personal safe for years and forgot about it. In the late 1990s, he came across the file while going through his papers.

"I called the Christiansen home and told them I still had this file and was told that he'd had a stroke," Ott continues. "He was still alive but in bad shape. The insurance policy was handled in-house by that time and since I was in a different line of business I asked what they wanted me to do with the file. They told me to just throw it away. So I chucked into my office garbage bin.

"That night while I took out the trash, I decided to bring it back and open it. I found there was one of the seven files called Gemstone which was all about the assassination of JFK and how it had been a contract hit by the CIA. We're talking about cancelled checks, bank accounts, travel vouchers, orders on CIA letterhead, personnel lists of participants, disposition of witnesses, letters from [George H.W.] Bush on Zapata [Off-Shore Oil] letterheads, the whole nine yards, and it was pointing to Bush. At the time I was a tried and true conservative, so I thought, 'This can't be right.'"

Bush has been implicated as complicit in the JFK assassination by some researchers for several reasons. There is strong evidence that he already worked for the CIA in 1963, while Bush headed his Zapata Off-Shore Drilling Company, based in Houston, Texas. Much of the funding for the disastrous Bay of Pigs invasion of Cuba in 1962 reportedly was raised through Bush's company (the code name for the invasion actually was Operation Zapata, according to the transcript of a Cabinet Room briefing of JFK by Richard Bissell of the CIA on March 29, 1961). Add to this the coincidence that two of the seven armed ships supporting the invasion were named *Houston* and *Barbara,* the home office of Zapata and the wife of George Bush.

The placement of the Zapata oil drilling sites also is interesting, because the rigs were located just 30 miles north of Cuba, in the midst of ongoing CIA operations that had been underway against the Castro government since 1959. This places Bush close to the anti-Castro Cubans who were directed by former CIA operatives Howard Hunt and Frank Sturgis, both of whom were placed in Dallas on the eve of the JFK assassination by Marita Lorenz and other witnesses.

Lorenz had been trained by the CIA to become Castro's mistress and murder him, but obviously failed in the latter task. She claimed that she rode with Sturgis from Florida to Dallas in a two-car caravan filled with men and guns on the eve of the assassination. When she became suspicious that the mission was to be against Kennedy rather than Castro, she fled back to Florida on November 21, 1963.

Bush's friendship with wealthy Russian émigré George DeMohrenschildt and his wife also is a red flag. DeMohrenschildt was close to Lee Harvey Oswald and there is evidence that he was also a CIA agent. It has been established that DeMohrenschildt was extremely close to Oswald and his wife between October 1962, just four months after Oswald returned from the USSR, and April 1963. Many researchers believe there is enough evidence to regard DeMohrenshildt as a case officer, handler or control agent for Oswald representing some intelligence agency.

Bush's name was in DeMohrenshildt's address book, found after DeMohrenshildt died of a gunshot wound in March 1977 on the eve of being interviewed by the House Select Committee on Assassinations. Much of DeMohrenshildt's head was blown off by a shotgun.

His death quickly was ruled a suicide, which was denied by his wife Jeanne who told a journalist in 1978 that her husband "was eliminated before he got to that committee." The address book listed Bush in Midland, Texas, where Zapata Offshore had an office until 1959 before relocating to Houston, indicating a long relationship between the two men.

The early Bush connection to the CIA was again mentioned in a July 16, 1988 article in *The Nation* by journalist Joseph McBride, who wrote "a source with close connections to the intelligence community confirms that Bush started working for the agency in 1960 or 1961, using his oil business as a cover for clandestine activities."

This corroborates an explosive memo titled "Assassination of John F. Kennedy" written by J. Edgar Hoover regarding a meeting that took place between the FBI and the CIA immediately following the murder of JFK. In the memo, Hoover identified one of the CIA representatives as "George Bush." The memo also identified Bush as a CIA supervisor of the anti-Castro Cuban forces that fought during the Bay of Pigs invasion.

In later years, Bush claimed that it was another George Bush who represented the CIA at the Hoover meeting. Although there was indeed another George Bush who worked then for the CIA, this one proved that he was a low-level analyst with the agency and signed an affidavit swearing that he was not at the Hoover meeting.

Author Webster Tarpley in his book, *George Bush: The Unauthorized Biography,* claims a reliable source told him 10 years before the book's publication that a meeting between JFK and retired General Douglas MacArthur occurred in 1961. MacArthur allegedly warned Kennedy of elements in the US government that sought to destroy his administration. The general said they were "centered in the Wall Street financial community and its various tentacles in the intelligence community."

Kennedy and MacArthur definitely did meet in late April 1961, following the Bay of Pigs, as confirmed by presidential aides Theodore Sorenson and Arthur Schlesinger.

"Kennedy was considering moves to limit or perhaps abolish the usurpation of authority over the national currency by the Wall Street and London interests controlling the Federal Reserve System," Tarpley added. "If re-elected to a second term, Kennedy was likely to have reasserted presidential control, as distinct from Wall Street control, over the intelligence community."

If Bush actually was working for the CIA at this early date, then a JFK reelection would concern him as it did the rest of the Agency.

There is evidence that Bush may have been in Dallas on November 22, 1963, along with a rogue's gallery that included Richard Nixon and Howard Hunt. When asked about his whereabouts, Bush claimed he didn't recall it, which makes him perhaps the only sentient American of 1963 who doesn't remember where he was that day.

This loss of memory becomes more suspicious in light of the FBI memorandum filed on November 22, 1963 by Special Agent Graham W. Kitchel, stating: "At 1:45 p.m. Mr. George H.W. Bush, President of the Zapata Off-Shore Drilling Company, Houston, Texas, residence 5525 Briar, Houston, telephonically furnished the following information to writer by long distance telephone call from Tyler, Texas. Bush stated that he wanted to be kept confidential but wanted to furnish hearsay that he recalled hearing in recent weeks, the day and source unknown. He stated that one James Parrott has been talking of killing the President when he comes to Houston....Bush stated that he was proceeding to Dallas, Texas, would remain in the Sheraton-Dallas Hotel and return to his residence on 11-23-63...."

The strangest part of this report is that Bush telephoned his warning more than an hour *after* Kennedy had been shot and a *full day after* Kennedy already had visited Houston. If he truly was in Tyler, Texas, which cannot be proved, he was only a short drive from Dallas.

The man Bush implicated as a political activist and potential assassin, James Parrott, was described as a right wing member of the Houston Young Republicans who had been discharged from the Air Force for psychiatric reasons in 1959. Nearly three decades after being implicated, the same James Parrott allegedly worked in the Bush re-election campaign against Bill Clinton.

During the 1975 Senate Select Committee on Assassinations, senators questioned then-CIA director William Colby, who admitted that Howard Hunt and George Bush were both in Dallas the day Kennedy was murdered. Colby claimed Bush was in charge, although he added that both were taking orders from others like Allen Dulles and the Rockefellers. This is remarkable, as Dulles had been fired by Kennedy as CIA director and had no authority to give orders to agents.

Nelson Rockefeller was vice president at the time of the hearings, so it comes as no surprise that Colby soon was fired. The surprise was his replacement, George Bush.

CIA cooperation with the committee abruptly ended with the promotion of Bush. Colby died many years later under suspicious circumstances that will be detailed in a subsequent book.

True Ott was unwilling to tell the author the details of the Gemstone File he discovered, specifically names and companies that appeared on the cancelled checks, bank accounts and other evidence that he says point to Bush and his Zapata Offshore firm, due to the incendiary nature of the information. However, Ott explains, the reason why Christiansen had this material was that he too was implicated in the assassination.

"There was a contingent of Mafioso Jews tied to the Mormons who were part of this deal," he told the author. "The specific names of [high ranking LDS church members] including Hartman Rector Junior's brother, were deeply involved with this whole group of Nazis who came over [to the US] through Operation Paperclip. One of them actually piloted the plane that brought these people over. They knew everything, and they were part of the CIA.

"Howard Hunt was reporting directly to Hartman Rector Junior's brother. When I read this, I thought, 'This is my church. They're dirty.' And Christiansen was using [this information] as a bargaining chip with the mob. Basically he was saying, 'If you kill me, this information will go to this law firm on Wilshire Boulevard.'"

According to Ott, in addition to evidence linking Bush and the CIA to the murder of JFK, the file also revealed CIA orders to murder witnesses of the assassination, naming 10 targets.

Ott phoned the law firm to clarify the import of the file he'd read. According to Ott, the attorney responded: "'Are you a Mormon?' I said, 'Yes.' 'Are you an elder?' I said, 'Yes.' 'Do you honor your priesthood?' I said, 'Yes.' 'Then throw the file away.' And he hung up. I kept the file anyway, because it revealed a dirty FBI with implications about [J. Edgar] Hoover, who had full knowledge of the [JFK] assassination and was playing both sides.

"The most surprising thing was that Lee Harvey Oswald was FBI. This was all in the file. He was FBI/double agent CIA. He was their [the FBI's] mole in the CIA."

Declassified secret documents gathered by the Warren Commission support Ott's contention. The Texas attorney general and the Dallas district attorney both testified that Oswald was FBI Informant Number 179 during the time of the assassination, and that he earned a monthly stipend of $200. When Oswald was arrested, Dallas police discovered in his wallet the name, phone number and license number of Dallas FBI agent James Hosty.

As early as 1960, J. Edgar Hoover wrote a memo complaining that someone was using Oswald's identity while the real Oswald was in Russia, and that the imposter was buying trucks for anti-Castro Cubans being trained by the CIA. JFK later ordered Hoover to shut down the anti-Castro training camps that were being run by the CIA, because it was a condition of the agreement with Russian Premier Kruschev that ended the 1962 Missile Crisis.

Following his return from Russia, Oswald was seen at the secret CIA training camp in Lake Ponchartrain, Louisiana, by Delphine Roberts, secretary of ex-FBI Chicago bureau chief Guy Bannister, who helped to direct the camp. Just a few days afterward, the FBI raided the camp and permanently closed it.

This leads some researchers like documentarian John Hankey to assume that Oswald was the source who pinpointed the Lake Ponchartrain training camp for the FBI raid. Hankey believes the CIA deliberately framed Oswald, obviously an important FBI asset who had betrayed them, for the murder of JFK, which they themselves committed. If true, one has to admit the dual acts of revenge dovetailed nicely for the

CIA.

Not long after Ott read the file, he was working with *George* magazine on a totally different topic — an article on his protest against expansion of the Circle 4 Farm's hog factory. A *George* magazine editor had flown to Ott's locale for a spread that included aerial photos and an interview with him. Afterward, Ott and the magazine's editor went out for a steak dinner. During the salad course, the editor told Ott that John Kennedy Jr. owned and published *George* magazine, which was a complete surprise to Ott.

"I asked him, 'Do you know John Junior?'" Ott told the author. "He said, 'Oh, yeah, we're best friends.' I asked if he was friendly enough that he could call him right now and he said yes. I said, 'Let me ask you. Does he believe the Warren Commission conclusion about his father's death?' He said, 'No, of course not.' I asked him who he thinks did it and he said they have their suspicions but can't prove it because there's no hard evidence.

"I told him [what] I knew about the Gemstone file and he immediately became electrified. I told him I might just have a copy of it. He said, 'Can I see it right now?' I said, 'Let's eat first,' and he said, 'No! Right now!' Then he gets up and yells to the waiter to put our steaks in a box."

Ott and the editor returned to his office, where he allowed the editor to take the file with him back to New York. At five o'clock the following morning, Ott received a phone call from the editor stating that they'd read the file and that John Kennedy had authorized him to write Ott a check, because Kennedy was positive its contents were valid. Ott refused to take payment, due to the heartache he felt about the involvement of the Mormon Church.

The editor promised that the facts in the file would be fully investigated. Later, on July 4th weekend, 1999, Ott received a phone call from John Kennedy Jr.

"He said, 'I just want to thank you for this file,'" Ott told the author. "He said, 'I've spent six figures on a private investigation to verify the contents, and I want you to be the first to know that in 10 days we will be convening a Federal Grand Jury. We will be indicting George Herbert Walker Bush for conspiracy to commit the murder of my father. And if George W. [Bush] thinks he can run for dog catcher after I'm done with his family, he is sorely mistaken.'

"Then he asked me for my bank information because he said he wanted to wire me some money. He asked, 'Would $15,000 be enough?' and I said, 'I don't want money.' He actually asked, 'Are you for real?' I told him I just don't want to take money for this information, but I want to know what happens with it.

"He gave me his personal phone number and told me I could call him anytime and added, 'I want to meet you some day.' I asked him, 'How do you feel now?' and he got emotional. He choked up and said the personal demons have been exorcised by knowing the truth. He said, 'I feel free. I feel angry that these people have gotten away with it for this long.'

"I told him, 'These people took out the most powerful man in the world in a *coup d'etat*. What makes you think you can go through with this?' He said, 'I've taken every precaution. I'm very precise.' I said, 'With all due respect, you're not the Secret Service.' He said, 'Justice will prevail.' Days later, he was dead."

John Fitzgerald Kennedy Jr. died on July 16, 1999, when his Piper Saratoga II HP private aircraft crashed into the Atlantic Ocean off Martha's Vineyard, also claiming the lives of his wife Carolyn and her sister Lauren. Their bodies were recovered following a five-day search.

The National Transportation Safety Board (NTSB) ruled probable pilot error "which was the result of spatial disorientation," as the cause of the crash. Ott firmly believes that it was no accident, and that the same people who had murdered JFK had also killed his son.

Just before the plane crash, George W. Bush was campaigning for the Republican Party nomination and was losing in the New Hampshire primary. Bush dropped out of sight on the morning of the Kennedys' death and was not seen by the press for three days. His staff members said they didn't know his whereabouts.

Ott admits that the Gemstone file still exists (Kennedy had sent a copy of it to Ott's attorney) and that he's duplicated the Christiansen gambit in threatening to release it should he meet an untimely or suspicious death.

"This is my bargaining chip," he told the author. "It's why I think I'm a little bit protected. After [John Kennedy] died, I knew I was in danger. I was being stalked and watched. My phone was bugged, so I deliberately spoke to my attorney about how the file was in his hands and with the Justice Department. We talked philosophically about balance of power and how it's not in my interest or anybody's interest to hurt the country. We basically told the listening ears that we were not a threat. We knew what we knew, but we knew that nobody would believe me anyway. We said that if I remained healthy and happy that this file would remain locked up. The cabal doesn't care that we know, as long as we don't do anything about it."

In Ott's opinion, JFK was murdered for two reasons: "First, he promised to disband the CIA. Also, he was going to discontinue the Federal Reserve by executive order."

A week after the plane crash, Ott received calls from various news publications including *Time* magazine and the *Wall Street Journal* asking if it was true that he'd provided a file to John Kennedy Jr. Ott denied the allegations and made no further comment.

At the same time *George* magazine called Ott and said that the publication was folding and that the JFK assassination story was dead. The editor added that the magazine's offices had been burgled and that the evidence went with John. There was not another issue of *George* published, not even a tribute issue to its late owner.

According to Ott, he was not the first to see the file. Jack Anderson, the late newshound and syndicated columnist of the *Washington Post,* had seen it five or six years earlier and even he refused to open Pandora's Box.

"The crime cartel in this country is simply too big and too powerful for the common man to fight," Ott adds.

FIFTH MOVEMENT – *BASSO CONTINUO*

KONTROLL

"Patriotism is supporting your country all the time and your government when it deserves it."

—Mark Twain

Education

"There is an organized effort today in our schools to indoctrinate our children in internationalism, in other words, belief in the United Nations, and the thought that we should do away with national sovereignty. There is an organized effort in our schools today to teach the children about collectivism and to rely on government to change our society. There is an organized effort in our education to destroy the belief in absolutes among our children and destroy belief in God. The purpose of education today in America is not education. It is indoctrination in internationalism, in collectivism, and in atheism. And they're doing a wonderful job."

—Dr. Stan Monteith, Physician, Author.

"You think the purpose of education is reading, writing and arithmetic? The purpose of education is to change the thoughts, actions and feelings of students....You have to get hold of the minds of the young [and] break the person's values. You break their understanding of their individuality. You bring them to consensus with the group. They become a member of the collective. It's the Soviet education, basically....There's no right and no wrong anymore....Sidney Simon's book, The Value Clarification, *[discusses] decision making, role playing...these are all psychological techniques to strip the child of any religion....Brock Chisolm, the Canadian psychiatrist [who was a] friend of Alger Hiss, [suggested to] retrain the teachers as little psychiatrists. [Soviet NKVD Director Lavrenty] Beria, going back to the 1930s, said the most important goal in the United States was to destroy Christianity."*

—Charlotte Thompson Iserbyt, Senior Policy Advisor, US Department of Education, Reagan Administration.

129

These are not the idle opinions of radicals. The people quoted on the previous page have studied the changes in American education over the past two decades, and they do not like what they see. They represent a consensus by many experts who believe that America's tax-supported educational system has begun to attack the idea of the nation and also the sanctity of family. They charge that the current educational system intends not to educate, but to indoctrinate.

The National Education Association (NEA) concocts and implements most of America's educational programs. The NEA was created by John D. Rockefeller, who once said, "I don't want a nation of thinkers. I want a nation of workers." Critics of the NEA and modern American education claim the goal now is to dumb down students.

This is not a new philosophy. In 1928, Ross Finney, a professor at the University of Minnesota, wrote in his book, *A Sociological Philosophy of Education:* "If leadership by the intelligent is ever to be achieved, followership by the dull and ignorant must somehow be assured. Followership, quite as much as leadership, is therefore the crucial problem of the present crisis. The safety of democracy is not to be sought, therefore, in the intellectual independence of the duller masses, but in their intellectual dependence."

The National Council for Social Studies (NCSS) provides a stark example of this philosophy in action. An offshoot of the NEA, this council claims the power to dictate what students should and should not be taught about history, political science, economics, religion, geography, psychology and the various other topics that have been gathered for decades under the term "social studies."

The NCSS is atop a bureaucratic pyramid, passing its regulations down to the various state councils, which in turn push for legislation that make NCSS curriculum a legal requirement in state-funded schools. Once this is achieved, parents and local school boards are hamstrung. Schools that do not meet the NCSS standards are denied state, federal and foundation funds, and even can be closed.

In 1992, Congress passed the Goals 2000: Educate America Act, which was signed into law by President Clinton on March 31, 1994. The bill provided federal funds to state and local schools with the high-minded goal of ensuring that all students reach their full potential. The legislation stated that by the year 2000, all American children would start school ready to learn, a 90 percent high school graduation rate would be achieved, US students would rank first in the world in mathematics, every adult American would be literate, and all schools would be free of drugs, violence and firearms.

That not one of these lofty goals was achieved by 2000, or by 2011, is not surprising, because they never were intended to be met. The real purpose of the legislation was to grab control of what students are taught by legalizing federal jurisdiction over curriculum. And when educators and activist groups complained about the failures, blame was shifted to parents, accusing them of taking little interest in their children's schooling, and to overcrowded classrooms and students who wouldn't work hard enough.

The solution in Washington was to pass the No Child Left Behind Act (NCLB) of 2001, signed into law by George W. Bush on January 8, 2002. It requires states to assess students through standardized testing as to which basic skills should be given to them, in exchange for federal funding.

Since its passage, the Department of Education has issued glowing results, based on its own statistics, but these statistics are misleading. An early report compared 2005 with 2000, even though the new legislation didn't take effect until 2003. Also the reported increase in scores between 2003 and 2005 was about the same as between 2000 and 2003, meaning NCLB had no appreciable effect. What the NCLB *has* achieved is greater control over what is taught, and to whom, at the expense of teacher and parental control.

The NCLB screening process of students was followed by the companion bureaucracy, the New Freedom Commission on Mental Health, a federal program which mandates screening and compulsory medication of children from infancy through the age of 18. The commission uses the Texas Medication Algorithm Project on school children to test for possible mental illness or emotional problems. The children identified with potential disabilities are to receive treatment, including new psychoactive drugs.

This program has drawn howls of protest from parents and citizens' groups. They claim the screening techniques are totally inappropriate and are designed to single out any child who does not think in harmony with a prescribed program. Critics abhor the power this program would give to government workers to medicate children against the will of their parents.

Many in the medical field also have charged that the proposed psychiatric medications to be used on children are unproven. Yet schools have asked children to sign an "assent form" which passively consents to participating in such programs as Teen Screen, even though they are not of legal age. Incentives like pizza parties are used to lure children to participate in screenings that include questions like: "Have you ever been depressed?" "Are you afraid to speak in a group?" "Do you feel your parents abuse you?"

After analyzing the answers to these questions, government-paid therapists make a diagnosis. As this program was initiated without parental permission or knowledge, families currently are suing schools that have instituted Teen Screen.

Clearly, a sea change has occurred in the federal government's approach to education, beginning in 1992. It is curious that this coincides with the end of the Cold War and the collapse of the Soviet Union in 1991.

Lech Biegalski, a former activist in the Polish Solidarity movement who has taught in schools both behind the Iron Curtain and in Canada, believes there is a definite relation between this change and the end of the Cold War. He wrote that after the West won the Cold War that "the ideological competition was over. 'Restructuring' was implemented promptly and our 46-year-old magic carpet [in Canada] began to roll back. And so did job security, high standard of living, decent social programs, full-time jobs, paid holidays, job security, benefits, democracy and the focus on human rights and human dignity in general. It seems that all the goodies we enjoyed in the 1970s and 1980s were not given to us out of a genuine support for decent life of working families. It seems they were not 'won' in a struggle between the workers and the capitalists. Rather, they were temporarily used by the elites as weapons in the ideological war between the West and the East. The war is now over, and so is 'capitalism with [a] human face.'"

From his perch in Ontario, Canada, Biegalski noticed an immediate change in Canada's educational policy shortly after the collapse of the Soviet Union. In a speech delivered to Toronto business leaders, the president of a major Canadian bank said, "Our education has outgrown the capacity of our economy in terms of employment." Biegalski took this to mean, "We had too many educated people. Our economy did not need them. We should not over-invest in education."

The actions of Canada's government seem to buttress Biegalski's take. School funds were cut. The role of parents in school council activities was minimized to fundraising. The schools had to institute a new curriculum, a new evaluation and reporting system, while cutting programs and special education services.

The industrial arts program was completely eliminated, meaning students would not learn to use simple tools and become more dependent upon the state. The family studies program was eliminated. Computer education was drastically cut. Libraries were reduced and in some cases eliminated. The number of textbooks was cut, forcing students to share. The workload on teachers, including greatly increased administrative and bureaucratic demands, grew to a point where they have much less time to prepare academic materials and lessons.

The Canadian situation mirrors that of the US. Students are learning less while being indoctrinated into a mindset where nations must give way to globalism, family must give way to the state, and religion must give way to reason.

Tax-Exempt Foundations

In 1952, Norman Dodd claimed that the president of the Ford Foundation told him its purpose was to "use our grant-making power so as to alter our life in the United States that we can be comfortably merged with the Soviet Union." Dodd was the director of research for the House Select Committee to Investigate Foundations and Comparable Organizations at the time he made this remarkable accusation.

Obviously, the US-USSR merger never took place, as the Soviet empire collapsed in 1991, but the goal of a centralized global control system remains a perceptible reality today. And there are more than 40,000 tax-exempt foundations similar to Ford, some linked to the CFR, in existence now. Many have the same stated purpose.

The CFR-linked charities include the ACLU, the Anti-Defamation League, the Center for Advanced Studies in Behavioral Sciences, the Communist League, the Fabian Society, the Hudson Institute, the Mellon Institute, the NAACP, the National Council of Churches, the Rand Institute, the Stanford Research Institute, the International Red Cross, and even the YMCA, in addition to the Ford Foundation.

This collection represents just a fraction of the charities with ties to the CFR, the Trilateral Commission, and other secret groups. For example, Paul Anderson wrote of the Aspen Institute in the *Aspen Times Weekly* that it "regularly hosts presidents, prime ministers, philosophers, statesmen, advisors, educators, journalists, artists, activists and a roster of corporate representatives to rival the Fortune 500 list." Anderson added that this internationally prominent organization "remains an enigma to the majority of local residents and visitors."

The Institute was founded by a collection of powerful men related to the CFR, including Time-Life publisher Henry Luce and Robert Maynard Hutchins, president of the University of Chicago (a Rockefeller institution) during the 1940s.

Another foundation, the Institute for Policy Studies (IPS), which has helped to shape America's foreign and domestic policies for decades, was founded by James Warburg and known Rothschild-connected holdings in the US. Much of the "New Left" of the 1960s was created by the IPS, which fostered the social unrest and drug use that marked that decade.

Author and former intelligence agent Dr. John Coleman claims that the IPS founders controlled and instigated the Black Panthers, Daniel Ellsberg and the Weather Underground, all of which represented radical socialism. Its activities clearly benefited the Soviet Union during those chaotic times. And research indicates that funding for the IPS comes from the Rubin Foundation, which is CFR-connected, owing to its affiliation with the law firm Lord, Day & Lord. Winston Lord was chairman of the CFR in 1983.

The Fabian Society is perhaps one of the most interesting of the foundations in that it had enough influence to form Britain's Labor Party in 1906. Itself founded in London in 1883, Fabian drew its name from the ancient Roman general Fabius, who defeated the army of Hannibal through guerilla tactics. The Society's stated purpose in its own tactics of avoiding pitched battle is "the reorganization of society by the emancipation of land and Industry Capital from individual and class ownership." Its members included George Bernard Shaw and economist John Maynard Keynes, author of the government-controlled economy theory that dominated American domestic policy from Franklin Roosevelt's administration to that of Jimmy Carter, and has returned in the administration of Barack Obama.

Another Fabian Society member, H.G. Wells, accused his cohorts of "a conceit of cunning" in believing "that the world may be maneuvered into socialism without knowing it." A Fabian Society creation, the London School of Economics, educated David Rockefeller, John Fitzgerald Kennedy, Robert Kennedy Jr., and Daniel Moynihan, who would become a powerful US senator.

The influence that tax-exempt foundations have on government foreign, domestic and economic policy is obvious. Less obvious is the awesome power these foundations wield over medicine and science. Researchers are enslaved in both of these fields by the rich grants their studies receive. Findings and opinions obnoxious to the plans of those who control the foundations are met with loss of funding and, in some cases, destruction of careers.

The Corporate Media

"We are grateful to the Washington Post, *the* New York Times, Time *magazine and other great publications whose directors have attended our meetings and respected their promises of discretion for almost 40 years. It would have been impossible for us to develop our plans for the world if we had been subjected to the lights of publicity during those years. But now the world is more sophisticated and prepared to march towards a world government. The supranational sovereignty of an intellectual elite and world bankers is surely preferable to the national auto-determination practiced in past centuries."*

—David Rockefeller

The above quote sums up the reason why the American, indeed the world, public receives no information on the secret conferences held by the CFR, the Bilderberg group, and other entities in the world's invisible government. It remains invisible because the entire mainstream media is under the control of the people who are in this government.

Any news story that promotes the globalist agenda is stressed in the media, whether it is true or false. Any fact that exposes or debases the globalist agenda is generally ridiculed or spiked and squelched. This is because nearly everything Americans read, watch or hear today is controlled by just six multinational corporations. The evidence:

Time Warner Inc. holds America Online, *Time* magazine, Time Warner Cable, Warner Bros. Studios, Hanna-Barbera Productions, HBO, CNN, Time-Life Books, Little, Brown and Company publishing, the Turner Entertainment Company, *Fortune* magazine, 11 movie production companies and 52 record labels.

The Walt Disney Company owns the ABC network, Walt Disney Pictures, Touchstone Pictures, MGM, Miramax, Buena Vista, Disneyland, Disney World, ESPN networks, Soap cable channel, Lifetime cable networks, and even the Jim Henson Muppets.

Viacom owns the CBS network, Paramount Pictures, MTV,

Nickelodeon Movies, Nickelodeon cable network, Dreamworks, TV Land channel, CMT, Spike TV, VH1, Comedy Central, BET, several book publishing houses and nearly 200 radio stations.

Vivendi Universal Entertainment owns Universal Music Group, Studio Canal+, five Universal Studio theme parks, Vivendi Universal Publishing (now called Editis, the umbrella for more than 60 publishing houses), and mobile phone companies.

News Corp. owns the entire Fox network family, England's Sky TV, Australia's Foxtel, Asian mega network Star TV, 20th century Fox (movies and TV), Fox Searchlight Pictures, MySpace, Photobucket, IGN Entertainment, *TV Guide,* Harper Collins Publishing, the *New York Post, The Times* of London, the *Daily Telegraph,* and many other newspapers around the world.

Bertelsmann AG, a Germany-based corporation, is the world's largest publisher in English whose holdings include BMG Music Publishing, Napster, RCA Records, the RCA Victor Group, Arista Records, television networks, radio stations, production houses, newspapers, magazines including *Family Circle, Parents, Geo* and *Stern,* Random House, Ballantine Books, Del Rey Publishing, Fawcett, Bantam, Delacorte Press, Dell, Delta, Spectra, Dial Press, Crown Publishers, Harmony Books, Broadway Books, Doubleday, Doubleday Religious Publishing, Main Street Books, Alfred A. Knopf, Pantheon Books, Vintage, The Modern Library, Random House Children's Books, Fodor's Travel Publications, and the Princeton Review. Bertelsmann also owns YES Solutions (media service), and in partnership with Time Warner directs the world's largest book clubs.

In addition, General Electric was a major player following its purchase of Universal Studios and the NBC network, the latter having recently been sold to another media giant, Comcast.

In the 1990s, Conrad Black made important inroads among media moguls with his company, Hollinger International, at the time the third largest newspaper chain in the West with a combined circulation of more than 10 million. Among the 650 dailies and weeklies owned worldwide by Black were the *Daily Telebraph* and the *Chicago Sun-Times.*

Black was a member of the Bilderberg group and served on the International Advisory Board of the CFR. He wielded tremendous influence in fostering the plans of these groups until December 2007, when Black was convicted of defrauding his stockholders by skimming millions of dollars from Hollinger International. He was sentenced to six and a half years in federal prison.

The loss of Black has not affected the corporate control of news, however. Anthony Holder, former UN correspondent with the London *Economist,* admitted, "The Bilderbergers have been removed from our assignment list years ago by executive order."

William Glasgow, the *Business Week* senior writer tasked with covering international organizations, complained, "We are barely aware of the Bilderbergers' existence, and we don't report on their activities. One cannot help but be a little suspicious when priorities for the future of mankind are being considered by those who have real influence over that future, in total secret."

But there are a number of very familiar media and journalist names who are more than aware of the Bilderbergers and their plans, because every year, as evidenced by David Rockefeller's thankful comment, the group invites members of the fourth estate to its conferences. Over the years, media and journalist attendees included Katherine and Donald Graham of the *Washington Post,* columnists Charles Krauthammer and Jim Hoagland, *New York Times* editor Arthur Sulzberger, Knight-Ridder newspaper director Arthur Knight, *U.S. News and World Report* editor-in-chief Mort Zuckerman, William F. Buckley of the *National Review,* and PBS director Bill Moyers. These are just a few of the journalists and media moguls thanked for their silence by David Rockefeller.

It is not surprising that few Americans realize that the *Washington Times,* the pre-eminent conservative newspaper in the capital, is owned by the Reverend Sun Myung Moon through his international media conglomerate, News World Communications. Moon is the Korean-born founder of the Unification Church, which is true to its title in pressing to unify all creeds into a one-world religion under Moon, who his church members believe is the Second Coming of Christ, fulfilling the unfinished mission of Jesus.

Despite the copious tales of abuse suffered by some of his followers at the hands of Moon and his congregation's elite, the Unification Church continues to flourish internationally with solid connections to virtually every major evangelical Christian church in America. Jerry Falwell accepted $2.5 million from Moon in 1994 to bail out his financially troubled Liberty University in Lynchburg, Virginia. Falwell repaid the favor by speaking at many of Moon's gatherings, giving him full support.

Other evangelical speakers at Moon affairs included Robert

Schuller, Beverly LaHaye and Gary Bauer. In 1981, LaHaye's husband Tim founded the Council of National Policy (CNP) with a $500,000 donation from Bo Hi Pak, Moon's chief lieutenant and an alleged former South Korean intelligence officer. The CNP, ostensibly a Christian organization, boasts a wide membership that includes CFR members.

Soon after Moon was arrested and jailed for tax evasion in 1984, he supplied funds to form the Coalition for Religious Freedom (CRF), whose executive committee members included Jerry Falwell, Jimmy Swaggart, Rex Humbard, and James Robison — all leaders in the Christian evangelical movement. These people are important and influential media personalities, so their connection to a church that wishes to create a one-world religion and to members of the CFR which has the same agenda, is troubling.

The Emergent Church Movement poses a similar problem. Beginning in the late 20th century, this supposedly Christian attempt to meld doctrine with what it considers a postmodern world seeks to create a one-world religion that crosses many theological boundaries. The "emergent" term was coined by Catholic political theologian Johann Baptist Metz in 1981, although he used it in a completely different context. But in the 21st century, the current Emergent Movement has exploded via the Internet.

One of the chief proponents of the Emergent Movement is Brian McLaren, a controversial evangelical pastor who believes it is vital for Christianity to join the cultural shift in the world toward postmodernism and to accept non-Christian doctrines in the name of unity. Others involved in the movement include Doug Pagitt, Rick Warren, Tony Jones and Chuck Smith Jr. in the US, Jonny Baker and Ian Mobsby of Great Britain, and Mike Riddell in New Zealand. Warren, founder and pastor of the huge Saddleback Church who was tabbed "America's most powerful religious leader" in the August 18, 2008 issue of *Time* magazine, is a member of the CFR.

Linda Harvey, president of Mission America, has accused the movement of mutilating Christian doctrine into whatever suits its political purposes for a one-world religion. "The Democratic Party's newest and closest consultants are many of these religious celebrities," said Harvey. "They are the prophets now speaking live to power...Tony Campolo served on the Democratic Platform Committee. Why would a minister be writing the platform for the Democratic Party for this [2008] election? [He's there] only to provide strategic input critical to a vital voting block...Campolo also served as a faith advisor to Bill Clinton."

Harvey also points out that Sojourners founder Jim Wallis crafted Barack Obama's faith-based policy for his election campaign. The Church of the Sojourners, a communal Christian movement, is heavily funded by organizations controlled by George Soros and Bill Moyers, both of whom support a variety of globalist causes that are in direct opposition to Christian doctrine.

The crux of the one-world religion is Mother Earth, in other words, nature. This is simple paganism, rendering the center of Christianity, Jesus, insignificant. Yet Christianity's most influential and popular American, Billy Graham, proposed this very thing in his Embrace America 2000 radio show in 1992, when he told his audience they needed to embrace the New World Order.

Graham has been accused of being a 33rd degree Freemason and despite his rather flaccid denials, Internet alternate news sites like HardTruth.com claim to have powerful evidence that this is indeed the case. Several Freemason-owned web pages actually listed Graham as a member until they were forced to remove his name under threat of lawsuit. Graham's close association with Norman Vincent Peale, an admitted high ranking member who wrote an article titled "Why I Am Proud to Be a Freemason," is another red flag. It certainly contradicts the supposed incompatibility of Freemasonry and Christianity.

Graham's *Christianity Today* is recognized as the most influential Christian publication in the world. Founded in 1955 by Graham and his father-in-law, Dr. L. Nelson Bell, the paper has been a consistent supporter of the Lausanne Movement to unify the religions of the world by spreading Christian doctrine overseas.

Initiated by Graham and John Stott in 1974, the Lausanne Covenant is a required adherence in numerous Christian organizations. Behind the Lausanne Movement is Stott's World Evangelical Fellowship (WEF), which is simply a revived version of the US Evangelical Alliance, originally created in London in 1846 at the United Grand Lodge of England headquarters at Freemason Hall — the recognized headquarters of international Freemasonry.

Principal financing of *Christianity Today* comes from Pew Charitible Trusts, owned by J. Howard Pew of the Sun Oil Corporation (Sunoco), which is part of the Rockefeller petroleum cartel. The main concern of the Pew Trusts in this matter is to foster a conjunction between evangelical Christians and American intellectual leaders by placing evangelical scholars in top universities.

Luis Lugo, religion program director for Pew Trusts, wrote of "increasing religious diversity" and developing "an appreciation of various religious traditions that hold deep meaning for so many Americans." To many of the faithful, this sounds like a departure from Christian doctrine and a channel through which the churches will become an arm of the state.

Pew Trusts also funds the CFR, and there are a number of CFR-connected persons on the *Christianity Today* masthead — advisory editors Michael Cromartie, Diane Knippers, Steven McFarland, Richard John Neuhaus, and Michael Novak. It is impossible to underestimate the influence Graham — whose career was vitalized on orders from William Randolph Hearst through his newspaper empire beginning in 1949 — and his *Christianity Today* have on American opinion. If, as critics claim, it has been corrupted, then this influence would be a tool of the globalist planners.

The Public Broadcasting System in the US also faces claims of corruption. Most Americans imagine that the PBS stations must offer a fair and objective viewpoint since the network is "publicly funded." However, most funding comes from CFR-run corporations like AT&T, PepsiCo and Smith Barney.

Archer Daniel Midland, another PBS donator, is chaired by Dwayne Andreas of the Trilateral Commission. Jim Lehrer, anchor of the network's cornerstone evening news broadcast, is a member of the CFR, and many journalists who participate in *NewsHour* — David Gergen, William Safire, William Kristol, Paul Gigot — belong or have belonged to the Bilderberg group, the CFR or the Trilateral Commission. Recall the Rockefeller domination of all three groups.

Author Gary Allen wrote in his book, *The Rockefeller File,* "The involvement of the Rockefellers with the media has multiple implications. One is that the Rockefeller gang's plans for monopolistic World Government are never, but never, discussed in the machines of mass disinformation. The media decides what the issues will be in the country. They can turn on the poverty issue or turn it off. The same holds true for population explosion, pollution, peace, détente, or whatever. The media can take a man like Ralph Nader and make him an instant folk hero. Or they can take an enemy of the Rockefellers (like Goldwater) and create an image that he is a cretin, a buffoon, a bigot, or a dangerous paranoid."

Allen's reference to Nader, an independent presidential candidate in two elections and a supposed hero of the anti-establishment sector, is important because Nader has been financed by the Rockefeller network and the CFR-linked Ford Foundation. Nader's mantra calls for the destruction of free enterprise, a balm to the Rockefeller monopolists.

Allen also submits that the Trilateral Commission has created its own formula for subjugating and then controlling the media. According to him, the commission wants to limit freedom of the press. The formal Trilateral proposals, taken from the commission's own minutes, include "prior restraint of what newspapers may publish in unspecified unusual circumstances, the assurance to the government [of] the right and the ability to withhold information at the source…moving promptly to reinstate the law of libel as a necessary and appropriate check upon the abuses of power by the press, and press council enforcing 'standards of professionalism,' the alternative [to which] could well be regulation by the government."

Control of our media by a handful of corporations has led to some disturbing occurrences. In 1998, ABC News spiked a report that showed Disney World to have some embarrassing safety and hiring issues. The AOL/Time Warner merger of 2000 somehow managed to escape anti-trust laws, perhaps owing to the political contributions of both firms. Similarly, Viacom probably broke FCC rules on media ownership when it purchased CBS, but Senator John McCain came to the rescue in one week by proposing a change in those rules. Viacom reportedly is among McCain's largest financial patrons.

Another example is the Fox News spiking of a story in 1996 that would have been damaging to the Monsanto Corporation. The Fox station in Florida, WTVT, had hired the husband-and-wife journalist team, Jane Akre and Steve Wilson, to be its much-publicized special investigative unit.

One of their first stories concerned a dangerous genetically engineered recombinant bovine growth hormone called rBHG which was being given to cows in the US. The hormone had been FDA approved, despite the fact that Canada's food and drug watchdog had refused approval in that country due to the carcinogenic properties of rBHG. The hormone is the flagship product in Monsanto's drive to dominate the biotechnology marketplace, and the firm stressed how injecting Posilac (the brand name of rBHG) creates much higher milk production in dairy cows.

The story produced by Akre and Wilson never aired, and the pair was fired after they independently published their script. Akre and Wilson have sued WTVT and Fox, claiming that rather than kill the story, the station ordered them to broadcast a "demonstrably inaccurate and dishonest" version. The reporters also claim in their suit that the Fox affiliate station bowed to high level lobbying by Monsanto, and perhaps also by the Florida dairy industry.

The aggressiveness of Monsanto in marketing rBHG is clear in the company's lawsuits against stores that carried milk and dairy products advertised as not containing the hormone. As early as 1989, Monsanto hired the PR firm of Carma International to monitor and analyze every story aired or written about rBHG, and to compile a list of friendly or unfriendly reporters.

Leaked internal Dairy Commission documents show that reporters who write negative pieces on dairy products, and scientists who provide opinions supporting such pieces, are systematically smeared. A case in point is that of Dr. Samuel Epstein, who linked milk to cancer in a press conference, which was covered by a *Boston Globe* reporter. The Dairy Commission used its scientific contacts to accuse Epstein of having "no standing among his peers," and also went after the *Globe* reporter by pointing out that the *Washington Post, Wall Street Journal,* and *New York Times* chose not to print their coverage of the press conference.

Even smaller audience radio shows have been targeted for suppression when they cross the line to report on incendiary topics. Witness the demise of Dr. A. True Ott's weekly two-hour talk radio show, "The Story Behind the Story," on the Republic Broadcasting Network.

The program apparently was on the radar of corporate leaders for its award-winning revelations in the late 1990s about the "Phen-fen" diet fraud perpetrated by American Home Products, Inc., and the CIA's MK-ULTRA program. In August 2001, Ott interviewed former naval intelligence agent Milton William "Bill" Cooper, author of *Behold a Pale Horse,* who warned of a coming attack on a major American landmark.

"He said it would not be what the government would claim it to be," Ott told the author. "[He said] they would blame it on a terrorist group, but it would be a 'false flag' [attack]. I took notes, but I didn't think it would happen. When the events [of 9/11] unfolded, I talked to him again and he had the contact who gave him this information call me. He said [the contact] is one of the top three demolition experts in the world, who claims he was contacted by Larry Silverstein [then owner of the World Trade Center] to do a schematic on how to bring it down."

When Ott pre-interviewed Cooper's building demolition expert, the man told him that the four pillars of the World Trade towers were too strong to be demolished by thermite. In order to bring down the towers, he said, according to Ott, "It had to melt the core pillars. The only way to do it, he said, was to use a bunker-buster mini nuke to take out those interiors. I got all of his documents.

"After the collapse, [the University of] Cal Berkeley went in there with Geiger counters measuring the dust and it was radioactive. It was full of Tritium. The government response to the Berkeley report was to say it [the radioactivity] was due to all of those thousands of Exit signs that have small amounts of radioactivity."

The show arranged for an on-air interview in late 2001, and according to Ott, "We advertised that this was going to be the most amazing true story in radio history. He would only talk on air through a voice scrambler, and we agreed. We broadcast from Cedar City, [Utah] and were five minutes into the broadcast when the lights flashed like there was a power surge.

"The signal was cut, and they shut down the station. They flat out shut it down. Then my show was cancelled. The station said they wouldn't be able to keep their FCC license if they continued broadcasting my show. Afterward I got so much hate mail, telling me to leave the country. Shortly after that, Bill Cooper was killed. He had been harassed for a time by federal agents and finally he was gunned down and killed in front of his house."

Cooper had a long-running battle with the IRS and a history of revealing information embarrassing to the US government, through his books, his public appearances and his shortwave radio show. The official police version of his death accuses him of brandishing a handgun and shooting at Apache County, Arizona, sheriff's deputies when they attempted to arrest him on a threat complaint warrant. But the official report is problematic, as the deputies were not in uniform and had been lurking near Cooper's remote home before gunning him down on his front porch.

This isn't the only instance of violence against members of the media who reveal uncomfortable truths about the government and those who control it from the shadows. In October 2009, CNN anchor and journalist Lou Dobbs revealed on his radio show that someone had fired a bullet into his home.

"Three weeks ago this morning, a shot was fired at my house, where

I live," Dobbs reported. "That followed weeks and weeks of threatening phone calls....The New Jersey State Patrol responded instantly...I decided not to report the threatening phone calls because they've become a way of life....But it's taken a different turn when they fire a shot at my home while my wife is standing next to the car."

Police found the bullet outside, noting that it marked the exterior of Dobbs' home but didn't penetrate it. Dobbs has been an outspoken critic of the push for a one-world government and a New World Order. He frequently used his show on CNN to issue warnings about globalization policies and to oppose illegal immigration, corporate control of politicians, and offshore outsourcing.

Dobbs twice quit CNN because he felt the network had become "clearly partisan" toward liberal Democratic policies. He clashed repeatedly over this with CNN President Rick Kaplan and finally resigned from the network in 1999. The following year, Kaplan left and Dobbs returned in 2001, continuing his anti-globalist reports. He also reported on the evidence that Barack Obama was born in Kenya, not Hawaii, and that his birth certificate is a forgery. Dobbs quit CNN again in 2009, less than two weeks after someone shot at his home.

The numerous instances of corporate pressure affecting news coverage would require a separate volume. Suffice it to say that corporations have the power to control what we read, watch and hear, and have acted in their own interests, even when those interests are opposed to public safety.

There is an old saying: Freedom of the press belongs to whoever owns the press. Media critics often have written that the task of the news business no longer is to tell it like it is, but to tell it like the media owners want it. One critic, Michael Parenti, pointed out the nomenclature that the news media use in order to skew the opinions of viewers. For instance, he uses the example of stories that use the term "labor disputes," but never "management disputes." Also, he said that in these stories management always makes "offers" but the unions always make "demands."

Reporter Britt Hume of Fox News chastised his fellow journalists, saying what reporters "pass off as objectivity is just a mindless kind of neutrality," and that they "shouldn't try to be objective, they should try to be honest."

Also important is the fact that large banking interests hold tremendous amounts of stock in the media conglomerates today. Some of these bankers are CFR members, and there also are CFR members sitting on the boards of the media corporations, according to the 2009 edition of

Standard & Poor's Corporation Records. With secret society members sitting in positions of power among the media giants, it becomes clear why coverage of the Bilderberg, CFR and Trilateral Commission meetings is sparse to non-existent in the mainstream media.

Another reason for the lack of coverage is that many of the friendly faces who report the news daily into our living rooms are either CFR or Trilateral members, or have joined both groups. They include Diane Sawyer, Bill Moyers, Ted Koppel, Barbara Walters, Marvin Kalb, George Will and former anchors Dan Rather and Tom Brokaw.

There are organizations that supposedly monitor the media for the public's sake, like Accuracy in Media, but in 1990 it was reported that the organization's founder, Reed Irvine, received a yearly salary of $37,000 from the Federal Reserve System in an advisory capacity. It is no surprise that this watchdog organization never focuses on topics that may be uncomfortable for the secret international groups.

One holdout may be AlterNet, a news service launched in 1998 which offers reports from alternative media outlets, mainly culled from the Internet. Among its staff is executive editor, Don Hazen, who used to publish *Mother Jones* magazine. However, AlterNet relies on donations from such entities as the Ford Foundation, which has strong connections to the same globalists who run the mainstream media.

Still, in AlterNet's customary "Top Ten Most Censored Stories" from year to year, most involved corporate malfeasance of some kind, including accountability in human rights violations, blame for health hazards in products, environmental threats and accidents, monopolization, medical industry fraud, and other business-oriented incidents. We can add to this censorship list the missing reports on who owns the corporations that control nearly all of the mainstream media.

Television news used to be run as a kind of public service, often at a deficit, by the big three networks until the 1960s. But having been gobbled up by large corporations, today they are expected to draw ratings and profits like any other offering, and there is pressure from the top to toe the company line with the choice of stories and how they're reported.

It is Paddy Cheyefsky's prescient script, *Network,* come to pass. Perhaps it's time everyone gets "mad as hell."

The National ID

In 2005 the Emergency Supplemental Appropriations Act for Defense, the Global War on Terror, and Tsunami Relief legislation, known simply as the Real ID Act, sneaked through Congress as a rider on a military spending bill. Prior to this, congressmen were extremely hesitant to sign on to a bill that would require every American to carry a national ID card, because of the outcry from their constituents.

Specifically, the Real ID Act calls for all state-issued driver licenses and all non-driver IDs to conform to a national standard. If a state-issued card does not meet the requirements in the Real ID Act, no federal agency will accept it.

Among other things, this means that any citizen that does not have this national ID card may be banned from flying on commercial aircraft. Absence of this card also could prevent citizens from being hired at a new job, as they would run afoul of the Social Security Administration requirement that states supply a new-hire directory. Even federally insured banks would be forced to deny customers without the proper new ID card, meaning these citizens would not be permitted to have banking services.

The pubic outcry in several states against the Real ID Act led to legislation there that opposed the national card, which was to go into effect in 2007. The federal government then announced the law would be delayed until December 2009. Continued popular and political resistance has delayed its implementation yet again.

Critics of the law insist it is unconstitutional and advances the globalist interests in this country, while doing little or nothing to safeguard Americans from terrorism, which was the stated purpose of the Real ID Act.

One of the possible results of a national ID is that it would allow the federal government to freeze assets of citizens whom they deem to be "anti-social," which could include political dissidents or anyone regarded as an enemy. Recall that the Nixon Administration had an "Enemies of the White House" list which was revealed in the Watergate hearings in 1973. Probably subsequent administrations have committed similar unconstitutional acts in which imagined "enemies" suddenly found themselves being audited by the IRS and having other problems with government agencies. Had Nixon's or other administrations possessed a weapon like the Real ID Act, would they not have used it literally to cause certain supposed enemies to disappear electronically?

By reprogramming databases on an individual, scanners no longer would recognize his card. That means no bank accounts, no ATM, no credit, no right to drive, no right to work, and no right to have medical care. And the federal government has other plans that go far beyond the Real ID Act, all the way into your own body.

The Chip

Applied Digital Solutions, Inc. is a high-tech company located in Palm Beach, Florida. In October 2002, the firm began promoting its new product, a personal verification microchip that can be implanted beneath a person's skin.

Called the VeriChip, it is a 12 millimeter by 2.1 millimeter Radio Frequency Identification Device (RFID) that contains a verification number which can be scanned via radio frequency energy. The scanner receives the verification number and transmits it to a secure data storage site. The VeriChip could thus be utilized in all financial, business and travel transactions, in addition to every other instance that requires identification with personal, criminal, and financial information.

In short, it's a one-stop method of instantly knowing everything about a person, in the hands of others.

Applied Digital Solutions launched a happy promotion for its new Orwellian product under the slogan, "Get Chipped," and advertised VeriChip centers in various states. The Cincinnati video surveillance firm, CityWatcher.com, became one of the first VeriChip takers when it implanted the product into the arms of some employees, although it wasn't mandatory.

Applied Digital Solutions also supplied a "ChipMobile," to market the product and implant people eager to be tagged like wilderness beasts. The campaign began almost immediately after the FDA ruled that the product was not a medical device, and that there was "reasonable assurance" it was safe.

What Applied Digital and the FDA failed to mention was that chip implants induced malignant cancers in some lab rats and mice, according to several toxicology studies in the 1990s. A Dow Chemical Company study in 1996 led by Keith Johnson caused him to conclude flatly, "The transponders were the cause of the tumors." And while attempting to give the chip a benefit of the doubt by saying lab animal tests don't necessarily apply to humans, several cancer experts, when asked by an Associated Press reporter, admitted they would not allow their children to be chipped.

It's crucial to note that Tommy Thompson was running the Department of Health and Human Services when the VeriChip received its FDA non-medical classification. Thompson retired from government work to become director of the VeriChip Corporation until 2007, when he resigned to make his unsuccessful run as a Republican candidate for the presidency.

While citizens haven't flocked to be chipped, the firm also markets the VeriChip for consumer products like computers, autos, vital possessions and homes, saying it will limit theft, including identity theft. It also allows these items to be electronically identified and even tracked anywhere.

A number of hospitals in America have implanted chips into patients for medical purposes, especially those patients suffering from Alzheimer's disease. This is reminiscent of a chilling historical precedent in which the Nazis identified and classified people suffering from this and other debilitating physical and mental diseases for its euthanasia program. But even in Nazi Germany the outcry against euthanasia was so great that the authorities had to stop, although it is clear from documents that they fully intended to resume the activities when the political climate favored it.

The RFID tracking chip already is mandated to be placed in all new American passports. If it is placed within all citizens, it will allow the government to keep track of and control every single aspect of an individual's finances, transactions, travel and all other interaction with society. With the power to "turn off" the chip, an individual essentially will be deleted.

Perhaps most disturbing is the possibility that the RFID chip already has been mandated into law, buried in Section 2521 of the mammoth 2,000-page health care bill that Congress passed in 2010. The language stipulates that no medical care will be given unless patients have an RFID implant. Clearly many lawmakers were not aware of this rider that was buried in a bill too long for them to read in the time allotted, much the same way that the Real ID Act passed. While Section 2521 says the implant is not mandatory, anyone who wants the health care his or her taxes have paid for will need to do it. And the new health bill applies to all citizens.

Another recent legislation involves GPS tracking. In 2010, the US Court of Appeals for the Ninth Circuit ruled that the government may monitor citizens at any time without a search warrant. The law covers

California and eight other Western states. It will allow government agents to place GPS tracking devices beneath cars parked on streets or in driveways without warrants and without violating rights guaranteed by the Fourth Amendment.

The case was initiated in 2007 when DEA agents monitored Juan Pineda-Moreno, whom they suspected was growing marijuana. In the dead of night, they placed a GPS device beneath the Jeep in his driveway. Pineda, who was convicted of manufacturing marijuana, challenged the DEA's right to place surveillance devices on vehicles parked in private driveways, but two sets of judges ruled that citizens have no reasonable expectation of privacy in their driveways. The exception to this, as ruled by Judge Alex Kozinski, is that driveways and other properties bordered by electric gates, fences and security booths *are* to be considered private. In other words, rich people are not susceptible to this warrantless invasion of privacy. This issue likely will go to the Supreme Court, but in the meantime, the ruling stands in the Ninth Circuit.

California ordinarily is a trailblazing state in trends and legislation, even the disturbing ones like warrantless GPS tracking and GPS tracking of children. In August 2010, officials of Contra Costa County announced they will outfit pre-school children with tracking devices that will reveal a child's whereabouts. The kids must wear a jersey containing a small RF tag which sends signals to sensors informing the monitors where a child is located, whether they are absent, and even whether or not they have eaten. The system is funded by a federal grant.

The concept of tracking an entire population through identification techniques goes back to IBM founder Thomas J. Watson, who had sold his punch card computers and his technicians to Nazi Germany for use in the death camps. The familiar tattoos on concentration camp prisoners served as IBM computer identification numbers. Watson had perfected this system of punch card identification in 1928, when it was used in the Jamaica Race Crossing Study. One could say that the first computers were specifically designed for eugenics studies.

The future holds similar threats as new technologies come into use. Genetic information on most people in the developed world should be available in the next decade, according to Francis Collins, director of the US National Institutes of Health. This mass genome sequencing would identify individuals with greater genetic health care risks of heart disease, diabetes, cancer and other ailments, thus providing a national database of at-risk individuals from childhood. Coupled with mandatory prescribed drugs for at-risk persons, which has been broached legally, one can see where this may be going.

Keeping track of citizens through new technology also has included unpiloted drones flying in US airspace for the past several years, according to researcher John Whitehead. He cited a 2006 news story that one North Carolina county had been using a drone with low-light and infrared cameras to monitor gatherings at the Gaston County Fairgrounds, flying low enough to identify faces. Whitehead also reported that "the Federal Aviation Administration is facing mounting pressure from state governments and localities to issue flying rights for a range of [unmanned aerial vehicles] to carry out civilian and law enforcement activities."

In 2007, witnesses reported insect-like drones flying above political rallies in New York and Washington. "Unfortunately, to a drone, everyone is a suspect," Whitehead wrote, "because drone technology makes no distinction between the law-abiding individual and the suspect. Everyone gets monitored, photographed, tracked and targeted."

Eye-scanning technology of the type seen in the film *Minority Report* also will be widely used to monitor people in the very near future. In August 2010, Global Rainmakers, Inc. (GRI), a biometrics research and development company, announced its iris scanning technology will debut in the city of Leon, Mexico. The scanners will be placed around the city, which has a population of more than one million, and a database of citizens will be created. It will be mandatory to scan convicted criminals into the Leon database, although the plan does not specify whether this would include minor convictions. Those citizens without a police record may volunteer to enter the database. Police officers will monitor scans made at ATMs, trains, bus stations and other venues to track the movement of watch-listed people.

"In the future, whether it's entering your home, opening your car, entering your workplace, getting a pharmacy prescription refilled, or having your medical records pulled up, everything will come off that unique key that is your iris," boasted GDI officer Jeff Carter. "Every person, place and thing on this planet will be connected [to the iris system] within the next 10 years."

It now requires less than one second to scan the iris, a time frame that no doubt will be reduced as models are improved. In October 2010, a new model successfully scanned irises from a distance of six feet in a test at a US border station.

Facial recognition technology already is in place in several airports around the world, including Singapore. Using driver license photos, all adult citizens are facially mapped to a matrix of numbers based on features and the distance between facial structures taken from an algorithm applied to the photo. This information goes into a database to be used in closed circuit TV cameras, which have proliferated tremendously in all communities around the world. This allows authorities to identify and track nearly every adult citizen where there is a camera.

Few people are aware that their faces already have been mapped and placed into a database. But police everywhere have embraced this as a tool through which criminals can be tracked. The rub is that the facial recognition system is only 90 percent accurate, meaning innocent people whose faces resemble that of a criminal will be misidentified and probably suffer because of it. Its potential as a tool to track and harass non-criminal individuals such as political activists and dissenters is obvious.

In September 2010, the Department of Homeland Security (DHS) announced the creation of a national database that would centralize citizenship information for intelligence and law enforcement agencies. Called the Citizenship and Data Repository System of Records, it will include a search engine and real-time updates, supposedly targeting illegal immigrants, but with an added agenda to "allow officials to vet applications for fraud and national security concerns…and respond to classified requests for information that could assist intelligence and law enforcement investigations."

More importantly, the DHS wants to "exempt portions of the system of records from one or more provisions of the Privacy Act because of criminal, civil and administrative enforcement requirements."

The Privacy Act of 1974 came into being following revelations during congressional hearings of gross constitutional violations of citizens' rights by the FBI, CIA and law enforcement agencies. The Act mandates a Code of Fair Information Practices limiting the collection of personal information about individuals for deposit into federal agencies' systems of records.

The Act also requires that agencies give public notice of their systems of records by publishing them in the Federal Register. Without written consent of the individual, federal agencies are prohibited from disclosing information from their systems of records. The Privacy Act also allows subject individuals to access and amend their records. The new DHS database seeks to castrate this legislation, which was enacted to protect the privacy of all US citizens.

In yet another reflection of the sci-fi movie, *Minority Report,* the US and other nations are taking the first steps toward pre-crime technology. In August 2010, Washington DC law enforcement agencies implemented a system purported to predict when crimes will take place and who will commit them — before they occur.

The new software, developed by University of Pennsylvania professor Richard Berk, inspects a database containing thousands of crimes, and through algorithms and variables like location and criminal records, predicts where, when and by whom a crime will be committed. Earlier versions of the software already were in use in Baltimore and Philadelphia, but were limited to predicting murders by parolees and prisoners on probation. According to an ABC News report, the newer version predicts a much wider scope of crimes.

"People assume that if someone murdered then they will murder in the future," Berk told ABC. "But what really matters is what that person did as a young individual. If they committed armed robbery at age 14, that's a good predictor."

Critics maintain that using a risk scale rather than true events violates the US justice system, founded on the presumption of innocence until proven guilty. Nevertheless, police departments across the country are looking into using this software and similar technologies. The Memphis Police Department already uses an IBM system of predictive analytics called Operation Blue CRUSH.

The British government has debated using pre-crime legislation to combat terrorism. Suspects would be tried before an act of terrorism occurs, based on MI-5 and MI-6 intelligence of an expected attack. If the evidence is sufficient in the eyes of the court, the suspect would be found guilty "on the balance of probabilities" rather than "beyond reasonable doubt" and imprisoned. Britain also plans to collect records on all residents, starting at age five and continuing throughout lifetimes, to screen for individuals who are more likely to commit crimes.

Perhaps the most outrageous UK program now underway, called Family Intervention Projects, has removed 2,000 families from their homes and relocated them to what the press has dubbed "sin bins" — government housing in which they are under 24-hour surveillance by closed circuit TV cameras.

The families were chosen due to their histories of drug abuse and criminal behavior. The cameras record proof that the children are attending school, eating properly and going to bed on time.

In the next two years, Britain intends to increase the program to involve 20,000 families at a cost of between 5,000 and 20,000 pounds each, according to the *Daily Telegraph.* "There should be Family Intervention Projects in every local authority area because every area has families that need that support," said British Children's Secretary Ed Balls.

In the US, a disturbing marriage between Google and the CIA is underway as the Agency's investment arm, Q-In-Tel, has matched the reported $10 million Google investment in Recorded Future, a firm which uses analytics to scour Twitter accounts, websites and blogs for information on individuals. Recorded Future collects personal information like changes of employment, family problems, entertainment preferences, and myriad other seemingly innocuous attributes that may be used against individuals in a variety of ways.

The potential for abuse in these new technologies of data collection is clear in the recent case of Harrisburg, Pennsylvania resident Gene Stilp. Present at several protests against government excesses, Stilp learned that his name was on the state's Homeland Security list of possible terrorists. Homeland Security officials distribute the list to government and law enforcement officials in a bulletin.

The affair produced such outrage among state politicians that the contract with the organization that compiled the list for Homeland Security was not renewed. Stilp, who holds a Virginia law license, is preparing a federal lawsuit.

With the identification technologies like thumb scanners, retina scanners and facial recognition devices already in place, a national, mandatory RFID chip will close the circle of surveillance nearly completely around all citizens.

The Obama Administration

The people President Obama has appointed to important advisory and cabinet positions in his first term are mainly from Wall Street. None of them come from heavy industry, the auto industry, Silicon Valley, the major oil industry, labor or small business. Only Wall Street financial leaders have a voice in the Obama administration. And nearly all of the important posts are held by members of one or all of the three secretive organizations that have been making policy for nearly a century. Here is a partial list:

Lawrence Summers, director of the National Economic Council, helped dismantle the Glass-Steagall Act, the banking act of 1933 which established the FDIC and controlled speculation. Summers is a member of the CFR and the Trilateral Commission.

Timothy Geithner, a Robert Rubin protégé and former president of the New York Federal Reserve Bank, is secretary of the treasury. He is a member of the Bilderberg group and the Trilateral Commission.

Hillary Clinton, secretary of state, is a Bilderberg and CFR member. Her husband, former President Bill Clinton, is a member of the Trilateral Commission.

Susan Rice, US ambassador to the United Nations, is a Trilateral Commission member.

General James L. Jones, national security advisor, is a member of Bilderberg group, the CFR and the Trilateral Commission.

Thomas Donilon, deputy national security advisor, is a CFR and Trilateral Commission member.

Henry Kissinger, state department special envoy, is a member of Bilderberg group, the CFR and the Trilateral Commission.

Paul Volcker, chairman of the Economic Recovery Committee, is a member of Bilderberg group, the CFR and the Trilateral Commission.

Admiral Dennis Blair, director of national security, is a member of the Bilderberg group, the CFR, and the Trilateral Commission.

Robert Gates, secretary of defense, is a member of the Bilderberg group, the CFR and the Trilateral Commission.

James Steinberg, deputy secretary of state, is a member of the

Bilderberg group, the CFR and the Trilateral Commission.

Richard Haass, state department special envoy, is a member of the Bilderberg group, the Trilateral Commission and is president of the CFR.

Alan Greenspan, presidential advisor, is a member of the Bilderberg group, the CFR and the Trilateral Commission.

Richard Holbrooke, state department special envoy, is a member of the Bilderberg group, the CFR and the Trilateral Commission.

During the 2008 primary season, Barack Obama had scheduled speaking engagements in Chicago and the Midwest. He'd arranged to travel by plane with various members of the press. But when the plane load of press lifted off, Obama was not aboard. Angry reporters grilled Obama's press secretary, who lamely said, "Senator Obama had a desire to do some meetings. He had a desire to meet in a private way. We set up these meetings. They're being done tonight."

Initially the press assumed Obama was meeting with his rival for the Democratic nomination, Hillary Clinton, at her Washington DC home. The Obama camp denied this, but wouldn't say where or with whom he was meeting. The news blackout lasted for a day and a half, as reporters tried to learn the whereabouts of Clinton and Obama.

Having exposed three separate cover stories from the Obama and Clinton camps as false, the press never learned of the true locale and nature of their secret meeting. But at this time, the Bilderberg group was meeting at the nearby Westfields Marriott Hotel just outside Washington in Chantilly, Virginia. Armed security guards, local police and agents of various intelligence networks including the CIA, MI-6 and Mossad were standard at every annual Bilderberg meeting, and the one held in Chantilly in 2008 was no exception.

According to journalist Alex Jones, who was present outside the Westfields Marriott for the three-day Bilderberg conference in 2008, "internal sources" confirmed that both Obama and Clinton attended at least one meeting. If this is true, and the candidates discussed policy with a foreign-populated group of powerful financiers and royalty, then both Clinton and Obama violated the Logan Act. The clandestine meeting with the Bilderberg power brokers also has caused several researchers to assume a deal was struck, giving Obama support for the presidency.

Since his election, President Obama has failed to keep most of his campaign promises. He claimed that US troops would be pulled from Iraq within 16 months. After his inauguration, he changed his pledge, saying he would bring home "some of the troops." Several weeks later, the figure changed to 23 months. That time element has passed and US soldiers continue to die there. And during all of this, he escalated the Afghan war by sending an additional 30,000 American troops there, which didn't dissuade voters from awarding him a Nobel Peace Prize.

Another campaign promise assured voters that Obama would repeal the Patriot Act, but when the time came, he signed its reauthorization twice.

During the 2008 presidential campaign, he slammed the Bush administration for its "illegal" warrantless wiretapping of American citizens, but later he announced his support for renewing the Foreign Intelligence Surveillance Act (FISA) legislation in the Senate.

Obama also lined up blue collar votes by promising workers he would change the North American Free Trade Agreement (NAFTA) to their benefit. At the same time, his campaign insiders assured members of the press, Canadian officials and corporate leaders that this promise should not be taken seriously. In other words, they admitted he was lying.

Obama's other campaign promises — transparency of government, environmental responsibility, and keeping lobbyists out of his administration — were broken within one month of his inauguration.

His promise to close the Guantanamo Bay prison camp within a year has gone by the wayside, and he actually renewed the Bush policy of rendition, which the press has called "secret abductions and transfers of prisoners to countries that cooperate with the United States." When Great Britain announced that it would reveal information on the torture of prisoners by its country and the US overseas, Obama threatened to cut all intelligence ties, and the revelations were squelched.

The cornerstone of the Obama campaign was his promise to exclude lobbyists and donors from his administration. Within hours of his election, Obama filled his administration at all levels with lobbyists and donors.

William Lynn, chief lobbyist for Raytheon, received a high position in the Department of Defense. Timothy Geithner, former president of the Federal Reserve Bank of New York, was given the treasury secretary post and he immediately filled the department with lobbyists, including his chief of staff, Mark Patterson, formerly the top lobbyist for Goldman Sachs.

George Mitchell, top lobbyist for the Saudi royal family, was appointed by Obama as Middle East envoy. Leon Panetta, top lobbyist for Wall Street, received Obama's appointment to head the CIA. Tom Daschle, a ranking lobbyist for the health care industry, received the top post in the Department of Health and Human Services.

These appointees wasted no time in working their magic. Lobbyists for the large factory farming operations owned by Monsanto, Sodexo, Tyson, ADM and others have succeeded in getting Congress to introduce a bill that, if passed, would open the way to banning all private food production.

Bill HR-875 is so broad that a person growing a backyard garden could be fined up to $25,000 and have his or her property seized. It will apply even to people who grow vegetables or own a few chickens strictly for their own consumption.

Independent farmers and food producers will be forced out of business because of the high costs of conforming to the terms of HR-875. And a new government agency would be formed to enforce the measures which include mandatory industry standards such as pesticide and fertilizer use. Essentially, it will criminalize organic farming.

Also troubling is the fact that this legislation would increase the growing federal encroachment on states' rights, as it requires state agriculture departments to enforce federal guidelines. The bill also calls for appointing officials from the large factory farms to interpret and enforce the restrictions.

In short, HR-875 will legalize the monopolization of food production in the US. This unprecedented control is reminiscent of the collectivization policies of Josef Stalin in 1930s Russia, which resulted in millions of deaths through starvation. Total control of the food supply means total control of the population.

The bill is related to the food production lobbyists' attempt to make America compliant to the standards of Codex Alimentarius, an international trade-oriented commission which sets guidelines relating to food. Established in 1963 by the Food and Agriculture Organization (FAO) of the UN and the World Health Organization (WHO), its standards are expected to be met by all member nations of the World Trade Organization (WTO).

The more than 4,000 standards apply to all foods and food processing, labeling, additives, pesticides and hygiene, but do not apply to pharmaceuticals. Defenders of Codex Alimentarius claim these standards are for the protection of consumer health and to ensure fairness in the international food trade. However, critics complain that Codex has become mandatory with its adoption by the WTO, which automatically settles disputes in favor of Codex-compliant nations no matter how just the position of a non-compliant nation might be.

The commission also adopted a controversial guideline that no herb, vitamin or mineral can be sold for preventive or therapeutic purposes, and that these supplements should be reclassified as drugs.

Protests temporarily have halted implementation of this standard, which would restrict the usage of safe supplements like Vitamin C, which strengthens the human immune system. But the Central American Free Trade Agreement (CAFTA) signed in 2004 increases the likelihood that Codex guidelines will be imposed on America.

The Great Recession

In 2007 the price of oil spiked above $150 per barrel, up from less than $60 a barrel just weeks before. The tremendous price jump reverberated throughout the American economy, driving up food and energy prices. It got to the point where people were stealing gas from parked cars, siphoning in the dead of night.

The high gas prices came on the heels of a year-long slump in the housing sector. House prices dropped dramatically as sales dwindled to a fraction of previous years. Then, in September 2008, came the *coup de grace*. Fannie Mae and Freddie Mac, the leading mortgage brokers, issued a fire alarm on defaults that threatened to wipe out banks all over the country.

This financial catastrophe, more than anything else, insured the election of Barack Obama, for no Republican candidate could hope to win the presidency after the disaster took place during the Bush administration.

There is evidence that all of these mishaps, the housing slump, the oil price spike and the mortgage banking collapse, might have been manipulated by international bankers and businessmen in a plot to destroy the US economy as a step toward globalism.

The first step in the plan was to remove banking regulations like the Glass-Steagall Act, which was repealed in 1999. Enacted in 1933 to separate banking from securities underwriting, its repeal would allow banks to issue unlimited credit and open the door to endless Ponzi schemes, which inevitably took place. Congress ignored the warning of the General Accounting Office to "go slow" and repealed the act in its entirety.

Immediately, the corporate-controlled mainstream media touted schemes like "derivatives" and "hedgelets," which tempted small investors to gamble on mortgage investments. The initial returns were sparkling, and this caused more small investors, corporations, state and local governments to invest heavily.

But in 2007, the bankers began to issue warnings about the schemes they had created. An article planted in *Barrons* in April of that year, for instance, warned that American real estate shares were overvalued. The bankers followed this by stopping the flow of fiat money that had inflated the real estate bubble, and when Congress would not vote for bailout money, the bankers launched what amounts to financial terrorism.

Through mouthpieces like Treasury Secretary Henry Paulson and Federal Reserve Chairman Benjamin Bernanke, the bankers promised an economic meltdown. The warnings pointed to another great world depression unless Congress met their demands for enormous bailout money.

This news alone plummeted the Dow Jones 777 points on September 29, 2008, the biggest one-day stock market drop in history. Congress continued to resist voting for the bailout, however. Senators James Inhofe of Oklahoma and Brad Sherman of California led the counterattack against the bankers, adding that Congress had been threatened by the White House and the Treasury Department with "martial law" if the banker bailout bill was not passed.

"The only way they can pass this bill is by creating and sustaining a panic atmosphere," said Sherman. "That atmosphere is not justified."

The bailout bill was written and its final version went unseen by Congress until a few minutes before the October 3, 2008, vote. The bill passed with the solemn promise by the Federal Reserve Bank that every dime of the $700 billion bailout money would be accounted for.

Five weeks after the bill passed, Paulson announced that he was changing the thrust of the original plan to buy troubled mortgage assets and instead would concentrate on nonbank financial institutions and consumer finance. This indicated that the bill was actually a Wall Street-manipulated coup, which amounted to a blank check.

To date, Congress has raised the government commitment to solving this financial "crisis" to the staggering and unimaginable figure of more than $10 trillion, much of it unaccounted for by the Federal Reserve Bank. At one point, when Bloomberg News Service requested to see the list of recipients for more than $2 trillion in the emergency loans from US taxpayers, the Federal Reserve refused to disclose the names. Bloomberg has since filed a Freedom of Information Act lawsuit requesting details on 11 federal lending programs. This did not dissuade the Federal Reserve Bank from lending the government $780 billion of this taxpayer money at interest to finance the Obama stimulus package.

Paulson's change in strategy was a tacit admission that the sub-prime mortgage crisis was not the cause of the banking system breakdown. His decision to buy up toxic assets indicates that derivatives were at the center of the crisis. And the bailout money that the banks received did not go to relieve the mortgage crisis, but toward buying other banks. Clearly, the banks were hoarding the bailout money instead of issuing new loans, which was the primary purpose of the bailout bill. Firms like J.P. Morgan Chase used the money to buy smaller healthy banks and insurance companies.

It is noteworthy that major polls taken during the crisis showed that a whopping 98 percent of the American people were opposed to the bailout bill, and yet leaders of both parties saw to its passage, including both President Bush and President-elect Obama.

In 2009, Congress passed the so-called Obama stimulus bill, committing trillions of taxpayer dollars to the continuing bailout. The bill contained more than 1,070 pages, and yet Congress was given just one hour to read it before voting. It put the lie to another Obama campaign promise that no bill would be voted upon without allowing Congress and US citizens at least five days to study it.

Obama's defense was that the bill needed to be passed immediately to prevent a crisis from becoming "a catastrophe." But when the bill railroaded to passage, Obama went on vacation for four days, saying there was "no rush" for him to sign it into law.

Nearly all analysts recognize the bailout policies as a return to the economic tenets of John Maynard Keynes, which call for deficit government spending backed by future tax dollars to control current business cycles. Keynes was an important architect of Franklin Roosevelt's New Deal attempt to pull America out of the Great Depression, recognized by nearly all economists today as a miserable failure which actually prolonged the Depression. But globalist bankers favor it for a variety of reasons, not the least of which is the destruction of US currency.

In 1919, Keynes said, "Lenin is certainly right. There is no more positive, or subtler, or surer means of overturning the existing basis of society than to debauch the currency. By a continuing process of inflation, governments can confiscate, secretly and unobserved, an important part of the wealth of their citizens....The process engages all of the hidden forces of economic law on the side of destruction, and does it in a manner that one man in a million is able to diagnose."

Keynes was an important member of the delegation that created the International Monetary Fund (IMF) and the World Bank in 1944 at a meeting in Bretton Woods, New Hampshire. Harry Dexter White, a CFR member, represented the US at the conference. A member of the US Treasury Department and a close confidante of Keynes, White was investigated by the House Committee on Un-American Activities in 1948 under suspicion that he was spying for the Soviet Union. Later, these allegations were supported by National Security Agency (NSA) cryptographers in the Verona Project decrypts.

Keynes himself was a member of the Marxist-leaning Fabian Society and the globalist Royal Institute for International Affairs (RIIA), in addition to his affiliations with secret societies like the Cambridge (University) "Apostles" and the Bloomsbury Group, which also counted Bertrand Russell and Victor Rothschild among its membership.

The "Apostles" became the eye of a media hurricane in 1951 when four of its members, Kim Philby, Guy Burgess, Donald Maclean and Anthony Blunt were exposed as a homosexual spy ring working for the KGB. The loss to British intelligence, especially due to Philby's high rank in MI-5, was shattering. Years later, in 1994, author Roland Perry named Victor Rothschild as a member of this KGB secret cabal in his book, *The Fifth Man.*

Economists who look at the latest Obama spending bill feel it was essentially a federal takeover maneuver aimed at reducing the power of individual states as guaranteed in the US Constitution. They also note that bankers were able to use the bailout money to buy various businesses at vastly reduced prices due to the recession they themselves helped to create. Swimming in new fiat capital, banks bought new sectors of the world economy not already under their control.

Some economists have gone so far as to charge bankers with artificially engineering a global depression and bankruptcy in order to achieve their goal of a single world bank that controls all aspects of world economy. This plan is evidenced in the June 1991 address by David Rockefeller before the Trilateral Commission, in which he stated that a supranational sovereignty of an intellectual elite and world bankers "is surely preferable to the national determination practiced in the last centuries."

It didn't take the bankers long to announce their opinion that the only way to solve the economic crisis would be to set up a Bank of the World, and a World Government — of course, owned and controlled by the big bankers. The corporate-controlled mainstream media published a flurry of articles supporting this New World Order. *Time* magazine published a piece saying a new privately owned offshore "Superbank" would control the world's currencies and set interest rates and that it would "knock the heads of bad countries like the United States."

A meeting called Breton Woods II: The Plan for World Government, consisting of central bank heads, finance ministers and national leaders, discussed how sovereign countries would pay taxes directly to such a world banking cartel. Hundreds of new carbon taxes were proposed that would draw revenue from every type of human activity under the aegis of reducing carbon dioxide emissions which supposedly are causing global warming. The revelations that environmental scientists were fudging or suppressing facts that did not support the man-made carbon dioxide threat to the planet have temporarily shelved the carbon tax and cap-and-trade legislations.

But already, a new campaign is underway in the mainstream media to promote this fallacious concept. More than 100 new taxes are in development with the stated intent to curb greenhouse gases. These new taxes would go directly to the private offshore bank consortium. They include such preposterous notions as a "cow tax" on livestock-produced methane gas through flatulence.

Consumers would see taxes on meat. Cars fitted with satellite tracking devices, which would be made mandatory, would allow for a tax levied on citizens based upon the miles they drive. (This was proposed by Obama as a replacement for the Federal Gas Tax, which would be a most welcome change for the oil companies).

Plastic products would be taxed due to the carbon emissions created by their manufacture. New taxes would be placed on fireplaces and outdoor space heaters. Customers receiving electricity from coal-powered plants would see those new taxes passed to them in their monthly bills.

The cap-and-trade proposal would require citizens to pay additional taxes on thousands of products to privately owned cap-and-trade service companies, including those owned by Al Gore. New taxes would be placed on light bulbs, trash pickup, water, airline and train travel, medicine, steel production, clothing and asphalt, to name just a few.

All of these proposals are based on the scientific fraud that claims global warming is caused by human carbon emissions. Among the theory's many critics is Dr. William Happer of the Princeton University physics department, who said the carbon emissions increase might be benefiting mankind. Happer, who once worked for the Gore project, was fired after stepping away from the company line.

These and other strategies that led to the collapse of the housing market and the worst econimic crisis since the Great Depression were deliberate attempts to destroy the American economy, according to a number of economic experts, including Senior Economics Editor John Hoefle. As far back as 2001, he reported: "The effect of all this deregulation and speculation has been the decimation of the physical economy of the United States. Over the last three decades, the productive capacity of the US economy has been cut in half, measured in terms of market baskets of goods on a per-capita, per-household, and per-square-kilometer basis. At the same time, the monetary claims on that declining production have risen hyperbolically."

As the American economy limps into the third year of the Great Recession, its destruction apparently will continue.

SIXTH MOVEMENT – *CACOPHONY*
THE DARK AGENDA

"All truth passes through three stages. First, it is ridiculed. Second, it is violently opposed. Third, it is accepted as being self-evident."

—Arthur Schopenhauer, German philosopher 1788-1860

The Dispatch From Iron Mountain

In 1963, President John F. Kennedy called for a special study group to work out the possible problems of peace following a theoretical end to the Cold War. He helped to choose 15 men, none of whom has ever been identified, but they reportedly were men of great stature in the fields of economics, history, psychology, sociology and science.

Most of their meetings took place in a large underground nuclear shelter near Hudson, New York, called Iron Mountain. The facility was designed to act as protected corporate offices for the Rockefeller-controlled Standard Oil of New Jersey, Dutch Shell Oil (then controlled by Prince Bernhard, founder of the Bilderberg group), the Morgan Bank, and Manufacturers Hanover Trust.

Kennedy's study group completed its report in 1966, three years after his murder, but it remained under wraps until leaked to Dial Press the following year by a man called "John Doe." This anonymous individual claimed to be a member of the study group, and told the publisher that while he agreed with the group's findings, he disdained the decision to keep it from the public.

Upon reading the Report from Iron Mountain, it is immediately clear why the authors wished to hide it from the American people. It professed the shocking central theme that "war itself is the basic social system, within which other secondary modes of social organization conflict or conspire. It is the system which has governed most human societies of record, as it is today."

In other words, the study concluded that war is necessary as "the principal organizing force" and that it is "the essential economic stabilizer of modern societies."

The report then turned its attention to leadership, expressing fear that ambiguous leaders could lose the ability to rationalize a desired war, which would lead to the breakdown of military institutions. The men of letters viewed this eventuality as "catastrophic."

The conclusion of the study group clearly stated: "We must first reply, as strongly as we can, that the war system cannot responsibly be allowed to disappear until (1.) we know exactly what we plan to put in its place and (2.) we are certain, beyond reasonable doubt, that these substitute institutions will serve their purposes…The elimination of war implies the inevitable elimination of national sovereignty and the traditional nation-state…The basic authority of a modern state over its people resides in its war powers."

Class relationships are controlled by war, the report further stated, and the anti-social elements of a society are given acceptable roles in the social structure by service in the military. Keep in mind that this study was made during the escalation of the Vietnam War, when anti-war protests were beginning and race riots had become commonplace. In this atmosphere the group opined, "The younger, and more dangerous, of these hostile social groupings have been kept under control by the Selective Service System."

The study went further, and much darker, in its solutions for the "culturally deprived" class, saying a "possible surrogate for the control of potential enemies of society is the reintroduction, in some form consistent with modern technology and political process, of slavery… The development of a sophisticated form of slavery may be an absolute prerequisite for social control in a world at peace."

In addition to the new slavery motif, the Iron Mountain "boys" made a list of possible substitutes for the "functions of war" that included a comprehensive social welfare program, a large space program aimed at unreachable goals, a permanent disarmament inspection system, an omnipotent international police force, a recognized extraterrestrial menace, massive global pollution and environmental menace (like "global warming"), fictitious enemies, programs modeled on the Peace Corps, new religions or mythologies, socially oriented violent games, and a program of eugenics.

The report concluded by proposing a permanent top-secret "War/Peace Research Agency" that would be answerable only to the president and not to Congress, the media or the public. Its purpose would be to institute the recommended substitutes for war and to create others as needed.

The Report from Iron Mountain still serves as a blueprint and an instruction manual, as you will see in the proceeding pages.

The Cancer Dance

What if today the press announced that a research team definitely has found the cure for all cancers? It would cause the entire world to rejoice, right?

Not the *entire* world. The specter of a cancer-free world would cost billions in profits to the enormous medical, pharmaceutical and insurance interests that are vitally involved in treatment, coverage and research on this disease, which is the second largest cause of death in America.

At this time in our history, more people are employed in cancer treatment and research than those who suffer from cancer. With this information — that so many livelihoods and so much money depends upon this disease remaining relatively incurable — it certainly is tempting to wonder whether any true cures that already have been discovered may have been suppressed.

According to the Barry Lynes book, *The Cancer Cure that Worked,* this is exactly what happened in the 1930s to Dr. Royal Raymond Rife. During the pre-war years, Rife experimented with precise electrical frequencies and their effects on viral and bacterial cells. As all cells are controlled by their DNA and their chemical action is controlled by electromagnetic frequencies, each cell possesses a weak electromagnetic field. Rife's experiments disrupted these fields in viral and bacterial cells.

The University of Southern California Research Committee repeated the Rife experiments and confirmed that the frequencies he used reversed many ailments, including cancer. In 1934, Rife announced that he'd bombarded a cancer-causing virus with electromagnetic frequencies and went on to use this process to kill sarcoma and carcinoma cancers in more than 400 lab animal tests. The press became interested and reported that Rife, Dr. Milbank Johnson and Dr. Avin Foord cured 16 terminal human cancer patients with electromagnetic frequencies during the summer of 1934.

Rife announced that the patients suffered no tissue damage, no pain and no discomfort during treatment by his frequency machine. "A tube lights up and three minutes later the treatment is completed," he added.

"The virus or bacteria is destroyed and the body then recovers itself naturally from the toxic effect of the virus or bacteria. Several diseases may be treated simultaneously."

The Rockefeller Institute immediately sprang into action, unleashing its member, Dr. Thomas Rivers, to debunk the procedure without even having seen Rife's equipment in operation. The underfunded Rife group could not defend itself against false claims and altered test procedures that opponents in the medical research field used against it.

Demonstrations were organized to fail. Astounding demands were made on Rife to prove his research by the International Cancer Research Foundation, which "broke their agreements, insisted on procedures with inexperienced people which were doomed from the outset, and ignored the larger goal which Rife was achieving — the cure for cancer in human beings," wrote Lynes.

Morris Fishbein, then head of the American Medical Association (AMA), offered a partnership to Rife if he agreed to advertise in *JAMA*, the AMA journal. Fishbein had been accused of giving the AMA approval to drugs and treatments that advertised in the journal, whether they worked or not, and for withholding AMA approval from any that did not advertise.

Rife refused. Lawsuits followed and the Special Research Committee's work was terminated. In 1971, broken and bitter, Rife died. A few doctors and private individuals offer his device today, which is still not FDA-approved, but only as an expensive research instrument.

The incidence of soft tissue cancer has spiked since the 1950s with more than one million new cases reported each year in the US. Prior to the mid-20th century, soft tissue cancer was quite rare, which raises questions about what might have changed in that time frame.

Edward Haslam produced compelling evidence for the answer to these questions in his book, *Mary, Ferrie & the Monkey Virus.* His convincing argument is that the polio vaccine introduced in 1955 was tainted with highly carcinogenic monkey viruses.

Polio had been a terrible epidemic by the early 1950s, because it mainly attacked children, crippling them for the remainder of their lives and often killing them. As President Franklin Roosevelt had been a polio sufferer, a campaign was launched to cure this malady with public support, the most successful program being the March of Dimes. The money helped to fund research that produced a workable polio vaccine developed by Albert Sabin in 1955, and a massive vaccination program got underway targeting children at early ages.

Soon after the polio vaccination program, word leaked that the Sabin vaccine may contain a cancer-causing monkey virus called Simian Virus (SV)-40, because it was incubated on monkey kidneys. This interested the military and intelligence communities as well as the polio vaccine researchers in labs run by Dr. Alton Ochsner.

Further study proved that there were several carcinogenic monkey viruses in the Sabin vaccine including SV-40, which meant that a deadly cancer virus had been injected into an entire generation of American children. The medical profession remained mum about this, but clearly had a new mandate: find a cure for cancer, because it would become epidemic in the decades ahead.

At the same time, several of the new polio vaccines quietly were removed from distribution. Sabin spread the word to his colleagues that "There is too much scaring of the public unnecessarily. Oh, your children were injected with a cancer virus and all that. That's not very good."

Predictably, the military and intelligence arms fastened on this tragic mistake in the new polio vaccines and began research into weaponizing these carcinogenic monkey viruses. By the end of the 1950s, the Cold War had become electrified when Fidel Castro established a communist regime in Cuba, just 90 miles from Florida, vowing to spread the creed throughout Latin America. The CIA immediately took the point in trying to assassinate Castro, and funded research into using the monkey viruses, among other things, as bioweapons.

In a large laboratory created for this purpose in New Orleans, researchers experimented with radiation to mutate the cancerous monkey viruses. Haslam claims this secretive project was located in Louisiana "to keep it out of the Bethesda [Maryland]-Washington DC area and to have it close to the people who they wanted to supervise it, particularly Dr. Ochsner.

"It's necessary to understand Ochsner's connection to the polio vaccine," Haslam adds. "There were six laboratories producing the vaccine and Ochsner was one of the major stockholders in one of them. He also had been one of the people promoting the release of the vaccine.

"It was assumed the vaccine was safe, but at the last minute they asked Bernice Eddy at the National Institute of Health, the official national vaccine safety tester, to test the vaccines. When she injected these vaccines into her monkeys, she got back dead and crippled monkeys. She tried to delay the release of the vaccine, but the problem was that every day they waited, there were another 100 children getting polio.

"Ochsner was so convinced that the vaccine was safe that he decided to publicly inoculate his own grandchildren in front of the faculty of Tulane Medical School. The result of this bold and courageous action was that his grandson died from polio and his granddaughter got polio. That's what put it in New Orleans."

What interested Ochsner's researchers most was SV-40, which still is one of the most carcinogenic agents known. Dr. Mary Sherman was a leading cancer researcher in the US at that time and she held a high position at Oschner's clinic. She died under extremely suspicious circumstances in 1964, and the subsequent investigation of her death was shut down, according to Haslam.

"They found her body in her apartment and [the investigation] concluded that she died in her apartment," Haslam said. "But I was able to get hold of the autopsy protocol from the medical examiner's office and it is very obvious that Mary Sherman did not die in her apartment. There was nothing in her apartment that could have created the damage to her body that they found. Her entire right arm was burned off. All that was left was about a six inch carbonized stump. Immediately next to that was unburned human hair.

"The bone is the hardest thing to burn on a body. Technically, it doesn't even burn. It just dehydrates. But hair is the easiest [part to burn], so how do you get the thousands of degrees of temperature required to disintegrate a bone next to [unburned] human hair? The only answer to that is very high voltage electricity."

Haslam believes the electrocuting instrument could have been a five-million-watt linear particle beam accelerator, which is used in cancer research and treatment, and probably was present in the Infectious Disease Laboratory building of the US Health Service Hospital in New Orleans, the main site of the secret monkey virus research.

Mary Sherman also had suffered multiple stab wounds, one of them to the heart, which hemorrhaged. There were six other stab wounds, one to her liver, which did not hemorrhage. A person hemorrhages only when alive, meaning the two sets of stab wounds did not occur at the same time. Haslam proposes that Mary Sherman was electrocuted in such a way that the high voltage charge passed through her right arm and out the rear of her shoulder without crossing her heart, which would mean that she did not die from this incident.

"Someone stabbed her in the heart very precisely with a very slim surgical instrument to kill her," Haslam concluded. "It's a mercy killing at that point. Then they put her body in a body bag, brought it back to her apartment, dumped it on her bed and piled underwear from her bedside drawer on top of her. They stabbed her again repeatedly at that point, making sure there would be cuts in the underwear. Then they started a fire to create an explanation for the burns on her body. The fire did not burn the curtains next to her bed or the underwear lying atop her, so it was not capable of burning off her arm."

The main fact of the case, Mary Sherman's obliterated arm was never was mentioned in the newspapers. Her death could have been the result of an industrial accident which was covered up for liability issues, but Haslam has concluded from the evidence that it was an act of sabotage to expose the secret laboratory.

It is interesting that Mary Sherman died on the same day the Warren Commission began the New Orleans phase of its investigation into the Kennedy assassination. Also, the secret US Health Service Hospital lab was immediately closed and dismantled upon Sherman's death.

We now know that the lab was just one mile from the New Orleans apartment of Lee Harvey Oswald. It also was one mile from the home of Ochsner, who in mid-1963 had organized the media coverage of Oswald-as-Marxist through the International Council of the Americas (INCA).

This organization was intended to protect the interests of the wealthy industries of New Orleans, specifically fruit and shipping companies dependent upon stability in the Latin American nations. Naturally, the communizing of Cuba under Castro was seen as a disaster, and INCA became an anti-communist propaganda outlet that shipped audio tapes to radio stations in Latin American countries.

Alton Ochsner, a tremendously influential man who once headed the American Cancer Society, was a virulent right wing anti-communist who founded INCA. In August 1963 Oswald began receiving publicity for his membership in the Fair Play for Cuba Committee, which demonized him as a former Soviet defector and a pro-Castro traitor. It is known today that INCA actually arranged this publicity, and that Ocshner himself produced and released a record album of the radio debate Oswald had with an anti-Castro spokesman. Ochsner's picture is on the back of the album.

Immediately following the assassination of JFK on November 22, 1963, INCA stepped up its portrayal of Oswald-as-Marxist and leaked information to the press that Castro was behind the president's death. INCA sprang into action again during the Jim Garrison investigation in 1967, but the New Orleans district attorney would have none of it. Ochsner became worried that Garrison would target him in the probe and attempted to smear investigators he believed were looking into his Oswald connections.

The Garrison probe also unearthed a second secret underground medical lab where cancer-causing viruses were studied. This lab was under the direction of right-wing extremists and located in the apartment of David Ferrie, who had been connected to Oswald since the latter's youthful days in the New Orleans Civil Air Patrol.

Ferrie was a pilot who had been fired by Eastern Airlines for homosexual behavior, and who had been active in training and aiding the anti-Castro Cubans before and after the Bay of Pigs. When the Garrison investigation targeted Ferrie, he turned up dead in his apartment under suspicious circumstances. His death was ruled as being caused by a berry aneurysm.

Haslam agrees with True Ott and researcher John Hankey that Oswald probably was an FBI mole who had infiltrated the CIA/Mafia/Anti-Castro Cuban cabal and provided information on its secret cancer research as well as pinpointing its secret training camp at Lake Ponchartrain.

Judyth Vary Baker, who had an affair with Oswald in New Orleans during 1963, told the producers of the documentary, *The Men Who Killed Kennedy,* "Lee Oswald was an innocent man who gave his life for this country. [He] was a loyal Marine to the very end and he deserves better in history than the vile portrait that has been painted."

Baker, who displayed an outstanding talent for science beginning in high school, attracted attention from the military for her work in cancer research and experiments in extracting metals from sea water. Immediately upon graduating high school she was recruited to work in the prestigious cancer research center, Roswell Park Memorial Institute, where she continued her experiments under Dr. Alton Ochsner.

"I was getting specialized in deadly cancers," she recalls. "It was made clear to me that, by the time I entered the University of Florida, they didn't want people knowing that we were working on projects that might have to do with eventually competing with Russia on the matter of using cancer as a bioweapon."

Baker joined Ochsner's staff in the spring of 1963. Ochsner had many military connections at the time, according to Baker, who worked in the cancer lab with Dr. Mary Sherman. She met Oswald soon after her arrival and he quickly introduced her to David Ferrie, who impressed Baker with his knowledge of cancer research. Ferrie also revealed that he knew Dr. Ochsner and Dr. Sherman, and that the three of them were working on a secret government medical project targeting Fidel Castro.

Oswald also introduced Baker to Guy Bannister, the former FBI bureau chief who was coordinating the training of the anti-Castro Cubans. Bannister affirmed to Baker that Oswald was working with him. In addition, before Baker met Ochsner, Oswald preceded her into his office, indicating that he already had an association with Ochsner.

When Baker finally met Ochsner, he briefed her on the research into deadly cancer strains that were intended to sicken and kill Castro through apparently natural causes. Being a staunch conservative and anti-Castro, Baker readily embraced the assignment.

She and Oswald received cover jobs at the downtown New Orleans Reily Coffee Company, which has been verified by payment receipts. Baker's real work took place in the secret lab located in the apartment of David Ferrie, developing deadly carcinogenic viruses on mice.

Baker admits to having bred a "vicious, galloping cancer," and claims she took her reports and samples to the apartment of Dr. Mary Sherman. Baker also claims that Oswald sometimes acted as the liaison between her and Dr. Sherman at the US Public Health Service Hospital, where Sherman and her colleagues used radiation on the Baker viruses to change their genetic components.

Oswald and Ferrie soon introduced Baker to a man they called Sparky Rubenstein. "Only much, much later did I learn that this was Jack Ruby, and I never connected the two when Lee was murdered," Baker says. "He was very interested in what we were doing in the lab and David Ferrie openly showed him what was going on, which surprised me."

Baker claims that Ruby told her he'd known Oswald since he was "a little boy."

Clay Shaw, who was unsuccessfully prosecuted during the Jim Garrison investigation years later, arranged for Oswald and Baker to meet in hotels for their love trysts, according to Baker. The connections between Oswald, Ferrie, Ruby, Bannister, Ochsner, Sherman and Shaw never have been officially affirmed in the various government investigations.

Aside from his anti-Castro work, Ferrie also had "infiltrated" groups that were interested in killing Kennedy, according to Baker, and she soon realized that the president posed another target. She claims that these conspirators saw Kennedy as an obstacle to doing what they pleased with Cuba. "A lot of these people had a lot of power," Baker added. "It was a frightening thing for me to hear about all these things."

Baker believes that Oswald's pro-Castro cover was intended to allow him to infiltrate Cuba itself if the opportunity arose. To avoid discovery that he worked for Bannister's anti-Castro organization, Oswald was fired on a pretext and Baker's work at the Ferrie lab ended.

She became upset when she learned that her cancer virus would be tested on human guinea pigs taken from the nearby Angola Penitentiary and infected at a mental hospital in Jackson. Baker wrote a note to Ochsner protesting the use of unwitting human volunteers. Ochsner was furious that Baker had committed this to paper and in a phone call told Baker that she and Oswald were both "expendable."

Oswald, Ferrie and Shaw, in the meantime, escorted the prison convoy from Angola to the Jackson mental hospital, where Ferrie himself made the injections. After this, Oswald was to take the cancerous material to Mexico City where he would hand it to a medical technician contact. From Mexico, the material would go to Cuba and be given to a member of Castro's medical team who had been turned.

On August 31, 1963, Baker says that Oswald drove her to the mental hospital in Jackson to inspect the results of the injections on the prisoners. She remembers the first man she saw already was so ill that he didn't know where he was, just 72 hours after receiving the injection. He would die 25 days later.

She filed her report on the "success" of the treatment, but Ochsner reneged on his promise to get her into Tulane Medical School, convincing her to return to her Miami home. Before leaving New Orleans, Baker had a last meeting with Oswald in their favorite hotel and he suggested they meet again some day in a special Yucatan location he knew through his CIA contacts.

Oswald traveled to Mexico City to hand over the materials, but his contacts were nowhere to be found. His attempts to bring the material to Cuba himself failed when he couldn't secure a transit visa, so he returned to the US in early October. When he arrived in Dallas, his handlers informed him the Castro mission had been aborted due to the damage a recent hurricane had caused in Cuba. Instead, Oswald received a new cover job, this time at the Texas School Book Depository.

Oswald continued to speak with Baker via a special phone line set up by Ferrie through his mafia contacts, which allowed for at least 14 conversations at no cost between Dallas and Miami, where Baker resided. Baker claims that Oswald's tone became more desperate as time went by. He told her he had penetrated a ring with the help of Shaw and Ferrie that required him to pretend he wanted to see the president eliminated.

"It was pretty well known to me that, just a little bit before the assassination, Dealey Plaza, the airport and the Trade Mart were the three sites that they were going to try and kill Kennedy," Baker says. She claims Oswald called her again on November 17, and said he was willing to save the president and that it was worth dying for. According to Baker, Oswald said he wasn't scared of dying, but that he was scared to leave his children behind with the impression he'd killed Kennedy, because he thought he would be blamed.

The pair spoke by phone again on November 20, and Baker claims that Oswald tried to assure her that he was not alone in trying to save Kennedy, but that there was at least one and perhaps two others who had the same goal. Oswald also told her there was no way he could remove himself from the situation he had penetrated, because his family would be murdered and eventually, himself too.

"And then he said, 'If I stay, there will be one less bullet fired at Kennedy,'" Baker remembers. She also claims that Oswald connected Billie Sol Estes and Bobby Baker, both close associates of then Vice President Lyndon Johnson, to the plot to kill Kennedy.

She recalls that Oswald told her he suspected that his handler, who used an alias, was David Atlee Phillips of the CIA. His association with Oswald was confirmed by Antonio Veciana, founder of the Alpha 66 organization of anti-Castro Cubans. Phillips also was the CIA officer in charge of the Mexico City station at the time of Oswald's visit there.

Oswald and Baker ended their final phone conversation by reciting the Lord's Prayer together, according to Baker. On the night of the assassination, Baker says she received a frantic call from Ferrie telling her to "keep your mouth shut and your head down." Ferrie told her that everything had gone wrong and that he would do all in his power to get Oswald out of jail.

Oswald was murdered on national television two days later by the man who claimed he had known him since his childhood, Jack Ruby.

Today, the weaponizing of cancer is an apparent success, because the Center for Disease Control states that 10 of the top 12 biological agents used in warfare produce skin cancers and other deadly soft tissue cancers. Does this mean the decades-long "war on cancer" is a sham?

Haslam's book raises dark specters based on the results of the soft tissue cancer epidemic. For one, it has created a monstrously lucrative arena for big pharmaceutical companies, insurance companies and the medical profession with an open-ended market among the population. Secondly, it fulfills the population control agenda that has been stated openly by the elitists promoting a New World Order, who have spent billions of dollars over the years on eugenics studies. This will be covered in detail in an upcoming chapter.

FEMA

Although the roots of the Federal Emergency Management Agency (FEMA) can be traced to a disaster legislation bill passed in 1803 that allowed the federal government to give assistance to a town in New Hampshire that was partially destroyed by fire, the Agency officially came into being during the Carter administration when he signed Executive Order 12127. The legislation merged 10 separate federal agencies into one, FEMA, with instructions to respond and aid in all domestic disasters, natural and manmade, including acts of terrorism.

George W. Bush signed another order in March 2003 which merged FEMA with other federal agencies as part of the US Department of Homeland Security, whose prime and stated objective is to "Protect Our Nation from Dangerous People." This new institution received its first challenge in 2005 when hurricane Katrina slammed into New Orleans.

The department didn't fare well. Its first mistake was to urge those homeless people who stayed in New Orleans to collect in the Louisiana Superdome where federal assistance would care for them. The media covered what became a human dumping ground. It was clear that the promised assistance was not immediately forthcoming.

The FEMA director at that time, Michael Brown, claims that he told President Bush that 90 percent of the population of New Orleans had been displaced. "I really thought that would get the whole mechanism of the federal government to come charging in," Brown said on NBC's *Today Show.* "It is once again this mentality that it's a natural disaster. It's a hurricane. It's not al-Qaeda."

The incompetence of FEMA became more apparent in the years following the Katrina disaster, when an estimated $1 billion of taxpayer money was wasted in fraudulent survivor claims that the agency never bothered to investigate before cutting the checks. Two years after the disaster, Katrina homeless were still being housed in 76,000 trailers that contained high levels of formaldehyde.

Widespread incidence of respiratory illness among the trailer dwellers prompted a congressional investigation. A Senate panel concluded FEMA should be scrapped and a new agency restructured, outside of the mammoth Homeland Security bureaucracy, and answerable directly to the president. This was not done.

The example of New Orleans becomes more frightening when one considers the potential powers of FEMA during any occurrence deemed an "emergency." Following the Katrina hurricane disaster, law enforcement officers confiscated all firearms from citizens. In the wealthy neighborhoods, where citizens had armed themselves to protect their property and families, police handcuffed the homeowners until the house searches led to weapons' discoveries. They did allow these residents to stay in their homes, however. In the poorer quarters, armed National Guard troops forced residents to evacuate their homes.

New laws signed in the wake of 9/11 to deal with emergencies like Katrina have police-state potential. For instance, Executive Order 10990 allows federal agencies to wrest control of all modes of transportation, including highways and seaports. Executive Order 10995 allows the federal government to seize and control all media.

Even the Internet came under federal emergency control in 2010 with the passage of the Protecting Cyberspace as a National Asset Act (PCNAA), which gives the government the power to shut down the entire web. The legislation requires all broadband providers, search engines and software firms to "immediately comply with any emergency measure or action developed" by the Department of Homeland Security.

Promoted by Senator Joseph Lieberman, the bill was combined with similar legislation offered by Senator Jay Rockefeller, who in 2009 during a congressional hearing cracked, "Wouldn't it had been better if we'd have never invented the Internet?" The PCNAA hands President Obama the ability to shut down the Internet for as much as four months during a "national emergency." The bill does not define what would constitute a national emergency.

Senator Lieberman was candid about his motive for this bill when he was interviewed by Candy Crowley of CNN: "Right now China, the government, can disconnect parts of its Internet in case of war and we need to have that here too."

In Britain, the government is pushing for full access to all email and Internet use by its citizens. Buried in the Strategic Defense and Security Review of 2010, security services and the police will receive the mandate to monitor every Briton's phone call, email and website visit if the legislation passes Parliament. This is despite the Coalition Agreement to "end the storage of Internet and email records without good reason."

Under the proposed terms, every communications provider would be required to store details of every phone call, email, text message and website visit made by the public for at least a year.

The Obama administration seeks a similar set of new regulations that would allow government intelligence and police agencies to tap into the Internet and email use of Americans. Scheduled to go before Congress in 2011, the change would improve the government's ability to eavesdrop on electronic communications, ostensibly to root out criminal and terrorist plots, by requiring service providers to make available the plain text of encrypted conversations over the phone, email and Internet.

The mandate would require providers to supply back doors and other changes that would permit wiretaps to receive an unscrambled version of communications. The target providers will be online services, networking sites such as Facebook and Skype, and cell phone systems such as Blackberry that deliver encrypted email. The government already has the ability to monitor any phone call and right now only the encrypted communications are out of its reach.

Marc Rotenberg, executive director of the Electronic Privacy Information Center, was blunt regarding this legislation in an interview with Yahoo News: "This is a short sighted and ill-conceived power grab by some in the administration. The balance has swung radically toward enhanced law enforcement powers. For them to argue that it's still not enough is just unbelievable. It's breathtaking in its hubris."

The Obama administration also began a campaign to make it easier for the FBI to force Internet providers to surrender records of individuals' online activity without a court order. The agents would only need to claim that the information is relevant to intelligence or terrorism investigations, according to a July 29, 2010 story in the *Washington Post*. It would require the addition of just four words — "electronic communication transactional records" — to the list of items the FBI already may demand under the existing law without a judge's approval.

With the entire media thoroughly controlled by a small collection of corporations, the Internet has become the last bastion of free speech in America, and these changes are the opening though which it finally can be squelched.

The Camps

In 1987, during the Iran-Contra hearings, the American public first learned of "Readiness Exercise 1984." Under the alternate title of "Rex 84," the plan called for suspension of the US Constitution and instituting martial law in which military commanders would take control of state and local governments. The plan provides for the military to detain large masses of US citizens deemed to be "national security threats" if the president should declare a "State of Domestic National Emergency."

On orders from the federal government, Oliver North, at that time the National Security Council's White House aide and liaison to FEMA, and John Brinkerhoff of FEMA, wrote the plan. Among the events envisioned that might cause such a national emergency was widespread opposition of citizenry to a US military invasion of a foreign country.

Rex 84 also authorized the military to relocate segments of the American civilian population at state and regional levels to safeguard against "subversive activities." This part of the plan originated in a 1970 Army War College report written by future FEMA Director Louis Giuffrida that proposed detaining as many as 21 million "American Negroes" in the event of a racial uprising in the US.

Rex 84 is simply one part of a general military contingency plan, Operation Garden Plot, for the US Army and National Guard to deal with major domestic civil disturbances. Hatched in response to the racial and anti-war riots of the 1960s, Garden Plot provides for federal and military intervention on the local and state level under the guidance of US Northern Command (NORTHCOM). It already has been activated twice: the 1992 Los Angeles riots and the 9/11 attacks.

On January 14, 2005, the US Army published its "rapid action revision" plan, Army Regulation 210-35, also called the "Civilian Inmate Labor Program." The document, signed by Army Chief of Staff General Peter J. Schoomaker, states, "This regulation provides guidance for establishing and managing civilian inmate labor programs on Army installations."

The plan supposedly is intended to make use of minimum and low security inmates under control of the Federal Bureau of Prisons as a labor force on installations controlled by the Army. The benefits described include supplying "a source of labor at no direct cost to the Army," while at the same time "alleviating overcrowding in nearby corrections facilities."

However, in January 2006, KBR, a domestic engineering and construction firm formerly known as Kellogg Brown & Root, received a contract from the Department of Homeland Security to expand the ICE DRO (Immigrations and Customs Enforcement Detention and Removal Operations) facilities "in the event of an emergency influx of immigrants into the US, *or to support the rapid development of new programs.*" (Emphasis added).

KBR, formerly a subsidiary of Halliburton, is the largest non-union construction company in America. The firm has been involved in building most of the 12 camps listed in Regulation 210-35, where federal and state prisoners already have become laborers under Army supervision. As an adjunct to Rex 84, Regulation 210-35 would also apply to emergency cases of civil unrest, which was admitted in the September 30, 2006 issue of the *Army Times:* "They [Army units] may be called upon to help with civil unrest and crowd control...."

This is a direct violation of the Posse Comitatus Act of 1878 which substantially limited the ability of the federal government to use military forces in domestic law enforcement. It prohibits "federal uniformed services" from maintaining law and order on non-federal property, "except where expressly authorized by the Constitution or by act of Congress."

However, the John Warner Defense Act (HR 5122) signed into law by President Bush in 2006 effectively nullified this legislation, allowing the president to station troops anywhere in the US without consent of state and local authorities in order to suppress "public disorder."

FEMA is in the process of building large camps in every region of the US. Some of these camps are refurbished military bases that had been closed. President George W. Bush also signed an order to refurbish World War II-era internment camps that were used to relocate Japanese, Italian and German Americans.

These camps are numerous, far too numerous to be intended for foreign terrorists awaiting trial. The logical suspicion is that these detention camps are to be used for American citizens in the event of an economic or political event which produces wide scale rioting and armed resistance.

The official explanation is that the camps are a contingency against widespread homelessness following an economic or natural catastrophe, but even this scenario is frightening based on the experience of the New Orleans Superdome residents following the Katrina disaster.

To aid in the maintenance of order in the camps, Congress has introduced the National Emergency Centers Act (HR 645) which combines local governments and local police to put them under federal control in emergencies. It mandates the use of the refurbished military and internment camps as relocation facilities providing temporary housing, and to "meet other appropriate needs as determined by the Secretary of Homeland Security." HR 645 also calls for adding public works and medical and educational facilities, reminiscent of the Japanese internment camps during World War II.

Videos of these now-empty camps reveal a consistent prison-like construction, with razor wire leaning inward to keep inmates from escaping. Watchtowers, presumably for armed guards, are present, as are double-row perimeter fences. These are not the hallmarks of sympathetic aid to homeless millions.

Enabling Acts

The Military Commissions Act of 2006 (HR 6166) established "procedures governing the use of military commissions to try alien unlawful enemy combatants engaged in hostilities against the United States for violations of the law of war and other offenses triable by military commission."

Defenders of HR 6166 say it is aimed specifically at foreign and resident non-citizens, but Section 948a refers to "unlawful enemy combatants" without excluding US citizens. The fear is that this Act could be used to arrest and imprison Americans without charges or trial, rights granted through *habeas corpus,* just for speaking out against government policy.

Critics of the Military Commissions Act have called it the American version of Germany's Enabling Act of 1933. Following an arson-caused fire in the Reichstag, which many historians suspect was a "false flag" operation perpetrated by the Nazis and blamed on communist radicals, the Enabling Act passed immediately by the Reichstag gave Adolf Hitler extraordinary powers. He used these powers to muffle or eliminate all opposition and to shatter the democratic elements of the Weimar Republic in just a few months.

Those who fear the ramifications of the Military Commissions Act believe American citizens can be secretly arrested, stripped of citizenship, flown to offshore torture camps and secretly executed. This is because Section 802 of the Patriot Act maintains that any violation of federal or state law during an emergency can result in designating the person as an "enemy combatant." In other words, even misdemeanors may be considered acts of terrorism. Elements of the Act also would allow VIPER (Visible Intermodal Protection and Response) teams of heavily armed federal police squads to randomly detain Americans and force them to show papers.

If the terms of Project Megiddo are applied, citizens may not even need to speak out to face incarceration. Submitted in 1999, Megiddo — a physical place in Israel related to the Hebrew word, "Armageddon" — was an FBI report warning domestic law enforcement agencies that

Christian groups, white supremacists, the militia movement, animal rights activists, groups campaigning against a New World Order, and apocalyptic cults were potential terrorists.

Criticized in the press as a polemic disguised in a threat report, Megiddo was aimed specifically at government fear of chaos with the turn of the new millennium in 2000. The fact that no such violence took place indicates clearly that there never was a threat, which then Attorney General Janet Reno admitted.

But the chilling thrust of the report, in which the FBI was in favor of pursuing citizen groups without establishing any evidence in court of plans or attempts to commit illegal acts, still exists as a precedent. What's more, additions have been made to the list of potential terrorists that include groups campaigning legally for gun ownership rights, private property rights, and home schooling rights, and even legal defenders of the US Constitution.

More recent reports have gone to absurd extremes. In February 2009, a Missouri Information Analysis Center (MIAC) "strategic report" on the modern militia movement urged police to follow up on red flags of potential terrorists, including those who sported bumper stickers supporting politicians like Ron Paul and Chuck Baldwin. There actually were instances when Missourians were pulled over and harassed for owning these bumper stickers.

This same report warned police that opponents of the Federal Reserve System, the North American Union, the UN, illegal immigration, and radio frequency identification cards are potential terrorists.

It is vital to remember that under the Patriot Act, any suspected terrorist, domestic or foreign, comes under the terms of severe restrictions such as the no-fly list and is liable for home searches and phone and Internet surveillance without court order.

On January 23, 2009, President Obama ordered the Defense Department to issue DOD 1404.10, the "Civilian Expeditionary Workforce." Its intent is to establish a civilian army of about one million to "deploy in support of combat operations by the military." It stipulates that "management retains the authority to assign civilian employees, either voluntarily, involuntarily, or on an unexpected basis." At the same time, the Obama administration launched the website, usaservice.org, a poorly disguised recruiting tool for a non-military private army answerable not to Congress but only to Obama and the men who control him.

Both Obama and his former chief of staff, Rahm Emanuel, have stated publicly their intent to conscript all Americans below age 64 into federal service. "Citizenship is not an entitlement program," Emanuel said with a smirk on one talk show. "It comes with responsibilities....Everybody somewhere between the ages of 18 and 25 will serve three months of basic training in some kind of civil defense."

Obama added in a talk that "it doesn't have to be service in uniform. If you talk to our generals, one of things they are desperate for is a civilian counterpart to our military forces." In other words, the plan of the Obama administration is to draft all Americans between the ages of 18 and 25 into a paramilitary domestic security force.

In a similar vein, Obama's transition site, change.gov, announced that middle school and high school students will be required to perform 50 hours of community service annually. College students will have to perform 100 hours a year. These ambitions have not passed into law, but if and when they do, it is another means of forcing American citizens to work for the federal government.

In the face of pressure, Obama has refused to rescind Presidential Directive 51 (NSPD 51) and Homeland Security Presidential Directive 20 (HSPD 20) which were signed by George W. Bush. These directives establish "a comprehensive national policy on the continuity of Federal Government structures and operations and a single National Continuity Coordinator responsible for the development of continuity policies. This policy establishes 'National Essential Functions' for all executive departments and agencies and provides guidance for State and local governments, and private sector organizations in order to ensure a comprehensive continuity program that will enhance the credibility of our national security position and effective response to and recovery from a national emergency."

Translated, the directives state that in an "emergency" the president becomes dictator and Congress is a rubber stamp. The details of these directives have been classified, and even members of Congress have not been permitted to read them.

Already, 10 bills have been introduced seeking to enforce gun control. Bill HR 1022 would allow Attorney General Eric Holder to ban any gun he wishes. During the Washington DC gun ban case heard by the Supreme Court in 2008 (District of Columbia vs. Heller), Holder argued for the complete disarmament of the American people, saying only the military and police should own firearms.

Bill HR 257 would ban all youth gun sports, including Youth Olympics shooting clubs. Bill HR 45 would require all gun owners to undergo federal psychological screening, testing and registration in order to keep their firearms. These are adjuncts to a gun confiscation law that has been lurking since 1961.

If Rahm Emanuel's stated intent is realized, any American whose name is on the no-fly list will not be permitted to own a gun. Each month, more than 25,000 Americans are added to the no-fly list. This list now tops one million people who have not been convicted or even charged with a crime.

The absurd possibilities of this situation crystallized in 2009 when a Matthew Gardner was not permitted to board a plane at Seattle-Tacoma airport because he was on the no-fly list. Matthew Gardner was five years old.

Security personnel insisted on searching the child. When Matthew began to cry and his mother hugged him to comfort him, security personnel threatened to separate them and re-search the child in case his mother secreted some contraband or weapon on him.

This preposterous situation keeps repeating itself in US airports. In June 2010, the Fox News affiliate in Cleveland reported that six-year-old Alyssa Thomas was temporarily stopped from boarding a flight to Minneapolis with her parents because her name was on the no-fly list. She eventually was permitted to make the trip with her family, who had to contact the Department of Homeland Security to remove their daughter's name from the list. They eventually received a letter from the government saying that nothing will be changed and refusing to confirm or deny any information they might have on the six-year-old girl or someone else with the same name.

The Obama Administration also continues to probe for ways to curtail free speech in the media through the Fairness Doctrine. Specifically targeting talk radio programming, the last bastion of on-air media which actively criticizes his administration, Obama has pressured Congress to pass laws that would effectively muzzle these popular and financially successful programs.

Another Obama policy, the federalization of health care, will allow the government to dictate what kind of care its citizens receive. The medical care of every American will be tracked electronically by the national coordinator of health information technology, with an eye toward making sure that doctors are treating patients according to what the system deems appropriate and cost effective.

This is an extension of the 2008 Tom Daschle book, *Critical: What We Can Do about the Health Care Crisis,* in which he called for doctors to give up their autonomy and "learn to operate less like solo practitioners."

The North American Union

With the EU in place, the globalist planners escalated their work on creating a North American Union, something they had been edging toward since the end of World War II.

At the 1996 Bilderberg meetings in Toronto, Canada, inside sources told journalist Daniel Estulin that the conference was literally "a staging ground for the imminent breakup of Canada." In his book, *The True Story of the Bilderberg Group,* Estulin writes, "This was to be secured through a Unilateral Declaration of Independence in Quebec, to be launched in early 1997. The declaration would fragment Canada, with the aim of achieving 'Continental Union' with the US by 2000, a date which has been pushed back at least twice since then."

Estulin and other Bilderberg watchers spread this news to various media outlets, which corroborated through government and private sources that Canada indeed was about to be partitioned. Writes Estulin: "They [the Bilderbergers] should have known that when people's own freedom is at stake, no amount of ownership of the press would prevent secretaries, copy editors, writers, investigative journalists and indeed, management of Canada's television, radio and print media from disseminating the truth for public consumption."

According to Estulin, a staff reporter told him that Kissinger completely lost his cool in the midst of the media firestorm, screaming at then Canadian Prime Minister Jean Chretien that he "would be damned if someone was going to screw this up for him."

Another source told Estulin that David Rockefeller asked Canadian media mogul Conrad Black to apply pressure to his employees to stop reporting the story. But even Black was unable to stanch the flow of news.

This victory for Canadian sovereignty is only temporary, Estulin claims. Plans are in place for a three-part process to break up Canada in this order: independence of French-speaking Quebec, breaking up the rest of Canada into separate states, and eventually integrating them into the US as new states.

"I have four independent confirmations from US and Canadian

191

officials working on the original NAFTA [North American Free Trade Agreement], which cited Canada as a fifty-first state," Estulin wrote. "My Bilderberg sources in 1996 told me that one of the proposals tabled at the 1996 King City, Toronto, Canada Bilderberg meeting have the Maritimes as the fifty-first state, Ontario as the fifty-second, the prairies as the fifty-third, and British Columbia with the northern territories as the fifty-fourth state."

The principal stumbling block to uniting Canada with the US is Quebec, the French-speaking separatist province, and globalist planners created an opportunity to solve the problem in 1995 when anti-Quebec nationalist Prime Minister Jean Chretien backed a referendum which would allow Quebec voters to decide upon secession and achieve independence. It seemed certain that Step One of a North American *Anschluss* would go smoothly, but 38,000 people from across Canada poured into Quebec a week before the referendum to plead with the French-speaking voters not to leave. It had an almost miraculous effect, as the people of Quebec voted to remain Canadians by the narrowest of margins.

"It is worth noting," Estulin wrote, "that Quebec Premier Jacques Parizeau had participated in briefings at David Rockefeller's Council on Foreign Relations in Washington, and that Lucien Bouchard, separatist PQ leader, had been brought into politics by [former Prime Minister] Brian Mulroney, whose last act in Ottawa was to host a black-tie dinner for 200 members of Rockefeller's Council of the Americas. In fact, what I uncovered was that every politician of note in Canada was somehow tied into the same New World Order interests: Power Corporation and Rockefeller corporations."

NAFTA was the initial step toward a planned North American Union of Canada, the US and Mexico. It is based on an agreement signed in Washington on October 3, 1987. Canada's Parliament received only a 33-page summary of the Agreement and to this date the original text has not been released publicly.

Responding to the items in the released agreement, a 1,500-page legal document was drafted in 1988 which detailed its ramifications. Those who have sought to see the original agreement, which is more than 200 pages, were told they could not have access because revealing 95 percent of it would threaten Canada's national security.

NAFTA went into effect on January 1, 1994, the same day that Congress committed the US to membership in the World Trade

Organization (WTO) in a "fast track" vote without debate.

"The free trade deal is in canisters sixteen miles outside of Ottawa and is not to be seen by Canadians for thirty years," wrote Estulin. Despite protests, the following steps toward North American Union continued:

In December 1994, heads of state from 34 Western Hemisphere nations held the first Summit of the Americas meeting and pledged to create a Free Trade Agreement of the Americas (FTAA) by 2005. This agreement eliminated barriers to trade and investment among the member nations.

President George Bush met in Washington with President Vicente Fox of Mexico in September 2001, just prior to 9/11, where they hammered out the terms of the Partnership for Prosperity Initiative. The attacks less than a week later gave the leaders a reason to add security to the initiative.

On October 7 of that year, the CFR added the word "security" to the initiative for the first time in its Atlanta, Georgia meeting headlined, "The Future of North American Integration in the Wake of the Terrorist Attacks." Discussions included Canada and also opened the issue of transportation among the three nations, which laid the groundwork for a NAFTA superhighway.

On December 12, 2001, a 30-point plan coordinating security and anti-terrorism regulations between Canada and the US, the Smart Border Declaration, was signed by Canadian Deputy Prime Minister John Manley and Homeland Security Director Tom Ridge without referring the matter to the legislatures of either nation.

The following year saw the creation of the North American Forum on Integration (NAFI) which was to solve issues arising from North American integration. Its board of directors included Robert Pastor and Stephen Blank, both CFR members.

On November 30, 2004, President Bush made his first visit to Canada, where he and Prime Minister Paul Martin birthed the idea of the Security and Prosperity Partnership of North America (SPP) in a joint statement called "A New Partnership in North America." The Agreement included cross-border law enforcement and intelligence sharing.

The CFR Independent Task Force on the Future of North America, formed in 2004, issued a report titled "Creating a North American Community" in March 2005. The report called for a continental security border which would screen foreigners entering North America rather than screening them nationally. Other recommendations of the task force included: harmonizing tariffs in Mexico, Canada and the US into a common North American external tariff at the lowest possible rate; establishing a common security perimeter by 2010; developing a North American border pass with biometric identifiers (like RFID chips) that would speed passage through customs, immigration and airport security; expanding NORAD to serve as a defense command for the three nations; establishing a North American Investment Fund to aid in developing Mexico; and "harmonizing" military, education, health, foreign policy, and energy issues among the nations while expanding migrant worker programs.

The next important step took place in Waco, Texas, at a Baylor University conference on March 23, 2005. President George W. Bush, Canadian Prime Minister Paul Martin and Mexican President Vicente Fox finalized the Security and Prosperity Partnership of North America (SPP) which would "establish a common continental security perimeter against outside threats while facilitating the legal flow of people and trade across shared borders and increasing cooperation on energy, the environment and bioterrorism." It is significant that this declaration does not mention the US as an entity.

"With very little fanfare," Estulin wrote, "over 300 initiatives have been included into the SPP aimed at harmonizing North American policies on food, drugs, security, immigration, manufacturing, the environment and public health. Few people realize that over 50 percent of these 'innocuous' initiatives have been cut and pasted from the original draft of the North American Free Trade Agreement."

The SPP is an updated version of an earlier agreement, and was made possible as a result of the 9/11 attacks. Robert Pastor, a leading proponent of the North American Union who directs the Center for North American Studies at American University in Washington DC, admits: "The 9/11 crisis made Canada and the United States redefine the protection of their borders. The debt crisis in Mexico forced the government to adopt a new economic model. Crisis…can force democratic governments to make difficult decisions like those that will be required to create a North American community. It's not that I want another 9/11 crisis, but having a crisis would force decisions that otherwise might not get made."

There was no legislative debate on the SPP. Publicly elected officials were ignored while corporate leaders and unelected cabinet members from each country received permanent spots on the directorship. Private sector dominance of the SPP became strengthened with the creation of the North American Competitiveness Council (NACC). This entity officially began its work on March 31, 2006, and features 30 large corporation CEOs at its helm. Texas Congressman Ron Paul immediately pointed out that the plan was hatched by a "quasi-government organization" (SPP) and that it was buried in "an enormous transportation appropriations bill," which was not noticed by most members of Congress.

Texas Governor Rick Perry, a past Bilderberg attendee, supported the superhighway project contained in the SPP agreement. Paul complained that the SPP agreement itself was not created by treaty, nor ratified by Congress, and called it "an unholy alliance of foreign consortiums and officials from several governments….Once again decisions that affect millions of Americans are not being made by those Americans themselves, or even by their elected representatives in Congress. Instead, a handful of elites use their government connections to bypass regional legislatures and ignore our Constitution, which expressly grants Congress sole authority to regulate international trade. The ultimate goal is not simply a superhighway, but an integrated North American Union — complete with a currency, a cross-national bureaucracy, and virtually borderless travel within the Union. Like the European Union, a North American Union would represent another step toward the abolition of national sovereignty altogether."

If NAFTA and SPP were official treaties among the three nations, a two-thirds vote of approval in the Senate would have been required. But as both are technically agreements and not treaties, only a majority is needed for ratification.

The march toward obliterating national sovereignties continued in July 2005 when the US House of Representatives narrowly approved the Central American Free Trade Agreement (CAFTA), which uses the NAFTA model to extend corporate rights over the undeveloped Central American nations like Nicaragua, El Salvador, Guatemala, Costa Rica, Honduras and even the Dominican Republic.

Later that same year the first meeting of the North American Forum took place secretly in Sonoma, California, where government and business representatives planned to enhance NAFTA as a "parallel structure" to the SPP. Its chairmen were former US Secretary of State George Schultz, former Canadian Alberta Premier Peter Lougheed and

Mexico's former Treasury Secretary Peter Aspe, who also co-chaired the CFR task force. In fact, the CFR task force amounted to about one third of the forum's attendees.

The North American Forum held its second meeting in September 2006, this time in Banff, Alberta, and discussed the "demographic and social dimensions of North American integration" and established a "North American energy strategy." Again, the meeting was secret, but a leaked document included a participant's statement that integration will succeed through "evolution by stealth."

The following June, Canada created its own no-fly list, called Passenger Protect, with the intent eventually to merge it with the US no-fly list.

On January 22, 2008, British Columbia introduced the "enhanced driver's licence" which was to be compatible with licenses from the neighboring US state of Washington. The new ID card contained an RFID chip that broadcasts a number linked to a computer database that allows border guards to obtain information on drivers as they approach. The new license will be compatible with the US Real ID card, which is yet to be implemented due to its immense unpopularity.

A month later, the US Northern Command signed a Civil Assistance Plan with Canada Command, permitting "the military from one nation to support the armed forces of the other nation...during floods, forest fires, hurricanes, earthquakes and effects of a terrorist attack."

The "evolution by stealth" continues today. Stephen Lendman of the Center for Research on Globalization opined: "NACC denies what's pretty clear about its aims. Saying its recommendations aren't meant to 'threaten the sovereign power of any of the three countries,' there's no doubt *that's* the central objective. It wants a North American Union headquartered in Washington with policies in place benefiting corporate giants at the expense of working people. They'll be hammered by the greater job losses, fewer social services, and the loss of personal security under militarized police state conditions in the name of 'national (continental) security' in the age of concocted global terror threats."

A North American Union would require the end of US sovereignty. Not only is this a Constitutional violation, it would destroy the US Constitution and the Bill of Rights, eradicating all rights and protections granted by those documents to American citizens.

All elected American officials and all American military personnel have sworn to uphold the Constitution. Therefore, participating in the dissolution of the United States would amount to high treason.

The Superhighway

On April 27, 2007, the transportation ministers of the US, Canada and Mexico met in Tucson, Arizona, to coordinate interconnected systems of transportation. This initiative grew out of the Waco meeting, in which the three national leaders called for an "adequate transportation infrastructure and efficient transportation services within and between" the three countries.

They proposed a 10-lane superhighway extending from the Mexican port of Lazaro Cardenas through Mexico, the US and Canada. A median strip between the north and south lanes would contain railway lines and oil and gas pipelines.

A portion of this superhighway came to be called the Trans Texas Corridor and to build it, unelected commissions have confiscated 584,000 acres of land from nearly one million Texas farmers through bogus condemnation rulings.

TV commentator Patrick Buchanan termed the proposed superhighway as the "Fox-Bush autobahn," and raised the scenario of container ships from China "unloading at Lazaro Cardenas, a port named for the Mexican president who nationalized US oil companies in 1938. From there trucks with Mexican drivers would run fast lines into the United States, hauling their cargo to a US Customs inspection terminal in Kansas City, Missouri. From there, the trucks would fan out across America or roll on into Canada."

The construction of the Trans Texas Corridor portion of the proposed superhighway was secretly handed to a Spanish firm, Cintra-Zachry, which will be permitted to collect tolls once the highway is completed. This was enacted without a vote by taxpayers in those counties through which the highway will run.

The Texas State legislature also was not aware of this secret agreement. When the story broke, Cintra's Australian subsidiary purchased the newspapers in every town and city along the planned Trans Texas Corridor. Polls show that more than 90 percent of Texans still oppose the plan, despite corporate control of the local press and its propaganda onslaught.

Foreign governments and corporations are seizing infrastructure throughout North America, concentrating first on Texas, where more than 8,000 miles of existing roads and land are being given to government-backed foreign companies. These foreign companies bribe local Texas legislators through campaign donations to turn over control of these roads and lands to them.

There is no cap on the amount of toll which can be collected on the superhighway once it is completed. Phase One of the toll road plan is expected to raise more than $200 billion in the first 15 years.

To be called the I-35 Highway, this artery cuts a swath through the American heartland. Asian imports could land duty-free on the West Coast of Mexico and then be shipped to I-35. The hub of the highway in Kansas City, the new Kansas City Inland Port, is now considered part of Mexico's sovereign soil.

RFID devices imbedded in toll tags and inspection stickers are already being used to track traffic. Highway off-ramps serving small rural communities have been walled off to create ghost towns in a move to force populations toward the cities. Under the NAFTA system, this is being accelerated with the goal of turning more than half of the US into a wilderness, as planned by the United Nations Convention on Biological Diversity and the Wildlands Project. The ultimate goal is to increase bureaucratic control and decrease individual independence.

Already in America, more than 80 federal and state highways have been designated as international arteries. Under current agreements, foreign companies are placing tolls on already existing roads that have been fully paid for. Federal and state documents prove that this toll money will be used to build up the transportation infrastructure of Mexico, so that foreign products can enter the US from Mexico faster and more cheaply. Other toll funds will go to finance the growing bureaucracy of the North American Union.

Originally, the US highway system was designed in the 1950s by the Pentagon to allow for rapid deployment of military ground forces in case of an invasion. Today, the Northern Command uses these highways as a force projection system that could allow military forces to overwhelm the population across the US. All this has occurred while county and city governments are being federalized nationwide.

Anyone who doubts whether these agreements threaten the sovereignty of the United States has only to look at the simple fact that NAFTA Headquarters is located in Mexico. Owing to this, the activities of NAFTA in the US are independent of Congress.

Eugenics Anyone?

In 1904, the Cold Springs Harbor research facility was launched by eugenicist Charles Davenport and funded by Andrew Carnegie, John D. Rockefeller and Edward Henry Harriman. Three years later the first sterilization laws were passed in the US. Citizens with deformities or children with low test scores on their report cards were arrested and forcibly sterilized. It was the beginning of an incredible and shameful chapter in American history.

The United States Eugenics Records Office was established in 1910. It aped the British system of creating a network of social workers whose job was to find and collect persons who fit their criteria for sterilization. These social workers also had the power to take children from families that fit their criteria for genetically undesirable individuals. In some cases, they had the power to euthanize, or murder, these persons.

The Rockefellers expanded their eugenics policies to Germany in 1911, funding the Kaiser Wilhelm Institute. This organization would outlast the Kaiser and become a centerpiece of the Nazi euthanasia program in the 1930s.

In 1912, the International Eugenics Conference was held in London. The roll call of respected scientists in attendance boosted eugenics to a level of widespread respect and admiration. Among its most ardent supporters was writer H.G. Wells, whose books and articles spread the gospel of eugenics worldwide. Wells was in favor of a single world government and aired his views in detail in his book, *Open Conspiracy: H.G. Wells on World Revolution.* In it he claimed his one-world government should be a scientific dictatorship, guided by the principals of eugenics.

Margaret Sanger, lover of H.G. Wells, promoted this philosophy in the US. By 1923 Sanger's eugenics campaign had received massive funding from the Rockefeller family.

In a letter to eugenicist Clarence Gamble, Sanger revealed a scheme to recruit African American religious leaders to their cause so they would act as Judas goats in luring black Americans toward sterilization programs and even extermination. She wrote: "The most successful educational approach to the Negro is through a religious appeal. We do not want word to go out that we want to exterminate the Negro population, and the Minister is the man who can straighten out that idea if it ever occurs to any of their more rebellious members."

The awful plan crystallized in 1939 with Sanger's "Negro Project," aimed at reducing the African American population because Negroes "still breed carelessly and disastrously, with the result that the increase among Negroes, even more than among whites, is from that portion of the population least intelligent and fit...."

Sanger, who founded the eugenics organization that would become Planned Parenthood, was an open supporter in the 1930s of the Nazi genetic engineering program designed to create a super race. In her published work, *The Pivot of Civilization,* Sanger promoted "the extermination of 'human weeds'" and "the sterilization of genetically inferior races." This would extend to Catholics, Fundamentalist Christians, Hispanics and American Indians as Sanger became more anti-religious. "Birth control appeals to the advanced radical," she wrote, "because it is calculated to undermine the authority of the Christian churches."

Eugenicist Madison Grant wrote *The Passing of the Great Race,* which became the bible of racial philosophy and forced sterilization. Among the fan mail he received for the book was a letter from Adolf Hitler, who later would employ his pseudo-scientific theories as justification for genocide. When he became Chancellor of Germany in 1933, one of Hitler's first acts was to pass eugenics laws that actually were modeled on those of the US. Within three years, Germany led the world in eugenics with an aggressive program that sterilized and euthanized citizens in the hundreds of thousands.

By 1927, eugenics was being touted in America's churches, schools and even state fairs. Contests offering cash prizes pitted churches against each other to see who could make the best case for eugenics in sermons. Some church fathers even went so far as to instruct their flocks that Jesus was pro-eugenics.

Also in 1927, 25 American states passed forced sterilization laws. When lawsuits against this legislation reached the US Supreme Court, it ruled in favor of the sterilization policies. Even Hollywood joined the pro-eugenics push, which was the theme of the 1934 film, *Tomorrow's Children.*

Charles Davenport and Professor Harry Laughlin were the scientists at the helm of the American eugenics program in the 1930s. The Rockefeller family funded their trip to Germany, to advise the Nazi government and scientists on ways to streamline their eugenics program, including their program of extermination.

Following the collapse of Nazi Germany, the Nuremberg trials did not prosecute the German scientists who had participated in the eugenics programs, apparently because the sheer scale of Nazi extermination was an embarrassment to American and British eugenicists. In an attempt to deflect the negative publicity that grew out of the revelations of German atrocities, the eugenics principals attempted to disguise their work. The publication, *Eugenics Quarterly,* became *Social Biology.* The American Birth Control League became Planned Parenthood. They invented new psychobabble terms like "trans humanism," "population control," "conservation," "sustainability," and "environmentalism" to disguise their dealings.

But their comments reveal the true nature of their intentions. National Park Service research biologist David Graber wrote in the *Los Angeles Times Book Review*, "Until such time as *homo sapiens* should decide to join nature, some of us can only hope for the right virus to come along."

And in the Council of Rome's publication, *The First Global Revolution,* the authors wrote, "In searching for a new enemy to unite us, we came up with the idea that pollution, the threat of global warming, water shortages, famine and the like would fit the bill. All these dangers are caused by human intervention....The real enemy, then, is humanity itself."

This philosophy has had awesome effects on policies and life around the world. In the early 1960s for instance, after the pesticide DDT was recognized as being responsible for killing mosquitoes in Guyana to a point where malaria had all but disappeared there, Club of Rome President Alexander King said, "My chief quarrel with DDT, in hindsight, is that it has greatly added to the population program."

In 1972, the US government outlawed the use of DDT, despite the fact that a six month EPA investigation had determined the pesticide was safe to humans and animals. The National Academy of Science in 1970 estimated that DDT had saved 500 million lives in the previous 20 years. Since banning the pesticide in 1972, at least that many lives have been lost to diseases like malaria.

The brazen statements of eugenics proponents continue without contrition. In November 1991, Jacques Cousteau wrote in the UNESCO *Courier,* "In order to stabilize world population, we must eliminate 350,000 people per day. It is a horrible thing to say, but it's just as bad not to say it."

Geneticist Julian Huxley said that since eugenicists had founded the environmental and conservationist movements, these movements should be used as vehicles in forming a world government. He helped to create the World Wildlife Fund with Bilderberg founder Prince Bernhard and Prince Philip of Great Britain. It was Philip who made the remarkable comment to *Deutsche Press Agentur,* "In the event that I am reincarnated, I would like to return as a deadly virus, in order to contribute something to solve overpopulation." Philip, the Duke of Edinburgh, is a Bilderberg member, a Freemason and a former director of the World Wildlife Fund.

Huxley's brother, Aldous, lectured at Berkeley in 1962, and admitted that his iconic book, *Brave New World,* was not based on fiction but on the research and planning that actually was underway. The book paints a gloomy picture of a future society in which entire populations are genetically engineered "test-tube humans" and the greatest insult would be, "Who was your mother?"

In his lecture, Aldous Huxley added, "I am inclined to think that the scientific dictatorships of the future — and I think there are going to be scientific dictatorships in many parts of the world — will be a good deal nearer to the *Brave New World* pattern than to the *1984* pattern. It will not be because of any humanitarian qualms in the scientific dictators, but simply because the *Brave New World* pattern is probably a good deal more efficient than the other.

"If you can get people to consent to the state of affairs in which they are living — the state of servitude, the state of being — it seems to me the nature of the ultimate revolution with which we are now faced is precisely this. We are in the process of developing a whole series of techniques which will enable the controlling oligarchy, who have always existed and presumably always will exist, to get people actually to love their servitude.

"People can be made to enjoy a state of affairs which, by any decent standard they ought not to enjoy....These methods combine methods of terror with methods of acceptance. There are various other methods that one can think of. There is, for example, the pharmacological method....You can imagine a euphoric that would make people thoroughly happy, even in the most abominable circumstances. These things are possible."

The Nazi doctors experimented in this and much more horrific programs during World War II. Not only did they escape prosecution at Nuremberg, they were recruited by Britain and America to continue their work in those countries at comfortable salaries. Some of them were part of the Crypto-Eugenics movement, which was an underground science featuring many respected anthropologists and geneticists.

A similar sweetheart deal was struck in Japan with the senior officers and scientists who had been conducting bioweapons research on a vast scale during the war. Their experiments claimed at least 3,000 human lives, many of them American and Chinese prisoners of war. Weapons were developed and used by Japan to spread diseases like anthrax in China.

But following the war, none of these biological weapons researchers were prosecuted in the war crimes trials. Instead, they continued their work under the guidance and protection of General Douglas MacArthur's military occupation administration. Several of the scientific murderers advanced to respected university positions in Japan.

Aggressive sterilization programs continued in the US until the mid-1980s. Its dark purpose was properly revealed by Bertrand Russell: "Gradually, by selective breeding, the congenital differences between rulers and ruled will increase until they almost become different species. A revolt of the plebs would become as unthinkable as an organized insurrection of sheep against the practice of eating mutton."

Sterilization research has been revitalized in recent years, according to Dr. True Ott, who says that currently patents are in place on a vaccine that causes spontaneous abortion.

"They've been doing this in the veterinarian segment for a decade or so," he told the author. "Instead of cutting and snipping a cat, they just give them a vaccine that makes them sterile. This vaccine is a porcine/bird virus structure. We have documented over 5,000 women that have aborted their fetuses after taking the vaccine, and that's just what we know about. And the majority of these aborted fetuses are African American. This is being covered up in Washington, where they say no women have had abortions using the vaccine. And yet you have Bill Gates last spring [2010] admitting that they have a new vaccination program that would cause a 15 percent reduction in the US population."

The primary agenda in population reduction may not only be related to reducing the number of mouths to feed. Russell, like Huxley, Wells and numerous eugenicists, frequently spoke of the oligarchs' belief that they are a separate and more advanced species than the common man.

Wells predicted that humanity would split into two distinct species in 100,000 years, and evolutionary theorist Oliver Curry of the London School of Economics has written that he expects a genetic upper class and a dim-witted underclass to emerge. Several geneticists have admitted that their goal is not to improve the human race, but to dumb it down so it would be more manageable.

Bertrand Russell, who won a Nobel Prize, wrote that vaccinations containing mercury and other brain damaging compounds could induce partial chemical lobotomies, creating a servile population. In his book, *The Impact of Science on Society,* Russell wrote, "Diet, injections and injunctions will combine, from a very early age, to produce the sort of character and the sort of beliefs that the authorities consider desirable. And any serious criticisms of the powers that be will become psychologically impossible."

Mind altering drugs intended to control populations are also part of the eugenics programs, going back more than a century. By 2007, more than 20 percent of Americans were taking prescription anti-depressant drugs. A quick study of the shocking instances in the last 15 years of children, postal workers and business employees killing others with guns reveals that in nearly every instance the perpetrators were taking or had just gone off prescription anti-depressant drugs.

Eugenicists even have initiated pre-crime policies, in which fetuses are screened according to family histories of criminal behavior. This policy was adopted by Great Britain in 2007, following the US example. Child protective services in Britain and America are now enrolling newborn children into criminal databases if they have a criminal family history. Beginning at age two, these children will be forced to attend probation hearings.

In 1974, the US government made a Third World population reduction an important national security issue. Titled "National Security Study Memorandum 200," the operation is an echo of the British Commission on Population created by King George VI in 1944, which stated that a Third World population explosion posed a threat to the international elite.

The US plan, created by Henry Kissinger, targeted 13 countries for massive population reduction. Kissinger recommended that the International Monetary Fund (IMF) and World Bank supply loans only if these nations agreed to begin aggressive population control programs, including sterilization. Kissinger also used "food diplomacy" to reach population reduction goals, and added that instigating wars also provided a solution.

Kissinger also was involved in the Nixon administration's 1972 eugenics policy, directed by George H.W. Bush, then ambassador to the United Nations. Bush advised China on creating its "one child" policy that has resulted, owing to the desirability of male children, to a preponderance of 30 million more men than women in that nation today. This was achieved in the scandalous murders by parents of female babies soon after birth, revealed by Steven W. Mosher in his book, *Broken Earth.* Bush also worked his magic in the US, directing the federal government to forcibly sterilize more than 40 percent of Native American women living on reservations.

The men who seek to create a global government now are aggressively working to get nations in line on a worldwide one-child policy. China's one-child policy was a graduated initiative, initially taxing couples who had more than one child. Later, this lenient policy was replaced by imprisonment of those having more than one child. Similar proposals are being made now in the US and Europe.

Heavy donators to population reduction organizations include Ted Turner, who gave $1 billion to the UN for its policies in Africa. Bill and Melinda Gates donated $2.2 billion to the UN Population Fund and other similar groups. By 2007, the Gates had donated more than $30 billion to population control groups. This amount was topped by the $37 billion given by Warren Buffett to various population control groups.

A chilling viewpoint on the eugenics movement came from Dr. Eric Pianka of the University of Texas biology department, who recently received a Texas Academy of Science award. He took advantage of the occasion to say in his speech that the AIDS epidemic was "no good" because it was "too slow." He instead praised the ebola virus, because it would kill 90 percent of the world's population much more quickly.

For this mad opinion, Pianka received a sustained standing ovation from the audience, which contained many other scientists. Pianka also praised China as the leading world superpower "because they have a police state and they are able to force people to stop reproducing."

These philosophies by elitists have led to the inevitable.

The Population Balm

The Club of Rome, dominated by Bilderberg members, decided that environmentalism would be the best cover in implementing population reduction. It's belief was that even educated Western populations would accept radical programs if they were packaged as saving the earth. They also believe that citizens would be willing to give up their nations' sovereignty if it would help the planet.

The Club of Rome continues to push for a global carbon tax, which will fund its global government aspirations. Its Global Biodiversity Assessment states plainly that the human population must be reduced from the current six billion humans to about one billion.

The process already is underway. South Africa developed bioweapons in the 1970s to target its black and Asian citizens, and then sold this technology to Israel in the 1980s.

In 2000, the Project for a New American Century report stated that "advanced forms of biological warfare that can 'target' specific genotypes may transform biological warfare from the realm of terror to a politically useful tool."

This "useful tool" already may have been applied. In the recent past, the media has spread alarm over the possibility of pandemics such as the H1N1 virus and Swine flu. In April 2009 the US departments of Health and Homeland Security declared a national health emergency based on the outbreak of Swine flu.

To prepare for such an outbreak, certain regional law enforcement agencies announced that it may be necessary to forcibly vaccinate and quarantine citizens. This was legalized by the US Emergency Medical Powers Acts, the Patriot Act and other federal legislation that calls for mandatory vaccination or drugging with no exemptions. At the federal and state levels, those who refuse vaccination are classified as felons and face immediate incarceration and quarantine, probably in one of the many FEMA camps that have been constructed around the nation.

Some states already have instituted mandatory vaccination and quarantine laws. Massachusetts, for instance, recently passed Bill 2028 allowing the governor to declare a state of emergency during a pandemic and authorize "non-health care licensed personnel" — police or National Guard — to vaccinate citizens against their will. Those adults who refuse to be vaccinated can be fined and imprisoned for up to 30 days without trial or even without charges under this new law.

The statute will allow police to enter private homes without search warrants and it does not spell out specifically what constitutes a pandemic. The statute also authorizes police to take children from their parents and vaccinate them against the will of the parents. Finally, the bill stipulates that the vaccinators shall be protected from legal liability. These authorizations are all violations of the US Constitution, and federal judges have the ability to declare the statute unconstitutional.

The national health emergency announcement in 2009 caused many Americans to voluntarily accept vaccinations despite the fact that doctors such as infectious disease specialist Kent Holtorf felt more uneasy about the vaccine than the flu.

"It's been rushed to market," Holtorf told Fox News. "There are high levels of adjuncts which basically make it more potent. It's kind of an unrefined method that they used....[One of the ingredients] has been shown to create autism in children....You also have to worry about people who have blood brain barrier dysfunction, which includes children, pregnant women, chronic neurological illnesses...I've seen people devastated by these effects." Holtorf added that he would not allow his children to receive the vaccination.

Fox News also aired a story on a young woman, Desiree Jennings, who developed a rare malady called Dystonia 10 days after receiving a Swine flu vaccination. Her condition, which severely hampers her speech and motor activity and produces frequent convulsions, has been diagnosed as irreversible.

The Swine flu vaccine contains aluminum and mercury, both of which are neurotoxins. Squalene, which can force the human immune system to attack itself, is added in some of the Swine flu vaccines.

Department of Health and Human Services Secretary Kathleen Sebelius currently is trying to get FDA approval for the use of Squalene additives Novardis MF59 and ASO3. According to Dr. Bill Deagle, a microbiologist who has worked with Special Forces and who was interviewed on Project Camelot radio, the additives are "laced with cancer viruses" and "a cleaning agent." He added that one company is testing a "live attenuated virus in the flu vaccine."

Deagle estimates the newly engineered virus will "have a lethality of around 70 percent. We're looking at a world-nation killer that in the next several years will become increasingly lethal and shut down international commerce. The government wants this....They're approving vaccines that are almost certainly going to make the virus evolve even quicker." He added that the new super-flu mutates 2.3 to three times faster than the 1918 pandemic flu.

A 70 percent plague lethality rate would be sufficient reason for the US government to declare an emergency and instill martial law. This high rate of susceptibility to disease might have been aided by a general reduction in the human immune system, caused by an additive in jet fuel called elthylene dibromide. It is a pesticide that was added to all jet fuel in the early 1990s ostensibly to improve combustion, but its side effects on humans is to act as a neurotoxin and an immune system suppressant.

"That's what is called a binary weapon system where you soften the target and then expose them to a pathogen," Deagle said. "They're getting ready for what I call The Hard Kill. These pandemics are to soften the population for a new economic order, a reduction in the population and more compliance by trackable national IDs....The keepers of civilization are ready to crash this civilization and resurrect it with their plans."

Deagle accused the US Armed Forces of instituting a vaccination program for all troops in which H1N1 RNA was inserted to modify their genetics so their immune systems would respond more readily to a second phase vaccine. "They want our troops to die so they can bring in foreign troops on American soil," Deagle said, "because they will shoot at American citizens and disarm them. American troops won't. That's already been established."

The case of former Marine David Faye bears out Deagle's accusation. On November 28, 2005, Faye and his platoon received what he described as undisclosed vaccinations.

"They asked us our names....and they gave us the shot," Faye had recalled. "Then we had the rest of the day off. After that shot I started swelling up. I gained 30 pounds of water [weight]. My eyes swelled up where I couldn't see."

Faye had to be hospitalized three weeks later, dying shortly after. The Department of Defense claims that "all service members vaccinated are documented in the individuals' permanent file," but Faye's mother Cindy found no such documentation in her son's record. She asked military administrators at the US Marine hospital in 29 Palms,

California, what was in the vaccination. According to Cindy Faye, an administrator said, "Ma'am, that's confidential. I can't say what that was." Then, 11 months later, a handwritten notation suddenly appeared on David Faye's Marine record, indicating the shot was a flu vaccine.

An anonymous military medical worker reported that there are thousands of service men and women who are suffering illness following vaccinations, ranging from arthritic symptoms to death. And despite the mandate to report adverse reactions to vaccinations to the Centers for Disease Control and Prevention (CDC) and the FDA, the military never did so in the case of David Faye and others.

Deagle claims that his whistle blowing has resulted in death threats and harassment from agencies like the State Board of Examiners. He reported the phoned death threats and tracked them to non-service phone numbers.

Another problem in recent years is that the number of vaccinations given to children has skyrocketed, much to the dismay of many health experts. One of them, vaccine researcher Dr. Andrew Wakefield, a Fellow of Britain's Royal College of Surgeons, said, "My concerns are the absence of any adequate safety studies looking at the long term detrimental effects of vaccinations in early childhood, and the almost cavalier continuance of the process of introducing more untested vaccines into a schedule of vaccination that is already appalling in terms of its scientific underpinning."

Dr. Stephen Marini, a microbiologist and immunologist, holds similar opinions. He warns that vaccinations are "not in the best interests of your children. You're going to be trading some innocent types of diseases that we now know how to handle better for other problems such as allergies, asthma, even autism for years to come."

There have been allegations against certain pharmaceutical companies as well, charging that they have deliberately infected certain nations, usually in the Third World, to boost sales of vaccines as well as to reduce populations. One accusation came from a surprising source, award winning public health expert Dr. Leonard Horowitz, regarding a new flu that appeared in Mexico recently.

He claimed that Novavax Inc., a British-based pharmaceutical firm, used an Anglo-American network of genetic engineers "in a conspiracy to commit genocide. Dr. James S. Robertson, England's leading bioengineer of flu viruses for the vaccine industry, and now the promoter of US government funding for lucrative bio-defense contracts, along with collaborators at the US Centers for Disease Control and Prevention (CDC), helped Novavax in Bethesda, Maryland, [to] produce genetically modified recombinants of the Avian, Swine and Spanish flu viruses H5N1 and H1N1.

"They are nearly identical to the unprecedented Mexican virus that has now spread to the United States. The outbreak was precisely timed to promote the company's new research and huge vaccine stockpiling contract. Scientists at the CDC are implicated through collaborations and publications involving private contracts with Novavax…[The] evidence to commit deadly duplicity in the vaccine industry includes the genetic markers on the virus."

Recently, the pharmaceutical company Baxter International was caught shipping live Avian flu viruses H5N1 and H3N2 mixed with vaccines to 18 foreign countries. The firm has to adhere to Biosafety Level 3, a set of failure-proof safety protocols intended to prevent contamination of vaccines. This indicates the inclusion of the Avian virus in its flu vaccine was deliberate, although Baxter spokespersons claimed it was an accident. The vaccines went to a number of Eastern European countries where authorities wonder whether Baxter deliberately tried to start a pandemic.

"If you were to cause a pandemic, that's the best way to do it," Dr. True Ott told the author. "I've shown how the 1918 flu pandemic was caused by a vaccine. I've got the research data given to President [Woodrow] Wilson to prove it. It's been covered up.

"In a nutshell, [the pandemic was caused by] typhus fever vaccination. They thought it was all bacteria [which caused disease] back then. They didn't know about viruses. So they took the basic Pasteurian theory of a bacteria-contaminated source. They took it [the virus] from an infected human who had the typhus fever blisters and other symptoms. They kept the infected fluid and injected it into pigs as hosts. They now had a whole mass of sick pigs. They harvested the infection from the pigs and put it into chickens. So you had a human virus that infected pigs, which caused a mutation that entered the host of the chickens, and then back to the humans [as a vaccine]. It's a meld between pig and bird. How did that happen? In nature, you don't have pigs mating with chickens. You don't have humans mating with pigs and chickens.

"John D. Rockefeller was the instigator of this typhus fever vaccination during The Great War through his big pharmaceutical companies, which manufactured it. He was the main mover and shaker for all vaccines back then and he was equal opportunity. He supplied the Kaiser's troops with it just as much as the British and the American troops.

"But the Germans got it first. All of them were sick when the Allies attacked [in summer 1918]. It was called a para-typhus in the military records. It wasn't full-blown typhus. It was more of a pneumonia with all of the symptoms of the 1918 virus. The Allied troops were able to win the war with that [1918 offensive] because the German troops were so deathly ill. Thus, the Allied victory was partially due to a vaccine. And the epidemic spread when the troops returned home with this mysterious para-typhus."

Ott believes that the 2009 H1N1 vaccine "is designed to be a eugenics program of the highest order." He maintains that the power elite of the world have targeted Third World nations, specifically Mexico and South America, for depopulation policies and projects. He also claims that depopulation policies have become a top priority for deliberation by the National Security Council, the Club of Rome and policymakers like Kissinger and Brzezinski, who are important advisors to President Obama.

Added Ott, "The elite have it in their agenda for what they call the New [World] Order to protect Mother Earth by killing off massive amounts of undesirable populations in Third World countries."

Only because of a fortunate precaution taken by a Czech laboratory to test the 2009 Baxter-produced vaccine on a dozen ferrets (all of which died within days) was a disastrous human pandemic avoided. There was no follow-up investigation of this matter by the World Health Organization (WHO) or the member states of the European Union.

On the same day the Baxter story broke, a FEMA conference announced that an Avian flu pandemic was a certainty at some point in the future, a suspicious coincidence.

Baxter currently is being sued by Austrian journalist Jane Burgermeister for deliberately and repeatedly contaminating vaccines with biological weapons designed to murder massive numbers of people. Burgermeister also has filed criminal charges of bioterrorism with the FBI against WHO, the UN, and several ranking government and corporate officials.

A story associated with the Baxter International scandal involves a whistle blower named Joseph Moshe, a Mossad agent and microbiologist specializing in biological warfare. In August 2009, Moshe claimed that the Baxter International facility in the Ukraine was creating a biological weapon designed to kill millions of Americans.

The episode began when Moshe called Dr. Ott, who guest-hosted a live radio show on Republic Broadcasting in 2009. "The whole topic of discussion on that show was exposing the bird flu-slash-swine flu as being a weaponized virus structure," Ott told the author. "I had a CDC insider on the show who shared with me the so-called gene plates of this novel virus.

"The gene plates could not have been natural. They had to be manufactured, probably in Fort Detrick. I had been hammering this home for a full week, two hours a day. I said, 'If anybody can come forward with hard evidence of the government's involvement in this, we would want to get indictments for mass murder, because murders are happening now. We know it's a government virus. What we don't know is who released it and how.'

"We were looking for eyewitness testimony that is verifiable. My attorney told me at the time that it was not illegal to make a weaponized virus. It's not moral, but it's not illegal. But when it is released, it becomes a criminal act."

Immediately following the show, Moshe called Ott, saying he wanted to give evidence to the US Attorney that Baxter BioPharma Solutions in the Ukraine was releasing a bioweapon in the form of a vaccine. He said the vaccine had an additive that weakens the human immune system and contains replicated RNA from the Spanish flu pandemic of 1918.

"He said, 'I have the documentation that I feel will put people behind bars,'" Ott remembers. They tried to arrange a quick meeting, but Ott's travel schedule prevented it and he referred Moshe to the US Attorney's office in Los Angeles.

Moshe also had informed the White House that he intended to go public with the information, but there is no evidence he made any bomb threats, an accusation that authorities used against him later. He was either en route to the US Attorney's office as Ott had suggested or to the Israeli embassy (he holds a dual citizenship) after noticing suspicious men in suits near his home.

FBI agents and LAPD SWAT units surrounded his car in Westwood, California, after disabling it with a microwave device. Moshe was accosted by dozens of FBI and police SWAT officers after a long standoff. Local news helicopters covered the incident. Despite the announcement that he'd been deported to Israel for threatening to bomb the White House, Moshe was imprisoned in the Twin Towers Correctional Facility on charges of violating a court order, a misdemeanor, and held without bond or bail.

Moshe's Mossad duties specialized in the study of plant diseases and he has written papers on the genetic manipulation of viruses, according to his profile on biomedexperts.com. It is known now that the suited men in front of his home were FBI agents with orders to detain and arrest him. But Moshe never was officially arrested. He was removed from his car after exhibiting absolutely no effects from the copious tear gas and pepper spray that police fired at him, an apparent result of his Mossad training and physical preparation.

Ott has never heard from him again, but managed to track down his whereabouts through sources in his network. "He was put into the Patton State Mental Hospital," Ott told the author. "As far as I know, he's still there. I tried to get permission to visit him, but I couldn't get permission to go."

The flu season that followed was relatively mild in the US, although in 2009 the Ukraine did indeed suffer a pandemic outbreak of Swine flu carrying Ukrainian Hermorrhagic Fever. Extremely lethal outbreaks also occurred in Chiapas, Mexico, and in Venezuela in 2009.

Reporter Wayne Madsen also has uncovered evidence that the Swine flu is a man-made biological agent. He said during a televised interview, "It's very apparent that there are three research centers involved in the development in a laboratory of the 1918 Spanish flu, which was actually resurrected...from the DNA extracted from an Inuit woman who died of this pandemic in 1918 in Alaska. The material was taken to several laboratories and what I've discovered is that three particular laboratories are very much involved in this research: the University of Madison at Wisconsin, the National Microbiology Laboratory in Winnipeg, Manitoba, and the St. Jude Research Laboratory in Memphis, Tennessee."

Dr. Ott added, "Jeffrey Taubenberger was the lead scientist who re-created the 1918 virus. His colleague did an article on this whole process, and he basically admits that five 1918-like viruses were created. The first couple caused high fever, aches and pains. They were shown not to be lethal at all through their lab experimentation. But one strain was more viral than the 1918 killer, with an estimated 70 percent lethality."

The obvious question is: why would these funded labs want to resurrect a virus that killed more people in one year than all the bullets, bombs and shells killed in the four years of World War I? The answer could be that the labs want to develop an antidote vaccine for the Spanish flu in case it resurfaces. It also could be that the labs are resurrecting it as a biological weapon.

"First of all, it's to make a lot of money," Ott says. "They patent vaccines through the big pharmaceutical companies, which are Rockefeller-controlled. They're not out to kill people. They're just trying to see what they can get away with. The whole vaccine thing is a hoax, so it's a worldwide multibillion dollar scam for vaccine. But that's not to say they can't use it as a blackmail chip."

Ott went on to explain that key members of congressional committees can be threatened into voting favorably for interest groups under fear of having a weaponized virus released among their constituencies. "I think that goes on much more than we would ever believe," he told the author.

Wayne Madsen also maintains that the genetic material gained from the Spanish flu is present in the H1N1 virus, which has already killed many people around the world. "Right now it doesn't appear that the FBI or any other law enforcement agency is actively investigating it," Madsen added, "which brings up the anthrax case. Some people say that was not adequately investigated, either."

Some health researchers charge that the H1N1 virus is a product of laboratory gene splicing, because it contains bird flu, two forms of human flu, and various forms of Swine flu. H1N1 has another unusual aspect in that it does not target children or the elderly like most flu viruses, but affects people between ages 20 and 45. Another suspicious aspect is that pigs are unaffected by this flu, which spreads strictly through human contact.

Other disturbing examples of deliberate and illegal transportation of pathogens have occurred recently. Madsen mentions a case in Maine where a scientist from the National Microbiology Laboratory was caught bringing Ebola and HIV DNA across the US border. He was arrested in North Dakota where he was apparently en route to the National Institutes of Health (NIH) outside Washington DC. There also is the case of the Japanese researcher who was caught taking H1N1 DNA out of Surabaya Airport in Indonesia to Japan.

Another form of unauthorized drug propagation for depopulation purposes may lie in our drinking water. On March 11, 2008, the Associated Press reported that tests on the water in 50 major American cities over a period of five months revealed the presence of pharmaceutical drugs in the drinking water of 24 cities. In just these tested metropolitan areas, more than 41 million people are being exposed to the drugs, according to the news story.

Philadelphia's drinking water contained at least 56 pharmaceuticals or pharmaceutical byproducts. The treated water in Southern California contained anti-epileptic and anti-anxiety medications. San Francisco's water contained sex hormones.

New York refused to cooperate with the AP test, but the state health department conducted its own tests and discovered the big city's water contained estrogen, heart medicine, tranquilizers, mood stabilizers and many more pharmaceuticals. The response of New York City health officials maintained, in spite of the evidence, that the water met all federal and state regulations.

Poisons such as arsenic, cadmium and lead have shown up in America's public water supply. In some cases, thermonium, a radioactive form of lead, has been discovered. These are not natural occurrences. Someone had to put them there.

No sufficient governmental testing program is in place at this time, and therefore no program to reduce the pharmaceuticals in city water supplies is available. Scientists quoted in the AP article warned that these impurities would cause widespread long-term side effects.

This study did not take into account the amount of sodium fluoride in water, which was part of a federally mandated program that began in the late 1940s. Sodium fluoride is a byproduct of the process to make aluminum. It is a toxin, which is used in rat poison.

Most tooth pastes contain fluoride and FDA guidelines make it necessary to list warnings on toothpaste tubes that if it is swallowed, individuals should call the nearest Poison Control Center. The American Dental Association actually recommends that fluoridated water should not be used by infants because baby formulas using tap water contain 250 times more fluoride than is contained in mothers' milk.

About 65 percent of the public water in the US is fluoridated, despite the known effects this compound has on bone cancer and bone strength. Dannon and several other companies are fluoridating bottled water now, so it is becoming harder to avoid.

One side effect of fluoride is that it calms aggressive tendencies. The drinking water in the Soviet *gulags* was heavily fluoridated for this reason.

Tooth damage known as fluorosis has become a widespread dental problem, due to the intake of high fluoride amounts during childhood. The damage to teeth indicates also that too much fluoride has passed into skeletal bones and organs.

Currently about one-third of individuals between the ages of six and 19 suffer from enamel fluorosis of their teeth. In addition, aluminum has been connected to the rise in the incidence of Alzheimer's Disease, and since fluoride is a byproduct of aluminum manufacture, fluoridated water becomes a chief suspect.

A study conducted by toxicologist Dr. Phyllis Mullenix revealed that fluoride is responsible for lowering the IQs of children. Several days after Dr, Mullenix learned that her study had been approved for publication, her employer, the Forsythe Dental Center, fired her. Since then she has received no financing to continue her study.

As of early 2008, more than 1,250 medical and environmental health professionals have signed a petition that calls for an end to water fluoridation. Interested parties may also sign by visiting the website, FlourideAlert.org.

All of this may be part of the population control programs spoken of earlier, which are nothing short of genocide. The US has been complicit in these programs and its leadership took a dark turn three decades ago.

During his presidency in the late 1970s, Jimmy Carter commissioned the Global 2000 Report, whose findings targeted the population growth of non-white peoples as the source of most problems in the world. The report recommended eliminating at least two billion people in Third World nations by the year 2000.

Shortly after the report's publication, an AIDS epidemic began to claim lives in Africa. The official explanation for the plague was that the pathogen had been passed from green monkeys to humans either through sexual contact or by consuming the monkeys as food. To date, the AIDS plague has claimed millions of lives, mostly in Third World nations but also in the industrialized West.

A *Los Angeles Times* article in 1988 cast doubt that the AIDS virus originated with green monkeys. The piece demonstrated that the AIDS DNA was inconsistent with the DNA of those primates. In addition, the article maintained that the AIDS virus could not be found anywhere in nature. This raised suspicion that the virus was man-made.

The charge first found its way into print on July 4, 1984, when the *New Delhi Patriot* offered detailed evidence that AIDS was laboratory-created as a biological warfare agent. The piece quoted an anonymous US anthropologist that AIDS was genetically engineered at the US Army Biological Warfare lab in Fort Detrick, Maryland.

In January 1986, French biologists Jakob and Lilli Segal published a pamphlet, *AIDS: USA Home-Made Evil; Not Imported from Africa.* They reported that after examining the genes in the HIV retrovirus, it "could not have come about by a natural way known to biologists." They tagged the virus as a "chimera" that was created in Fort Detrick in 1977.

A Soviet journal repeated these charges a year later, and in October 1986, the *London Sunday Express* ran a front page story confirming the findings of the Indian and Soviet publications. This was repeated by the *London Times* in its 1987 front page article, "Smallpox Vaccine Triggered AIDS." The article established a direct correlation between the smallpox vaccine administered by the WHO to between 50 and 70 million people in several central African countries and the subsequent AIDS outbreaks there.

The AIDS plague is related to vaccination programs conducted worldwide by the WHO. Scientists who have studied the virus and believe it was man-made all note that HIV has structural similarities to visna virus, a pathogen found in sheep. These scientists believe the visna virus was combined artificially with HTLV-I virus, another pathogen that causes human lymphoma, the cancer that attacks white blood cells.

Scientists also speak of the possibility that, in developing bioweapons and vaccines to combat them, some day this could lead to discovering an agent that boosts the human immune system to a point that it becomes thoroughly disease resistant.

Robert Booth Nichols, an international businessman who worked with US military and intelligence branches, considered this possibility in his unpublished manuscript, *Acceptable Casualty.* In it he posed the dilemma of releasing such a marvelous discovery to a world already facing overpopulation. He guessed that it would be withheld and granted only to the few elite who were needed to run the world.

Nichols reportedly died in Geneva, Switzerland, on St. Valentine's Day 2009 of a heart attack, but there were reports that he exhibited a blow to the head. Verification of this became impossible after the quick cremation of Nichols' body, arranged by a New York stockbroker "friend" who reportedly had been helping him move a large sum of cash, bonds and gold.

All of the aspects of population control through genocide harken back to the Georgia Guidestones, a huge granite monument erected in that state's Elbert County in 1980. A message engraved in eight different languages on the four stone supports of the capstone contains 10 "Guides" or commandments. They call for a number of globalist changes like a world court, a new world religion and a single world language.

But most chilling is the statement, "Maintain humanity under 500,000,000 in perpetual balance with nature." Mixed with a number of Masonic symbols, this call for reducing the world's human population to a small percentage of the present number is nothing short of a desire for mass extermination.

No one knows who financed this "American Stonehenge." The only certainty is that a man calling himself R.C. Christian in June 1979 hired the Elberton Granite Finishing Company to build an edifice with a message to mankind. It is clear now that he used an alias, but he said he represented a group of men who wanted to offer direction to humanity.

That the monument cost millions of dollars makes it clear that this group of men were wealthy globalists in the vein of the Rockefellers, Rothschilds, Harrimans and other elite families that have donated billions of dollars to radical eugenics and population control organizations.

Exterminating 6,500,000,000 people is a tall order, but instituting a mandatory vaccination that contains a deadly virus would do the trick.

SEVENTH MOVEMENT – *BATTAGLIA* WAR AND REVOLUTION

"We are not going to achieve a New World Order without paying for it in blood as well as words and money."

—Arthur Schlesinger Jr., US historian

The Business of War

In his excellent script for the movie *Patton,* Francis Ford Coppola quoted the outspoken general when he observed his army pouring into Germany: "Compared to war, all other forms of human endeavor shrink to insignificance." He was quite correct, and he might also have said that compared to war, all other business shrinks to insignificance.

When nations go to war, they must borrow enormous sums of money from international banks at high interest in order to field armies and equip them. Then they spend this borrowed money with its high-interest tag on munitions. The munitions companies often are run by the very same groups of men who lent the money to governments in the first place. In other words, they get their money right back by selling munitions at vastly inflated prices for great profits, and the governments still are required to pay them that same amount of borrowed money, plus the interest.

It's not difficult to realize then, that warfare is a tremendous boon to the small cabal of men who control the banks and the munitions factories. Since many of these men are members in secret societies like the CFR and Bilderbergers, and clearly have great influence on the policies of governments, is it not in their interests to promulgate warfare?

Armed conflict has many advantages for a small ruling class that wishes to increase its power and wealth, in addition to the enormous profits realized. War is a control system. The Report from Iron Mountain cited earlier in this book flatly states that war is the supreme social organizing force. It allows governments to impose new laws that reduce personal freedom with the acceptance of the population which feels that all citizens, rich and poor, are in an emergency situation. This creates a false sense of bonding between the poor, the middle class and the oligarchy — a feeling that everyone is in this trouble together. It also creates the impression that these new, freedom-reducing enactments are temporary.

Americans need only look to the results of 9/11 and their acceptance of extraordinary governmental abilities to interfere in their lives through legislation like the Patriot Act. This was intended to be a temporary situation, but as the "War on Terror" completes its first full decade of existence, so does the Patriot Act. An intriguing story indicates that this could have been premeditated.

Film and TV producer Aaron Russo was welcomed into the sanctum of powerful oligarchs like Nicholas Rockefeller, owing to his great successes with the films *The Rose* and *Trading Places* and the TV series, *Wise Guys*. This was despite Russo's anti-globalist documentary, *Mad as Hell*.

Russo's friendship with the banking elite ended when Nicholas Rockefeller divulged certain plans nearly a year prior to 9/11. According to Russo, "He said to me one night, he said, 'There's going to be an event, Aaron, and after that event your [sic] going to see that we'll go into Afghanistan so we can throw in [oil] pipelines through the Caspian Sea. We're going to go into Iraq to take the oil and establish a base in the Middle East. And we're going to go into Venezuela and then get rid of Chavez.'"

Russo also claimed that Rockefeller predicted he'd see troops searching caves "looking for people they're never going to find," and added that "by having a war on terror you can never win it. It's an eternal war and you can always keep taking people's liberties away."

Russo claimed he asked Rockefeller how he intended to convince people it was a real war and he responded, "By the media." Russo said he then asked why, with so much money and power, would the elite want to hurt people and that Rockefeller responded, "What do you care about the people?"

Answering a question about what the ultimate goal of these plans might be, Russo claimed Rockefeller said, "The goal is to get everybody in this world chipped with an RFID chip," in order to track all financial transactions. Russo claimed Rockefeller added that in the cases of those who protest, "We'll just turn off their chip."

In an even more remarkable statement, former FBI senior special agent in charge of Los Angeles, Memphis and Dallas, Ted Gunderson, maintains that the CIA had actually organized some of the most heinous attacks that were portrayed as Muslim terrorism.

"Look at the terrorist acts that have occurred," he said. "The CIA is behind most if not all of them. You have the Marine barracks [in Beirut, Lebanon], our embassy in Kenya, you have Pan Am [Flight] 103 [which crashed in Lockerbee, Scotland, following an alleged bomb explosion]. We had the USS Cole. We had Oklahoma City. We had the World Trade

Center in 1993."

Gunderson said of the latter incident that a government-paid infiltrator of a terrorist cell, Emad Salem, reported to an unnamed FBI supervisor that he would place a dummy bomb in the World Trade tower, and that this supervisor said no, a real bomb would be planted instead. This was corroborated in an October 28, 1993 front page story in the *New York Times,* which reported that Salem was to have helped the plotters build a bomb using harmless powder.

Salem, a 43-year-old former Egyptian army officer, claimed an FBI supervisor told him to call off that plan because he had other ideas about how the infiltrator should be used. Salem's story is buttressed by the transcript taken from hundreds of hours of tape recordings he secretly made during his talks with law enforcement agents.

On February 26, 1993, the plotters successfully detonated their bomb, killing six US citizens and injuring more than 1,000 others. Damage to the World Trade tower came to more than $500 million.

Salem told the *Times* that he spoke with an FBI agent after the bombing, complaining that the unnamed supervisor "came and messed it up." Salem told agent John Anticev that he wanted to file a complaint about this with FBI Headquarters in Washington, but was dissuaded. According to Salem, Anticev said, "I don't think that the New York people would like the things out of the New York office to go to Washington DC."

What all of this means is that the FBI had full knowledge of the plot to bomb the WTC in 1993 and the capability to foil it, but chose not to do it. Gunderson added that, since the bombing killed "only" six people, it was "not enough to pass the [anti-terror] legislation," which came into effect after the Oklahoma City bombing that killed 168 people two years later. Gunderson investigated the Murrah building bombing and developed information that the truck bomb was not an ammonia nitrate fuel oil bomb as claimed in the official government report, but a highly classified weapon called an Electro-Hydro Dynamic gaseous fuel bomb. Developed in the early 1980s for the CIA by scientist Michael Riconsciuto, the device was manufactured in Salt Lake City by Dyna Nobel, a leading commercial explosives firm, according to Gunderson.

He also learned there were other bombs that hadn't exploded and were removed after the initial explosion blew the face off the Murrah building. This was corroborated in the September 1995 issue of *Firehouse Magazine,* which said four additional explosive devices had been removed.

On the day of the bombing, five Oklahoma City TV news station reporters on the scene all said that unexploded devices were removed from the debris after the initial explosion. One news reporter even claimed that one of the unexploded devices bore a US Army stencil. These statements were written off as a result of the confusion that day.

Gunderson claims he learned from a defense investigator that at least 11 other individuals besides Timothy McVeigh and Larry Nichols were involved in the bombing. Potentially important evidence that may have shed more light on the Oklahoma City bombing could not be gathered because the Murrah building was quickly destroyed.

If Gunderson is correct that these attacks were "false flag" actions intended to implicate terrorists, then it paints a frightening portrait. But it is not a new gambit. Our history is rife with examples of wars and revolutions instigated and manipulated to enrich a small elite and to increase their control.

The American Revolution

When Sir Francis Bacon, the 17th century scientist, politician and writer, finished his book *New Atlantis,* he refused to publish it until after his death in 1626. The book, which described a utopian social structure in a new land, probably revealed too many aspects of secret societies like the Freemasons and the Rosicrucian Order, to which Bacon belonged.

New Atlantis has been construed as Bacon's attempt to discuss the desirability of creating an "ideal commonwealth" in the colonizing land of America. As the book hints that this ideal commonwealth has been the goal of secret societies like the Freemasons for thousands of years, it is clear why Bacon wished to keep it under wraps until after he died of pneumonia. But seen in the light of a Masonic plan for America, *New Atlantis* would have its prediction come true in the next century.

Many of the men who made the American Revolution were Freemasons. These included Benjamin Franklin, who was grandmaster of the Philadelphia lodge as early as 1734, George Washington, Thomas Jefferson, Alexander Hamilton, Ethan Allen, James Madison, John Hancock, Paul Revere and Patrick Henry. Also, a large segment of the officers in the Continental Army were Freemasons.

Many of the inciting incidents leading to the revolution were either instigated or performed by Masons. The Boston Tea Party was the work of men belonging to St. John's Lodge, according to *A New Encyclopedia of Freemasonry.*

In 1764, Britain forbade its colonies to continue printing Colonial Scrip — paper money printed free of interest and not backed by gold or silver — demanding instead that settlers use notes printed by the Bank of England, which charged interest. In the wake of four costly wars, Britain was deeply indebted to this privately held bank and needed money from its colonies to help pay the interest on its loans.

The 1764 Currency Act passed by Parliament not only ordered the colonies to cease printing Colonial Scrip, it decreed that all future taxes must be paid in gold and silver coin. In just one year, putting America on a gold standard resulted in economic depression and set the colonies on a path toward rebellion.

According to Benjamin Franklin, it was not taxation but this law that caused the revolution. "The colonies would gladly have borne the little tax on tea and other matters had not it been that England took away from the colonies their money, which created unemployment and dissatisfaction," wrote Franklin. "The inability of the colonists to get power to issue their own money permanently out of the hands of George III and the international bankers was the prime reason for the Revolutionary War."

When the first shots were fired in 1775 at Lexington, Massachusetts, the colonies were all but drained of gold and silver coin and had to return to printed money. At the outset of the war, the colonial money supply totaled just $12 million. By the war's end, the supply had ballooned to almost $500 million, making the currency virtually worthless. Inflation had hiked prices to a point where a pair of shoes cost $5,000. George Washington complained, "A wagon load of money will scarcely purchase a wagon load of provisions."

Before the fighting started, rebellious-minded settlers formed secretive groups. The backlash in New England was led by the Freemasons, who flocked to the Sons of Liberty and Samuel Adams' other organization, the Committees of Correspondence. They boycotted British goods and perpetrated violence.

When England instituted the Stamp Act in 1765, Boston Freemasons, along with merchants, formed a group called the Loyal Nine, which organized a large popular demonstration march that ended in the effigy burning of the local stamp master. The organized march disintegrated into an angry mob that destroyed property.

It is no coincidence that the source of trouble between England and her colonies, printed money, was resolved in victory when the new United States could print its own dollars, and that these dollars were rich in Masonic symbols. On the reverse side of the modern $1 bill there is a pyramid missing its capstone beneath the "All Seeing Eye." Both are well-known Masonic symbols. Every bill also contains the Latin inscription, *Novus Ordo Seclorum,* meaning New World Order.

Similarly, the Great Seal of the United States contains Masonic imagery, almost certainly because its designer, Charles Thompson, was a Freemason. Author William Bramley claims that this seal originally featured a Phoenix rising from its own ashes, which the Freemasons commonly used as one of their many references to ancient Egypt. This myth was not well-known to Americans of the early 19th century, who mistook the Phoenix for a turkey, and so the bird was replaced by the bald eagle in 1841, according to Bramley.

The Masonic influence on America clearly can be seen by the number of presidents who were high degree members: Washington, Monroe, Jackson, Polk, Buchanan, Andrew Johnson, Garfield, Taft, Harding, Teddy and Franklin Roosevelt, Truman, Ford and Bush Sr. Other post-revolutionary Masons who gained power or fame include Sam Houston, Jim Bowie, Davy Crockett, Douglas MacArthur and J. Edgar Hoover.

Since so many Freemasons held power in the US, it stands to reason that the Illuminized Masonic plan for a New World Order was in play. And this plan took its greatest steps toward realization through another more vicious conflict.

The American Civil War

The fierce division between North and South in the mid 19th Century clearly was heading toward conflict. Knowing this, a meeting in London of the International Banking Syndicate concocted a strategy of divide and conquer.

A war would force the federal government to spend vast sums of money, therefore borrowing at interest and creating debt. The plan further had provisions for a possible Southern victory and independence, in which case, individual Southern states would receive their own European-controlled banks. These states in turn could be instigated into wars with one another, creating more loans and debt.

It was nothing short of a roadmap for fracturing, fragmenting and destroying the United States through the chaos of war. From his perch in the Prussian chancellorship, Otto von Bismarck saw the plot clearly: "The division of the United States into federations of equal force was decided long before the Civil War by the high financial powers of Europe. These bankers were afraid that the United States, if they remained in one block and as one nation, would attain economic and financial independence, which would upset their financial domination of the world. The voice of the Rothschilds prevailed."

American businesses, North and South, had been penetrated by the Rothschilds well before the Civil War. Nathan Rothschild purchased major cotton exports from the South for his English textile business. At the same time, he made loans to several states in the North and for a time was an official banker of the US government.

The complete story of Rothschild complicity in the start and prosecution of the Civil War never will be known, because the private family correspondence between 1854 and 1860, especially those letters emanating from London, is missing. According to Rothschild biographer Niall Ferguson, the letters deliberately were destroyed by subsequent senior partners in the family firm in London.

In any case, it is clear that the foreign bankers took advantage of the economic friction between the North and South. The Southern businessmen rankled at the stiff tariffs on European imports that were imposed by Congress at the behest of Northern manufacturers. European businesses retaliated by ceasing to import cotton from the South, which heightened the economic hardships there. When the Southern states seceded, a federal naval blockade strangled all Confederate imports and exports.

Seven years before the opening guns fired on Fort Sumter, a surgeon and writer named Dr. George Bickley founded the first chapter of the Knights of the Golden Circle (KGC) in Cincinnati, Ohio. Comprising mostly local Freemasons, the society patterned itself on Masonic lodges in its organization and its rituals. Initiates were sworn to secrecy.

Bickley's dream was to found a circular empire encompassing the southern US, Cuba, Mexico, Central America and the West Indies. His "Golden Circle" would be a bastion of slave labor to create a monopoly on cotton, tobacco, sugar, coffee and rice production.

Financial support for the KGC came from the American Colonization and Steamship Company in Veracruz, Mexico, which was capitalized for $5 million despite the fact that Bickley had no visible personal fortune. Who were Bickley's benefactors?

Bickley's ties to England are undeniable. He claimed to be a University of London graduate and after the Civil War he lectured in England. But by 1860, he had made remarkable progress in building the KGC society to a membership of more than 65,000 "Knights."

The KGC by this time was headquartered in San Antonio, Texas, where Bickley hoped soon to march his Knights into Mexico. But, he said, if Abraham Lincoln were to win the 1860 presidential election, he would order a march on Washington instead.

Bickley's Knights actually made two abortive invasions of Mexico that spring. Each failed miserably when Bickley didn't send reinforcements and supplies. The following year, with the beginning of the Civil War, Bickley's Knights passed into the Confederate Army as an organizing command force.

He also had plans to create a Northern Confederacy by utilizing his Knights in Michigan, Ohio, Indiana, Minnesota and Illinois (which boasted an amazing 20,000 KGC members) to seize federal arsenals and take control. The state governments took the threat seriously enough to indict 60 KGC members in Indiana for treason. Although they were eventually released, the federal government was thereafter attentive to KGC plots.

President Abraham Lincoln during the Civil War enacted all the emergency powers available to his office in the US Constitution, including the suspension of *habeas corpus.* In the course of the war, more than 13,000 citizens — businessmen, local politicians, newspaper editors — went to prison without trial on charges of treason or simple "disloyalty." Lincoln's political opponents accused him of using the KGC threat as an excuse to create a dictatorship.

The emergency legal statutes finally ensnared Bickley in 1863, when he was arrested on charges of spying in Indiana. He was released only after the war's end in 1865 and died two years later. But the KGC lived on after the war, going underground as the Ku Klux Klan.

When the Civil War began, France and England were quick to see opportunities for renewing their power in North America. Britain sent an additional 11,000 troops to Canada, positioning them along America's northern border, and Canada became a hotbed of Confederate agents. The British fleet went on alert, in case it would have to quickly intervene.

Napoleon III of France, after receiving a loan of 210 million francs from the central bankers of Europe, sent a French army to Mexico, and installed a puppet, Archduke Maximilian of Austria, as emperor. Maximilian promptly arranged for transportation of vital supplies to the Confederacy through Texas, circumventing the federal blockade.

French and British troops stationed on the northern and southern borders of the US were ready to move when the warring sides exhausted themselves. The central bankers of Europe hoped that a weakened America would allow them to circumvent the Monroe Doctrine and reopen the Central and South American territories to be looted by them.

Lincoln parried this threat in a piece of political genius, issuing the Emancipation Proclamation on January 1, 1863. The document, which declared all slaves in the Confederacy to be free men, cut the legs from beneath the British and French interests by making slavery the central issue of the war. The populations of both countries were fiercely opposed to slavery, that institution having been abolished in France and England nearly three decades earlier.

But the danger still existed that the governments of France and England might diplomatically recognize the Confederate government and attempt to ship supplies through the Union blockade. It was one of several schemes the two countries had plotted against other nations, and one of the plots — instigating a war that would allow them to divide up the Russian empire — came to the ears of Czar Alexander II.

Already a supporter of the Union cause in the Civil War, Alexander sent two Russian fleets to the United States in late 1863 — one anchored off Virginia and the other moored in San Francisco harbor — to threaten any French or British naval intervention. Britain and France remained neutral.

In the meantime, prosecution of the war created the necessity to impose the first income tax in American history. By 1862, there was a five percent tax on all income of more than $10,000. But this would prove insufficient to meet the spectacular costs of the war, so in 1862 Lincoln instructed the US Treasury to print paper money. The Treasury did this without charging interest, Lincoln stating that government "need not and should not borrow capital at interest."

An estimate made much later in 1910 put the total cost of the American Civil War at an incredible $12 billion, a figure that would amount to many trillions in modern terms. The federal government at first sought to borrow from the European bankers, who, sensing their opportunity to ruin America, charged outrageous interest fees of between 24 and 36 percent. Lincoln refused to borrow under such extreme conditions, and instead tabbed Colonel Dick Taylor of Chicago to take charge of financing the war.

Taylor advised Lincoln to induce Congress to pass a bill authorizing the treasury to print its own legal tender in notes that would pay the military. Lincoln's concern over whether Americans would accept the new money was quelled by Taylor, who told him, "The people or anyone else will not have any choice in the matter, if you make them full legal tender. They will have the full sanction of the government and be just as good as any money, as Congress is given that express right by the Constitution."

In 1862 and 1863, the US Treasury printed $450 million worth of the new money, and to distinguish it from other bills, green ink was used on the back side, causing them to be called "greenbacks." These bills went into circulation without any need for the government to pay interest.

Lincoln explained his reasoning to Congress, saying, "The government should create, issue and circulate all the currency and credit needed to satisfy the spending power of the government and the buying power of consumers. The privilege of creating and issuing money is not only the supreme prerogative of government, but it is the government's greatest creative opportunity. By the adoption of these principals...the taxpayers will be saved immense sums of interest. Money will cease to be master and become the servant of humanity."

The *London Times* quickly spouted the central bankers' viewpoint in an editorial: "If this mischievous financial policy, which has its origin in North America, shall become endurated down to a fixture, then that government will furnish its own money without cost. It will pay off debts and be without debt. It will have all the money necessary to carry on its commerce. It will become prosperous without precedent in the history of the world. The brains and wealth of all countries will go to North America. That country must be destroyed, or it will destroy every monarchy on the globe."

Several authors have claimed that Lincoln may have been assassinated because of his bold monetary policy. The man who murdered him, John Wilkes Booth, was a famous actor who was known to have joined the foreign-funded KGC.

Theorists also point to a possible connection between Booth and Confederate Secretary of State Judah P. Benjamin, who had established relations with the House of Rothschild to finance the Southern states. The Rothschilds and other European bankers certainly saw Lincoln's policy of creating interest-free capital as a catastrophe.

"Greenbacks," however, were not sufficient to fully finance the tremendous cost of the Civil War. In 1863, with the war reaching its turning point, Lincoln allowed the bankers to establish the National Banking Act, in which banks could operate free of taxation while creating the new "greenbacks" bank notes.

After this, the entire US money supply was created from debt by bankers who bought US Government Bonds to issue them as reserves for bank notes. Treasury Secretary Salmon P. Chase later bemoaned his role in creating this situation: "My agency in promoting the passage of the National Banking Act was the greatest financial mistake in my life. It has built up a monopoly which affects every interest in the country."

Rothschild agent August Belmont took advantage of the situation by financing both the North and South. He convinced European bankers to buy federal bonds while he bought Southern bank bonds at knockdown prices, gambling that the South would have to honor them at higher prices following the war. In 1863, the *Chicago Tribune* attacked Belmont, the Rothschilds, "and the whole tribe of Jews," for buying Confederate bonds.

Salomon Rothschild actually came to America at the beginning of the war. Clearly pro-Confederate, he criticized Lincoln for being "uncompromising." Rothschild almost certainly referred to Lincoln's refusal to borrow at interest rather than his uncompromising policy of maintaining the Union.

But maintain the Union he did, and for that Lincoln was murdered immediately after the war ended. Otto von Bismarck in Germany understood the implications, and wrote, "The death of Lincoln was a disaster for Christendom....I fear that foreign bankers, with their craftiness and tortuous tricks will entirely control the exuberant riches of America, and use it systematically to corrupt modern civilization. They will not hesitate to plunge the whole of Christendom into wars and chaos in order that the earth should become their inheritance."

The subsequent investigation of the Lincoln assassination revealed a complicated plot that included smuggling and kidnapping by agents of the KGC with overseas financing. The trail led to KGC and British agents in Canada.

Booth could not enlighten the investigators, because he'd been shot and killed by federal troops. Four additional conspirators from Baltimore — one of them having wounded Secretary of State William Seward and another having lost his nerve to assassinate Vice President Andrew Johnson — were hanged. The plot clearly intended to behead the entire US executive branch.

Allegations that international bankers were behind the Lincoln assassination emerged 70 years later in Canada when in 1934, Vancouver attorney Gerald Grattan McGeer presented evidence to the House of Commons Committee on Banking and Commerce. McGeer studied the unexpurgated testimony of secret service agents during the posthumous Booth trial, which had been deleted from the public record, and concluded, "The evidence discloses that, instead of being a patriot, John Wilkes Booth...was a mercenary."

McGeer offered evidence that the plot to murder Lincoln originated in Montreal and Toronto, where, "a group of men representing the Confederacy were operating in Canada with headquarters in those cities. During the winter of 1864 and 1865, they were approached by an unknown group with a proposition to assassinate Lincoln. They [the unknown group] were not from the South nor connected with the Southern government, because representatives of the South in Canada hesitated to consider the proposal until it had been submitted to the South for approval. Booth was engaged to organize the assassination."

Although the instigators of the murder were unknown, McGeer revealed that "they were described as a group which could undertake anything without regard to cost." One of Booth's co-conspirators did indeed return from Canada with "plenty of gold." This and other evidence convinced McGeer that the plotters were "the men opposed to [Lincoln's] national currency program, and who had fought him throughout the whole Civil War on his policy of greenback currency. They were the men interested in the establishment of the gold standard system and the right of bankers to manage the currency and credit of every nation in the world. With Lincoln out of the way, they were able to proceed with that plan, and did proceed with it in the United States. Within eight years of Lincoln's assassination, silver was demonetized and the gold standard money system set up in the United States."

The international bankers at this time controlled much of the world's gold, while silver was plentiful in the US.

It is one of history's great curiosities that so many aspects of Lincoln's assassination are identical to the assassination of John Kennedy. Both men had made many powerful enemies who certainly had the means to murder them by subtle methods like poisoning. This, after all, was a time-tested and safe way to achieve regime change.

But Lincoln and Kennedy were publicly executed while in office, as if to send a message. The fact that both men are the only presidents to have ordered the US Treasury to create money at no interest may be a clue as to where the message originated.

The result of the Civil War was a failure for the European bankers' ambitions, however. More than 600,000 Americans had died, but the nation was undivided and suddenly a world power. No foreign-controlled central bank had been established. The country was not deeply indebted to foreign bankers.

But the foreign bankers would continue to try. Almost exactly one year after Lincoln's murder, Congress passed the Contraction Act, authorizing the Treasury Department to begin removing greenbacks from circulation, thereby contracting the money supply. While no direct connection between the passage of this act and the influence of international bankers has come to light, it is clear that it benefited them tremendously.

By 1876, two-thirds of America's money supply had been called in by the bankers. The tightening of money produced hardship in the South and a series of money panics in the North. This pressured Congress eventually to put the US banking system under centralized control.

World War I

For many years prior to the outbreak of hostilities in the First World War, the major European nations were locked in an arms race, particularly the German and British navies. German policy had moved to an aggressive quest for colonies, grabbing lands in Africa, the Pacific and China. Kaiser Wilhelm II, long an admirer of the British navy, decided that Germany would need a large naval force to protect its new colonies, so he embarked on a campaign of dreadnought construction.

The dreadnought was considered the ultimate naval weapon at the turn of the 20th century. Its all-steel construction and greater speed than the previous generation of battleships made it a necessary centerpiece for any true naval power. It also made it very expensive. In order to keep a two-to-one ratio against Germany, Britain began an aggressive dreadnought-building program of its own.

All of this was good news to the central banks in Europe, as kings and parliaments approved taking on large loans at interest. It was clear to the Rothschild bankers that these loans would escalate to historic levels once the debtor nations began using these new arms in warfare.

To prepare for this in America, President Wilson named Wall Street financier Bernard Baruch to head the War Industries Board, a position which netted him and the Rockefellers more than $200 million in war profits, according to author James Perloff.

When the shooting started, business boomed. The DuPont company, owing to its gunpowder manufacture, saw profits soar from $6 million in 1914 to $58 million by the war's end. U.S. Steel's yearly earnings went from $105 million annually before the war to $240 million annually between 1914 and 1918. One of the most astonishing profit increases, more than 7,200 percent, was enjoyed by the International Nickel Company, which soared from $4 million annually to $73.5 million.

With national treasuries footing the bill for this boon, the belligerent nations faced bankruptcy. England and France would be ruined if Germany won, which seemed to be probable during the first two years of war.

The Great War simply had no benefit to anyone, except for a

handful of bankers and industrialists. But surprisingly, as early as 1909 in the United States, there was a scheme to get the country into a war. That year the trustees for the Andrew Carnegie Foundation's Endowment for International Peace met to discuss America's changing social structure.

Among the trustees was the former president of the foundation and ex-Skull and Bones member, Daniel Gilman. He had a good deal of influence on the conclusion reached during the meeting that war is the most effective means of altering the life of an entire people. Since Americans were stringently isolationist at that time, the trustees asked, according to one researcher, "How do we involve the United States in a war?"

When war broke out in Europe, the French Rothschild bank floated a $100 million loan to Morgan and Company in New York, most of which paid for purchases of American goods by France. J.P. Morgan Jr. handled the loan as the new head of the Morgan empire, following his father's death in 1913. He became President Wilson's choice as chief purchasing agent for the United States, rewarding the younger Morgan for his help — along with bankers Jacob Schiff, Cleveland Dodge and Bernard Baruch — in getting Wilson elected. Morgan added this new portfolio to his positions as sole purchasing agent for Canada, Britain, France, Russia and Italy.

As the war continued, his positions allowed Morgan to oversee transfers of unprecedented monies, including more than $3 billion from the Entente powers to purchase American supplies. Morgan also gathered together more than 2,000 American banks to underwrite over $1.5 billion in Allied bonds.

As noted, Wilson rewarded Bernard Baruch's political and financial support by giving him charge of the War Industries Board, allowing him to control all domestic munitions contracts.

America managed to stay out of the European conflict that began in 1914. During the presidential election campaign of 1916, Woodrow Wilson ran on the slogan, "He kept us out of the war."

Five months after his inauguration, following a narrow re-election victory, Wilson asked Congress to declare war on the Central Powers and Americans headed for the front in France.

In his book, *None Dare Call It Conspiracy,* Gary Allen places the blame for America's involvement squarely on the vested interests: "The same crowd which manipulated the passage of the income tax and the Federal Reserve System wanted America in the war. J.P. Morgan, John

D. Rockefeller, 'Colonel' House, Jacob Schiff, Paul Warburg and the rest of the Jekyll Island conspirators were all deeply involved."

If the terms of a secret agreement reached in March 1916, eight months before the presidential election, are true, Wilson never intended to keep his campaign promise to maintain American neutrality. According to a German sympathizer named George Viereck, Wilson advisor Colonel House arranged the president's agreement to put America into the war on the Allied side. After the war, the text of this agreement was leaked by Sir Edward Gray, with subsequent corroboration by US Ambassador Walter Hines Page and Colonel House himself.

At this point, the vested interests only needed to change the isolationist attitude of the American public. They owned or controlled the instrument to do this: America's newspapers. The Congressional Record of 1917 states, "In March 1915, the J.P. Morgan interests...got together 12 men high up in the newspaper world and employed them to select the most influential newspapers in the United States...to control generally the policy of the daily press...They found it was only necessary to purchase the control of 25 of the greatest papers. An agreement was reached; the policy of the papers was bought, to be paid for by the month; an editor was furnished for each paper to properly supervise and edit information regarding the questions of preparedness, militarism, financial policies and other things of national and international nature considered vital to the interests of the purchasers."

The enormous purchasing power of the Rockefeller-Morgan advertising dollars kept the papers not directly under their control from publishing isolationist articles. Also, these interests occasionally paid newspapers not to publish such stories.

The initial attempt by newspapers to inflame the American public for war occurred in May 1915, when a German submarine sank the British liner *Lusitania,* drowning 128 US citizens. The press campaign was nearly hysterical and set off a wave of anti-German feeling in America, but it failed to galvanize the populace for a European war.

Later it would be learned that the *Lusitania,* far from being just a passenger liner, was carrying 600 tons of gun cotton explosive, 1,248 cases of artillery shells and six million rounds of small arms ammunition. There is little doubt, based on the evidence, President Wilson knew of this cargo. Despite this, Germany temporarily suspended its unrestricted submarine warfare so as not to antagonize America.

The tripwire that finally nudged the American public into war fever was the Zimmerman Telegram, which was intercepted by British cryptographers, decoded, and presented to the US Ambassador. On March 1, 1917, American newspapers revealed the story to the public.

It involved a note from German Foreign Secretary Arthur Zimmerman to the German ambassador in Mexico, authorizing him to advise Mexican President Venustiano Carranza that Germany was about to resume unrestricted submarine warfare. The note added that, in the event this led to war with the US, Germany was willing to ally with Mexico and Japan, and promised Mexico the return of its lost territories of Texas, Arizona and New Mexico.

Although Japan and Mexico were at odds with America at this time — a US military force had invaded Mexico in pursuit of Pancho Villa, and Japan still smarted over the American-brokered peace that ended its victorious 1905 war with Russia — there was no realistic danger that the two nations would jump at the German offer. But the effect on the American public was electric.

America officially declared war on April 6, 1917. Slightly more than a week later, Congress passed the War Loan Act authorizing $1 billion in credit to the drained banks of Britain and France. The total expenditure by the United States in World War I came to a staggering sum. Combined with the much lower amount of paper money circulating in America, this caused the dollar to sink to about half of its prewar worth. The war had created a tremendous debt, much to the pleasure of those institutions that received interest on that debt.

After the Armistice in November 1918, the victorious Allies gathered at Versailles to dictate the peace terms. Representing the US banking interests there was Paul Warburg, chairman of the Federal Reserve System. Representing the banking interests of Germany was Warburg's brother, Max.

Nearly every signatory of the peace treaty secretly believed it would lead to another war, and so promises of demilitarization lasted only a few years before all the belligerent nations began to rearm themselves.

The international bankers took advantage of the war weariness resulting from the global conflict they helped to create by centralizing. Claiming to seek means that would insure peace in the future, the bankers pushed for an international world government propped up by a central bank they called the Bank for International Settlements. They also strove for a World Court, located in The Hague, and a world executive called the League of Nations.

Carroll Quigley in his book, *Tragedy and Hope,* revealed the bankers' true intentions: "The powers of financial capitalism had [a] far-reaching [plan], nothing less than to create a world system of financial control in private hands able to dominate the political system of each country and the economy of the world as a whole. This system was to be controlled in a feudalistic fashion by the central banks of the world acting in concert, by secret agreements arrived at in frequent meetings and conferences. The apex of the system was to be the Bank for International Settlements in Basel, Switzerland, a private bank owned and controlled by the world's central banks which were themselves private corporations. Each central bank...sought to dominate its government by its ability to control treasury loans, to manipulate foreign exchanges, to influence the level of economic activity in the country, and to influence cooperative politicians by subsequent economic rewards in the business world."

These plans were dashed when the US, thanks to senators like Henry Cabot Lodge, refused to participate. Congress voted against US membership in the new League of Nations, dooming it to failure. But despite America's official position to avoid participating in the Bank for International Settlements, the Federal Reserve sent representatives to this institution in Basel. These men actively took part in meetings until the US officially became a member in 1994, when it had become the World Bank.

Following World War I, it would take another war to pull the US into full participation in the globalist agenda, but in 1944 at a meeting in New Hampshire, the International Monetary Fund and the World Bank came into being with American approval. A year later, the League of Nations was resurrected as the United Nations, this time with committed US membership.

The Russian Revolution

It is well known that during its war with Czarist Russia in 1914-17, Germany did many things to instigate a revolution in St. Petersburg that would knock its Eastern enemy out of the conflict. Russia already had been a cauldron of revolutionary activity for decades, owing to the cruel dictatorship of the czars and the chronic famines that starved the populace.

In 1905, this fervor produced a widespread revolution and general strike immediately following the ignominious defeat of the Czarist military forces by Japan. The revolution was brutally put down, but its currents remained strong in Russian society.

When war came with Germany, Russia shocked the Kaiser's High Command by mobilizing an enormous army quickly and invading German-held territory in Poland. The German military had counted on a quick victory in the West before having to deal with a second front, so the early Russian victories in August 1914 were a potential catastrophe. The German government wasted little time in siphoning aid to Russia's revolutionaries, and actually transported Vladimir Lenin by train from his exile in Switzerland to his Russian homeland.

What is not well known are the many instances in which certain influential men of the United States and Great Britain also aided the successful Bolshevik Revolution. Aside from the profit motive, the bankers of Britain never forgot how Russia's monarchy had intervened on the side of Abraham Lincoln and the North during the American Civil War. Russia also was the last major European nation to hold out against establishing its own privately owned central bank.

For these reasons, international bankers actively aided Bolshevik revolutionaries. One of them, Leon Trotsky, lived in New York and worked as a reporter for *The New World* at the outset of 1917 with their financial help.

Trotsky's journey to New York bears attention. With the failure of the 1905 Revolution in Russia, Trotsky escaped to Paris, but his radical literary polemics proved too much for the French government. Police escorted him to the Spanish border, where he made his way to Madrid.

Police in that city arrested him but put him in a "first class cell," charging him a small fee. Later the authorities escorted him to Cadiz and finally Barcelona, where they put Trotsky and his family on a steamer bound for New York.

Arriving in America on January 13, 1917, Trotsky and his family moved into a well-appointed New York apartment, paid three months in advance, which contained a telephone and a refrigerator, rare luxuries at that time. He also admitted that his family occasionally traveled in a chauffeured limousine, all of this on a total savings of $310 that he possessed when he left France.

Trotsky met several Wall Street bankers who revealed they would be willing to finance a Russian revolution. Jacob Schiff was one of these bankers. His family had close connections with the German Rothschilds, and even lived with them at one time in Frankfurt. Jacob's grandson, John Schiff, revealed years later to the New York *Journal-American* newspaper that his grandfather donated an estimated $20 million toward the triumph of Bolshevism in Russia.

Elihu Root, who represented Paul Warburg with the law firm of Kuhn, Loeb & Company, contributed an additional $20 million to the communist cause in Russia, according to the Congressional Hearings on Russian Bonds (HJ 8714.U5) and the Congressional Record of September 2, 1919. The money came from the $100 million voted by Congress as a Special War Fund for Wilson, and Root took it to Russia with his Special War Mission.

Root was a charter member of the CFR. J.P. Morgan & Co. also sent millions of dollars in cash to the revolutionaries through Henry Davison, using the head of the Red Cross Mission to Russia, Colonel Raymond Robins, as the emissary.

Trotsky left New York for Russia on March 17, 1917, along with nearly 300 other communist revolutionaries, loaded with Wall Street funds. Just prior to sailing, he stated, "I am going back to Russia to overthrow the provisional government and stop the war with Germany."

This statement probably caused his internment, along with his funds and his cohorts, in Halifax, Nova Scotia, by a Canadian government that rightfully understood that a Russian withdrawal from the war would free German armies to be transferred to the Western Front. But Trotsky's New York sailing and arrest occurred just a short time before America declared war.

Less than a month after the arrest, British Prime Minister Lloyd

Battle Hymn

George ordered Trotsky released, based on President Wilson's demand as communicated by Colonel House to Sir William Wiseman, chief of the British Secret Service. The British prime minister clearly was frightened that the Trotsky affair would scotch the much-needed US entry into the war on the Allied side.

The Canadians still refused to free Trotsky. It took John D. Rockefeller's labor expert, Mackenzie King, to convince the Canadian government to release the revolutionary, who then continued to Russia with an American passport personally authorized by President Wilson at the behest of Rockefeller.

King's generous reward for his efforts was the top position in the Rockefeller Foundation Department of Industrial Research, and a $30,000-per-year salary at a time when the average annual American wage was well under $1,000. As to the Canadian agents who detained Trotsky, all were dismissed from service.

By the 1920s, the directors of the Federal Reserve Bank were funneling huge sums of money to the Bolshevik regime through an entity called the American International Corporation. As early as 1915, a familiar collection of American bankers and businessmen established the American International Corporation through various directors. These directors represented the Rothschilds, Rockefellers, DuPonts, Harrimans and even Federal Reserve bankers like Frank Vanderlip and George Herbert Walker, the father and grandfather of the two Bush presidents.

"In the Bolshevik Revolution," wrote author Gary Allen, "we have some of the world's richest and most powerful men financing a movement which claims its very existence is based on the concept of stripping of their wealth men like the Rothschilds, Rockefellers, Schiffs, Warburgs, Morgans, Harrimans and Milners. But obviously these men have no fear of international communism. It is only logical to assume that if they financed it and do not fear it, it must be because they control it."

Allen explained the apparent conundrum: "If one understands that the true nature of socialism is not a share-the-wealth program, but is in reality a method to consolidate and control the wealth, then the seeming paradox of super-rich men promoting socialism becomes no paradox at all. Instead, it becomes logical, even the perfect tool of power-seeking megalomaniacs. Communism, or more accurately, socialism, is not a movement of the downtrodden masses, but of the economic elite."

That the men most threatened by the goals of communism would

241

nurture it into existence also can be explained by the likelihood that Russia's industrial development would have rivaled that of the US and Western Europe if there had been no Bolshevik revolution. By financing its success, American and British magnates retarded Russian industrial growth tremendously, while the debt created by this financing permitted Wall Street bankers and investors to gain some control over what industrial development did take place.

Prior to the revolution, Russia already had become the world's top petroleum producer, surpassing the US. As early as 1900, the Caucasus oil fields produced more petroleum than the US, and two years later accounted for more than half of the world's oil.

But the 1917 revolution and its subsequent civil war in Russia obliterated its oil industry. By 1922, half the wells were idle and the remainder barely functioned due to lack of equipment. In short, the Russian Revolution essentially crushed the chief competition to the Rockefeller-owned Standard Oil Company. And through its loans to the Soviet Union, reportedly totaling $75 million, Standard eventually received a piece of its petroleum industry.

The Rockefeller-owned firm built an oil refinery in Russia in 1927, with the promise to refine 50 percent of the Caucasus oil production. And when Josef Stalin nationalized a large number of foreign investors' assets in 1935, he allowed the Standard Oil properties to continue unmolested.

Noticing this, Congressman Louis McFadden commented, "The course of Russian history has, indeed, been greatly affected by the operations of international bankers....The Soviet government has been given United States Treasury funds by the Federal Reserve Board... acting through the Chase Bank. England has drawn money from us through the Federal Reserve banks and has re-lent it at high rates of interest to the Soviet government....The Dnieperstory Dam was built with funds unlawfully taken from the United States Treasury by the corrupt and dishonest Federal Reserve Board and the Federal Reserve banks."

Winston Churchill, no stranger to back room political intrigue, stated in 1920 that he saw the Russian Revolution as the greatest success of a plan that was more than a century in the making. He named 18th century Illuminati head, Adam Weishaupt, as the early culprit in a list that included Trotsky, Marx and other communists in a "worldwide conspiracy for the overthrow of civilization."

Churchill continued: "It played a definitely recognizable role in the tragedy of the French Revolution. It has been the mainspring of every subversive movement during the nineteenth century, and now at last this band of extraordinary personalities from the underworld of the great cities of Europe and America have gripped the Russian people by the hair of their heads, and have become practically the undisputed masters of that enormous empire."

Churchill was aware that British interests also participated in this "worldwide conspiracy," as Lord Alfred Milner of Cecil Rhodes' Round Table had contributed more than 12 million rubles to the Bolshevik cause.

Almost as soon as the Bolsheviks took control in St. Petersburg in November 1917, the British and American governments organized military expeditions to "liberate" Russia from communism. For several years following the successful overthrow of the Kerensky government, which succeeded the Czar, Russia was embroiled in a civil war between the White and Red Armies that would claim an estimated 28 million lives.

Capitalist nations financed the Whites, and sent troops to join its fight. It began a conflict between East and West that would last 70 years and continues in many ways to this day, causing both sides to borrow trillions at interest and spend that money on weaponry. In short, the success of Bolshevism birthed a new and lasting political force in the world — anti-communism. It also enriched and empowered the bankers and business oligarchs to new heights.

In aiding both the Bolsheviks and the czarist elements of Russia, the bankers remained true to the teachings of 19th century German philosopher Georg Hegel (1770-1831) and his "dialectic theory." Hegel's dialectic was a constant attempt to reconcile opposites, bringing them together as a systematic whole. He was influenced by another German philosopher of his time, Johann Gottlieb Fichte (1762-1814), who was a Freemason and apparently a member of the Illuminati as that group definitely supported his work.

When Karl Marx studied Hegel's treatises later in the 19th century, he applied them to the material and economic aspects of society. He used the Hegelian dialectic, reconciling thesis and antithesis to form a synthesis or compromise. To the bankrollers of the Bolshevik Revolution, this philosophy called for the success of a thesis (communism) to create an antithesis (anti-communism) among the capitalist nations, in order to have an open-ended conflict and produce enormous profits in arms and financial markets. The synthesis, exhaustion of both sides, theoretically would allow the powerful, unelected few to gain control through a one-world government.

This Hegelian dialectic, applied to the idea that social upheaval and war can be created and manipulated by a few powerful men for their benefit, could be the key to understanding history since the American Revolution.

As to the revolution in Russia, the Red Army claimed victory in the civil war by 1922. The Bolsheviks seemingly had full control of Russia. But after a short time as premier, Vladimir Lenin admitted the truth.

"The state does not function as we desired," he wrote. "A man is at the wheel and seems to lead it, but the car does not drive in the desired direction. It moves as another force wishes."

The Nazis

Is it possible that World War II was arranged by a few powerful men in secret societies like the Illuminati and Freemasons of Germany and Britain? Surprisingly, there is some evidence to support this radical theory, which flies in the face of the standard histories of the Second World War.

It's almost universally accepted that the Nazis are to blame for the outbreak of war in 1939, but the occult nature of Nazism is not well understood to this day. Winston Churchill was well aware of the black magic rites that many Nazi leaders practiced and he did his best to keep it from the general public. Airey Neave, one of the prosecutors at the Nuremberg post-war trials, stated that these occult practices were ruled inadmissible because there were fears that the information would produce unwanted psychological reactions among the victorious nations.

Adolf Hitler put the deeper nature of Nazism into perspective when he said, "Anyone who interprets National Socialism merely as a political movement knows almost nothing about it. It is more than religion; it is the determination to create a new man."

In many ways, Hitler himself was the created new man. He was formed by certain early members of the Nazi cult.

Following World War I, secret societies and political armies flourished in Germany. This period also witnessed the republication of a harmful tract that originally appeared in 1864 in France, *The Protocols of the Learned Elders of Zion*. Written anonymously by Maurice Joly, a French attorney and Rosicrucian, it was intended as satire on the aggressive policies of Napoleon III, who ruled France at the time. The satire didn't tickle Louis Bonaparte, who upon discovering its true author, sentenced Joly to a 15-month prison term.

About 30 years later, Joly's tract was rewritten with fiercely anti-Semitic material added, at the behest of the Russian Ochrana, secret police of the czar. It was published deliberately to coincide with the 1897 World Congress of Jewry in Basel, Switzerland, which was recognized as the first Zionist movement aimed at creating a Jewish homeland in Palestine.

The purpose of the *Protocols* was to cast blame upon Russia's revolutionaries, portraying them as puppets of an "international Jewish conspiracy." The tract claimed that a cabal of Freemasons and Jews were plotting together to create a one-world government with themselves at its head.

"We are the chosen," the tract states, "we are the only true men. Our minds give off the true power of the spirit; the intelligence of the rest of the world is merely instinctive and animal. They can see, but they cannot foresee...Does it not follow that nature herself has predestined us to dominate the whole world?"

The document lays out a plan to indebt governments by means of monetary loans and warns that if any state dares to resist this scheme, "we will unleash a world war." The document also speaks of controlling how the public thinks by controlling what they hear, and by creating new conflicts, spreading hunger and plague.

Essentially, it was a plagiarized version of Adam Weishaupt's list of plans for the Bavarian Illuminati of the previous century, only with international Jewry cast as the culprits. In all, there were 24 protocols in this version, which have a strong connection to the philosophies of Freemasonry. They read like step-by-step instructions for world domination by a few powerful individuals.

No one knows who authored this forged document purporting to be written by a Jewish cabal. Despite its shady origins, *The Protocols* was taken quite seriously by a number of influential men, including Czar Nicholas II, Kaiser Wilhelm II, and Henry Ford, who used the tract as ammunition in convincing the US Senate not to join the League of Nations.

The immediate result of the tract in Russia was a pogrom against Jews by a group calling itself "The Black Guard." The public unrest reached a peak with the 1905 insurrection and general strike, during which *The Protocols* played an important role in furthering czarist propaganda and paving the way for a brutal putdown of the revolt.

The effect of the document in Germany was summed up by author Konrad Heiden, who said, "Today the forgery is incontrovertibly proved, yet something infinitely significant has remained: a textbook of world domination."

This textbook became an important guide for the early Nazis, as well as a weapon to be used against German Jews. One of the guided was an Estonian Jew named Alfred Rosenberg, who read *The Protocols* in

1917 and then fled to Germany after the Bolshevik takeover that year.

In 1918, Rosenberg showed the book to Dietrich Eckart, a Munich publisher and poet. Eckart embraced the world domination aspect of the book and introduced Rosenberg to fellow members of the Thule Society, which was a front for a more secret group, the German Order. The name was taken from the mystical German homeland, Ultima Thule, and its logo was a sword and a swastika. Both organizations mixed occult beliefs with anti-Semitism.

The Thule and the German Order owed many of their tenets to the Theosophist movement created by a mystic from Russia named Helena Blavatsky, who founded her society in New York in 1875. Madame Blavatsky spread her ideas through books like *Isis Unveiled,* which attempted to present a pseudo-scientific aspect to religious mysteries. The movement also popularized Eastern religions like Buddhism and Hinduism in the West.

The Christian churches saw it as a threat that specifically targeted their teachings. Especially obnoxious was the Theosophist claim that a "Great White Brotherhood" secretly directs the evolution of mankind.

This marriage of alien intervention and racial superiority would later become the theological foundation of Nazi occultism. And in the years immediately following World War I, these beliefs merged with political action groups in hotbeds like Munich, which survived a communist coup to become a center for right wing anti-communist organizations.

The Thule Society, in particular, perpetuated the myth of an ancient German homeland on an island much like the Atlantis legend, populated once by a lost civilization of extraterrestrials that had interbred with humans to create a Master Race. Many of the Thule rituals were attempts to contact this lost race of superior aliens.

According to author Trevor Ravenscroft, the inner core members of the Thule Society were Satanists who practiced black magic. They were "solely concerned with raising their consciousness by means of rituals to an awareness of evil and non-human Intelligences in the Universe, and with achieving a means of communication with the Intelligences," Ravenscroft explained. He added that the "Master-Adept of this circle was Dietrich Eckart."

It was at this time that Eckart republished *The Protocols* and the book's message spread throughout Europe and into the US. Its circulation in Germany revived the long-held bias there against the Jews, blaming them for losing the war and conspiring to spread international communism, which had become a major political force.

The inflamed situation resulted in hundreds of unsolved political murders in Munich alone, most of the victims being Jews and communists. Ravenscroft claimed that these people were "sacrificial victims who were murdered in the rites of 'Astrological Magic' carried out by Dietrich Ekart and the innermost circle of the *Thule Gesellschaft.*"

It certainly was no coincidence that during the short-lived communist takeover of Munich in 1919, members of the Bavarian Soviet Republic leadership rounded up and executed Thule Society members such as Prince von Thurn und Taxis. Nor was it coincidental that the right wing *Freikorps* units who overthrew the communists by force wore the Thule swastika on their helmets.

After ousting the communists, a program of winning over the masses to the Thule political line, led in secret by Munich's business and military elite, was initiated in meetings at the Four Seasons Hotel, and a new organization was born — the German Workers' Party. Hoping for blue collar appeal, the Thule appointed a railroad machinist and a sportswriter to head the party. It grew along with the dissatisfaction of Germans toward the Weimar government in Berlin, and soon collected a militaristic arm of roughnecks, the Storm Troopers, led by war veteran Ernst Roehm.

Eckart, who became an early member of the German Workers Party, sought a leader. "We need a fellow at the head who can stand the sound of a machine gun," Eckart told a party gathering in 1919. "We can't use an officer because the people don't respect them anymore. The best would be a worker who knows how to talk."

This leader arrived as an infiltrator, sent by the German Army to spy on the new political party. His name was Adolf Hitler, a decorated corporal who served in the Great War on the Western Front.

According to author Ravenscroft, the young man already was steeped in occult mysticism from his destitute years in Vienna. "It was in the small back office of the bookshop in the old quarter of the city that Ernst Pretzsche unveiled for Hitler the secrets hidden behind the astrological and alchemical symbolism of the search for the Grail," Ravenscroft wrote. "It was here too that the sinister hunchback handed his monstrous pupil the drug which evoked the clairvoyant vision of the Aztecs, the magic Peyotl venerated like a deity."

Ravenscroft's book, *The Spear of Destiny,* speaks of young Hitler's fascination with the lance on exhibit in Vienna's Hofburg Museum, purported to be the spear that Roman soldier Longinus used to pierce the side of Jesus on the cross as an act of mercy. Hitler, according to Ravenscroft, believed the legend of the Holy Spear — that whoever possesses it controls the world.

The author claims this knowledge came to him through Dr. Walter Johannes Stein, who knew Hitler in Vienna. Stein told Ravenscroft that he saw Hitler channeling a non-human entity while next to the spear in a trance state. Many witnesses to Hitler's subsequent speeches would comment how he seemed to be in a trance state while making his addresses.

Another little-known influence upon Hitler during his Vienna days was a former Cistercian monk named Jorg Lanz von Liebenfels, publisher of the occult magazine, *Ostara.* Along with Guido von List, Liebenfels founded the Order of the New Templars, an anti-Semitic attempt at re-creating the medieval Teutonic Knights. List eventually had to flee Vienna when it was revealed that his secret order committed sexual perversions during its black magic rites. But the order's beliefs would be revived later in the Thule Society.

These Vienna influences produced a sea change in Hitler, previously raised as a Catholic who once had ambitions of becoming a priest. His new attitude is clear in a poem he wrote during the war while at the front lines in 1915. The poem talks of going "to Wotan's oak" armed with "dark powers" that make the impudent people of the day "small by the magic formula!"

While recovering from temporary blindness caused by a British gas attack in 1918, Hitler experienced a vision. His eyesight returned and he heard voices like St. Joan, according to author John Toland, urging him to save Germany. Hitler wrote of this experience later, saying it was a command he obeyed, which was why he'd entered politics.

During the short-lived Bavarian Soviet rule, Hitler was a double agent for the German Army. He spied upon the communists, posing as one of them. When the Army and *Freikorps* reclaimed Munich, Hitler can be seen in photos walking along the lines of communist captives, pointing out the leaders for execution.

His reward was an assignment to the Press and News Bureau of the army's Political Department, which was actually an intelligence outfit. His orders were to spy on various political groups to learn of revolutionary activities.

During his first meeting with the German Workers Party at the

Sterneckerbrau beer hall, Hitler actually made a speech criticizing a previous proposal that Bavaria secede from Germany. A few days later, he received a postcard informing him that he'd been accepted as a member.

Eckart quickly noticed that Hitler contained exactly the qualities he'd been seeking in a party leader. He introduced Hitler to influential members of Munich society as well as to his cohorts in the Thule Society.

On his deathbed in 1923, Eckart delivered this testament to the party members: "Follow Hitler! He will dance, but it is I who have called the tune. I have initiated him into the 'Secret Doctrine,' opened his centers in vision and given him the means to communicate with the Powers."

According to Ravenscroft the "Secret Doctrine" that Hitler received was a mixture of occultism, Eastern mysticism and the hidden history of man's origin by genetic manipulation, executed by non-human visitors long ago. The doctrine taught that the Aryans were among seven sub-races of humans during the time of Atlantis. With the destruction of this legendary land, the races scattered around the globe, their godlike attributes diminishing with time. Life spans shortened. Thought processes became locked into the physical senses, causing the loss of magical powers. These new creatures had to be taught again that everything on Earth is directed by invisible gods who demanded their total fealty and obedience. Many of these beliefs are evident in Hitler's *Mein Kampf,* where he speaks of mental abilities "slumbering" in humans.

Armed with his new beliefs and supported by important members of the Thule Society, Hitler soon gained control of the party, which in 1920 he renamed the National Socialist German Workers Party — the German language abbreviation being Nazi. Along with other party leaders, Hitler created the "Twenty-Five Points" of the Nazi platform that same year. Is it coincidental that this number is identical to the number of protocols in Adam Weishaupt's 18th century manifesto?

German businessmen, who viewed the Nazi party as highly preferable to communism, provided much needed financial aid. And by the time the Nazi popularity had crested with its disappointing showing in the 1932 elections, 39 business leaders, including Fritz Thyssen and Alfred Krupp, convinced President Paul von Hindenburg to appoint Hitler as chancellor.

This arrangement took place at the home of Baron Kurt von

Schroeder, a powerful banking magnate whose firm, J.H. Stein & Company, was represented by the New York law firm of Sullivan and Cromwell. Two of its lawyers, Allen Dulles and John Foster Dulles, were present at the Schroeder meeting that day, according to author Eustace Mullins. The Schroeder bank would continue its service to Nazi Germany for the remainder of the Third Reich, acting as its agent in Britain and the United States.

Another America-based bank, the Union Banking Corporation of New York, also financed Hitler during his rise to power and continued financing the Nazis during World War II. The bank maintained this arrangement until press reports exposed the firm as a money laundering outlet for German businessmen like Fritz Thyssen, who had a reported $3 million tucked away in the New York vaults. Soon afterward, the federal government seized all assets of Union Banking for violating the Trading with the Enemy Act.

At the time, the Union Banking director and vice president was Prescott Bush, father and grandfather to the two Bush presidents.

Hitler also received important early and steady financial support from the Deutsche Bank, the *Deutsche Kredit Gesellschaft* and the insurance company, *Allianz.* Despite Hitler's speeches on the evils of loans at interest and other banking practices, the bankers supported him and his party, knowing that he would not act on his verbal promises to the nation.

Hitler wasted no time in grabbing extraordinary powers within the democratic Weimar government. Just one week after being named chancellor, a fire erupted in the Reichstag under suspicious circumstances. Hitler was quick to blame the communists and convinced the Reichstag to pass the Enabling Act that gave the chancellor emergency powers and set in motion the transition from democracy to dictatorship.

Opposition parties, not just the communists, were squashed. Labor unions were abolished. The catchword, *Gleichschaltung,* basically meaning "line up," replaced the many individual freedoms that rapidly disappeared.

Once the Nazis had sufficient control of the civilian institutions, Hitler turned to the only other threat to his power, the German Army. He brokered a deal with the General Staff, who feared the growing power and continued socialist revolutionary ardor of Ernst Roehm's brown-shirted Storm Troopers. In June 1934, with the aid of Heinrich Himmler and the black-shirted SS, the Storm Troop leadership was purged, most of them by murder.

When President Hindenburg died on August 2, 1934, Hitler took the final steps in achieving total power, combining the offices of chancellor and president and assuming the official title of commander in chief of the military forces. At this point, Hitler's relationships with international businessmen and bankers deepened.

Henry Ford admired the German Fuehrer for both his anti-communist and anti-Semitic philosophies (Ford had published a viciously anti-Semitic book in 1920, *The International Jew,* which Hitler paraphrased often in *Mein Kampf*). In 1938, Hitler repaid Ford's generous financial support by awarding him the Grand Cross of the Supreme Order of the German Eagle.

Ford claimed to trace his theory that international Jewish bankers plotted to start wars for profit to a ship voyage to Europe in 1915 with the purpose of bringing a negotiated end to World War I. He maintained that Jewish passengers on the ship revealed to him that his peace initiative was hopeless unless he could win over certain Jewish bankers in France and Britain, obviously referring to the Rothschilds.

Another influential American who admired the Nazis was Joseph Kennedy, father of President John F. Kennedy. Formerly the US ambassador to England, Kennedy donated money to Germany as late as May 1941, after he'd met with Hermann Goering in Vichy, France. At this time, Germany already had been bombing Britain for a year, after conquering and occupying France, Denmark, Norway, Yugoslavia, Greece and Poland.

Well before the Nazi takeovers, the Rothschild-dominated Bank of England bailed out the German economy from a disastrous inflation in 1924. In a meeting between Hjalmar Schacht, the Reich commissioner for National Currency, and Montagu Norman, governor of the Bank of England, it was agreed that Norman's bank would donate half the money to begin a new German credit bank that would issue notes in pound sterling. Norman approved the loan at a low interest rate and convinced fellow London bankers to accept German bills that exceeded the loan.

When the Nazi experiment surprised its doubters by showing progress, Norman advised his bank directors to provide Hitler with covert financial aid until he could convince the British politicians to abandon their pro-French policy for a pro-German one.

At this time, Paul Warburg, who had helped to create the American

Federal Reserve Bank, and his brother Max directed the immense petro-chemical conglomerate, I.G. Farben. One of their I.G. Farben lieutenants, H.A. Metz, became director of the Warburg Bank of Manhattan, which later became a division of the Rockefeller Chase Manhattan Bank.

Another Rockefeller holding, Standard Oil of New Jersey, had partnered with I.G. Farben before the outbreak of World War II, and one of the German firm's American directors, C.E. Mitchell, also served as director of the Federal Reserve Bank of New York. In Germany, the president of I.G. Farben was Hermann Schmitz, who also sat on the boards of the Deutsche Bank and the Bank for International Settlements. By 1929, Schmitz became president of the board of National City Bank, now known as Citibank.

The interwoven relationships between bankers and businessmen across the Atlantic is perhaps demonstrated best by a claim that Schmitz once owned as much stock in Standard Oil of New Jersey as the Rockefellers. The reach of I.G. Farben spanned the Pacific as well, and Schmitz controlled 11 of the firm's subsidiary companies in Japan.

These relationships did not cease with the outbreak of war between Germany and America. The I.G. Farben Company in the US and the American I.G. Chemical Corporation continued business as usual and even became an important source of intelligence to the Nazis regarding US government and economic issues.

Hitler's fortunes began to sour in 1941, especially when he launched a mammoth invasion of Russia. Just six weeks prior to that, Rudolf Hess, then deputy leader of the Nazi Party, flew a plane to England in order to broker a peace. Hess was imprisoned, first in England and after the war in Spandau prison in Germany, where former Reich Minister of Armaments and War Production Albert Speer also served his sentence. According to Speer, Hess told him in Spandau that the idea of his flying to England on a peace mission "had been inspired in him in a dream by supernatural forces."

Upon news of Hess' flight and subsequent imprisonment in the Tower of London, Hitler publicly denounced him as mad. That Hitler may also have washed his hands of the occultist aspect of Nazi philosophy could be suggested in his comment to Speer, blaming the Hess flight on "the corrupting influence of Professor Haushofer," who had influenced Hess with his teachings of the "Secret Doctrine."

Another reason for Hitler to turn against Hess was that he feared his former colleague would reveal the imminent plan to invade Russia. In any case, Hitler outlawed occult practices like astrology, séances and secret groups like the Theosophical Society, the Order of the Golden Dawn and other "Freemason lodge-like Organizations." He said it was time to stop "these stargazers."

Although Hitler often was duplicitous regarding the occultists, publicly criticizing them while secretly inviting their guidance, he may truly have turned his back on this former support group in 1941, resulting in its hostility toward him. His fortunes certainly changed immediately after the schism.

World War II

During the 1940 presidential campaign, Franklin Roosevelt, as Wilson did before him, ran on the platform of keeping America out of the war in Europe. But his cabinet and advisory board, populated by CFR members, had already begun to plan for war the previous year.

The State Department actually allowed the CFR to handle long-range planning via five study groups, financed by the Rockefeller Foundation. In the course of the war, they bombarded the State Department with 682 memoranda. Known as the War and Peace Studies Project, the intent of the CFR became public with the official members' announcement in the press in 1940 that the US should immediately declare war on Germany.

Author James Perloff charges that the CFR simply wanted to exploit the Second World War as it had done in the Great War, to justify and create a one-world government. "The globalists hoped to use the Axis threat to force the US and England into a permanent Atlantic alliance — an intermediate step to world government," Perloff added.

The "isolationist impulse" of the American public won out until Japan attacked Pearl Harbor on December 7, 1941. Ever since the revelations in the 1970s that American intelligence had cracked and was reading the Japanese naval codes, suspicions and outright accusations have been made that Roosevelt had foreknowledge of the Pearl Harbor attack.

Among the smoking guns was Roosevelt's ordering of the Pacific Fleet to an exposed position in Hawaii, over the strenuous objections of Admiral James Richardson, who refused to obey the order and had to be sacked. Also, General George Marshall, an associate of several CFR members, sent a message to Pearl Harbor on November 27, 1941, warning that "Hostile action [is] possible at any moment," based on the sailing and disappearance of a large Japanese task force. Marshall's message added that, "If hostilities cannot, repeat CANNOT, be avoided, the United States desires that Japan commit the first overt act."

Late warnings from Australian intelligence reported the Japanese task force moving toward Pearl Harbor on December 4, which Roosevelt dismissed as a rumor. Other warnings from a wide variety of intelligence and political sources — including Winston Churchill — were not acted upon, and long after the war it was revealed that Marshall and Navy Secretary Frank Knox met with Roosevelt on the night of December 6, despite their denials.

Finally, the fortunate absence from Pearl Harbor of America's only two aircraft carriers in the Pacific at that moment raises suspicions that these most strategically important weapons of the Pacific war were deliberately put out of harm's way.

Roosevelt, who'd spent his previous two terms centralizing the American government and socializing the economy, was clearly hostile to "the bandit nations," as he called the Axis members. And so, while foreknowledge of the Pearl Harbor debacle cannot be proved absolutely, it is clear that Roosevelt had embarked on a pro-British policy despite his claims of American neutrality.

The famous Lend-Lease Agreement with England in 1940 sent American warships to join the British navy; this policy was a result of a CFR-populated organization called the Century Group. Still claiming neutrality, Roosevelt then ordered American military forces to occupy Iceland, a key stepping stone to provide air protection from German U-boats for the convoys bound for Britain crammed with American military supplies.

Roosevelt's hostility toward Japan, which had invaded Manchuria in 1931 and the rest of China in 1938, resulted in American loans to the Chinese. He also allowed American "volunteers" to form the Flying Tiger squadron inside China, which successfully shot down Japanese war planes well before a state of war existed between the two nations.

It can be argued that all of these policies violated the US Neutrality Act as well as several international agreements. But Roosevelt's Machiavellianism should have been no surprise to those aware of his family roots. His uncle, Frederic Delano, was an original member of the Federal Reserve Board.

The Pearl Harbor attack galvanized the American public from an isolationist mass into a warlike horde. It was truly a world at war now and a situation seen as having gone out of control by the international bankers who were profiting.

Some of them, like Standard Oil of New Jersey chairman Walter Teagle, maintained their hold on companies associated with those of the new enemy, Germany. Teagle also directed the American I.G. Chemical

Corp., and so continued shipping American tetraethyl lead, a vital ingredient for aviation fuel, to I.G. Farben in Germany. The *Luftwaffe* would be unable to fly without it during the early stages of the war, meaning that American business was fueling the planes that would bomb London.

After the German declaration of war with the US, the Rockefeller partnership with the Schroeder Bank continued, with legal representation by the firm that employed the Dulles brothers. By 1942, the head of the US Justice Department Anti-Trust Division, Thurman Arnold, documented for Senator Harry Truman's defense committee that, "Standard [Oil of New Jersey] and [I.G.] Farben in Germany had literally carved up the world markets, with oil and chemical monopolies established all over the map."

Well into the war, the Rockefellers continued selling petroleum products to the Nazis through third party nations like Spain, while Americans suffered severe gas rationing at home. Solid evidence also reveals that Standard Oil sent Germany petroleum through Switzerland in 1942, and that the Chase Bank in German-occupied Paris conducted business as usual with the knowledge of its New York directors.

Ford produced trucks for the German army with full approval of its corporate leadership. The International Telephone and Telegraph Corp. (ITT) aided the Nazi improvements in telecommunications and even helped the "enemy" to produce fighter planes and the V-1 rocket bomb.

These outrages took place legally, owing to President Roosevelt's December 13, 1941 order to amend the Trading with the Enemy Act, allowing any business to transpire so long as it had the approval of Treasury Secretary Henry Morganthau, whose father had helped to create the CFR.

Many of the funds that paid for the war passed through the Bank for International Settlements (BIS), which was owned by the First National Bank of New York (a Morgan affiliate), the Bank of England, Germany's *Reichsbank*, the Bank of Italy, the Bank of France and several other central banks. In this way, the BIS provided an excellent tool for those who sought a global system of financial control that would take precedence over the political establishments of nations.

Shortly before the war, BIS came under the pro-Hitler control of Kurt Schroeder and Hjalmar Schacht, becoming a means to finance the German war machine. Interestingly, the first BIS president was Gates McGarrah, a former officer of the Rockefeller-owned Chase National

Bank and the Federal Reserve Bank. McGarrah's grandson was Richard Helms, future CIA director.

Switzerland became the hub of many interconnected financial transactions among businesses representing the war's belligerents. Oddities like patents jointly held by Krupp in Germany and the Chemical Foundation of New York became more prevalent as the war progressed.

One complicated maneuver partnered the Nazi government with ITT, in which the American firm supplied fuses for artillery shells that killed British and American soldiers, reaching a peak of 50,000 per month in 1944. And Opel, the largest manufacturer of armored vehicles in Germany, was owned throughout the war as a subsidiary of General Motors.

In his hallmark book, *Trading with the Enemy: An Expose of the Nazi-American Money Plot 1933-49,* Charles Higham wrote that these international, interconnected businessmen and bankers "sought a common future of fascist domination, regardless of which world leader might further that ambition." Higham referred to this cabal as "The Fraternity," adding that "the bosses of the multinationals as we know them today had a six-spot on every side of the dice cube. Whichever side won the war, the powers that really ran nations would not be adversely affected."

This explains the increased national "loyalty" of the American businessmen and bankers once it became clear in 1943 that the Germans were losing the war. And at war's end, under the Marshall Plan these business interests entered Germany to protect their assets there, while at the same time helping to provoke a Cold War between Russia and the West.

The Nuremberg Tribunal did little to reveal the wartime machinations of this fraternity of businessmen, although many of them certainly were guilty of war crimes. The I.G. Farben executives built concentration camps that killed millions and factories that used slave labor that killed millions more, and even invented and marketed Zyklon-B, the insecticide poison used to gas camp victims.

Attempts at Nuremberg to unravel the complex business dealings of the war, like those of US Justice Department attorney James Martin, met with so many roadblocks that Martin eventually quit. In his 1950 book, *All Honorable Men,* Martin blamed American business for his frustrations in Germany, pointing out that these actions were not approved by Congress or the president. "Whatever it was that stopped us, it was not the government," he added. "But it clearly had command of channels through which the government operates."

Multiple lawsuits against these firms, guilty of war crimes inside Germany and of aiding Germany in killing American soldiers, continue to be fought in 21st century courtrooms.

Perhaps the most significant result of World War II is the amount of debt it raised among the combatant governments. The US debt went from $43 billion in 1940 to $257 billion in 1950. The national debt of Japan during the war increased by more than 1,300 percent. The war caused a debt increase of 583 percent in France and 417 percent in Canada.

The war's outcome only served to continue increasing debt as an open-ended arms race between the communist bloc and the capitalist bloc got underway. This played smartly into the hands of the globalist international bankers who sought to centralize the world's economic systems as a first step toward creating a one-world government.

A world bank already exists in the guise of the International Monetary Fund (IMF) that today controls two-thirds of the world's gold reserves. It has the power to create a single world fiat money, called Special Drawing Rights (SDRs).

At this time, the IMF has created more than $30 billion worth of SDRs, while pressuring its member nations to make their currencies exchangeable with SDRs. Since 1968, the Federal Reserve has had Congressional permission to accept SDRs as reserve notes and to issue Federal Reserve notes in exchange for this new money. This means that today, SDRs are part of America's lawful money. And as the SDRs are backed by the huge gold reserves owned by the central banks, the bankers may structure the economic future of the world in any way that is most profitable to them.

The US Federal Reserve and the Bank of England are essentially in control of the IMF due to their voting power. And just as these two banks control the money supply in their nations, so does the world bank, the BIS and IMF control the money supply of the globe.

Tighter credit strategies by this troika of central world banks are creating havoc in nations with low monetary reserves. In 1989, Japan experienced a terrible crash due to these strategies, which has since wiped out more than 50 percent of its stock market value and 60 percent of its commercial real estate value. The Bank of Japan was forced to lower interest rates to below one percent in order to stimulate the economy there, but this gambit has not paid off. Also, Mexico is surviving on US bailout loans following its economic collapse. Mexico now borrows money from the US simply to pay the interest on the older loans.

All of this is part of an enormous power shift that is making nations subservient to a handful of the world's richest bankers. As the IMF creates more SDRs, more nations have to borrow in that currency to pay the interest on old loans. This increases the control that the world central bankers have over nations.

As the current worldwide economic depression spreads and deepens, the central bankers will have the power to decide which nations will be bailed out by new SDR loans, and which nations will collapse. This policy is simply a steady transfer of wealth from the debtor nations to the small group of central world bankers. In Third World nations like those of Africa, this has translated to famine, high infant mortality and increased disease-related deaths. This could be a prelude to what awaits the rest of the world.

As one Brazilian politician put it, "The Third World War has already started. It is a silent war, not, for that reason, any less sinister. The war is tearing down Brazil, Latin America, and practically all the Third World. Instead of soldiers dying, there are children [dying]. It is a war over the Third World debt, one which has as its main weapon, interest, a weapon more deadly than the atom bomb, more shattering than a laser beam."

This certainly is a result of World War II. Was it the goal?

Korea

The Korean "police action," sanctioned by the United Nations from 1950 to 1953, cost the lives of nearly 34,000 American soldiers. Evidence suggests that these boys died in a conflict that was arranged by a few men who had influence both in the United States and the Soviet Union.

Following World War II, an international peacekeeping organization modeled on the failed League of Nations of the 1920s came into being as the United Nations. The driving force behind the creation of the UN was John Foster Dulles, one of the founders of the CFR.

The seeds of the Korean War were sown at the Yalta Conference, attended by Winston Churchill, President Harry Truman and Josef Stalin in February 1945. The three leaders agreed to divide Korea along the 38th Parallel, the North being in the Soviet communist sphere, owing to the belated attack by Russian forces upon the Japanese in that country.

A year before Yalta, the CFR publication, *Foreign Affairs,* suggested a "trusteeship" of Korea by a group of powers, namely the US, Russia, China and Great Britain. That same year, an internal CFR memo approached the "difficulty" in "dealing with the Constitutional provision that only Congress may declare war," and that this might be sidestepped by creating a treaty to "override this barrier." The memo actually coined the term "police action," saying it could be precipitated by agreement within an "international security organization" and "need not necessarily be construed as war."

UN preparations began two months after Yalta in San Francisco during the United Nations Conference on International Organization. The charter, signed in June, went into effect on October 24, 1945.

Author Ralph Epperson states flatly that this new international organization was created "essentially by the Council on Foreign Relations," because 47 of its members were among the American delegation in San Francisco. Their senior advisor was John Foster Dulles, who in 1953 would dominate American foreign policy as secretary of state in the Eisenhower administration.

With the new decade, North Korean Premier Kim Il-Sung proclaimed 1950 a "year of unification." The US State Department, well populated with CFR members, sat idly while a North Korean army massed on its southern border. Secretary of State Dean Acheson even announced that Korea was beyond America's defensive perimeter, prompting Perloff to write that this gave a "clear signal to Kim, who invaded the South that June under Soviet auspices."

An emergency meeting of the UN Security Council took place among its permanent members: the US, Great Britain, France, Nationalist China, and the Soviet Union. But for some inexplicable reason, the Soviets didn't show up, and the wholly non-communist council passed a resolution condemning the invasion and determined to send troops to Korea under a UN mandate.

At the time of the invasion, the South was woefully unprepared. The South Korean Army consisted mostly of troops with no combat experience, supplied mainly with small arms. The American military presence consisted of just 16,000 troops. Even the four divisions sent by Truman couldn't stanch the flow of the North Koreans, and all the Southern forces soon were pushed into a tiny pocket around the port city of Pusan.

The outlook remained bleak until General Douglas MacArthur executed a brilliant end-run sea invasion far behind enemy lines at Inchon. By the time the UN troops went in pursuit of the routed North Korean Army, 90 percent of them were Americans.

The surging Southern forces crossed into North Korea and threatened to reach that nation's northern border with China at the Yalu River. China's new leader, Mao Tse Tung, massed 200,000 of his troops on that border, and warnings of this by MacArthur to the CFR-filled State Department were duly ignored.

On November 25, the Chinese army invaded, followed soon by an additional half a million soldiers. The overwhelming size of the Chinese force shocked and routed the Americans and their allies. The "great bug-out" ended where it all began as both sides dug in around the 38th Parallel and fought for the next three years in what resembled the trench warfare on the Western Front during World War I.

President Truman called General George Marshall, a CFR member, out of retirement to the post of secretary of defense. It was Marshall who forbade MacArthur to bomb the bridges over the Yalu River, which would have cut off the Chinese Army supply route.

After the war, Chinese commander Lin Pao would say of this order, "I never would have made the attack and risked my men and my military reputation if I had not been assured that Washington would restrain General MacArthur from taking adequate retaliatory measures against my lines of supply and communication."

When MacArthur tried to go around Truman and Marshall by appealing directly to the American public, Truman sacked him and replaced him with General Matthew Ridgeway, who later would join the CFR.

On the other side, Soviet General Vasilev was calling the shots for the North Korean Army. Vasilev's chain of command ran through Moscow and the UN undersecretary general for Political and Security Council Affairs, the same office as that of Ridgeway's chain of command. At the outset of the Korean War, the UN undersecretary for Political and Security Council Affairs was a Russian, Constantine Zinchenko. This led to the preposterous situation in which a Soviet officer was in the same UN office that commanded the American war plan.

The battlefield stalemate ended when both sides signed an armistice on July 27, 1953. A disgusted MacArthur commented, "Never before has this nation been engaged in mortal combat with a hostile power without military objective, without policy other than restrictions governing operations, or indeed without even formally recognizing a state of war."

The military aspects of MacArthur's complaint would be repeated a little more than a decade later in Vietnam with tragic results.

The ability to go to war without Congressional declaration is a Constitutional violation that has been repeated again and again, and dogs our nation to this day. The 1944 CFR goal to circumvent Congress has been achieved in spectacular fashion.

Vietnam

The prelude to the Vietnam conflict is a template in how to start a war. You take a Third World nation that has been arbitrarily divided into two halves, set them against each other in a civil war, and then pour in troops and military equipment to help one side while your global opponents aid the other side. Mix and serve.

The people of Vietnam had the great misfortune of being rich in a natural resource that the European and North American industrial magnates lusted after — rubber. With the onset of the 20th century and the surge in automobile manufacture, rubber became a commodity of need, and therefore of tremendous profit. Tiny Vietnam suddenly became a pearl of great prize, and among the colonizing nations of the West, France claimed that prize.

Following the First World War, Vietnam, like so many other colonies, began to strive for independence from its French masters. This desire was eloquently stated at the Versailles Peace Conference in 1919 by a young Vietnamese diplomat named Nguyen That Thanh.

Having lived in France throughout the war, Thanh came into contact with the intellectual socialists of Paris, some of whom derived their philosophies from the Illuminized Freemasons. This would color the young man's thinking for the remainder of his life, and he would become the fulcrum of Indochinese independence for decades under his *nom de guerre,* Ho Chi Minh, which means "he who enlightens."

Ho founded the Vietnamese Communist Party in 1930 and later changed the title to the Indochinese Communist Party at the behest of Josef Stalin, who cautioned against sounding like a national movement. This changed once again in 1941 when Ho finally returned to his country and created the Viet Minh, or the League for the Independence of Vietnam.

The French maintained a grip on Vietnam until 1940, when the German *Wehrmacht* smashed through its army and British forces to occupy France. Germany's ally, Japan, took quick advantage of the vacuum and invaded Vietnam from China, where its troops had been fighting for several years.

To the Japanese industrial planners, it was another step in wresting control of Asia from the colonial powers of the West, forming a hegemony — The Greater East Asia Co-Prosperity Sphere — under their tight, brutal control. To the Japanese military, it meant rubber for its war machine and a jumping off point for the rich oil reserves in the Dutch East Indies.

And to the Vietnamese peasants, it was the beginning of a bloody fight that would not end for 35 years. Guerilla war had come to Vietnam, and the Japanese army was simply the first of several opponents.

At this time, Ho and General Vo Nguyen Giap coordinated the communist insurgent fight with agents of America's Office of Strategic Services (OSS), precursor of the CIA. When the United States forced Japan to capitulate in 1945, a secret agreement reached at the Yalta Conference between Winston Churchill, President Harry Truman and Josef Stalin granted the Pacific to America as its sphere of influence.

Ho and his nation continued to receive aid from the US after the Japanese withdrew. General Charles de Gaulle became fearful that once Ho succeeded in creating an independent Vietnam, he would broaden his American relationship and allow the US rubber magnates to move in and set up a new monopoly on the nation's rubber resources.

In October 1945, de Gaulle sent French troops into Saigon and reclaimed Vietnam for France. Attempting to placate the Vietnamese, de Gaulle offered to reinstate Emperor Bao Dai, but Ho would have none of it. War returned to Vietnam, climaxing in the stunning surrender of French forces to General Giap's soldiers at Dien Bien Phu in 1954.

France was out of the picture.

In a Geneva conference later that year, diplomats from Europe and America wrangled over which faction should rule Vietnam: Ho and his communists or the French-backed Bao Dai. The delegates reached a fateful compromise, dividing Vietnam into two nations along the 17th Parallel, with Ho's delegation ruling the north.

The only reason Ho went along with this decision was the promise made in these Geneva Accords that a vote on reunification would be held at some future date. Confident the nation would agree to his leadership of a united Vietnam, Ho signed the accords. Significantly, the United States did not.

South Vietnam contained most of the natural resources in the nation. It would be ruled by Ngo Dinh Diem, a Catholic who left the country after the French defeat to live in the US. Now he returned to rule a land that was 95 percent Buddhist.

Diem had immediate support from the US Military Advisory and Assistance Group, headed by Colonel Edward Lansdale. The group was a conduit of US aid to create and finance the Vietnamese National Army, which soon numbered 234,000 soldiers.

Diem, with complete American support, indefinitely postponed the reunification vote. He also arranged to move nearly one million Tonkinese Catholics into the rich farmlands of South Vietnam, dispossessing nearly as many native Vietnamese from their ancestral homes.

According to Fletcher Prouty, this was done at the behest of the CIA, already well populated by CFR members, in order to cause conflict. It was a certain recipe for civil war. As the dispossessed farmers roamed the countryside trying to avoid starvation, they came to be known as "viet ca," which means "beggars." This term eventually would morph into Viet Cong.

Under this name, anti-Catholic Buddhists and Viet Minh veterans poured into the south from the north and began reclaiming areas. As violence escalated, the Allen Dulles-run CIA urged the addition of American military advisors to South Vietnam, and President Dwight Eisenhower approved, despite congressional balking. At the same time, the Soviet Union and China began sending aid to North Vietnam.

In 1960, when John F. Kennedy won the narrowest victory to that date in presidential electoral history, Allen Dulles remained as director of the CIA. In addition, many of the new president's top advisors were also CFR members.

The economist John Kenneth Galbraith, who held a special advisor post in the administration, wrote, "Those of us who had worked for the Kennedy election were tolerated in the government for that reason and had a say, but foreign policy was still with the Council on Foreign Relations people."

Among those CFR members were Secretary of Defense Robert McNamara and Walt Rostow, head of the Policy Planning Council in the State Department. McNamara and Rostow wasted little time in urging the president to send troops to support CIA-backed General Phoumi Nosavan in a fresh crisis in Laos, created by the communist Pathet Lao. When Kennedy refused, they turned their attention to the simmering cauldron of Vietnam, long a CFR touchstone.

As far back as 1951, Vietnam was the focus of a study group run by the CFR and the Royal Institute for International Affairs, which was funded by the Rockefeller Foundation. The study concluded that Southeast Asia should be dominated jointly by Britain and America. During the Eisenhower administration, in which CFR co-founders John Foster Dulles was secretary of state and his brother Allen headed the CIA, American military advisors made their debut in the region.

In 1954, John Foster Dulles arranged the Manila Conference, which created the Southeast Asia Treaty Organization (SEATO) that bound the US, the British Commonwealth, France and the Philippines into a pact of mutual defense for Indochina. According to *New York Times* writer C. L. Sulzberger, "Dulles fathered SEATO with the deliberate purpose, as he explained to me, of providing the US president with legal authority to intervene in Indochina. When Congress approved SEATO, it signed the first of a series of blank checks yielding authority over Vietnam policy."

President Kennedy, despite being the son of a wealthy New England businessman, soon showed he was not part of the Eastern Establishment. Angry with the CIA and Allen Dulles over the disastrous Bay of Pigs attempt to invade Cuba in 1961 — he vowed to break up the CIA — Kennedy began stepping on the toes of very powerful interests.

In 1962, when the major steel companies raised their prices, Kennedy forced them to rescind the increase by threatening to cancel Defense Department steel contracts and ordering his brother, Attorney General Robert Kennedy, to initiate a price fixing investigation of the industry. When U.S. Steel backed down, the other steel companies followed suit. But the U.S. Steel board members, many of them CFR and related to the Morgan interests, realized they had an enemy in the White House.

Kennedy and the globalists next banged heads over the Federal Reserve Board, which began to clash with Comptroller of Currency James Saxon because he sought more powers to invest and lend for the non-Federal Reserve banks. Saxon then allowed the non-Fed banks to underwrite state and local bonds.

The struggle came to a head in June 1963, when Kennedy hammered the Federal Reserve Bank by authorizing more than $4 billion in "United States Notes" to be printed by the Treasury Department at no interest. It was his solution to the soaring national debt, but was unprecedented since the creation of the Federal Reserve System.

Kennedy didn't stop there. He cracked down on foreign tax havens, proposed to eliminate tax privileges to the wealthy and to America-based global investment firms, and threatened to increase taxes on the large oil and mineral companies. The Rockefellers, Nelson (then governor of New York) and David attacked Kennedy's economic house cleaning.

Treasury Secretary Douglas Dillon, a CFR member, publicly agreed with David Rockefeller, opposing his president's policies. Interestingly, in 1965 after Kennedy's murder, Dillon joined Rockefeller in promoting the Vietnam War.

Kennedy's foreign policy also antagonized the globalists. His anti-colonial bias and support of Third World nationalism, even if it involved nationalizing American business holdings in these countries, inevitably put him into conflict with the moneyed elitists of America and Europe.

During his presidency, Kennedy went along with his cabinet and the CIA on some issues. He approved McNamara's proposal to add a new intelligence entity, the Defense Intelligence Agency, in August 1961.

A month later, McNamara and General Maxwell Taylor recommended the addition of 16,000 US military advisors to Vietnam. Undersecretary of State George Ball urged Kennedy not to do this, saying it would lead to the eventual deployment of at least 300,000 combat troops within two years. Kennedy didn't heed Ball's sage advice and approved the troop additions McNamara wanted.

But on October 11, 1963, he reversed course by approving National Security Action Memorandum 263, allowing for a possible pullout of all US troops from Vietnam by the end of 1965. He had never agreed to send combat troops to Vietnam, despite constant pressure to do so from the CIA, the Joint Chiefs and the CFR members who held high positions in his government — Robert McNamara, McGeorge Bundy, William Bundy and Dean Rusk.

It is revealing that McNamara, who would remain secretary of state through the height of the Vietnam War until 1968, and who hamstrung the US military with policies that forbade strategic air strikes in the north, became president of the World Bank in 1978. This United Nations bank was a CFR project that brokered a $60 million loan to the communist government of Vietnam.

But in 1963, the situation in Vietnam clearly was worsening, as Buddhist riots in the south coincided with Viet Cong military successes. Averill Harriman, a CFR member who had been intriguing for this secret society for nearly four decades, convinced Kennedy that Vietnam President Diem had to go. With Kennedy's approval, Harriman sent the so-called "green light" cable to Saigon and Diem's military generals assassinated him on November 2, 1963.

"The axis of [Henry Cabot] Lodge and Harriman was too strong for President Kennedy to thwart or overcome," opined Frederick Nolting, former US Ambassador to Vietnam. Lodge, too, was affiliated with the CFR.

Kennedy decided to wait until the 1964 elections when he was sure voters would give him the mandate he needed to completely disengage from the Vietnam imbroglio. But he never saw those elections, having been assassinated less than three weeks after Diem.

Reams of books and articles have been written about his death and who might be responsible. It is obvious that Kennedy had made many powerful enemies, and any one or all of them could have conspired to eliminate him. But one intriguing voice from that dark time resurfaced in 1994.

The former wife of accused assassin Lee Harvey Oswald, Marina, told author A. J. Weberman, "The answer to the Kennedy assassination is with the Federal Reserve Bank. Don't underestimate that. It's wrong to blame it on [CIA official] James Angleton and the CIA per se only. This is only one finger of the same hand. The people who supply the money are above the CIA."

LBJ's War

Almost immediately upon succeeding Kennedy, Lyndon Baines Johnson shredded the policies in place and reversed course on Vietnam. A White House memo dated December 2, 1963, from Johnson to General Maxwell Taylor, and only released to the public in 1998, stated, "The more I look at it, the more it is clear to me that South Vietnam is our most critical military area right now. I hope that you and your colleagues in the Joint Chiefs of Staff will see to it that the very best available officers are assigned to General Harkins' command in all areas and for all purposes. We should put our blue ribbon men on this job at every level."

General Taylor, a CFR member, gladly obliged.

The Navy took the lead in provoking the kind of incident necessary to arouse the public and Congress to the point where it would be appropriate to send combat troops into Vietnam. Johnson authorized the resumption of destroyer patrols in the Gulf of Tonkin on August 4, 1964.

US destroyers *Maddox* and *Turner Joy* received word that the National Security Agency (NSA) had monitored a planned attack upon them by North Vietnamese gunboats. Prior to this, a joint US Navy and South Vietnamese action called Operation Planning (OPLAN) 34-A raided the North Vietnamese coast with the endorsement of Secretary of State McNamara. North Vietnamese gunboats attempted to retaliate against the *Maddox,* to no effect.

Two days after the attempted North Vietnamese retaliation, the destroyer crews went to battle stations in response to the same NSA warning and opened fire. Naval Commander Wesley McDonald was flying combat patrol in his A-4 jet squadron over the gulf and admitted later that the destroyer crews could be heard "calling out where they thought the torpedo boats were, but I could never find the damn torpedo boats."

A number of researchers believe there were no North Vietnamese torpedo boats, yet based on this "attack," Johnson called a meeting of Congressional leaders to ask for permission to respond militarily. He said "some of our boys are floating around in the water" despite the fact there were no casualties.

Armed with this information, the House voted 416-0 to allow Johnson "to take all necessary steps, including the use of armed force…." This mandate, which came to be known as the Gulf of Tonkin Resolution, passed in the Senate 88-2.

Much like the so-called "police action" in Korea a decade before, this Resolution niftily sidestepped the Constitutional requirement that only Congress has the power to declare war.

A month later, acting on advice from McNamara and McGeorge Bundy, Johnson approved "Rolling Thunder," the first US bombing campaign against North Vietnam. By mid summer, 100,000 troops had been ordered to Vietnam by Johnson. The most tragic of all American wars was underway.

But it was far from the usual kind of war in which both sides strive completely to win. This is obvious in the *Congressional Record* at that time, declassified and published in 1985. The US military clearly was hamstrung by "rules of engagement," a list 26 pages long that prohibited bombing of strategic targets as determined by the Joint Chiefs of Staff, firing upon the Viet Cong unless fired upon first, bombing vehicles more than 200 yards beyond the Ho Chi Minh trail, attacking North Vietnamese fighter planes unless they were flying and behaving in a hostile manner, bombing SAM missile sites while they were under construction, and pursuing enemy forces when they cross into Laos or Cambodia. These and other restrictions were the American military's marching orders as it went to war.

This ridiculous situation has been repeated today in Afghanistan. The rules of engagement there have allowed the Taliban to regain strength while endangering the lives of American soldiers.

"If they use rockets to hit the [forward operating base] we can't shoot back because they were within 500 meters of the village," complained Spc. Charles Brooks, a US Army medic with the 4th Infantry Regiment in Zabul province, to a *Washington Examiner* correspondent. "If they shoot at us and drop their weapon in the process, we can't shoot back."

The article reported that a new order called for the watch towers surrounding US military bases to be dismantled because local village elders, many of whom support the Taliban, complained they disturbed the villagers' privacy. Brooks told the correspondent, "We have to take down our towers because it offends them and now the Taliban can set up mortars and we can't see them."

Another soldier, Spc. Matthew Fuhrken, told the correspondent, "I'm sick of people trying to cover up what's really going on over here. They won't let us do our job. I don't care if they try to kick me out for what I'm saying. War is war and this is no war. I don't know what this is."

It seems, like Vietnam, the invisible government is not committed to winning a war in Afghanistan, but to prolonging it.

In Saigon during the mid 1960s, US leadership swapped CFR members, General Maxwell Taylor replacing Henry Cabot Lodge as ambassador. Other CFR members intimately involved in the struggle became household names during the broadcasts covering the war: Cyrus Vance, Walt Rostow, William and McGeorge McBundy, Averill Harriman, Dean Rusk, Dean Acheson and Ellsworth Bunker. Among those advocating the war from behind the scenes, David Rockefeller, Allen Dulles, Henry Wriston and John McCloy all were on the CFR Board of Directors.

In 1964, William Bundy was appointed director of the CFR while also serving as Assistant Secretary of State for Far Eastern affairs. According to the *Pentagon Papers,* which Daniel Ellsberg leaked years later, Bundy was the architect of the Gulf of Tonkin Resolution and had a hand in OPLAN 34-A.

Later, Bundy would be editor of the CFR publication, *Foreign Affairs.* Bundy achieved the post of assistant secretary of war at the young age of 27. He served both Kennedy and Johnson as special assistant for National Security Affairs, and between 1969 and 1979, he was president of the Ford Foundation.

Dean Rusk once held the chairmanship of the Rockefeller Foundation. He guided policy for both Kennedy and Johnson. Rusk moved into the Kennedy administration based on the enthusiastic recommendations of CFR members Dean Acheson and Robert Lovett, former defense secretary to Harry Truman.

Author James Perloff claims that Walt Rostow, who was Johnson's national security advisor after 1966, had been rejected three times in his bid to work for the Eisenhower administration because he failed security checks. A hint as to why he failed lies in his 1960 book, *The United States in the World Arena,* where he revealed a globalist outlook by saying that nations, including the US, must lose the right to use substantial military force in pursuing their own interests, because it is "an American interest to see an end to nationhood as it has been historically defined."

Johnson literally surrounded himself with CFR members. He met daily with his 14 closest advisors and 12 of them were in the CFR. Many were bankers, and all of them urged increased commitment to the Vietnam War. Among his closest advisors, who Johnson called his "Wise Men," were State Department advisor Charles Bohlen and former US Ambassador to Russia George Kennan—both CFR members.

Louisiana Congressman John Rarick pointed a finger at the CFR in 1971, while the country was suffering through anti-war protests and the greatest domestic unrest since the Civil War. He said, "The My Lai massacre, the sentencing of Lt. Calley to life imprisonment, 'The Selling of the Pentagon,' and the so-called *Pentagon Papers* are leading examples of attempts to shift all the blame to the military in the eyes of the public. But no one identified the Council on Foreign Relations — the CFR — a group of some 1,400 Americans which includes as members almost every top level decision and policy maker in the Vietnam War.

"CBS tells the people it wants them to know what is going on and who is to blame. Why doesn't CBS tell the American people about the CFR and let the people decide whom to blame for the Vietnam fiasco — the planners and top decision makers of a closely knit financial-industrial-intellectual aristocracy or military leaders under civilian control who have had little or no voice in the overall policies and operations and who are forbidden by law to tell the American people their side....Who will tell the American people the truth if those who control 'the right to know machinery' also control the government?"

In 1968, Johnson's "Wise Men" turned against the Vietnam War. General Maxwell Taylor explained it with a flippant comment: "My Council on Foreign Relations friends were living in the cloud of the *New York Times*." Most interpret this to mean that the president's advisors finally realized the Vietnam War was destroying the country, perhaps even creating a revolutionary danger. And it simply did not make good business sense to let the conflict escalate into a nuclear war.

So the "Wise Men" harkened back to a concept that one of their members wrote in 1957 in their publication, *Foreign Affairs*: "We must be prepared to fight limited actions ourselves. Otherwise we shall have made no advance beyond 'massive retaliation' which tied our hands in conflicts involving less than our survival. And we must be prepared to lose limited actions."

Johnson, seemingly shattered by what he considered a betrayal, announced on television that he would not seek or accept candidacy for re-election. The subsequent 1968 contest for the presidency pitted CFR members Richard Nixon and Hubert Humphrey against each other, and when Nixon entered the White House, he brought with him a new collection of CFR cronies. Henry Kissinger, a member of both the CFR and the Trilateral Commission, assumed the position of national security advisor, which enabled him to control policy for Vietnam.

To many historians, the behavior of the Johnson administration during the Vietnam War presents a puzzle. But when seen through the eyes of the men who advised him, who were doing the bidding of globalist banking and business elites, the puzzle solves itself. The important thing was not to win the war, but to prolong it for profit and increased control.

For example, in 1964 David Rockefeller, then president of the Chase Manhattan Bank, went to the USSR and met with Nikita Krushchev. When he returned, he reported to President Johnson that the two countries should increase trade with each other. Rockefeller said Krushchev suggested that the US extend long term loans to the Soviet Union. The Chase Bank had a history with Russia going back decades and had participated in creating the American-Russian Chamber of Commerce.

In October, Johnson's administration acted on the Rockefeller initiative by removing restrictions on more than 400 items of export to the Soviet Union and Eastern Europe. This came just one week after a Soviet leaders' conference announced it was approving aid and munitions to North Vietnam totaling $1 billion.

Three years later, Rockefeller joined Cyrus Eaton, founder of the Republic Steel Corporation, in a venture to finance aluminum and rubber plants in the Soviet Union. Occurring during the height of the Vietnam War, this meant US dollars and material went to Russia while Russia sent material to North Vietnam to kill US soldiers.

Taking this, and the miserable conduct of the war into account, author Perloff wrote, "Viewed, however, as an exercise in deliberate mismanagement, [the Vietnam War] ceases to mystify, for its outcome fulfilled precisely the goals traditional to the CFR."

The Persian Gulf War

The Persian Gulf War of 1991 was a spectacular military and diplomatic success. President George H.W. Bush had cobbled together a coalition of disparate nations from the Muslim and Christian religions, and troops from Asia, Eastern and Western Europe, North Africa and North America.

The mission ostensibly was to evict the Iraqi army from neighboring Kuwait, which they had invaded and occupied under orders from their dictator Saddam Hussein. It was over quickly. Iraq had suffered 365,000 casualties, while the Allies suffered fewer than 800 troops and airmen killed, wounded or captured.

The root issue, of course, was oil, a business interest of great importance both to the Bush family and to Secretary of State James Baker. What was good news to them also was good news to the oil magnates who supported them with campaign funds, including the Rockefeller-controlled oil cartel.

What went unreported was the benefit this war seemed to promise the globalists, who had often stated their preference for a one-world military force. Some authors believe the Persian Gulf War was instigated by these men. Here are a few items that Jonathan Vankin and John Whalen used to back up these claims:

When George Bush was director of the CIA, he supported Saddam at the outbreak of the Iran-Iraq War in 1979. He continued his support when he became vice president in 1981, supplying Iraq with arms and equipment throughout the eight year struggle against the new fundamentalist Iranian government. He and much of the corporate media turned a blind eye to Saddam's use of deadly sarin and tabun nerve gas on the battlefield, which killed untold thousands of Iranian soldiers.

When the conflict ended with neither side achieving anything but carnage and death, Iraq was close to bankruptcy. OPEC refused to allow Saddam to raise the price of his nation's oil, and international bankers began to complain about his slow repayment of the loans he took to fight the war. The banks also refused to make new loans to Iraq. The simplest solution was on Iraq's southern border, where a nation that was the region's third largest oil producer resides — Kuwait.

Saddam decided to use the "stolen territory" gambit, as Kuwait had once been part of Iraq until created as a separate nation by mandate as a British Protectorate in 1914. Iraq previously had attempted to reclaim Kuwait in 1961, which prompted Britain to send troops there.

Deciding to try again in 1990, Saddam began massing troops on the Kuwaiti border that summer. US intelligence agencies were well aware of this and Saddam knew it, so he sounded out US Ambassador April Glaspie on July 25 about how the US would respond to his intentions.

"I have direct instructions from President Bush to improve our relations with Iraq," Glaspie said. "We have considerable sympathy for your quest for higher oil prices....We have no opinion on your Arab-Arab conflicts, like your dispute with Kuwait. Secretary Baker has directed me to emphasize the instruction, first given to Iraq in the 1960s, that the Kuwaiti issue is not associated with America."

Shortly after Glaspie issued what many diplomats would call a blank check to move on Kuwait, she left the region on vacation. This, too, could diplomatically signal Saddam that the US was disinterested in the crisis.

Saddam had several meetings with David Rockefeller after Chase Manhattan became the principal bank in major Iraqi credit syndications. There also were reports that a vice president of Henry Kissinger's firm, Kissinger Associates, Alan Stoga, met with Iraqi leaders in the two years prior to the Kuwait invasion.

On the eve of the invasion, a scandal surfaced concerning $5 billion in loans to Saddam during the 1980s through the Atlanta, Georgia branch of Banca Nazional del Lavoro (BNL), Italy's government-owned bank. The Atlanta branch manager, Christopher Drogoul, pleaded guilty in federal court to approving the $5 billion transfer without obtaining permission from BNL.

But many people found it incredible that Drogoul could make such a massive transfer of cash without the knowledge of his superiors in Italy. And during the trial, a Drogoul attorney claimed that his client was the victim of "a scheme orchestrated at the highest levels of the US Government." This charge was buttressed by the testimony of BNL official Franz von Wedel, who claimed that Drogoul had acted on advice from Kissinger Associates, the bank's consultants.

Of course, the supreme irony in this is that the $5 billion Saddam received in US taxpayer-backed money purchased weapons to kill

American soldiers. This is because the loan passed through the government-supported Commodity Credit Corporation as funds intended to buy grain from US farmers. Instead, some of this grain left the country to Eastern European nations in exchange for weapons, and the rest allowed Saddam to tap his limited cash reserves to buy more munitions.

Another smoking gun in this scandal involves the blocking of two indictments issued by the Atlanta attorney general following the FBI raid on BNL on August 4, 1989. The Bush Justice Department held up legal action against the bank for more than a year, and the indictments finally came down the day after George Bush issued his TV cease-fire speech to end the Gulf War.

Congressman Henry Gonzalez, chairman of the House Committee on Banking, Finance and Urban Affairs, was so incensed by what came to be known as the "Iraqgate Scandal" that he called for the impeachment of Bush Attorney General William Barr for obstruction of justice. House Judiciary Committee Chairman Jack Brooks then told Barr to appoint a special prosecutor to investigate, but Barr said he found no evidence of wrongdoing on his own part and refused. The scandal was not well covered in the press, which concentrated on the cease fire and the celebration that followed it.

Just days after Ambassador Glaspie took her vacation in 1990, the Iraqi army invaded Kuwait. Bush immediately ordered all Iraqi assets in the US frozen. But when asked by reporters whether he'd decided to intervene militarily in the Kuwait situation, Bush said he was not contemplating "such action."

His posture changed drastically after meeting with British Prime Minister Margaret Thatcher, a Bilderberg meetings attendee. Suddenly Bush demonized Saddam as a "new Hitler," adding that the presence of Iraqi troops in Kuwait was "unacceptable."

Bush contacted the Saudi Arabian royal family and warned them that Saddam was planning to invade their country, despite assurances from the Iraqi dictator that Kuwait was his only objective. The frightened Saudis gave as much as $4 billion to Bush and other world leaders in secret payoffs to protect them from Saddam, according to Sheik Fahd Mohammed al-Sabah, chairman of the Kuwait Investment Office.

When the war ended, al-Sabah answered critics of this enormous gift: "That money was used to buy Kuwait's liberation." Postwar audits discovered the gift money had been put into a London slush fund.

It is easy to speculate that the gift money prompted Bush to draw his "line in the sand," as he put it in a speech, and set the wheels of war in motion. But it's a fact that his son, future President George W. Bush, was a board member of the Harken Energy Corp. Just days before the shooting started in the Gulf War, Harken announced an oil production agreement with Bahrain, the island financial haven for international bankers just off the Saudi coast.

The Harken coup was a shock to the established oil men because the firm scored a lucrative contract with allegedly zero drilling experience. An even more surprising rider to the deal provided for American and multi-national forces to establish permanent bases in Bahrain to protect the Harken interests.

The younger Bush scoffed at reporters' questions that his father launched the Gulf War to protect his interests in Bahrain, and added that he'd sold his Harken stock before the start of hostilities. *Houston Post* reporter Peter Brewton checked on this claim and found no record of sale in the SEC files.

The record of the stock sale finally did turn up in March 1991, which was eight months after the SEC deadline for filing. But SEC records also revealed that Bush did indeed sell 66 percent of his Harken stock on June 22, 1990, weeks prior to Saddam's invasion of Kuwait, for $848,000 at $4 per share.

One week after the Iraq invasion of Kuwait, Harken stock dropped to $3.03 per share. Of course, all of this was buried in the media by the decisiveness of the victory against Saddam's army.

Iraq 2003

The US invasion of Iraq in 2003 was sold as a regime change to oust a murderous dictator who possessed chemical and biological weapons, and to replace him with a democratic government. As the world knows, Saddam Hussein was captured, tried and executed, but no weapons of mass destruction were discovered. Eight years into this military adventure, the new Iraqi government is unstable and American troops continue to occupy the country with more people dying each week.

The most cynical critics of the Iraq adventure claim that the US never had any intention of winning there, because that would interfere with the plans of American and British bankers to maintain control of the country's rich oil deposits and to establish permanent military bases from which attacks against renegade oil producing nations like Iran and Syria could be launched.

An indication that the so-called war against Iraq's insurgency is "being manipulated" occurred on September 19, 2005 when two British SAS officers were arrested by Iraqi police for shooting at civilians from a moving Toyota Cressida while dressed as insurgents. Iraqi authorities also accused the pair of planting bombs in Basra.

The arresting officers were fired upon by the undercover SAS men, killing one and wounding another. Iraqi police responded and made the arrests.

Iraqi National Assemblyman Fattah al-Shaykh told the press that the captured Toyota was booby trapped "and was meant to explode in the center of the city of Basra in the popular market." Initial BBC Radio reports also claimed the car contained explosives, but later said only light weapons were found.

The British Army demanded their immediate release, and when Iraqi officials refused, launched a helicopter and tank attack on the prison where they were incarcerated and freed them. Bear in mind that the attack took place against the supposedly friendly new regime of Iraq and not against terrorists of al-Qaeda. It resulted in the destruction of an Iraqi prison that released a large number of other prisoners, firefights with Iraqi policemen, popular demonstrations against the British, and a withdrawal of cooperation with them by the regional Basra government.

The US-British-supported Iraqi regime has made repeated accusations during the war that American and British forces have carried out bombings against civilian targets.

On April 20, 2004, American journalist Dahr Jamail wrote for the Countercurrents website, "The word on the street in Baghdad is that the cessation of suicide car bombings is proof that the CIA was behind them. Why? Because as one man states, '[CIA agents] are too busy fighting [amongst themselves] now, and the unrest they wanted to cause by the bombings is now upon them.'"

Two days later, Agence France-Presse quoted Shiite cleric Mogtada al-Sadr's accusation that British troops were responsible for the five car bombings in Basra, three of which exploded outside Iraqi police stations, killing 68 people including 20 children.

In May 2005, Iraqi exile physicist Imad Khadduri wrote of the story told him by a Baghdad cab driver whose license had been confiscated at an American military checkpoint. The driver obeyed the American soldiers' order to drive to a military base near the airport to be interrogated, after which he could retrieve his license. He spent about half an hour under questioning before being told he was free to leave and that he could pick up his license at the Iraqi police station at al-Khadimiya.

En route, the cabbie became concerned that his vehicle seemed to be carrying extra weight and he noticed a US helicopter flying overhead, as if trailing him. "He stopped the car and inspected it carefully," Khadduri reported. "He found nearly 100 kilograms of explosive hidden in the back seat and along the two back doors. The only feasible explanation for this incident is that the car was indeed booby trapped by the Americans and intended for the al-Khadimiya Shiite district of Baghdad."

According to Khadduri, the same scenario took place later in Mosul, only this time the driver's life was saved when the car broke down en route to the police station where he was to reclaim his license. A mechanic who had come to fix the car discovered its spare tire was crammed with explosives.

In April 2005, CBS cameraman Abdul Amir Younes Hussein received a wound from US troops who fired in his direction while he filmed the aftermath of a car bombing in Mosul. American military authorities initially apologized, but arrested Hussein three days later and incarcerated him in the Abu Ghraib prison on charges of "anti-coalition activity." Following the Abu Ghraib scandal, Hussein was transferred to Camp Bucca, the largest US prison in Iraq, holding more than 30,000 detainees. CBS President Andrew Heyward claimed his attempts to urge due process by stating the specific charges and evidence against Hussein received no cooperation from the military.

American and British military authorities have rejected claims that their troops engaged in "false-flag" terrorist attacks in Iraq. But if Allied troops and intelligence agents are behind some of the bombings, it only could be intended to continue and intensify strife and perhaps provide the impetus to partition Iraq into Sunni, Shiite and Kurd territories.

This solution would please former president emeritus of the CFR, Leslie Gelb, by his own admission. The former senior State Department member, Pentagon official, and ex-editor and columnist of the *New York Times* explained his views in a November 25, 2003 essay titled "The Three-State Solution." In it, Gelb supported the notion of a Sunni-led insurgency and proposed punishing the sect by separating its territory from the oil-rich Kurdish and Shiite lands. He offered the example of Yugoslavia's breakup into numerous ethno-centric states as a "hopeful precedent." Due to his impressive political and military positions in the past, Gelb's essay is interpreted by many as a signal of intent by at least one important faction within the US government.

Typically, the mainstream American media has not covered this possibility and barely a word has been mentioned or written about the apparent "false flag" attacks. If these attacks continue with impunity, it may be due to the possibility that the shadow government already has gotten away with history's biggest false flag operation.

CRESCENDO – *DIES IRAE*
9/11

"Sit down before a fact as a little child. Be prepared to give up every preconceived notion...or you shall learn nothing."

—Thomas H. Huxley

The Towers

The attacks of September 11, 2001, claimed the lives of 2,974 US citizens, the great majority of them civilians. Since that terrible day, thousands of other Americans who were present at the scene have died from respiratory ailments due to asbestos and other contaminant poisoning.

Today, an estimated 50,000 rescue workers who were dispatched to the World Trade Center on or soon after 9/11 suffer from lung-related maladies, including cancer. Most of them have not qualified for health care. Many of them will die within the next year.

In the absence of timely city, state and federal health assistance, John Feal, a 9/11 responder, created the Feal Good Foundation to help other fire and police personnel obtain proper health care.

The New York City Health Department, which ruled that the widespread health problems suffered by those present in the World Trade Center (WTC) on or soon after 9/11 had no relation to the events of 9/11, was investigated by Congressman Dennis Kucinich, chairman of the Domestic Policies Subcommittee. Unfortunately, congressional leaders continued to refuse medical aid to the sufferers, possibly because such aid would be an admission that the debris in the air was indeed toxic and that blame would boomerang on the federal government.

A $7.2 billion bill intended explicitly to aid the suffering first responders, the James Zadroga 9/11 Health and Compensation Act of 2010, failed to gain the necessary two-thirds vote in Congress. This prompted a firestorm of criticism, especially against President Barack Obama, who has remained silent about the Zadroga Bill while promoting the building of a mosque two blocks from the former World Trade Center.

Feal, who lost part of a foot when a steel beam fell on him during the WTC cleanup, wrote a letter of protest to Obama stressing the dire health situations of firemen, policemen and citizens who breathed the toxic cloud of debris on 9/11. The House finally passed a new version of the Zadroga Act, the 9/11 Health Bill, in December 2010, providing $7.4 billion in free health care and compensation to rescue and recovery workers in the trade center who have fallen ill. It came nine years too late for thousands of the men and women who have died, however.

On the day of the tragedy, Environmental Protection Agency (EPA) Director Christine Whitman announced that the dust and asbestos-filled air in and around the World Trade Center was safe to breathe. Her pronouncement caused rescue workers and citizens to labor in the area wearing no respirators. Rescue workers who suffer now from respiratory ailments charge Whitman with diminishing the threat in order to reopen Wall Street as soon as possible.

Based on the charges against Whitman, medical aid for the 9/11 sufferers became a possibility when New York Mayor Michael Bloomberg asked the federal government for $150 million each year to cover their treatments. Five days later, however, an appeals court ruled that Whitman should not be punished for her false assurance that the toxic contaminants in the air at Ground Zero were safe to breathe after 9/11.

It is painful for Americans to realize their government has treated citizens so shabbily. It is absolutely traumatic to consider that the government may have played either a passive or an active role in the 9/11 attacks. To think that our own leaders would concoct such a mad scheme as a "false flag" terrorist attack on its own territory, in which so many things could go wrong and reveal such a plot, flies in the face of logic.

And yet, numerous polls have shown that about half of the Americans questioned believe that some members of the federal government at least had prior knowledge, if not complicity, in the 9/11 attacks. In addition, the official version in the *9/11 Commission Report* has received severe criticism from senior military, intelligence and government personnel, along with more than 100 professors, 200 pilots and hundreds of architects and engineers. Even a member of the 9/11 Commission, former Senator Max Cleland, resigned from that investigation in 2003 due to its lack of access to White House documents.

"It should be a national scandal," Cleland said during an interview with salon.com. "A minority of the commissioners will be able to see a minority of the [President's Daily Brief] documents that the White House has already said is pertinent."

Cleland specifically complained of the Bush Administration's refusal to release pertinent White House, FAA and NORAD documents in what he charged was a coverup. He concluded: "This investigation is now compromised."

Former FBI Director Louis Freeh also challenged the report's credibility and added that it "might just render the Commission historically insignificant...."

Retired General Albert Stubblebine, who as commander of Army Intelligence and Security, had to oversee photographic interpretation, said in a videotaped interview, "I look at the hole in the Pentagon and I look at the size of an airplane that was supposed to have hit the Pentagon, and I said, 'The plane does not fit in that hole.' So what did hit the Pentagon? What hit it? Where is it? What's going on?"

Retired Colonel Robert Bowman, former director of Advanced Space Programs Development, called the Commission Report "hogwash," and accused the Bush Administration of a coverup. He added that the best that could be said of the administration was that it had foreknowledge of the attacks and allowed them to happen, which, he added, is still "high treason and conspiracy to commit murder."

Former Italian President Francesco Cossiga went so far as to accuse the CIA and the Mossad of carrying out the 9/11 attacks. In a November 2007 article in *Corriere della Sera,* Cossiga said these agencies organized and carried out the attacks "to falsely incriminate Arabic countries and to persuade the Western Powers to intervene in Iraq and Afghanistan....All [the intelligence services] of America and Europe know well that the disastrous attack has been planned and realized from the Mossad, with the aid of the Zionist world, to put under accusation the Arabic countries...."

Cossiga served as president of Italy from 1985 to 1992, when he was forced to resign after revealing the existence of Operation Gladio and his part in creating it. As mentioned earlier in this book, Operation Gladio was a NATO-controlled series of "false flag" bombings throughout Europe during the 1960s, '70s and '80s that were blamed on leftist terror groups.

Cossiga's revelations were corroborated in 2001 by a Gladio agent named Vincenzo Vinciguerra, who said in sworn testimony, "You had to attack civilians, the people, women, children, innocent people, unknown people far removed from any political game. The reason was quite simple: to force the public to turn to the state to ask for greater security."

Reverse reasoning certainly provides and fulfills those motives. After all, without 9/11 there would be no Patriot Act, which gives the federal government extraordinary powers in domestic spying and enforcement, subverting most of the Bill of Rights. The attack also gave President Bush the opportunity to mount a military invasion of Afghanistan, deposing and replacing its Taliban government.

Indirectly, 9/11 also led to US forces invading and occupying Iraq. Other government entities like the Homeland Security Department and the Transportation Security Administration exist as direct results of the claimed terrorist attack. And finally, since 9/11 the US government has increased its military spending by $1 billion, and at least 250,000 civilians have died in the Afghan and Iraq wars.

Immediately following the 9/11 incidents, President George W. Bush explained the need for creating the Patriot Act and other measures reducing individual Constitutional rights by saying, "An evil exists that threatens every man, woman and child of this great nation. We must take steps to insure our domestic security and protect our homeland."

Oddly, this speech is identical in every word to Adolf Hitler's 1933 speech in the Reichstag announcing the creation of the Gestapo.

The import of the post-9/11 legislation is not lost on US citizens. In a June 2010 Rasmussen poll, 48 percent of American adults said the federal government is a threat to their individual rights.

It is never pleasant to suspect that the government of the United States might have helped to organize what amounted to a second Pearl Harbor in order to achieve these goals and create these entities, but there are some disturbing red flags in the 9/11 story. These have prompted the creation of credible organizations seeking to investigate the tragedy and find the truth, among them Architects and Engineers for 9/11 Truth (ae911truth.org), Pilots for 9/11 Truth (pilotsfor911truth.org) and Scholars for 9/11 Truth (911scholars.org).

There is precedent for the US government to plan fake attacks in order to justify a counterattack, some of which already have been covered in this book. Here are a few more:

In 1962, Lyman Lemnitzer, chairman of the Joint Chiefs of Staff, proposed to Secretary of Defense Robert McNamara a plan code-named Operation North Woods. The now declassified document called for staging terrorist attacks at Guantanamo Bay to "provide justification for US military intervention in Cuba."

The scheme included landing expatriate Cubans inside the Guantanamo base to stage attacks and riots, start fires and blow up ammunition. Other aspects of the plan called for sabotaging aircraft and ships at Guantanamo, sinking a ship to block the port entrance to the base, and blasting the base with mortar fire. Mock funerals for fictional US personnel were to be staged for cameras.

Terrorist attacks in Florida and Washington DC also were part of the plan, as well as shooting down an aircraft over Cuba, whose reported passengers, college students on vacation, would be posing as federal agents. The plane was to be stationed at Eglin Air Force Base, where it would be painted to resemble a civilian aircraft twin plane that had been converted into a drone. The document states: "At a designated time, the duplicate would be substituted for the actual civil aircraft and would be loaded with the selected passengers, all boarded under carefully prepared aliases. The actual registered aircraft would be converted to a drone."

The two planes were to rendezvous south of Florida, at which time the passenger-laden plane would land at Eglin and unload. The drone was to assume the flight plan and transmit a Mayday signal over Cuban waters before being blown up by remote control. McNamara rejected the plan and President Kennedy removed Lemnitzer from his post on the Joint Chiefs.

Such "false flag" attacks have been employed by this and other nations. The infamous Gulf of Tonkin incident, which never occurred, provided an excuse to ramp up the American military commitment to the Vietnam War. More recently, three British SAS troops were caught firing on Iraqi citizens in Basra, while dressed as Arabs. These incidents have been covered in greater detail in the appropriate chapters of this book.

The Israeli intelligence organization, Mossad, engaged in a false flag operation code-named "Susannah" in 1954, using its agents, dressed as Muslims, to bomb American, British and Egyptian targets in Egypt. The scheme intended to keep Britain in control of the Suez Canal, preventing a hostile Egyptian government from occupying the strategic waterway. The plan derailed when a bomb prematurely exploded in the pocket of one of the Mossad agents as he was about to enter a movie theater.

There also are disturbing occurrences prior to 9/11 that may point to some kind of foreknowledge. Here are some of them:

The August 1997 cover of the *FEMA Emergency Response to Terrorism* handbook contained an illustration with cross-hairs on the World Trade Center. This same picture was repeated in June 2000 on the cover of a Justice Department terrorism manual.

In 1999, the North American Aerospace Defense Command

(NORAD) conducted exercises simulating hijacked airliners, deliberately crashing into targets, which included the World Trade Center and the Pentagon. When the press revealed this, the Defense Department claimed the drill never was performed because it was deemed unrealistic.

One year before 9/11, the Project for a New American Century, whose members included Dick Cheney, Paul Wolfowitz, Donald Rumsfeld and Jeb Bush, released a report titled *Rebuilding America's Defenses: Strategy, Forces and Resources for a New Century.* The report summarizes: "...the process of transformation, even if it brings revolutionary change, is likely to be a long one, absent some catastrophic and catalyzing event — *like a new Pearl Harbor.*" (Emphasis added)

On October 24, 2000, the Pentagon conducted the first of two training exercises simulating a Boeing 757 crash into the building. Former naval airman Charles Burlingame participated in this exercise before joining American Airlines after his military career ended.

Burlingame was the pilot of the hijacked 757 that allegedly crashed into the Pentagon on 9/11, less than a year later.

In June 2001, the Department of Defense published new instructions for military intervention in case of domestic airline hijackings, which stated that permission from the secretary of defense must be given before any military action may take place.

The French newspaper *Le Figaro* reported that on July 4, 2001, Osama bin Laden traveled to Dubai and spent 10 days getting treatment in an American hospital, where he received a visit by the local CIA bureau chief. At this time, bin Laden had been on the FBI Most Wanted List for more than three years.

On September 10, 2001, National Security Advisor Condoleeza Rice phoned San Francisco Mayer Willie Brown and warned him not to fly the next morning. Initially, Brown claimed the warning came from his "airport security," and that he simply was advised that Americans should be cautious about air travel at that time, but Pacifica Radio revealed the call came from Rice.

That same day, the Tokyo, Japan headquarters of Goldman Sachs released a memo warning its employees to avoid American government buildings.

In his book, *The Terror Conspiracy,* author/journalist Jim Marrs makes a strong case that more than a dozen nations tried to warn our leaders that America was about to be attacked. According to Marrs, some of these warnings came from the Taliban itself in Afghanistan and from

Fidel Castro.

After the tragedy, the press reported that British intelligence had warned the White House of an impending terrorist attack. Egyptian President Hosni Mubarak claimed that he had warned the US of an al-Qaeda plot prior to 9/11. The American press also revealed that warnings of large-scale terror attacks came from Russian intelligence and Israeli security.

Among the most suspicious occurrences indicating that some had prior knowledge of the attacks took place near the World Trade Center. Fox News reported that "a group of five men had set up video cameras aimed at the Twin Towers prior to the attack on Tuesday, and were seen congratulating one another afterwards."

It is known now that war game exercises were underway the morning of 9/11. Initially, the military denied that any war games took place at that time, but National Security Council Counter-Terrorism Chief Richard Clarke admitted they indeed happened, this coming a year after the fact. The exercise, code-named Vigilant Guardian, was intended to "pose an imaginary crisis to North American Air Defense outposts nationwide," according to Lieutenant Colonel Dawne Deskins.

The fact these exercises took place that day is vital. They potentially confused and prevented a response by US defense systems to the incoming airliners. The war games also involved participation of the great majority of US fighter-jets, leaving just 14 F-16s to guard the entire eastern seaboard.

The testimony of a Sgt. Lauro Chavez, who participated in the war games as part of the US Central Command Headquarters staff, has electrified some researchers. Chavez said it was the first military exercise in which he was involved that was classified Top Secret. He also said that Vice President Dick Cheney became the first civilian to have command of NORAD, and that this took place just one week before the attacks.

Chavez insisted that a superior officer told him that Cheney issued an order for interceptors to stand down.

Finally, Chavez claimed that the war games included a scenario in which a hijacked commercial airliner crashes into a World Trade Center tower. He maintained that false radar images of several hijacked planes were created as part of the exercise and that these caused confusion over what was real. Oddly, these war games were mentioned only in a single footnote to the *9/11 Commission Report.*

Since the attack, seven of the 19 men still listed by the FBI as participants in the 9/11 hijackings were found to be alive overseas long after they supposedly died in the crashed airliners or were confirmed to have died before the attacks. They include: Abdul Azia Omari of Saudi Arabia, who claims his passport was stolen while he traveled through Denver, Colorado; Ameer Bukhari, who died in a plane crash prior to 9/11, according to his brother who passed a lie detector test; Waleed al Shehri, a Saudi pilot who now lives in Morocco; Saeed al Ghamdi, a Saudi airline pilot who says he was shocked when he heard his name connected to the hijackings; Abdul Rahman al Omari, a Saudi who went to the US Embassy in Jeddah to proclaim his innocence; Ahmed al Gambi, who complained, "I have never even heard of Pennsylvania," when he was named as a hijacker of Flight 93; and Salem al Hazmi, a Saudi who said, "I have never been to the United States."

Although the passport of one of the men who hijacked Flight 11 allegedly was found in the World Trade Center rubble, neither his name nor any names of the other hijackers appeared on the flight manifests of all four airliners. In fact, there were no Arabic names at all on any of the manifests.

The discovery of the miraculously undamaged passport wasn't announced until weeks after the attacks, at which time the passport owner, Abdul Omari, turned up alive in Saudi Arabia. He told the *London Telegraph*, "I couldn't believe it when the FBI put me on their list...I am not a suicide bomber. I am here. I am alive. I have no idea how to fly a plane."

The stories of all the above men were vouched for by the Saudi Arabian embassy and the Saudi foreign minister. Despite the newsworthy aspect of this story, the American news media did not cover it. Nor did the official investigation of the attacks look into the fact that $100,000 was wired to alleged hijacker Muhammad Atta prior to 9/11 by Omar Sheikh at the request of General Mahmood Ahmed, director of Pakistan's intelligence organization, the ISI. Sheikh, the accused paymaster behind the terrorists, admitted that he was supported by the ISI.

The *9/11 Commission Report* concluded that the financing of the attacks was "of little practical significance." Strangely, General Ahmed breakfasted with several US government officials on the morning of 9/11.

Some researchers have theorized that the airliners that struck the North and South towers were remote-controlled. This radical opinion is not shared by even the most ardent conspiracy theorists, although the technology certainly exists.

A firm called System Planning Corporation (SPC) offers what it calls "flight termination" and a "command transmitter system," designed to fly an airliner safely by remote control after the pilot and co-pilot have been incapacitated. The technology allows a ground control or airborne operator to fly as many as eight different airborne vehicles simultaneously. One of the SPC marketing campaigns boasts that this system could wrest control of an airliner from hijackers while in flight and land the plane safely.

The CEO of SPC International until just four months before the 9/11 attacks was Dov Zakheim, an Orthodox Jewish rabbi who also is a member of the CFR. His work within the US government extends back to the Reagan presidency when he served in various Department of Defense posts.

Zakheim also served as a foreign policy advisor to George W. Bush during his 2000 presidential campaign. He is co-author of the Project for a New American Century study, "Rebuilding America's Defenses," which concluded that "a new Pearl Harbor" would be the "catalyzing event" that would bring about "revolutionary change."

On May 4, 2001, Bush made Zakheim undersecretary of Defense and Comptroller of the Pentagon. More will be said about Zakheim's possible connection to the attacks later in this section.

Al Qaeda continues to be the villain in the 9/11 attacks, but it's important to remember that al Qaeda was the indirect creation of the CIA in the 1980s, when the Agency supplied weapons and training to the *mujahideen* fighting the Soviet invasion of Afghanistan. This group of battle-hardened Muslims later trained and armed the Kosovo Liberation Army during the US bombing of Serbia in the late 1990s. The CIA oversaw its role in Kosovo.

Britain's foreign secretary at that time, Robin Cook, went so far as to call al Qaeda a CIA creation, pointing out that its translation to the term "the base," actually refers to an Agency computer database.

In January 2001, the Bush administration ordered the FBI and other intelligence agencies to "back off" from their investigations of the bin Laden family, according to a news story broken by the BBC on November 7, 2001, and published later in the *London Guardian.* The report also revealed that two bin Laden relatives, Abdullah and Omar, lived at that time in Falls Church, Virginia, near CIA headquarters.

On the morning of 9/11, former President George H.W. Bush met in the Washington DC Ritz-Carlton Hotel with Shafig bin Laden, Osama's older brother, to discuss mutual business interests they had with the Carlyle Group. This firm is linked to powerful defense contracting companies.

Business connections regarding investments in Texas between the bin Laden family and the Bush family date back to the 1990s.

Another suspicious occurrence involves the fact that more than two dozen members of the Osama bin Laden family flew across the US during the "no fly" period immediately following the 9/11 attacks. This was confirmed by former Counter-Terrorism Chief Richard Clarke. "Someone brought to us for approval the decision to let an airplane filled with Saudis, including members of the bin Laden family, leave the country," Clarke told *Vanity Fair* magazine.

The collapse of the two towers of the World Trade Center was covered from nearly every angle, and yet there are many problems concerning how and why these buildings went down. Responsibility for investigating the cause of the collapses fell to FEMA, which proceeded to haul away much of the evidence before any investigation could be made.

Bill Manning, editor of the iconic fireman's publication, *Fire Engineering,* complained in the January 2002 issue that the publication, "has good reason to believe that the 'official investigation' blessed by FEMA and run by the American Society of Civil Engineers is a half-baked farce that may already have been commandeered by political forces whose primary interests, to put it mildly, lie far afield of full disclosure."

Why would certain "political forces" have reason to destroy evidence in the World Trade Center collapses? The official account claims the towers collapsed due to heat generated by burning jet fuel that caused the steel supports to soften, leading to a sequential collapse of each floor in the 110-story buildings. This conclusion was supported by experts in the structural engineering field.

There are, however, other experts in this arena who disagree. They wonder, for instance, how structural steel giving way on one side of a building could cause the entire tower to collapse straight downward at almost free-fall speed.

Other dissenting experts wonder how jet fuel, basically kerosene with added ingredients that burns at a temperature of 1,517 degrees

Fahrenheit in open air, could buckle structural steel, which has a melting point of 2,750 degrees Fahrenheit. In addition, it's obvious from the black smoke captured on video pouring out of the tower windows that the fires burned in an oxygen-starved environment, and not in open air.

Although jet fuel was not involved, there was an earlier plane crash into a New York building that bears mention. On July 28, 1945, a B-25 bomber flying in thick fog smashed into the 79th floor of the Empire State Building, causing a fire and killing 14 people including its three crew members. The building was not structurally damaged, and after speedy repairs, it remains an icon of the New York skyline today.

In 1975, a three-alarm fire burned fiercely on several floors of the WTC North Tower, which led the New York Port Authority to install sprinklers throughout both buildings. There was no damage to the structural steel.

Then on May 4, 1988, fires raged through four floors in a 62-story Los Angeles skyscraper. It burned for three hours before firefighters extinguished the blaze, and the repaired building continues to stand today.

A skyscraper in Venezuela survived a 2004 fire that burned for more than 17 hours over 26 floors. The building, which was constructed in 1974, still stands today.

Perhaps most interesting of all is the February 12, 2005 blaze in the Windsor Building in Madrid, Spain, a 32-story steel-reinforced concrete tower that burned for nearly 24 hours. The top 10 floors of the building, thoroughly engulfed in flames, fell, but the building itself did not collapse.

Completed in 1970 and 1973, the Twin Towers contained 200,000 tons of steel and 425,000 cubic yards of concrete. The core of each tower contained 47 box columns, 36-by-16 inches thick.

With this knowledge and having studied the tapes of the collapsing towers, a number of engineering experts weighed in. Van Romero, vice president for Research at the New Mexico Institute of Mining and Technology, said, "...after the airplanes hit the World Trade Center there were some explosive devices inside the buildings that caused the towers to collapse." He added that "the collapses were too methodical to be a chance result of airplanes colliding with the structures."

Then, just 10 days later, Romero did an about-face, saying, "Certainly the fire is what caused the building to fail."

Hyman Brown, construction manager of the World Trade Center, said, "It was over-designed to withstand almost anything, including hurricanes, high winds, bombings, and an airplane hitting it."

He later said, "Although the buildings were designed to withstand a 150-year storm and the impact of a Boeing 707, jet fuel burning at 2,000 degrees weakened the steel."

Responding to Brown's strange turnabout, Kevin Ryan of Underwriters Laboratories, supplier of the World Trade Center steel, wrote in a letter to the National Institute of Standards and Technology:

"We know that the steel components were certified to ASTM E119. The time temperature curves for this standard require the samples to be exposed to temperatures around 2000F for several hours. And as we all agree, the steel applied met those specifications. Additionally, I think we can all agree that even un-fireproofed steel will not melt until reaching red-hot temperatures of nearly 3000F. Why Dr. Brown would imply that 2000F would melt the high-grade steel used in those buildings makes no sense at all…If the steel from those buildings did soften or melt, I'm sure we can all agree that this was certainly not due to jet fuel fires of any kind, let alone the briefly burning fires in those towers."

Kevin Ryan was fired by Underwriters Laboratories several days after writing this letter.

Bystander videos shot during the evacuation of NYFD personnel from the Twin Towers quite clearly show firemen repeatedly saying, "There's a bomb in the building." At one point, a fireman within a few feet of the camera says to its operator, clearly, "There's a bomb in the building. Start clearing out." An adjacent bystander asks, "I'm sorry. You say there's a bomb? What did you say?" The fireman turns and repeats, "There's a bomb in the building. Start clearing out."

Another group of firemen appear in the video as it pans right and one is overheard saying to another, "There's a report of a secondary device in the area." Following this, another rescue worker says, "I got a secondary device."

This is in addition to the numerous live news broadcasts that reported secondary explosions long after the airlines crashed into the towers. In a live interview at the scene with Stephen Evans, a correspondent for North America Business, the BBC broadcast him saying, "Then an hour later [following the airliner impact] we had that big explosion from much, much lower. I don't know what caused that."

An MSNBC reporter was on the scene that morning and stated live, "At 10:30 I tried to leave the building, but as soon as I got outside I heard a second explosion and another rumble, and more smoke, and more dust. I ran inside the building. The chandeliers shook, and again this black smoke filled the air...And then a fire marshal came in and said we had to leave because if there was a third explosion this building might not last."

A Fox News reporter on the scene reported that the FBI had roped off the area around the towers and were taking photographs "just prior to that huge explosion that we all heard and felt."

Witnesses outside the building who'd been injured by debris testified to hearing three explosions preceded by a series of sounds that resembled rapid gunfire. Another Fox News reporter issued a live report that he'd been talking to a policeman when they both heard a huge explosion and looked up to see the building begin to collapse.

NBC reporter Pat Dawson on the scene spoke to Chief Albert Turrey, in charge of safety for the New York Fire Department, who told him he "had received word of a secondary device, that is, another bomb going off. He tried to get his men out as quickly as he could, but he said there was another explosion which took place. And then an hour after the first hit here, the first [air] crash that took place, he said there was another explosion that took place in one of the towers here. He thinks there were actually devices that were planted in the buildings. The second device, he thinks, he speculates, was probably planted in the building."

Teresa Veliz was on the 47th floor of the North Tower when the building was struck by Flight 11. Long after the initial impact, she said, "There were explosions going off everywhere. I was convinced that there were bombs planted all over the place and someone was sitting at a control panel pushing detonator buttons."

Fireman John Schroeder was among the first responders to the fires in the Twin Towers, because his ladder company was across from the World Trade Center. From his place, he witnessed the first airplane impacting the tower and so was the first fireman to call for emergency rescue vehicles.

He and fellow firemen entered the tower lobby and suddenly "the elevators exploded....People come running out of the elevators on fire. Fireball. We were in there for maybe five minutes, five minutes and the elevators exploded on us. We said, 'Something's wrong here. The plane hit up on the 80th floor. In five minutes all of a sudden the elevators are exploding on the first level?'"

Schroeder claims he and his fellow firemen reached the 24th floor when a warning blared from their portable radios: "Mayday! Mayday! Second plane!" After the impact of the plane on the adjacent tower threw them around, the firemen decided to evacuate the building. They made it to the third floor when the stairwell collapsed.

"When we got to the lobby," Schroeder continues, "everything was blown out, exploded."

Video taken in the lobby of the North Tower before its collapse supports his statements. The windows were blown out and marble panels had been blown off the walls. Attempts to explain this blamed a fireball that traveled down the elevator shafts, but these shafts were hermetically sealed and airtight, making it somewhat impossible for a fireball to have sufficient oxygen to travel 1,300 feet downward and destroy the lower eight floors of the building.

Fireman Louie Cacchioli, among the first responders to arrive in the second Tower, told *People* magazine, "I was taking firefighters up in the elevator to the 24th floor to get in position to evacuate workers. On the last trip up, a bomb went off. We think there were bombs set in the building."

Ginny Carr was in a business meeting on the 36th floor of One Liberty Plaza across the street from the World Trade Center and caught the entire first impact on audio tape. Her audio reveals a second, greater explosion about nine seconds after the first one.

Willie Rodriguez was working as a janitor in Sub Level One of the North Tower when it was hit. He said of the initial explosion, "I thought it was a generator that blew up in the basement." Seconds later he heard another explosion, "right on top [of the building], pretty far away. So it was a difference coming from the basement and coming from the top."

Rodriguez added that he heard many explosions, which someone tried to explain away as blown propane canisters in the building's various kitchens. "I don't believe that," Rodriguez said on tape, "because there are very strict guidelines on what you can put in the kitchens."

Literally every news crew on the scene recorded eyewitness reports from police, firemen and civilians of one or more secondary explosions in the Twin Towers. One eyewitness who was standing two and a half blocks from the South Tower said he saw "a number of brief light sources being emitted from inside the building between floors 10 and 15." He added that he saw six of these brief flashes and "a crackling sound" before the building collapsed.

The testimony of Stephen Gregory, commissioner of the NYFD Bureau of Communications, concurred: "I saw a flash, flash, flash and then the building came down."

Captain Karla de Shore of NYFD Battalion 46: "Somewhere around the middle of the WTC there was this orange and red flash...initially it was just one and then [it] just kept popping all the way around the building and [it] started to explode. As far as I could see, these popping sounds and the explosions were getting bigger, going both up and down and then all around the building."

The NYFD lost 343 fire fighters in the World Trade Center on 9/11. Yet for more than a year the Port Authority blocked the release of recordings made by firefighters inside the World Trade towers that day. A tape finally was released in November 2002. On it at one point, a fireman says, "I got, uh, an eyewitness who said there was an explosion on floors seven and eight." Another fireman says later, "Battalion 3 to Dispatch, we've just had another explosion." Yet another fireman reports, "We've got numerous people covered with dust from the secondary explosion." Then an excited fireman shouts, "We've got another explosion on the tower, 10-13, 10-13." Finally another fireman reports, "Tower Two has had a major explosion and what appears to be a complete collapse surrounding the entire area."

The most troubling recording came from fire Chief Palmer, who had reached the 78th floor lobby command post of the South Tower and said, "We've got two isolated pockets of fire. We should be able to knock it down with two lines."

The fact that Palmer reached the 78th floor, the heart of the plane crash, and felt the fire could be controlled indicates that part of the building was not the intense inferno that official reports indicate. In August 2005, additional hours of fire department tapes finally were released to the press, supporting the earlier tapes.

Engineers have claimed that a high-rise steel-reinforced building never has collapsed due to fire. On 9/11 there were three. Videos from a number of angles show the towers in collapse. They also show puffs of black smoke belching from the windows on the floors lower than the collapsing portion of the building. These puffs of smoke are sequential, always leading the main collapse by about 10 stories or more.

Close inspection of WTC videos shows molten material pouring out of windows of the South Tower as fires raged above. After studying the video, metallurgical experts like Professor Steven Jones of BYU insist the molten material is iron from thermite or Thermate and not aluminum melting from the heat of the fire in that building.

After Jones proved his point in lab demonstrations and analyzed a sample of the molten material from the South Tower, he concluded that the material was indeed iron and not aluminum. He added that the only way to explain the presence of that much molten iron is that several tons of thermite had to be placed in either the tower or the airliner.

This study also inspected samples of the WTC melted steel through an electron microscope. Not only did Jones discover traces of thermite explosive compound, he recognized the high sulphur signature of a patented brand of industrial explosive called Thermate, commonly used in the demolition business.

After his findings were published, BYU forced Jones to take an early retirement.

Mark Loizeaux, president of Controlled Demolition, Inc., told the *American Free Press* that in the basements of the World Trade Center, where 47 central support columns connected with the bedrock, hot spots of "literally molten steel" measuring more than 2,000 degrees Fahrenheit were discovered more than a month after the buildings had collapsed. At 70 feet below street level, Loizeaux said that a persistent and intense residual heat would be required to melt steel in such an oxygen-starved environment, and that this could explain how the structural supports of the towers failed.

The hot spots were located "at the bottoms of the elevator shafts of the main towers, down seven [basement] levels." He added that molten steel also was discovered in Building 7, which never was struck by a plane but collapsed in the afternoon of 9/11.

The highest recorded temperature in the towers was less than 1,400 degrees Fahrenheit, but the temperature required to melt the steel in the basement was more than double that figure.

If explosives were pre-set in the World Trade towers prior to 9/11, the question arises: how could they be planted without notice by those who worked in those buildings daily? Ben Fountain, a financial analyst who worked in one of the towers told *People* magazine that during the weeks prior to 9/11 there were several unusual and unannounced drills in which sections of the towers and Building 7 were evacuated for security reasons.

A North Tower security guard named Daria Coard told *Newsday* that she and her colleagues had been working 12-hour shifts in the weeks leading up to the attack due to a flurry of threatening phone calls. During the week of 9/11, Coard said the bomb-sniffing dogs abruptly were removed from the building.

A firm called Securacom provided electronic security for the World Trade Center at that time and therefore had control over measures such as shift lengths and bomb-sniffing dog use. Among the recent Securacom board directors was Marvin Bush, brother of President George W. Bush. Marvin Bush served on the board soon after the 1993 WTC bombing, when Securacom acquired its $8.3 million contract to upgrade the security there and held that post until June 2000.

Wirt Walker III, cousin of Marvin and George Bush, was the CEO of Securacom from 1999 to January 2002, so he was at the helm during the attacks. Walker also ran the aircraft company, Aviation General, that had a contract to sell planes to the National Civil Aviation Training Organization (NCATO) of Giza, Egypt. Touted as "the first civilian pilot training organization in the Middle East," NCATO was headquartered in the home town of alleged 9/11 terrorist ringleader Muhammad Atta.

Based in Sterling, Virginia, Securacom changed its name to Stratesec after 9/11, before going bankrupt in 2002. Aside from the World Trade Center, Securacom/Stratesec provided security for Dulles Airport — departure point for Flight 77, which allegedly struck the Pentagon — and United Airlines. The firm also had work with the Department of Defense, and it was capitalized by the Kuwait-American Corp., also known as KuwAm, an investment firm that has been linked to the Bush family since the Gulf War.

After leaving the Stratesec board in 2000, Marvin Bush joined the board of HCC Insurance, formerly the Houston Casualty Company, which was one of the insurers of the World Trade Center on 9/11. Bush left HCC in November 2002 on the same day that Congress passed the 9/11 insurance bailout legislation at urging from the White House. And in a final suspicious note, Wirt Walker's Aviation General company was bankrolled by KuwAm.

Some suspicious "eyewitness" reports aired on 9/11 require attention, too. Take the Fox News interview in the street near the WTC with a man identified as Mark Humphry, who calmly stated he saw the collapse and repeatedly added the same phrase, that it was due to "structural failure because the fire was too intense."

The collapse had just occurred. People were walking around in a daze, covered gray with dust, and this witness calmly spoke in his pristine state about structural failure due to fire? So suspicious was his account that researchers performed a search and claimed to learn that Humphry is really an actor named Harley Guy whose work is readily available on YouTube.

Also on that morning, CBS anchor Dan Rather interviewed Jerome Hauer, listed on screen as a "Terrorism Expert." Hauer stated flatly that the collapse of the towers was due to the velocity of the airplanes and the heat from their burning fuel, long before any investigation had been organized.

Subsequent research indicated Hauer to be a bio-warfare expert for Kroll Inc., which received a WTC security contract following the 1993 bombing. On 9/11 Hauer was an advisor with the Department of Health and Human Services (HHS), an appointment he received from HHS Secretary Tommy Thompson of the Bush Administration. Hauer also ran New York Mayor Rudolph Giuliani's Office of Emergency Management between 1996 and 2000, and he was the key reason why this organization was headquartered in Building 7.

In his work for Kroll, Hauer named former FBI special agent John O'Neil to take charge of WTC security. O'Neil had quit the FBI in frustration over the obstruction he received from the US Embassy in Yemen during his investigation of the USS Cole attack, and had serious doubts that bin Laden and al Qaeda were responsible. O'Neil died on his first day of work at the WTC, on 9/11.

Hauer would surface again weeks after the attacks when he advised White House members to take the antibiotic, Cipro, to counteract the effects of anthrax — one week before any anthrax arrived in the mail.

Finally, there is the odd MSNBC broadcast at 9:34 a.m., just 33 minutes after the second airliner struck, blaming Osama bin Laden and the Taliban in Afghanistan for the attack.

The strange comment that then-New York Mayor Rudolph Giuliani made to Peter Jennings of ABC News on the day of the attacks also bears notice. Giuliani said he had been in a temporary command center, and not the newly completed and hardened command center located in Building 7 of the World Trade Center, which collapsed later that day. He added that someone told him he must evacuate because the towers were going to come down.

The interesting question here is who this person was and how he knew of the imminent tower collapses. It also begs the question as to why the first responders were not given the same warning. Later, when

Giuliani was in the midst of his campaign for the presidency, a man asked both of these questions during a campaign event. He was arrested and removed.

Giuliani also was responsible for the lack of investigation of the World Trade Center debris. He ordered the remains shipped to overseas recycling yards before investigators, including FEMA, could examine it. Instead, Controlled Demolition, Inc. oversaw the clean-up, the same firm that oversaw the clean-up of the Alfred Murrah Building in Oklahoma City after it was bombed in 1995.

Finally, there is the witness testimony regarding a white van parked on the New Jersey side of the Hudson River, where the view of the attacks was fairly clear. Witnesses saw men dressed in traditional Muslim outfits jumping on the van to celebrate the destruction of the towers. Some called police, reporting the van and its license plate.

When New Jersey police responded to the all-points-bulletin, they pulled the van over as it approached the George Washington Bridge headed toward Manhattan. To their surprise, the occupants turned out to be Israelis named Sivan and Paul Kurzberg, Yaron Schmuel, Oded Ellner and Omer Marmari. One of them, Sivan Kurzberg, told the officers, "We are Israelis. We are not your problem. Your problems are our problems. The Palestinians are your problem."

Police and FBI agents remained suspicious, however, after discovering maps of New York City and box cutters in the van. They also found $4,700 in cash stuffed into a sock.

Although no explosives were found in the van, bomb-sniffing dogs reacted to indicate that there had been explosives there recently. Among the confiscated photos was a picture of Sivan Kurzberg flicking a cigarette lighter in front of the smoking ruins of the World Trade Center which, according to the *Bergen Record,* appeared to be celebratory.

According to the *Jewish Daily Forward,* the FBI determined that at least two of the van's detainees were Mossad agents. This was corroborated when the FBI learned the men were employed by Urban Moving Systems, known to be a Mossad front company.

The Israelis remained in custody for 71 days before quietly being released. A CIA source claimed, "There was no question but that [the order to stop the investigation] came from the White House. It was immediately assumed at CIA headquarters that this basically was going to be a cover-up so that the Israelis would not be implicated in any way in 9/11."

Once back in Israel, the detainees appeared on a talk show during which one of them admitted, "Our purpose was to document the event."

In the early days following 9/11, more than 60 Israelis were arrested or detained under the new Patriot Act or for immigration violations, as reported by Fox News. Some were active members of the Israeli military who failed polygraph tests when asked about alleged surveillance activities in the US.

An unnamed source told Fox, "Evidence linking these Israelis to 9/11 is classified. I cannot tell you about evidence that has been gathered." The report also claimed that more than 140 Israelis had been arrested prior to 9/11 during an investigation into Mossad spying activity inside the US.

Evidence that Israelis may have had prior knowledge of the 9/11 attacks appeared at the Israeli Odigo instant messaging service. At least two Israel-based Odigo employees received warning of an attack in New York City more than two hours before the first plane struck, but the warning was not forwarded to any American authorities.

The US headquarters of Odigo was just two blocks from the WTC. Two weeks after the attack Odigo Vice President Alex Diamondis said, "It is possible that the attack warning was broadcast to other Odigo members, but the company has not received reports of other recipients of the message."

The FBI supposedly received the Internet tracking number of the person who sent the Odigo message, but there has been no announcement of his or her identity to this day. Interestingly, the research and development headquarters of Odigo is in Herzliya, Israel, which is where Mossad headquarters is located. The firm has since changed its name to Comverse.

Another curious connection between Israel and 9/11 is the fact that an Israeli company, ICTS International, had charge of security for all passengers boarding flights from Boston's Logan Airport, where the hijacked airliners departed. Years later, this same security company failed to prevent "shoe bomber" Richard Reid from boarding a Tel Aviv to Paris flight. And yet a rider in the Patriot Act declared that foreign security companies such as ICTS could not be targeted for 9/11 lawsuits. In this way, ICTS was excused from providing any evidence it may have gathered on 9/11, including the airport video surveillance tapes.

The behavior of Zim Integrated Shipping Services just prior to 9/11 also bears attention. Days before the attacks this firm broke its lease and vacated its offices on the 16th and 17th floors in WTC's North Tower, costing Zim $50,000 in unused lease time. The state of Israel owns close to 50 percent of the parent company, Zim Israel Navigation with the remainder of ownership being held by Israel Corp. One of the world's largest shipping container firms, Zim has since relocated some of its offices to Houston, Texas.

An investigation by FBI special agent Michael Dick into why Zim broke its lease and vacated the North Tower just a week prior to the attacks resulted in his removal from the case under orders from then-Justice Department Criminal Division head Michael Chertoff. Chertoff holds a dual citizenship in the US and Israel.

A CIA "non-official cover" source who worked with Agent Dick claimed that Israeli movers transferred explosives into the vacated Zim office space. The FBI eventually transferred Dick to Pakistan, where he investigated the kidnapping of *Wall Street Journal* reporter Daniel Pearl who, according to the CIA source, was murdered when his investigation threatened to identify those who financed the 9/11 attacks. According to Special Agent Dick, the CIA source said, "The same people that beheaded Pearl in Pakistan did the beheadings in Iraq," and added that al-Qaeda was not responsible.

The FBI received curious tips as early as October 2000 from a retired Israeli Defense Forces officer who claimed he overheard men speaking in Hebrew while he was visiting the Gomel Chesed Jewish Cemetery near Newark, New Jersey. He said one of the men stated that Americans would learn what it's like to live with terrorists when "the planes hit the twins." As this was just one month before the Bush-Gore presidential election, one of the men expressed concern over how the voting outcome would affect matters. According to the source, another man said, "Don't worry. We have people in high places, and no matter who gets elected, they will take care of everything." The FBI did not follow up this lead.

Dr. A. True Ott, a researcher and author who hosts an Internet radio show, has been an outspoken proponent of the Israeli connection to the 9/11 attacks. "Steven Jones has all this forensic evidence of the superthermite, but what good is it if you don't have a suspect with a motive?" he told the author. "Steven Jones never addresses how these al-Qaeda operatives got hold of superthermite. Few talk about the September 10, [2001] announcement by Donald Rumsfeld at a press conference revealing that $2.3 trillion was missing from the Pentagon.

He's forced to announce this because there's an ongoing 18-month investigation into it and the key player in it is Dov Zakheim."

Zakheim served as the Pentagon comptroller after being appointed to the post by President George W. Bush, and held the position from May 4, 2001 to March 10, 2004, despite the audit early in his tenure that revealed actually $2.6 trillion was missing from the Pentagon books.

Zakheim attained a vice president's position with one of the world's most prestigious strategy consulting firms, Booz Allen Hamilton, on May 6, 2004, just two months after leaving the Pentagon. He holds a dual Israeli-American citizenship, is an ordained rabbi, and also is a member of the CFR and the Center for Strategic and International Studies.

As mentioned earlier, Zakheim contributed to writing "Rebuilding America's Defenses," the position paper for the Project for a New American Century, which stressed that a Pearl Harbor-type incident might be needed to incite Americans to support war against its Muslim enemies. He also served as vice president of System Planning Corp., which specializes in remote control technology for airplanes.

This piqued the interest of some researchers who believe the two Boeing 767 airliners that hit the Twin Towers were empty, remote-controlled military tanker planes. As Pentagon comptroller, Zakheim earlier had leased more than 30 Boeing 767 tanker planes to MacDill Air Force Base in Florida.

"To me, Zakheim has 2.3 trillion motives to take out the World Trade Center and Building 7, where the [Pentagon missing funds] investigation is centered," Ott told the author. "He had civilian control of the Pentagon budgets. The attacks destroyed the whole area where the paper trail would be. The FBI, the SEC and all the other investigations into what happened to these trillions of dollars were centered in the World Trade Center. That, to me, is a motive.

"It's not a matter of bin-Laden hating Americans. It's an Israeli operation to cover up their theft. A lot of heads would have rolled among the Joint Chiefs if this became public, and there is a lot of pro-Zionist feeling among the Pentagon staffers. Now the guilty parties have no physical evidence to prosecute them."

The section of the Pentagon that was hit also contained physical evidence. The 2001 budget files were there, as well as some of the involved accountants, bookkeepers and budget analysts who died that day.

The cleanup of the WTC rubble involved several firms. One of them, Metals Management, hauled away the steel that so many witnesses claimed had remained molten for weeks after 9/11. This vital evidence quickly went to Japan, where it was smelted and sold to a Shanghai company in China. Metal Management, owned by Alan Ratner, has since merged with the Sims Group, after showing a handsome profit in selling a reported 50,000 tons of WTC steel to the Chinese.

It troubles many investigators that Philip Zelikow, a dual Israeli-American citizen, was executive director of the 9/11 Commission, the most powerful position in that probe. Henry Kissinger originally was named to that post, but surrendered it to Zelikow after protests.

Zelikow had a long association with Bush staffers Condoleeza Rice, Paul Wolfowitz and Karl Rove as well as Vice President Dick Cheney. He guided an investigation that is littered with red flags.

Building 7

Another red flag involves the Salomon Brothers Building, or Building 7. It was a 47-story steel and glass structure that collapsed straight downward into its own foundation at 5:25 pm on 9/11 in just six seconds, without critically damaging the adjacent US Post Office and Verizon Buildings.

The Salomon Brothers skyscraper was not struck by the airliners, and FEMA's *WTC Building Performance Study* concluded that the "loss of structural integrity was likely a result of weakening caused by fires on the 5th to 7th floors. The specifics of the fires in WTC 7 and how they caused the building to collapse remain unknown at this time."

Later, another report surmised that burning debris from the Twin Towers started fires in Building 7 that ignited fuel tanks inside the building.

The tale of Building 7 becomes muddled with the revelation that a BBC reporter announced its collapse 20 minutes before the fact. Video even shows the structure still standing behind the reporter as she makes her announcement. Just as troubling are the YouTube videos that show firemen telling bystanders to move away from Building 7, saying it was about to come down.

Richard Gage, founder of Architects for 9/11 Truth, himself an architect with more than two decades of building experience, stated, "Once you get to the science, it's indisputable. Building 7, a 47-story skyscraper not hit by an airplane on 9/11, fell symmetrically, smoothly at virtually free-fall speed into its own footprint — a perfect controlled demolition. There's only graphic evidence for two or three fires in that building on the 12th and maybe 13th floor. The official story tells us that the steel was softened, but if that was the case and if the building fell due to fires, the fires by their nature creep from place to place, leaving one area cool and burning another area. That would force an asymmetrical collapse. The building would tip over."

Building 7 was constructed by real estate developer Larry Silverstein, who also leased all the buildings in the World Trade Center on July 24, 2001. He made the purchase just six weeks before the 9/11 attacks for a total of $3.2 billion under the aegis of the Silverstein Group, with a down payment of $124 million, $14 million of which was Silverstein's own money.

The terms of the lease stipulated that Silverstein had the right to rebuild the structures if they were somehow destroyed. Some researchers point out that the first step in preparing the WTC buildings for demolition in a false flag attack would be to take them out of the hands of the New York Port Authority and put them under private control.

Silverstein gushed about his "dream come true," but the WTC was hardly a real estate dream. According to *Business Week*, the WTC, "subsidized since its inception, has never functioned, nor was it intended to function, unprotected in the rough-and-tumble real estate marketplace."

Silverstein knew that the Twin Towers alone would require an immediate $200 million expenditure for improvements such as removal and replacement of building materials considered to be health hazards. The New York Port Authority, prior to the Silverstein sale, tried several times to obtain permits to tear down the towers for liability reasons, since they were widely considered an "asbestos bombshell." These requests all were refused.

Instead of beginning renovation, however, Silverstein took out two insurance policies — covering acts of terrorism — on the Trade Center buildings for the maximum amount, with a potential payout of $7.1 billion. This payout was based, in Silverstein's opinion, on the possibility of two terrorist attacks.

According to the *Washington Post*, the insurer, Swiss Reinsurance, went to court, arguing that 9/11 was just one attack, which would reduce the payout to $3.55 billion. In 2004, a federal jury ruled that, for insurance purposes, 9/11 involved two attacks. In a settlement, the insurers agreed to pay $4.55 billion.

Silverstein and his investors had scored a huge profit on their original cash investment of $124 million.

In April 2006, an agreement was reached allowing Silverstein to build three office towers on the World Trade Center site. These are currently under construction.

Returning to Building 7, Silverstein admitted in the PBS documentary, *America Rebuilds*, aired in September 2002, that he and the FDNY jointly decided to demolish the structure late in the afternoon of 9/11.

"I remember getting a call from the fire department commander," said Silverstein, "telling me that they were not sure that they were going to be able to contain the fire, and I said, 'We've had such a terrible loss of life. Maybe the smartest thing to do is pull it.' And they made that decision to pull and we watched the building collapse."

A spokesman for Silverstein Properties later claimed that "pull it" referred to pulling out the firefighters. However, according to the FEMA report, "No manual firefighting actions were taken by FDNY [in Building 7]." The *New York Times* reported that Assistant Chief Frank Fellini, the fire commander for that area, ordered his firemen away from WTC 7 at 11:30 a.m. for safety reasons — six hours before the building came down.

Barry Jennings, an emergency coordinator for the New York Housing Authority, was in Building 7 shortly after the first plane struck the North Tower across the WTC plaza. Jennings had been called there along with Michael Hess, a corporate council appointed by Mayor Giuliani, and they were in the building before the second plane struck the South Tower.

Jennings detailed what occurred that day in a videotaped interview conducted years later by documentary director Dylan Avery. Jennings claimed that he and Hess encountered a large number of policemen in the lobby when they first entered the building. The pair rode to the 23rd floor, the FEMA office, in a freight elevator after a previous attempt to enter that floor from a stairwell failed. Jennings claimed the FEMA office had been evacuated recently, as evidenced by half-eaten sandwiches and coffee still steaming in cups.

Jennings used the phone until an unnamed individual told him and Hess they had to leave "right away." He and Hess descended on a stairwell and were on the 6th level when an explosion caused the stairs to collapse under their feet. Jennings claimed that he actually hung in the air while grasping a pole.

The pair went back up and on the 8th level Jennings looked out a window and saw that the Twin Towers were still standing. This is an important point, because it proves that there was an explosion in Building 7 *prior* to the collapse of the towers, which have been blamed for the building's own eventual collapse.

When they returned to the lobby, it had been utterly destroyed. By this time Jennings had been in Building 7 for some time and he claimed that he heard explosions inside the structure throughout his stay there.

Later it would be suggested that Jennings had heard the building's fuel oil tank exploding, but he stuck to his story.

"I know what I heard," he told Avery. "I heard explosions." Jennings also claimed that when he tried to exit through the lobby he had to step over bodies, another contradiction to the official 9/11 report that claims there were no fatalities in Building 7. Jennings said the lobby was so wrecked that "I didn't know where I was. [The lobby was] so destroyed that they had to take me out through a hole in the wall that I believe the fire department made to get me out."

Once outside, Jennings told his story to news cameras. Years later, he repeated it to Avery for the *Loose Change* documentary, but asked that it not be included in the "Final Cut" version because he had been getting threats regarding his job security and his pension. Avery kept the Jennings interview from public view until a subsequent BBC documentary twisted Jennings' words to fit the official version of the Building 7 collapse. Avery then released the Jennings video he'd made.

In August 2008, just one week before the NIST (National Institute of Standards & Technology) report on Building 7 was made public, Barry Jennings died. There was no official report on the cause of death. Avery hired a private investigator to look into this and was shocked to hear the investigator's response after just 24 hours:

"Due to some of the information I have uncovered, I have determined this is a job for the police. I have refunded your credit card. Please do not contact me ever again about this individual." A second investigator learned that Jennings' death certificate was not properly filled out. Avery referred the matter to the police, and no new information has become available.

Jennings' tale is supported by news video shot outside WTC 7 that afternoon, which shows firemen clearing the area with the warning, "It's blowin' boy," and "The building is about to blow up, move it back."

A witness, Kevin McPadden — veteran of the Air Force Search and Rescue unit — has said in taped interviews that he saw a Red Cross representative listening to a hand-held radio and that he and other witnesses clearly heard a voice on the radio saying "three, two, one," just before the building came down. Other witnesses have testified that the fire in Building 7 was confined to the lower floors when suddenly a sound like a thunderclap echoed, followed by a shockwave through the structure that blew out windows.

"A second later," said a witness, "the bottom floor caved out and the building followed after that." Another witness, NYPD officer Clay Bartmer, claimed he heard a series of explosions from Building 7.

These facts cast serious doubt on the Silverstein Properties claims that "pull it" referred to pulling out firefighters. It is well known in engineering circles that "pull it" is common jargon for demolishing a structure.

It is obvious, of course, that if the evidence indicating that Building 7 was deliberately demolished by explosives is true, those explosives could not have been placed in the short time span between the attacks and the collapse. Explosives would have had to be in place before 9/11. One point of interest is that WTC 7's fire alarm system was placed on "test" at 6:47 am on the morning of 9/11. When in this mode, any alarms received from the system are considered the result of maintenance or testing and are ignored.

It's also intriguing to note that WTC 7 contained the offices of the FBI, IRS, Department of Defense, Secret Service, Securities & Exchange Commission, Citibank's Salomon Smith Barney, and Mayor Giuliani's Office of Emergency Management. The IRS office contained enormous numbers of files on corporate tax fraud, including Enron, and the SEC office was crammed with more stock fraud records. The SEC has not said how many of those files were destroyed, but Reuters estimated the number at between 3,000 and 4,000.

Included among these was the SEC inquiry into how investment banks divided shares of public offerings during the high-tech boom of the 1990s. Max Burger of the Bernstein, Litowitz, Burger & Grossmann law firm called the paper loss "a disaster for these cases."

As mentioned earlier, files important to the investigation of the $2.6 trillion missing from the Pentagon books under Dov Zakheim's watch also were lost.

In February 2002, Silverstein Properties received $861 million from Industrial Risk Insurance for WTC 7. The firm's estimated initial investment of $386 million means a realized profit of $475 million on the building's collapse.

After all of the evidence is inspected, one has to ask who exactly is the man some call "Lucky Larry"? Born in Brooklyn, NY, in 1931, Silverstein entered the real estate business with his father, establishing Silverstein Properties in 1957. Being Jewish, Silverstein holds important positions in such organizations as the Anti-Defamation League, the Museum of Jewish Heritage in New York, and the United Jewish Appeal, which he formerly chaired. It is obvious that these positions aided Silverstein, who, like Zakheim, holds dual Israeli-American citizenship, in obtaining the lease agreement for the WTC. This is because Lewis Eisenberg, chairman of the New York Port Authority, was on the planning board of the United Jewish Appeal.

It is an accepted fact that all of these charitable organizations have direct ties to Israel and have been used by the Mossad in a variety of ways. If the Mossad had prior knowledge of the 9/11 attacks (and perhaps even participated in them, as some evidence presented previously has indicated), could this be the key to "Lucky Larry's" luck? It is vital to remember that Silverstein had such a close relationship with former and current Israeli Prime Minister Benjamin Netanyahu, that he received a phone call from him every Sunday morning.

Silverstein made a point to breakfast in the Windows on the World restaurant, located on Floor 107 of the North Tower, every morning. He skipped that meal on the morning of 9/11. Two of his children worked in the WTC. Both took the day off on 9/11.

The preceding evidence is not included in the official report. Instead, the responsibility of Osama bin Laden and his organization for the 9/11 attacks seemed to be proved by his own words in a tape released by Al-Jezeera on December 14, 2001. The low-quality recording, claimed by authorities to have been found in a house in Jalalabad, Afghanistan, shows bin Laden confessing to the attacks.

But there are reasons to be skeptical that the man in the tape is Osama bin Laden. Firstly, the FBI website that listed bin Laden among its Top Ten Most Wanted plainly claimed that he is left-handed. The man in the video is writing a note with his right hand. On the fourth finger of that same hand, the man in the video wears a gold ring, which is forbidden by Islamic law. And although the resemblance is quite strong, the man in the video has a much fuller face than the drawn bin Laden who appears in FBI photos.

The jubilantly celebrated killing of bin Laden in Pakistan on May 2, 2011, provided punctuation to the 9/11 tragedy in the mainstream media, despite the curiously rapid dumping of the alleged body in the sea and the instantaneous DNA results that positively identified him. It bothered none of the press that the body never would be inspected by independent experts, or that DNA testing does not produce instantaneous results.

The 9/11 attack in Washington only adds to these troubling riddles.

The Pentagon

The official story of the 9/11 attack on the Pentagon claims that Hani Hanjour and other terrorists hijacked American Flight 77, and that Hanjour flew the Boeing 757 into the building's Western wall at full speed. The impact and fire killed 64 people making up the plane's crew and passengers, as well as 125 people in the building. The official report goes on to claim that the airliner bored through the Pentagon's steel-reinforced exterior wall, its wings and tail folding to form a cylindrical missile that burst into flames.

The lack of debris has been explained away by the heat intensity of the fire. Yet this supposedly high intensity fire failed to damage wooden tables, plastic computers and a paper book, all of which were clearly seen in photos of the crash area.

Prior to 9/11, no other airline crash in history had resulted in the complete vaporization of plane parts, specifically engines and wings. This history-making result would be repeated shortly in the alleged crash of Flight 93 in Pennsylvania, also claimed to have been vaporized in official reports.

Comparisons to crashes under similar conditions to those of Flight 77 bear out this anomaly. On August 15, 2005, Greek-owned Helios Airways Flight 522 was a Boeing 737 headed to Athens that crashed at full speed into a hillside, killing all 121 passengers aboard. The crash site revealed a fire, but also sections of the airliner's tail, engines, wings and cockpit. Bodies were retrieved.

Oddly, within a few days of the Pentagon attack the FBI announced that 184 of the189 people who died in the alleged crash of Flight 77 had been identified by their fingerprints. No explanation was offered as to how human remains could have been preserved so well in a fire so hot that it consumed an entire Boeing 757, including its wheels, and engines. The identifications were made by the Armed Forces DNA Identification Laboratory, the same organization that identified the victims of the alleged Flight 93 crash.

Another troubling aspect of this attack involves the photos taken of the Pentagon before the West wall collapsed. They show a hole about 15-

by-20 feet in the ground floor. The Boeing 757 has a 124-foot wingspan and a height of 44 feet — about four stories. The plane has two Rolls Royce or Pratt & Whitney turbofan engines that weigh close to six tons each, made of a steel and titanium alloy.

Titanium has a melting point of 1,688 degrees Celcius. Jet fuel, which consists mostly of kerosene, burns at 1,120 degrees Celcius. This makes the vaporizing of the engines physically impossible. Some vestiges of the engines should have been among the debris at the Pentagon, but there were no signs of them. Instead, a single turbo jet engine measuring just three feet in diameter was discovered inside the Pentagon.

The official report claimed this small engine part came from the APU in the 757's tail section, but a Honeywell Aerospace Division expert, upon inspecting the engine photo, said, "There's no way that's an APU wheel." Also, John W. Brown, a spokesman for Rolls Royce said the turbine in the photo was "not a part of any Rolls Royce engine that I am familiar with."

Carl Schwartz, president and CEO of Patmos Nanotechnology LLC, wrote an article in which he suggests the turbo jet engine in the Pentagon photographs comes from a US Air Force A-3 Skywarrior, specifically the front shaft bearing housing of that engine. The A-3 is an older and obsolete fighter-bomber and there are few left in the US, most of which are stored at the Hughes Aircraft facility, now known as Raytheon, in Van Nuys, California.

Other experts, like French army battle damage assessment officer Major Pierre-Henri Bunel, suspect the turbo jet engine may have been part of a cruise-type missile. Bunel points to the fact that the Pentagon damage was too deep and collimated to have been caused by airliner fuel, and suggests instead that a shaped charge warhead cut the hole.

Logic indicates the heavy 757 engines would make their own holes in a wall, but no such holes existed. The fuselage of the 757 is made of aluminum, which more probably would squash itself against a steel-reinforced wall. And yet the impact hole passes completely through 16 feet of the building, making a hole on the inner side.

These suspicious facts were underscored in a CNN live report from the scene in which the correspondent says, "From my close-up inspection there's no evidence of a plane having crashed anywhere near the Pentagon....The only pieces left that you could see are small enough that you could pick [them] up in your hand. There are no tail sections, wing sections, fuselage sections anywhere around which would indicate that the entire plane crashed into the side of the Pentagon and then caused the side to collapse."

Whatever debris was not carried off by FBI agents soon was deliberately buried by trucks and tractors.

Some theorists are convinced that a Tomahawk cruise missile struck the Pentagon on 9/11. This is partially corroborated in an odd comment made by Defense Secretary Rumsfeld to *Parade* magazine when he was interviewed inside the Pentagon in October 2001. Rumsfeld referred to "the missile damage done to this building."

Norman Mineta, who was US secretary of transportation at the time, testified to the National Commission on September 11th Attacks that he was in the White House Presidential Emergency Operations Center (PEOC) bunker with Vice President Dick Cheney after the first plane hit the WTC but prior to the strike on the Pentagon. Mineta testified:

"There was a young man who came in and said to the Vice President, 'The plane is 50 miles out, the plane is 30 miles out.' And when he got down to 'The plane is 10 miles out,' the young man also said to the Vice President, 'Do the orders still stand?' The Vice President turned and flicked his neck around and said, 'Of course the order still stands. Have you heard anything to the contrary?' At the time I didn't know what all that meant."

Mineta claimed that the standing "order" was to shoot down the approaching plane, but as no such order was carried out, investigators suspect the "order" was *not* to shoot down the plane. Author David Ray Griffin posed the question: "If the orders were to shoot down an unidentified aircraft headed toward the Pentagon, would it not have been abundantly obvious that they would still stand, especially given what had just happened in New York City?"

A three-year study by Craig Ranke and Aldo Marquis of the Citizen Investigation Team (CIT) concluded that the Pentagon incident was not caused by a hijacked airliner, "but rather a false flag military black operation involving a carefully planned and skillfully executed deception."

The results of their investigation appear in an 81-minute video called *National Security Alert*. The producers interviewed eyewitnesses, many of them in exactly the same spots where they stood when the Pentagon was struck on 9/11.

All the witnesses testified that the plane's flight path was radically different than what the official story claims and one of them, a Pentagon policeman named Roosevelt Roberts, said he saw an airliner fly away from the Pentagon immediately after the explosion. As neither the official report nor eyewitness reports speak of a second low-flying airliner, the plane Roberts saw flying away had to be the same one all the other witnesses described.

Officer Roberts' testimony is supported by Arlington National Cemetery employee Erik Dihle in his December 13, 2001 interview with the Center for Military History. Dihle did not see the plane, but said that other witnesses told him a bomb had exploded and that a jet flew away.

Five light poles were knocked down by the low flying airliner before it struck the Pentagon, according to the official report. But since eyewitnesses interviewed by Ranke and Marquis unanimously testified that the flight path was further to the north, the downed poles must have been dropped deliberately.

One of them supposedly fell through and shattered the windshield of Lloyde England's taxi cab, according to the official report, but not one witness saw the pole on the cab or saw England lifting it from the cab. England claims a "silent stranger" helped him remove the pole minutes after the Pentagon explosion. His cab's hood had no damage, not even a scratch.

When confronted with photographic evidence that conflicted with his story, England said, "I can't explain it." He also revealed that his wife works for the FBI. And while England didn't know he was being recorded, he said on videotape, "This is a world thing happening. I'm a small man."

April Gallop, a Pentagon employee, was working in the building's west side when it was struck. She and her son received a ride to a nearby hospital, where she claims she was repeatedly visited by men in suits.

In an interview with Jim Marrs for his book, *Inside Job,* April said, "They never identified themselves or even said which agency they worked for. But I know they were not newsmen because I learned that the Pentagon told news reporters not to cover survivors' stories or they would not get any more stories out of there. The men who visited me all said they couldn't tell me what to say. They only wanted to make suggestions. But then they told me what to do, which was to take the [Victim Compensation Fund] money and shut up. They also kept insisting that a plane hit the building. They repeated this over and over. But I was there and I never saw a plane or even debris from a plane. I figure the plane story is there to brainwash people."

Other witnesses inside the Pentagon described the impact. Air Force Lieutenant Colonel Marc Abshire told the *Washington Post,* "There was a huge blast. I could feel the air shock wave of it. It didn't rumble. It was more of a direct smack."

Master Sergeant Noel Sepulveda, who was only 150 feet from the impact point, said the blast was so tremendous that it threw him 100 feet backward and slammed him into a light pole, which caused internal injuries. Other witnesses more than one and a half miles away at the Sheraton Hotel reported a blast that shook the whole building.

Don Perkal of MSNBC said he smelled cordite in the Pentagon building and added, "I knew explosives had been set off somewhere."

Test crashes of airliners have been conducted over the years. None of them produced a shock wave, a cordite smell or the bright silvery flash that many eyewitnesses reported that day.

After the attack, the *Los Angeles Times* discovered that the portion of the Pentagon struck by the plane was the only section of the building that had been renovated to resist just such an impact. The new windows were blast resistant, weighing 2,500 pounds each and remained intact during the crash and fire, according to the report.

The building foundation was only slightly damaged with two supports bent outward rather than inward, which would be the case when struck by a 757 airliner. Also, there was no extensive charring in the alleged crash site, which is inconsistent with all known airline crashes and especially one in which the official report claimed that the fire obliterated nearly all of the wreckage.

A number of witnesses claim to have seen an aircraft resembling a military C-130 four-engine cargo plane above the Pentagon minutes after the crash. But press accounts claimed the plane was above the Pentagon during the explosion and that it made a steep descent and turned away from the Pentagon following the explosion. Eyewitnesses have denied seeing this. A second plane, a four-engine airliner painted white with no markings, was captured on a private video camera flying in circles above the White House, a highly restricted air space.

The terrorist who reportedly flew Flight 77, Hani Hanjour, was so unskilled at controlling even small planes that one month before the attack he was not permitted to fly after demonstrating difficulty in controlling and landing a single-engine Cessna 172 at Freeway Airport in Bowie, Maryland. Marcel Bernard, chief flight instructor at Freeway

Airport, said Hanjour already had been flight certified. According to Bernard, in order to rent an aircraft, "our insurance required that he fly with one of our instructors...The consensus was that he was very quiet, [with] average to below average piloting skills."

More suspicious is the fact that Hanjour did not have a ticket for Flight 77.

The laws of aerodynamics pose another problem for the official story. A plane the size of a 757 has to slow almost to stall speed in order to land, because flight speed causes an air cushion that prevents touch down. If it is true that Flight 77 was traveling full throttle at about 500 mph, the air cushion would prevent it from getting closer than 50 feet from the ground. Yet, the hole in the Pentagon wall is on the ground floor.

In an interview with Wing TV, former Air Force and commercial pilot Russ Wittenburg, who had flown two of the planes used in the 9/11 attacks, said Flight 77 "could not possibly have flown at those speeds which they said it did without going into a high speed stall. The airplane won't go that fast when you start pulling those high G maneuvers. That plane would have fallen out of the sky...."

Pilotsfor911truth.org claims that data from Flight 77 showed an altitude of 180 feet. The site goes on: "This altitude has been determined to reflect Pressure altitude as set by 29.92 inHg [inches of mercury] on the altimeter. The actual local [barometric] pressure for DCA [Ronald Reagan Washington National Airport] at impact time was 30.22 inHg. The error for this discrepancy is 300 feet. Meaning, the actual aircraft altitude was 300 feet higher than indicated at that moment in time. Which means aircraft altitude was 480 feet above sea level (MSL, 75 foot margin for error according to Federal Aviation Regultions)....The aircraft is too high, even for the official released video of the five frames where you see something cross the Pentagon lawn at level altitude. The five frames of video captured by the parking gate cam are in direct conflict with the Aircraft Flight Data Recorder information released by the NTSB [National Transportation Safety Board]."

This discrepancy increases the credibility of witnesses who said they saw a jumbo jet fly over the Pentagon without hitting the building. The mystery would be cleared up if the video from the 82 security cameras trained on the Pentagon were to be released, but these were confiscated by the FBI that day and never have been shown to the public. The only video released is a series of frames taken from two security cameras close to one another showing an explosion in the Pentagon but not a large airliner.

The clips begin in synchronization, but the explosion seen from one camera takes place two frames before the other camera. The cameras remain out of sync for a total of eight frames until a sunburst effect puts them back into sync.

Technicians who have studied the clips believe at least two frames are missing. And a study of the video as released by NBC shows a cylindrical object, supposedly the front of the 757 fuselage, entering from the right and standing still for several frames, one of which shows it on the right of the frame at the same moment there is an explosion on the Pentagon wall at the left of the frame. This indicates editing of the released security camera videos.

A video taken from a helicopter in flight near the Pentagon shows a cylindrical object crashing into the wall and exploding. Study of the video indicates no frames are missing. The object impacts and enters the building and the resulting fire billows outward a full 15 seconds later than it appears on the officially released security video.

In 2002, video from a security camera located outside a hotel in Arlington, Virginia, was made public after the FBI had confiscated it, according to the hotel manager. It shows in the distance the explosion on the Pentagon wall, but there is no sign of Flight 77. A lawsuit forced its release.

Other videos of the crash, including those taken at a nearby Citgo gas station, the Virginia Department of Transportation and the Sheraton Hotel, were confiscated by the FBI within minutes of the crash. Employees also said that the FBI agents warned them not to discuss what they had seen.

To date the FBI has not released the voice or cockpit recordings from the Flight 77 black boxes, and the NTSB never investigated the alleged crash, as required by law.

The official report on Flight 77 has still other problems. It claims the airliner struck the Pentagon lawn before striking the building. Photographs taken immediately after the impact show no damage at all to the lawn outside the impact zone. Finally, transcripts of the conversations between the Flight 77 crew and the Indianapolis Control tower, the last contact with the plane, show absolutely no indication of a hijacking.

Flight 93

The official report states plainly that United Flight 93 crashed in a rural area near Shanksville, Pennsylvania, at 10:06 a.m., following an attempt by passengers to overcome the hijackers. Evidence, however, suggests that this did not happen.

A live Fox News report from the crash site of Flight 93 in Pennsylvania stated: "We have rescue vehicles that came in earlier in the day and they have turned up nothing." The reporter then said to news photographer Chris Kanicki, who had been to the crash site, "I've seen the pictures. It looks like there's nothing there except for a hole in the ground." Kanicki responded, "Basically that's right. The only thing you could see from where we were was a big gouge in the earth and some broken trees."

When asked if he saw any large pieces of debris, Kanicki responded, "No, there was nothing that you could distinguish that a plane had crashed there." The photographer added there was no smoke or fire and that "it was actually very quiet." Kanicki estimated the gouge made by the plane crash at 15 to 20 feet long and 10 feet wide.

Wally Miller, the coroner for Somerset County, was dispatched to the crash site. Later he told the *Houston Chronicle,* "It looked like somebody just dropped a bunch of metal out of the sky." To the *Washington Post,* Miller added, "It looked like someone took a scrap truck, dug a 10-foot ditch and dumped trash into it. I stopped being coroner after about 20 minutes, because there were no bodies there." And the *Pittsburgh Review* quoted Miller as saying, "I have not, to this day, seen a single drop of blood. Not a drop."

Thus, in a single day, there were not one but two previously unprecedented occurrences of planes disappearing upon impact.

If Flight 93 didn't crash in the rural Pennsylvania plot as the official report states, then where did it go? If the plane crashed on land someplace else, it would be nearly impossible to keep it secret.

In the late morning of 9/11, WCPO-TV in Cincinnati broadcast a strange report, quoting Cleveland Mayor Michael White that a Boeing 757 made an emergency landing at Hopkins International Airport in

Cleveland due to fear that a bomb was on board. The report also stated, "[Mayor] White said the plane had been moved to a secure area of [Hopkins] Airport, and was evacuated. United identified the plane as Flight 93."

At around 10 a.m. that same morning, Hopkins Airport was evacuated due to the imminent landing of a reportedly hijacked plane. Evacuees had to walk for miles, because airport security prevented anyone from driving their cars from the parking lots. Even buses were forced to remain. Freeway exits closed. Still, the people were ordered to go home.

The Associated Press reported that one plane landed at Hopkins at around 10:45 a.m. It was identified in the report as a Delta flight from Boston and that no explosives were found on board. Delta Airlines, however, claimed that their Flight 1989 landed at Hopkins at 10:10 a.m.

The Delta plane underwent a two-hour search by FBI agents, who also questioned passengers individually. Bomb-sniffing dogs were used during the search. The passengers finally were allowed to leave the plane at 12:30 p.m. However, the *Akron Beacon* reported that a plane at Hopkins was evacuated at 11:15 a.m.

Mayor White claimed the plane carried 200 passengers, but one of the passengers on Flight 1989 said there only were about 60 passengers on board. This same passenger claims she was taken from the plane straight to the headquarters of the Federal Aviation Administration (FAA).

Other passengers were taken to the NASA Glenn Research Center, located at a far end of Hopkins Airport, which had been previously evacuated. If the passengers sent to NASA Glenn were from Flight 93, what happened to them?

Searchers recovered the plane's cockpit voice recorder, and in April 2002, the victims' families were permitted to listen to it. But before this, all of the listeners had to sign an agreement promising not to talk about what they heard. Despite cooperating with this odd demand, the family members did not hear the last three minutes of the recording, which still has not been explained.

According to the official government 9/11 report, the black boxes on all four airliners (except the cockpit voice recorder on Flight 93) never were found and are presumed destroyed. This is despite the fact that these recording devices are sheathed in the strongest metal available today.

NTSB spokesman Ted Lopatkiewicz stated to CBS News, "It's extremely rare that we don't get the recorders back. I can't recall another domestic case in which we did not recover the recorders."

On that day the unprecedented happened again. Like the vertical collapse of three steel-reinforced high-rise buildings, all of the black boxes from four plane crashes allegedly were destroyed beyond recognition.

The official stance was directly contradicted by Nicholas DeMasi, a fireman who was at the World Trade Center and revealed in his book, *Behind the Scenes: Ground Zero,* "At one point I was assigned to take Federal agents around the site to search for the black boxes from the planes. There were a total of four. We found three."

A similar admission by FBI Director Robert Mueller indicates that at least one of the black boxes was found. Mueller said the data recorder of Flight 77 gave information on altitude, speed, headings and other facets, but added that the voice recorder box provided nothing useful. Donald Rumsfeld corroborated this statement when he said the data on the voice recorder was unrecoverable.

One last chapter in the Flight 93 riddle occurred at Chicago's O'Hare Airport on April 10, 2003. David Friedman, a United Airlines worker whose task was to record flights landing at O'Hare, logged a tail number, N591UA, on United Flight 1111, a Boeing 757. Flight 93 bore the N591UA tail number on 9/11. According to the FAA, this tail number is still "valid."

Further combing of FAA records reveals that American Flights 11 and 77 were not scheduled to fly at all on 9/11.

The cell phone calls made by passengers and crew on all the crashed flights that day also bear scrutiny. Betty Ong, a flight attendant on American 11, placed an Airfone call to the American Airlines Southeastern Reservations Office that lasted 23 minutes, and only four and a half minutes were recorded, according to the 9/11 Commission. Ong reported multiple stabbings on board the flight, adding that no one was able to enter the cockpit or reach it by phone. She did this in a calm and steady voice, and there were no sounds of panic or disturbance in the background, despite the catastrophic nature of events in her report.

Madeline Sweeney, an attendant on the same flight, called the American Flight Services Office in Boston and allegedly spoke for 25 minutes. She said there were four men who had hijacked the plane. The FBI report claims there were five. Sweeney claimed the hijackers had been seated in rows nine and 10, while the official FAA version puts all of them in row eight.

Sweeney calmly said that a passenger in first class had his throat slashed, and that two flight attendants had been stabbed. She also claimed there was a bomb in the cockpit, maintaining a calm demeanor until she became upset at the end of the call. Her last words were, "I see water. I see buildings. I see buildings! We are flying low. We are flying very, very low. We are flying way too low. Oh, my God we are flying way too low. Oh, my God!"

One of the passengers on Flight 93, Mark Bingham, allegedly called his mother during the flight and according to his mother, said, "Mom, this is Mark Bingham." How often have any of us called our mothers and identified ourselves with our first and last names? Then Bingham told his mother the plane has been hijacked by three men claiming to have a bomb. When his mother asks who the men are, there is a long pause before Bingham finally says, "You believe me, don't you mom?"

The phone calls from passenger cell phones on the hijacked flights are problematic, owing to the research of A.K. Dewdney of the scientific panel investigating 9/11, Physics 911. In his reports on the cell phone and Airfone calls from Flight 93, and from his Project Achilles cell phone altitude experiments, Dewdney concluded that placing cell phone calls from heights above 30,000 feet, the standard cruising altitude of commercial airliners, would be practically impossible.

"An aircraft, having a metal skin and fuselage, acts like a Faraday cage," wrote Dewdney, "tending to block or attenuate electromagnetic radiation. One can make a cell phone call from inside an aircraft while on the ground because the weakened signal is still close enough to the nearest cell site [relay tower] to get picked up. Once above 10,000 feet, however, calls rarely get through, if ever."

Dewdney's Project Achilles experiment measured the success rates in placing calls from a number of cell phones inside a Cessna-172 airplane at varying altitudes. At 4,000 feet, the phones displayed just a .4 success rate. At 8,000 feet, the success rate dropped to .1, which led to the calculation of a .006 success rate in placing calls above 30,000 feet.

Passengers and crew on Flight 93 allegedly placed at least 13 cell phone calls, more than all the other hijacked flights combined. Dewdney wrote that Flight 93 "reached its cruising altitude of approximately 30,000 feet about 40 minutes into the flight...And at about this time, the aircraft was 'hijacked' according to several cell phone calls. Note that at this altitude the calls were flat-out impossible."

One of the Flight 93 passengers claiming to be Jeremy Glick asked during his call whether it was true that planes had crashed into the World Trade Center. He claimed he got this news from another passenger, who'd heard it on their cell phone. In a subsequent call, the passenger told Lyz Glick that he and others were planning to do something to overcome the hijackers. When Lyz asked about weapons, the passenger managed a joke: "I have my butter knife from breakfast." Aside from glibness in the face of disaster, this comment also is suspicious because breakfast would not begin to be served until the airliner reached cruising altitude, which was when the hijackers allegedly made their move.

Aside from simple voice mimicry, there are two electronic means to duplicate a person's voice. One uses software that was available before 9/11, synthesizing a caller's voice with that of the intended person through a tape recording of that person in nearly real time. This was accomplished years earlier for all to hear during a Los Alamos demonstration when the mimicked voice of General Colin Powell said, "I am being treated well by my captors."

The other technique involves voice transformers like the Spook 2004 and the SeeStorm 2004. When someone speaks into a microphone, the sound pattern is digitalized and a computer within these devices produces a signal that is reconstituted as sound in real time. These devices literally can transform the voice of an old man into that of a young girl. The fact that this technology wasn't available to the public until 2004 does not mean it couldn't have been in the hands of military and intelligence personnel in 2001.

Dewdney theorized a scenario for faking cell phone calls that were electronically impossible to make from an aircraft flying at more than 500 miles per hour at around 30,000 feet of altitude:

"On the fateful day, the calling operation would take place in an operations center, basically a sound studio that is equipped with communication lines and several telephones. An operations director displays a scripted sequence of events on a screen so that the voice operators know what stage the 'hijacking' is supposed to be at. All calls are orchestrated to follow the script...To supplement the calls with real sound effects, an audio engineer would have several tapes ready to play."

In conclusion, Dewdney wrote, "Under the weight of the evidence that the cell phone (not the Airfone) calls were essentially impossible as described by the Bush White House and the major media on the day in question, we have no alternative but to give serious consideration to the operational possibilities, as outlined here."

American Airlines in 2004 installed cell phone relays in some of their planes to allow passengers to make cell phone calls in flight at cruising altitudes, another indication that calls had previously been impossible under similar conditions.

Suspicious Stock Trades

Just prior to the 9/11 attacks, an unusually high number of "put" options were purchased for the stocks of AMR Corp. and UAL Corp., the parent companies of American and United Airlines. A put option gives the buyer the right to sell at a specified price before a certain date, basically betting that the stock price will fall.

Put options are similar to selling stocks short. This scenario involves having a broker sell shares you don't own yet at a set price, gambling that those stocks can be acquired later at a lower price. The price difference represents profit in these cases.

It's a risky strategy, but if you have foreknowledge of an event or insider information, you can make huge profits. Historically, when unusual short selling precedes a disastrous event, it indicates foreknowledge.

Between September 6 and 7, 2001, the Chicago Board of Options Exchange reported 4,744 put options on United Airlines and just 396 call options, which are gambles by investors that the stock will increase in value. On September 10, the exchange listed 4,516 put options placed on American Airlines, and only 748 call options. The put options on American Airlines stock the day before 9/11 represented a 6,000 percent increase and was unmatched by the stocks of any other airline. Of course, American and United were the two airlines involved in the 9/11 attacks.

Morgan Stanley, which occupied 22 floors of one of the World Trade towers, reported 2,157 put options during the three trading days prior to 9/11, up from a mere 27 per day before September 6. Merrill Lynch & Co., also housed on 22 floors of the World Trade tower, reported that 12,215 one-month put options were purchased during the four trading days prior to the attacks, as opposed to the normal average of just 252 per day.

These spikes almost certainly were monitored by the CIA, which carefully tracks the market transactions for signs of an impending attack. To date, no such information has been made public.

And who made the put purchases? The *San Francisco Chronicle* pointed a finger at Deutsche Bank. Alex.Brown, the American investment banking division of Deutsche Bank, purchased some of the options on United Airlines. A.B. Krongard, executive director of the CIA during the 9/11 attacks, was until 1998 the chairman of Alex.Brown, the oldest investment bank in the US. His first position after Alex.Brown was as counselor to CIA Director George Tenet. In spite of this information, the media harped on the stock activity of Osama bin Laden, completely ignoring the CIA connection.

Sifting through the rubble of the World Trade Center, searchers recovered more than 400 computer hard drives. These were given to a German firm, Convar, which specialized in recovering data from damaged computers. The firm successfully recovered data from 32 of the hard drives, some of which suggested that various 9/11-related stock transactions were illegal cases of insider trading.

According to Convar investigator Richard Wagner, "There is a suspicion that some people had advance knowledge of the approximate time of the plane crashes in order to move out amounts exceeding $100 million. They thought that the records of their transactions could not be traced after the main frames were destroyed."

The FBI received the Convar investigation results and, although legally bound to pursue information on the suspects of insider trading, the Bureau has not proceeded.

Few people realize that there was an immense gold bullion deposit stored beneath the World Trade Center, belonging to Kuwaiti interests and amounting to more than $1 billion. Kuwait later announced it had retrieved its gold from the site, but Mayor Giuliani revealed the discovery of gold in the Ground Zero debris totaling more than $230 million. Reuters reported the gold was discovered in the back of a 10-wheel truck that was buried in the rubble beneath Building 5, even though the precious metal had been stored beneath Building 4. Curiously, Building 5 is more remote from the South Tower, which was adjacent to Building 4.

Once the gold was discovered, FBI and Secret Service agents began to restrict access to the site. Heavy machinery operators, still necessary to the cleanup, worked under the scrutiny of nearly 100 armed officers.

News reports also revealed that the Comex metals trading division of the New York Mercantile Exchange stored 3,800 gold bars, then valued at more than $100 million, in vaults beneath the World Trade Center. Comex held gold for other interests as well, like the Chase

Manhattan Bank and the Bank of New York, totaling nearly 800,000 ounces at a value of roughly $220 million. The firm held silver in the same vaults, valued at $430 million.

Some rumors put the total gold storage beneath the World Trade Center as high as $167 billion. If this is true, less than one percent of the gold and silver has been accounted for.

The Anthrax Mailings

Shortly after 9/11, weapons-grade anthrax arrived in the mail of Democratic Congressmen Tom Daschle and Patrick Leahy, as well as some media outlets, infecting 23 people and killing five. Daschle and Leahy both had voiced opposition to the upcoming vote on the Patriot Act.

Despite the fact that one of the anthrax-laced letters carried the phrase, "Allah is great," it was clear that the biological agent had not been manufactured in any Afghan cave. It was a highly concentrated, electro-magnetized, silica-laced strain of anthrax that was most likely manufactured in the Fort Detrick, Maryland, biochemical weapons lab. In all, about 10 grams of this weaponized substance arrived in various letters, an amount large enough to make experts doubt it could have been stolen from the high security lab in Fort Detrick.

In 2002, the media identified Steven Hatfill, a government scientist involved in biological research, as a suspect in the anthrax affair. Hatfill and some of his associates were under constant scrutiny by government agents until 2008, when he was exonerated by the Justice Department. Hatfill later sued the government for harassment and won $5.8 million.

That same year, the government turned its attention to Bruce Ivins, a Fort Detrick scientist specializing in anthrax weaponization. Ivins actually was part of the government team investigating the 2001 anthrax attacks. But before Ivins could be arrested and charged, he allegedly killed himself with an overdose of acetaminophin, the active ingredient in Tylenol. The official theory stated that Ivins probably mailed the anthrax in order to test his cure for the pathogen. Ivins, of course, was unable to speak for himself.

According to papers filed in court by a social worker named Jean Duley, Ivins had a history of making death threats against his therapists, and Dr. W. Russell Byrne, a member of the bacteriology division at Fort Detrick, said police forcibly removed Ivins from the workplace shortly before his death because authorities feared he had become a danger to himself and to others. But Byrne also said he did not believe Ivins was behind the anthrax attacks.

Ivins' attorney, Paul F. Kemp, insisted upon his client's innocence and said that he'd been cooperating with investigators for more than a year prior to his death. "We are saddened by his death, and disappointed that we will not have the opportunity to defend his good name and reputation in a court of law."

The Justice Department's investigative documents pertaining to the case remain sealed. Later, it emerged that social worker Duley was on probation for minor criminal offenses and reportedly needed money.

Dr. Meryl Nass, an Ivins associate, said after the alleged suicide, "There has been a tremendous amount of innuendo and information put forward that has never been backed up and never been attributed to anyone." The Justice Department closed the case, declaring that Ivins had acted alone — another lone nut assassin.

Families of the Lost

Shortly after the attacks, the US Justice Department and Kenneth Feinberg established the $7 billion September 11th Victim Compensation Fund of 2001, awarding fees to the families of those victims in the four crashed airliners. The average compensation was around $2 million, depending on a variety of factors set down in the fund's rules.

In exchange, families accepting the compensation agreed to forego any lawsuits claiming damages against the involved airlines, Boeing or the airport security firms. About three percent of the families refused to sign off on their rights to sue. This was because the victims were without spouses, dependents, and/or had not worked in high-salaried jobs. Feeling compensation as low as $250,000 was unacceptable when the high-end compensation to some families reached $7.1 million, these people filed suits that have been settled over time for about $500 million.

The nearly total rate of settlement as opposed to trial was partially due to the action of judges, who ordered that trials to determine damages take place before the trials on liability. This encouraged settlement prior to liability trials.

The only family to refuse settlement and file for a civil trial is that of Mark Bavis, who was a passenger on United Flight 175, the second plane that crashed into the World Trade Center. In October 2010, a federal judge in Manhattan established the timetable for the wrongful death lawsuit. The suit named United, Boeing and the security firm responsible for screening passengers at Logan Airport in Boston for negligence.

The rest of the victims' families have remained strangely silent regarding the circumstances of their loved-ones' deaths, especially those who lost someone on Flights 77 and 93. This is in spite of the evidence that these flights may never have crashed into the Pentagon or in Pennsylvania.

This behavior is in stark contrast with the families of the Ground Zero victims who were not airline passengers. They have been eager to delve into the inconsistencies in the official *9/11 Commission Report*. It raises the question: Are the many hundreds of relatives and loved ones who lost someone on the planes that day afraid of something?

Recent events may signify a change, as family members begin to voice their doubts about the official version, 10 years after the fact. Bill Doyle, head of the Coalition of 9/11 Families, claims that "a large number" of his organization's members disbelieve the official version of events.

"It's mostly because they know that pre-9/11 there were warnings [of an attack] which our president did nothing about," Doyle told the author. "It's been proved that there were warnings pre-9/11. The August 6, 2001 memo said bin Laden would attack the United States with hijacked planes. Condoleeza Rice testified to this at the [9/11 Commission] hearings and explained they just didn't know the date and time."

Doyle lost his son Joey in the WTC collapse. After forming his coalition, the largest of the organizations representing the victims' families, he delved into the evidence that the official report neglected.

"It looks like there was a conspiracy behind 9/11 if you really look at all the facts," Doyle said. "A lot of families now feel the same way. What bothers me the most is that our US government knows who financed these hijackers. There were 28 pages of the independent commission's book that were all blanked out. It concerned who financed 9/11. I've had whistle blowers contact me and send me information that proves certain people who financed 9/11 were actually Saudis."

Doyle is involved in a pending lawsuit to discover and expose this information, under the case title, *Thomas Burnett Sr., et al, Plaintiffs, v. al Baraka Investment and Development Corporation, et al, Defendants.* The attorney Doyle recommended to his member families to file the suit, Ronald Motley, is famous for his successful lawsuits against Big Tobacco in South Carolina, in which he won hundreds of billions of dollars in settlements.

The suit remains in the Rule 12 stage while Motley attempts to convince the judges that he has established causes for action against various individuals, charities and banks. The judges already have dismissed the charges against some of the 200 defendants, including the al Baraka Corporation and two Saudi princes who, due to their official connection with a foreign government, are protected from claims. But Motley's international investigative team has collected more than two million documents that trace the money trail to the hijackers from a variety of Middle Eastern banks, institutions and individuals.

"We want it to be known what they did," Doyle told the author. "We want to hold them accountable. If you block 28 pages of who financed [the hijackers] and our government, including senators and congressmen who saw the original version of the 9/11 Commission report and who all say to me, 'Bill, you're right on in who you're accusing,' then why isn't that information known?

"I've seen the evidence. I've seen a blank check. I've seen a $10,000 check drawn by certain Saudi princes and given to two of the hijackers in San Diego. We went all the way to the Supreme Court trying to get the 28 pages known and to hold certain Saudis liable in the lawsuit.

"Two days before the Supreme Court was to hear the merits of our case, Solicitor General Elena Kagan recommended that the justices not hear our case about the Saudis. Because [Saudi Arabia] is not a state that sponsors terrorism in our government's eyes, we can't hold them accountable. This is wrong. Why are we protecting these people?"

According to Doyle, Motley explained the US government motive behind the apparent coverup in a single word — oil. He points to the example of the Holy Land Foundation, formerly the largest Islamic charity in the US, which was successfully prosecuted by the federal government in 2009 for funding Hamas and other "Islamic terrorist organizations."

"The Holy Land Foundation pleaded guilty if that information would be sealed and never known," Doyle told the author, "Our government accepted that."

The founders of the organization received sentences ranging from 15 to 65 years.

Doyle also admitted that some of his coalition members believe there may not have been plane crashes at the Pentagon and in Shanksville, Pennsylvania. "There are people out there who think that it was more of a missile that went into the Pentagon," Doyle told the author. "But what happened to all the people?"

It's important to note that Doyle does not subscribe to this theory, but some families of the victims do.

One of them, Marion Kminek, lost her daughter, Mari-Rae Sopper, on Flight 77 when it allegedly plowed into the Pentagon. Mari-Rae was en route to California where she was to begin a new career as coach of the women's gymnastics team at the University of California at Santa Barbara.

"One of the men in our grief group who had lost his daughter in the towers asked me, 'Do you really believe that her plane hit the Pentagon?'" Kminek told the author. "I said, 'Yeah.' I thought he was kind of crazy. But the more we learned, the more we thought, 'Well, who knows?' And now we got to really believing that Bush and Cheney and Rumsfeld and all [the rest] were involved....We don't want to believe that somebody would actually do this.

"And if the plane didn't crash [into the Pentagon], then where is it? Where are the people? And you know they're dead. It's impossible to keep someone as a prisoner for 10 years. I just don't believe that....I still believe they [our government] were involved. It's just so hard to accept that they'd be that evil....You don't allow a plane to fly into that air space. It just doesn't make sense that that plane wasn't shot down....My husband always has believed that there was no plane crash [at the Pentagon]. He thought maybe they landed at another military base, but there are too many people involved to do that because somebody's going to talk."

Earl Dorsey is dealing with the same conundrum. His wife Dora Menchaca also was aboard Flight 77, and he's spent a decade delving into the evidence.

"The conclusion that I have come up with from either books that I have read or documentaries that I have seen is that the official account is inaccurate," he told the author. "My other family members, after viewing the same information, have come to the same conclusion. I don't know what to do with it, though."

Dora, a research scientist and associate director for Amgen, a leading biotech firm, had flown to Washington to meet with FDA officials regarding approval of a new prostate cancer drug. She was returning to her Santa Monica home on 9/11.

Dorsey is most troubled by the official account that Flight 77 was incinerated upon hitting the Pentagon. He believes this is impossible due to what the FBI gave to him personally after the alleged crash.

"The FBI gave me [some of my wife's] personal belongings," he said. "Like there was a hand-written note, and it seems impossible that a hand-written note would survive that [crash]. It's clearly her handwriting. And there were some other personal items that wouldn't have survived the crash. When the FBI came to my house to bring me these personal items, I asked where was this found. They said [it was found] in the seat next to her. That didn't make sense to me."

There were no signs of seats, or any other sizable debris at the alleged crash site. When asked whether he has any thoughts about where, if there was no plane crash at the Pentagon, might the Flight 77 passengers be, Dorsey said, "I don't know what to think. I have a lot of questions and I'm not able to come to any larger conclusion. All I have are some personal effects that belonged to my wife. Like, I have her driver's license, and that wouldn't survive [a crash]."

Dorsey feels that the thought his wife and the other passengers are still alive somewhere "seems impossible as well. If there is something else going on, or some other story as to what happened to the plane, why would they even provide me with this information?"

Another of the victims' families went public with their doubts in 2007. John and Beverly Titus, parents of Alicia Titus, who was a flight attendant on Flight 175, have publicly expressed their views that the truth has not been revealed in the official version of the 9/11 attacks.

"It will be our lifelong goal to find the truth about September 11 and the real story behind it," said Beverly Titus, "because we know that what we've been given is only a glimpse of it and distortions of it, and my daughter deserves better than that. There's still no answer to so many questions that we have that have not been given the truth, and we're going to continue to search and support people that are out there asking the same kinds of questions and demanding the truth."

According to the Bureau of Traffic Safety (BTS) there is no record of Flights 11 and 77 taking off on 9/11. There is no record of elapsed runway time, wheels-off time or taxi-out time for either flight that day, although records of all these items are present for 9/10 and 9/12. No explanation has been given for the missing BTS data.

It seems odd, too, that families of the victims haven't complained that none of the airport surveillance video of the four doomed flights of 9/11 are available to the public. Only one victim family member, Ellen Mariani, who lost her husband on Flight 175, has demanded an investigation into the BTS records and the unreleased surveillance tapes.

The case of Joseph and Samia Iskandar also deserves attention. A year after 9/11 they were told by the Ground Zero recovery team that they had found the Wells Fargo ATM card belonging to their son Waleed, who allegedly was a passenger on Flight 11. The card was pristine after supposedly being involved in the inferno of the first plane to crash into the WTC. What's more, Waleed, a 34-year-old Harvard graduate, never was on the Flight 11 passenger lists, including the original manifest and the official list provided by American Airlines. His name only appears on the Flight 11 passenger lists of newspapers and Internet memorials. Despite this, the Iskandars have remained completely silent and have refused to return phone calls from researchers.

A similar story involves the miraculous recovery of the driver's license and wedding ring of Suzanne Calley, an alleged victim in the Pentagon crash of Flight 77. The items were found in the Pentagon in perfect condition and sent to Calley's husband, Frank, who fully accepts the official version of the crash and his wife's autopsy despite disturbing evidence to the contrary.

The autopsy investigation on the victims of Flight 77 was conducted by the Armed Forces Institute of Pathology (AFIP), a military organization. Its report, dated November 16, 2001, claims to have identified 184 of the 189 persons who died at the Pentagon, including all but one of the airline's passengers. Yet, Frank Calley claims that a private Pentagon attaché who was sent to him said only 19 passengers were positively identified.

More troubling is the fact that not one of the 184 identified victims on the AFIP list has an Arabic name. This caused Dr. Thomas Olmstead, a medical investigator, to file a Freedom of Information Act (FOIA) request to see the government autopsy reports and lists.

"A list of names on a piece of paper is not evidence," said Olmstead to journalist Greg Szymanski, "but an autopsy by a pathologist is. I undertook by FOIA request to get the autopsy list. Guess what. Still no Arabs on the list. It is my opinion that the monsters who planned this crime made a mistake by not including Arabic names on the original list to make the ruse seem more believable….It seems very unlikely to me that five Arabs sneaked on to a flight with weapons."

Olmstead also discovered that three names on the AFIP autopsy list were not on the airline manifest passengers list. This did not include the alleged five Arabic hijackers.

"The AFIP suggests these numbers," Olmstead added. "189 killed. 125 worked at the Pentagon and 64 were passengers on the plane. The [airline] list only had 56 [passengers], and the list just obtained has 58.

"They did not explain how they were able to tell victims' bodies from hijacker bodies. In fact, from the beginning no explanation has been given for the extra five [passengers] suggested in news reports, except that the FBI showed us the pictures to make up the difference, and that makes it so. No Arabs wound up on the morgue slab. However, three additional people not listed by American Airlines sneaked in. I have seen no explanation for these extras. I did give American the opportunity to revise their original list, but they have not responded. The new names are Robert Ploger, Zandra Ploger and Sandra Teague."

To date, this discrepancy, like so many others from that terrible day of wrath, has not been addressed.

GRAN FINALE – *LAMENTO*
THROUGH THE LOOKING GLASS

"There are more things in heaven and earth, Horatio, than are dreamt of in your philosophy."

—William Shakespeare, *Hamlet*

Secret Experiments and Mind Control

A multitude of Congressional investigations has revealed that more than 20,000 secret experiments and tests were performed on American citizens between 1910 and 2000. One of them, the Tuskeegee Syphilis Project, lasted 40 years and killed hundreds of African Americans. Doctors told the patients they were receiving treatment for syphilis when in reality they gave them placebos while monitoring the course of the disease and its awful effects on the unwitting men. The program only ended when whistle blowers exposed the project in 1972.

A few other examples:

Starting in 1947, Great Britain ran a program testing lethal nerve gas on its military personnel, killing a number of them instantly and causing many others to suffer for years before dying.

In 2006, a secret experiment in Detroit testing a blood substitute killed two people. The blood substitute was administered to victims of auto accidents, shootings and other trauma without their knowledge or consent.

Between 1944 and 1994, the US Department of Defense conducted secret radiation experiments on thousands of unsuspecting citizens. American hospitals injected uranium and plutonium into healthy persons, the dosages ranging from non-therapeutic to lethal.

In one secret experiment, the pregnant wives of American soldiers received "vitamins" from base doctors containing Uranium 239 and Plutonium 241. The women had violent miscarriages, resulting in their deaths.

The many nuclear bomb tests conducted by the US during the Cold War deliberately exposed American servicemen to radiation. Pilots also were ordered to fly through mushroom clouds of exploded nuclear weapons to test the radiation results.

Between 1951 and 1961 the US Army paid the Israeli Health Ministry 3 million *lira* to conduct radiation testing on immigrant Sephardic children. The children were told by the government-run schools that they were getting medical exams, which included an X-ray. More than 110,000 dark-skinned Jews received head X-rays 35,000

338

times greater than the maximum safety level. Many died within months. All of them lost their hair. Some continue to live with severe health problems.

The Pentagon had previously performed its own version of this experiment, radiating 4,000 institutionalized children in the US, many of them dying.

From 1940 to 1979, the majority of Britons were exposed to agents sprayed by aircraft on more than 2,000 separate occasions. In 2002, the *London Times* reported that lethal chemical weapons, including sarin, tabun, soman and VX, were sprayed on citizens in the Wiltshire countryside during the 1960s by crop duster planes flown by British and American military personnel from the secret Porton Down facility.

In 1968, the Pentagon tested a deadly bioweapon in the New York subway system, while placing medical personnel in local hospitals to monitor the effects.

Currently, the US is testing pesticides and toxic experimental drugs on thousands of foster children. The drugs include experimental AIDS vaccines being used on HIV-positive children under New York State supervision. Many of the foster children have died due to these experiments.

Other experiments require the children to take a cocktail of psychotropic drugs. Joe Burkett, chairman of the Texas Society of Psychiatric Physicians, testified to the State House Select Committee on Psychotropic Drugs and Foster Care that two-thirds of foster children in Texas had been placed on psychiatric drugs because "they were very, very sick from a bad gene pool."

Many prisons in America have forced inmates to participate in experiments with pesticides and other potentially lethal agents. In one experiment, inmates had tablets of dioxin sewed into their backs.

In the late 1960s, Dr. James Hamilton, a San Francisco psychiatrist, was hired by the CIA to conduct clinical testing of behavioral control materials on prisoners at the Vacaville Medical Facility. Hamilton experimented on at least 400 inmates and perhaps as many as 1,000 between 1967 and 1968. The deliberate infection of unwitting inmates from Angola State Prison in New Orleans with a galloping cancer during 1963 already has been detailed in a previous chapter of this book.

The military repeatedly has used unsuspecting subjects in its quest for better poisons and bioweapons. The Special Operations Division (SOD) at Fort Detrick produced an arsenal of different germ weapons for the CIA under a program called MK-NAOMI. A pill was developed from deadly shellfish toxins that would kill in several seconds.

Botulinum was weaponized as one of the many poisons that would appear as natural death on the target. Roughly a dozen diseases and toxins were designed to incapacitate a target for days or weeks. Two different types of "brucellosis" toxin could incapacitate a person for months. SOD also produced deadly aerosol sprays that could be fired by remote control. One scheme fired the spray when someone turned on a fluorescent light.

George White, a narcotics agent, was recruited by the CIA to test LSD on unsuspecting people in a San Francisco safe house located on Telegraph Hill. The house had been bugged with microphones disguised as electrical wall outlets and monitored by agents in an adjacent house. Prostitutes brought in their "johns" and gave them LSD and other more exotic drugs in their drinks. Many of the subjects became ill for days and one had to be hospitalized. This operation received cooperation from the San Francisco Police Department, which protected the activities in case critical situations arose.

Years later, George White wrote a letter to his CIA superior, Dr. Sidney Gottlieb, boasting, "I was a very minor missionary, actually a heretic, but I toiled wholeheartedly in the vineyards because it was fun, fun, fun. Where else could a red-blooded American boy lie, kill, cheat, steal, rape and pillage with the sanction and the blessing of the All Highest?"

When revelations of these experiments became public knowledge through a Senate Select Committee, the Fort Detrick projects temporarily shut down and were transferred to the Scientific Engineering Institute in Boston, which up to that time had been a CIA proprietary company used in radar research. Here, research continued in gene splicing and other exotic genetic manipulation to create new viruses.

One of them may have been the mysterious Gulf War Syndrome that affected so many troops returning from Iraq after 1991. In November 1996, KREM-TV News in Spokane, Washington, did a series on the subject, in which microbiologist Dr. Garth Nicholson claimed that Gulf War Syndrome contains "altered genetic structures" similar to AIDS. He went on to say he believed the syndrome was a genetically engineered bioweapon that was contagious.

This was confirmed by Dr. Larry Goss of Walters, Oklahoma, who claimed that his wife contracted the syndrome while treating Gulf War veterans. In addition, Dr. William Baumzweiger, a neurologist at the Veteran's Hospital in Los Angeles, found brain stem damage in the soldiers suffering from the syndrome, and learned that the virus actually causes the human immune system to turn on itself.

These veteran victims were warned not to have unprotected sex and not to have children. Over the years, undeniable evidence of the syndrome's contagious aspect lies in the many cases in which wives and children of the vets have been infected.

The aforementioned programs and countless others are documented and available online for those who seek proof and more detail. They reveal callous attitudes among our nation's leaders in applying the aged philosophy of secret societies and shadow governments, in which the end always justifies the means.

We list them here because secret experiments on unwitting citizens continue to this day, and to prepare the reader for the difficult revelations we will make in this section.

The queen-mother of all secret US government experiments on its unsuspecting citizens is the mind control project, code-named MK-ULTRA, and its many offshoots. Disclosed through several congressional investigations during the 1970s, the program involved "brainwashing" through various means, including electroshock, sleep deprivation, physical and psychological torture and a variety of other means intended to create human robots programmed with specific talents, including prostitution, espionage and assassination. Quite simply, to investigate mind control and its victims is to enter a house of mirrors.

The 1973 Rockefeller Commission Report indicated that former CIA Director Richard Helms had destroyed 153 MK-ULTRA files before leaving office. However, many of these files subsequently turned up in other departments and painted a dark picture of government agencies using American citizens as just so many lab rats.

It is clear from the now-public files that the US has been involved in mind control experimentation at least since World War II. There even is some evidence that as early as World War I, the military attempted to improve the performance of couriers through hypnosis.

But it wasn't until the Soviet show trials under Josef Stalin during the 1930s that the American military establishment took serious notice of mind control and its potential. Witnessing defendants confessing to crimes they could not possibly have committed and begging to be shot as enemies of the state convinced American authorities that the Soviets were well ahead in mind control technology.

This fear sharpened during the Korean War, when American POWs confessed to having engaged in germ warfare against the North Korean communists. When the soldiers were repatriated through Russia to the US after the war, they had a disturbing trait in common. According to a now declassified 1953 Top Secret memo, they experienced a blank period, or a period of disorientation "while passing through a special zone in Manchuria." This no doubt was the inspiration for Richard Condon's classic novel, *The Manchurian Candidate,* which contained more elements of truth than most people realized when it was published in 1959.

Mind control research became a CIA top priority a decade before Condon's book, however, with the show trial of Cardinal Jozsef Mindszenty in 1949. As head of the Catholic Church in Hungary, which was occupied by the Soviet Union, Mindszenty was arrested for his anti-communist position and his outspoken criticism of brutal Stalinist persecution in his country.

While incarcerated, the Cardinal was tortured and during the trial, he confessed to various crimes he did not commit, including the preposterous claims that he had engineered the theft of Hungary's crown jewels and had plotted to instigate World War III.

Unknown to him or the Soviets, the CIA had an agent in the prison where Mindszenty was held, and knew of the programming process that included hypnosis and drugs along with physical and psychological trauma.

The trial drew worldwide condemnation, including a UN resolution demanding the Cardinal's release. This finally would happen without Soviet cooperation when Mindszenty was freed during the 1956 revolt in Hungary and given political asylum in the US Embassy in Budapest. Curiously, when Mindszenty wrote his memoirs years later, he claimed to have no memory of the programming he underwent in prison.

Stepped-up experiments in the US included sensory deprivation, in which scientists discovered the potential of this process to create "false memory." In one experiment held on college campuses, students simply were blindfolded and remained fastened to a bed. In just 48 hours, the subjects began hallucinating wildly through all five of their senses. One student thought a man was in bed with him, and actually claimed to feel him.

Other more hideous experiments involved giving massive jolts of electricity to subjects three to four times daily for periods of weeks. Some of the shocks were delivered to the stomach and back as punishments for behavior modification. Scientists learned that even dissociative subjects (those with Multiple Personality Disorder) could not block out the pain of electroshock initially, as it affects both the body and the brain. Experimenters also discovered that dissociative subjects are capable of withstanding pain by shutting off the tortured portion of the body from the brain.

Victims of these experiments have testified to Congress as well as to therapists that they underwent vile procedures that are almost incredible. They spoke of LSD and sodium amytal injections, which, along with hypnosis, created false memories and amnesia barriers. The false memories were effective in masking why a subject noticed welts and burn marks on their bodies afterward and could not remember getting them.

So effective were the drugs given before and after transit to a lab that the victims didn't remember the trip, and simply recalled suddenly being home again. Other drugs caused temporary physical paralysis while maintaining full consciousness.

Testimony also indicates that scientists used dog shock collars on patients to control subjects and condition them to believe their very throats and vocal chords are owned by their controllers. Other electrical devices, like a thick waist belt, were reported. Cattle prods and stun guns commonly pepper the testimonies of mind control victims.

The most disturbing part of this program involves children, which scientists were quick to realize are the best subjects for mind control. Tales of torture, of being caged like animals, of having to participate in cruelties toward animals and other children, including infants, are a common thread in the testimony of former victims. The fact that these memories come from a wide variety of victims who have had no contact with one another is an indication that these people are not delusional, even though many have been diagnosed with Multiple Personality Disorder (MPD).

Some of the testimony includes instances where a child is strapped to a table with electrodes connected to the body and head while an overhead projector flashes colored light. Others have spoken of being suspended and spun in astronaut-type training devices to induce feelings of weightlessness. Victims have testified that procedures called "traumatic baseline" took them to the point of near death.

Films and music were used to create "triggers" and implant impressions, according to many victims. When programming children, Disney films and childhood tunes often were used, as in the case of Susan Ford, whose story will be detailed later in this book. Films like *The Parent Trap* were screened to create the impression that the subject has "a twin," an alter-ego.

Researchers like Ron Patton trace the techniques used in MK-ULTRA all the way back to the ancient Egyptian priesthood and its *Book of the Dead,* which "is a compilation of rituals explicitly describing methods of torture and intimidation (to create trauma), the use of potions (drugs), and the casting of spells (hypnotism), ultimately resulting in the total enslavement of the initiate."

Patton points out that these same techniques have been constant ingredients in satanic rituals through the ages, as well as in MK-ULTRA and the more recent Monarch Project. All of the techniques, according to Patton, are a "form of trauma-structured dissociation and occultic integration in order to compartmentalize the mind into multiple personalities within a systematic framework." Some mental health therapists have termed the process "Conditioned Stimulus-Response Sequences."

Immediately after World War II scores of Nazi scientists and doctors came to America under the secret Project Paperclip. The press has amply covered the German scientists brought to America like Werner von Braun, who contributed mightily to the US rocket and missile programs, but still has not given much coverage to the Nazi doctors who experimented on concentration camp inmates.

These experiments covered a wide range of purposes, including mind control. Strangely, a number of American mind control victims have claimed that Dr. Josef Mengele oversaw their conditioning during the MK-ULTRA program, despite the evidence that this villainous figure spent the remainder of his life in Paraguay and Brazil after escaping Germany, and never traveled to the US. It is widely accepted that most of Mengele's work in Auschwitz concerned genetic studies like the creation of twins, but it certainly is possible that he also experimented with mind control.

Patton told the author that two of his sources have corroborated the tales of several mind control victims that Mengele indeed had traveled to the US and participated in mind control programs. "Both [sources] were in intelligence," Patton said. "One was a former CIA [agent] who was involved in the Secret Service for Lyndon Johnson. The other individual who I spoke to in person was in the Defense Intelligence Agency. He read my article about Mengele [being part of mind control research in the US] and he asked how [did] I know about this.

"Apparently Mengele went under false names like Dr. Green or Dr. Greenbaum. This is what survivors are saying. It certainly is plausible, because we know the US government was using Nazi doctors. There was one who surfaced in the Portland [Oregon] area named Dr. Heinrich Mueller. There are photos of him in his SS uniform and of him with a little girl sitting on his lap. This [latter photo] was supposedly taken in Portland during the early 1960s. I met this woman [the former little girl] and she was going through therapy at the time."

This Dr. Mueller is not to be confused with the Heinrich Mueller who headed the Gestapo during the Nazi regime.

One of the mind control victims who believes that Mengele directed his conditioning in the US is Peter Tscherneff, who has been diagnosed with MPD. He claims his condition is due to the trauma and drug techniques used during his childhood. He admits that his parents were pro-Nazi when they lived in Germany before moving to Harrisburg, Pennsylvania, where Peter was born. Tscherneff also had an uncle who was a member of the SS, and who eventually was executed by the Nazis. He believes that his parents also were subjected to mind control experiments.

"My most common memory of my mom was her sitting in a big chair with a wet cloth on her forehead with a migraine," Tscherneff told the author. "My dad's personality was curious, to say the least."

Although he has no specific memories of trauma conditioning during his childhood, Tscherneff recalls, "I used to have this daydream where I was in a wooded area, floating down a stream surrounded by flowers. I associated it with an area near my home in Pennsylvania, but it didn't make sense. Years later, in 1996, while I'm attending classes at a college in Santa Rosa, California, a guy invited me to his place in the mountain area. It was a gay compound. I walked around the area and I found this exact spot that I'd been having this daydream about for years.

"Apparently I was there when I was eight. I had flash memories of being in a hallway with a bunch of kids, and they were all kissing. Then I remembered another scene in the same time frame where I was in a classroom and it was very cold because I was sitting beneath a vent. All of a sudden the vent opens and a human head falls out and lands in my hands. When I remembered this, I started hyperventilating."

Tscherneff did not begin to recall these and other events until he spent several months in jail during 2003, which he refers to as his "fast" because he'd stopped eating and lost 50 pounds. He describes his memories as "bits of movies," which came to him in jail.

"I had some pretty interesting recalls," he told the author. "There were a variety of scenarios where kids were being abused and murdered in rituals to indoctrinate others into a mindset. I remember this taking place outdoors in parks. Typically there would be three to five men and one to three women along with five to eight kids. Sometimes there would be a big dog or two. It looked like a group of people going out for a picnic.

"Everything was pre-planned, including the kid that was going to be killed. It was intended to get us into the mindset that, 'You belong here. You don't belong out there with your parents.' They put narcotics in the drinks, and one of the adults would kill the kid. He'd slit the kid open. The adults would drain his blood and rub it on their genitalia, and then have sex with the other kids in a narcotic state.

"Then they would dispose of the body in a number of ways. Sometimes they would throw the guts out for the buzzards and crush up the body. If there was one or two big dogs, they would feed the remains to them and bury what was left. They would take the skull away in a burlap bag to crush it up later. It was a hybrid satanic/military mind control deal."

Tscherneff claims the central perpetrator in these events was Dr. Maurice Wolin, who was arrested in 2006 for child sexual abuse following a sting operation organized by the TV show *To Catch a Predator* and state police in Petaluma, California. Wolin and 28 other men were awaiting a rendezvous they'd arranged with under-aged boys and girls at an East Petaluma home.

Tscherneff also claims that his conditioning was orchestrated by Josef Mengele, who went by the name of Dr. Felix Polk. "At this time I was an adult," Tscherneff says. "I was a go-fer. I was a dupe. I was a program. I was used sexually and I was also the guy who did the dirty cleanup work with the kids. German being my first language, I understood when I heard these people speaking in German and referring to him [Dr. Polk] as Josef or Dr. Mengele."

Ron Patton believes the victims' statements regarding Mengele, but feels the more recent program, termed by victims as Project Monarch, is nebulous. "You're not going to find any official documentation saying that there was a Project Monarch," Patton told the author. "What you *will* find is information that relates to a trauma-based mind control program that was used on children to create Multiple Personality Disorder.

"The purpose was to create alternate personalities and give each one an assigned task. One personality would be like a human tape recorder. One personality would be an assassin and one personality does prostitution.

"[Monarch] was a joint effort by the CIA and Department of Defense. Allen Dulles, who was head of the CIA in the 1950s is who most likely approved it. [Monarch] probably is a combination of about three or four subprojects, so you won't find anything [about it] through the Freedom of Information Act. Some people speculate that [Monarch] was officially designated in either the late '50s or early '60s, so it's been going on for about 50 years."

One of the first documented instances of mind control involved the statuesque 1940s model, Candy Jones. Born as Jessica Wilcox in Wilkes-Barre, Pennsylvania, in 1925 to a wealthy family, Jones claimed she was repeatedly abused by her parents — an aspect that is present in nearly every case of claimed mind control victimization. Along with vague memories of sexual abuse, Jones said her mother used to lock her in a dark room for long periods, where she invented an imaginary friend named Arlene.

When she grew up, she changed her name and entered a highly successful modeling career in which she became a popular pin-up girl during World War II.

In 1945, Jones fell ill and was treated by two doctors, one of whom she finally identified shortly before her death in 1990 as Dr. William Kroger. This, according to Donald Bain in his book, *The Control of Candy Jones,* was the initial phase of a conditioning process that would turn Candy Jones into a mind-controlled courier.

Candy's past revealed itself during her marriage to radio host Long John Nebel, whom she married on her birthday in 1972. Nebel claims that shortly after their marriage he was shocked by Candy's mood swings into another personality that he called "The Voice." The alternate personality usually disappeared rapidly, but the change was so startling that Nebel decided to learn more by hypnotizing his new bride. He had reason to be concerned, as Candy once told him she worked for the FBI and might need to leave town on assignments occasionally.

Nebel's hypnosis sessions uncovered an alternate personality, "Arlene," who revealed she had been subjected to a long CIA mind control program that began in 1960, usually held at West Coast colleges. She claimed that she had to deliver a letter at this time to a man in Oakland, California, who turned out to be the same doctor who had treated her during her 1945 illness. This doctor, along with Kroger, offered her sums of money to continue being a courier. The "Arlene" alternate was groomed further by the doctors, to the point where Jones had no memory of Arlene's activities.

The courier trips continued, one time taking Jones to Taiwan, but under hypnosis she claimed that the two doctors often tortured her to strengthen her conditioning. This again is an aspect repeated in the claims of other mind control victims and will be covered in later parts of this book.

Jones revealed that many of her courier trips coincided with her tours to various Army units with the USO, which continued into the Vietnam War. Her puzzling absences reported by others who worked for her modeling schools verified some of Jones' claims.

Another important piece of evidence surfaced with the discovery of a passport for "Arlene Grant," which bore a picture of Candy Jones in a dark wig and dark makeup.

According to Bain, further evidence exists in the message left on the couple's telephone answering machine on July 3, 1973, purporting to be someone from Japan Airlines: "Please have Miss Grant call [phone number]…She is holding a reservation on Japan Airlines Flight 5 for the 6th of July, Kennedy to Tokyo, with an option on to Taipei. This is per Cynthia that we are calling."

Jones called the number and learned it was the Japan Airlines reservation desk, but that no one named Cynthia worked there. Bain theorized in his book that the name Cynthia might simply have been a trigger code word to put Jones into an alternate state.

In the forward of Bain's book, nationally recognized hypnosis expert Dr. Herbert Spiegel wrote that he believed Nebel did not plant the tales that Jones told during her successful hypnoses by him. Although not convinced the entire story was accurate, Spiegel admitted that the corroborative evidence made it difficult to dismiss the story.

"The big thing with [the Candy Jones case] is that you can effectively program a person who's older," Patton told the author. "The key ingredient to mind control programming is creating lots and lots of personalities or alters, and that only can be done prior to the age of six. After the age of six, if an individual goes through severe trauma for a long period of time, they'll develop PTSD [Post Traumatic Stress Disorder] or die of shock."

Dr. Donald Ewan Cameron, one of the foremost psychiatrists in the world and one-time president of the World Psychiatric Association, is known now to have worked on adults for the CIA in MK-ULTRA. His work in a CIA-funded Montreal operation was nothing short of torture with the aims of conditioning and extracting information from "resistant sources."

Cameron developed a system called "psychic driving," which attempted to erase memory and completely rebuild the psyche. The technique involved psychotropic drugs injected into a strapped-down patient, reducing him or her to a comatose state for months. During this time, the subject wore a football-type helmet with speakers that played taped loops of various noises and repeated statements, in a process Cameron called "depatterning."

The experiments continued between 1957 and 1964, and in 1977 released documents proved that thousands of unwitting patients were used in this program, many of whom were US citizens. Most patients had entered the Allen Memorial Institute, where Cameron worked, complaining of such minor problems as post-partum depression, and were harmed permanently.

These shocking revelations inspired Senator John Glenn in 1997 to put the Human Research Subject Protections Act before Congress, in an attempt to criminalize future experiments using humans. The matter passed to the Senate Committee on Labor and Human Resources, then chaired by Senator Arlen Spector, where it died.

The testimony of victims has been effectively counterattacked by a portion of the medical community that claims such "recovered memories" are the result of mental illness. The fact that many mentally ill people do believe that they are mind control victims has buttressed these arguments. But are all mind control victims delusional?

One particularly effective attack on the victims claims their recovered memories are created by their therapists through suggestion during hypnosis. The False Memory Syndrome Foundation (FMSF) is the principal outlet for this point of view, which has been used in courts quite successfully to debunk testimony by alleged mind control victims.

The foundation has filed lawsuits in many states and succeeded in disqualifying testimony by witnesses who have been hypnotized at any time in their lives. In addition, FMSF has successfully caused the revocation of medical licenses from many therapists and doctors who treat former child abuse/mind control victims.

The co-founders of the FMSF, Peter and Pamela Freyd, are connected to CIA-funded psychiatrists Martin Orne and Harold Lief, who were on the foundation's Scientific Advisory Board. FMSF co-founder Dr. Ralph Underwager was forced from the organization after an interview in which he defended pedophiles, and the Freyds were charged by their daughter Jennifer for sexual abuse.

It should be noted that most people who claim to be victims of mind control experimentation have MPD. (We will use this term rather than the newspeak medical jargon for the syndrome, Dissociative Identity Disorder, or DID, because it is much more descriptive and does not attempt to mask the condition). Indeed, victims claim that MPD is the immediate goal of mind control technology — to shatter the personality through intense, ritualized, repeated trauma in order to create alternate personalities which can be programmed as "structured multiples" with specific talents and tasks. Among these tasks and talents are:

* Picking locks
* Courier services in which messages are passed faultlessly and later forgotten
* Smuggling drugs, diamonds, arms, and even children (to pedophile networks)
* Bodyguard duties
* Sexual duties (called "Beta Programming" according to testimony)
* Hostage intervention
* Body disposals
* Photographic memory (called "Alpha Programming" according to testimony)
* Withholding information under interrogation
* Psychic ability (called "Theta Programming" according to testimony)
* Murder (called "Delta Programming" according to testimony)
* Suicide (called "Omega Programming," which is triggered when the victim begins to "remember")

The systematic purpose and conditioning process in creating MPD victims was documented in a July 1990 memorandum written by Bishop Glen L. Pace of the Mormon Church. Pace had been tasked by an LDS committee to investigate claims of Satanic Ritual Abuse (SRA) among church hierarchy.

He interviewed 60 alleged victims and concluded, "The basic objective is premeditated — to systematically and methodically torture and terrorize children until they are forced to dissociate. The torture is not a consequence of the loss of temper, but the execution of well-planned, well thought-out rituals often performed by close relatives.

"The only escape for the children is to dissociate. They will develop a new personality to enable them to endure the various forms of abuse. When the episode is over, the core personality is again in control and the individual is not conscious of what happened."

Because he learned that the child victims had no day-to-day recollection of the atrocities, Pace understood that they go through adolescence and into adulthood with no active knowledge of the trauma still taking place, which serves the cultists' desire for secrecy. The victims led relatively normal lives during all of this. Pace wrote that the traumatic memories do begin to surface years later.

"As they become adults and move into another environment," he wrote, "something triggers the memories and, consequently, flashbacks and nightmares occur. One day they will have been living a normal life and the next day they will be in a mental hospital in the fetal position."

From the interviews, Pace concluded there are two reasons why the memories return during adulthood in such detail. First, the terror they experienced is so stark as to become indelible. Secondly, the memory was compartmentalized, buried for years so that when it returns it is as though the traumatic experience has just occurred.

"The memories seem to come in layers," Pace wrote. "For example, the first memory might be of incest; then they remember robes and candles; next they realize that their father or mother or both were present when they were being abused. Another layer will be the memory of seeing other people hurt and even killed. Then they remember having seen babies killed. Another layer is realizing that they participated in the sacrifices. One of the most painful memories may be that they even sacrificed their own baby."

Most of the victims are suicidal, according to Pace, programmed to kill themselves if and when they begin telling secrets.

"They have been threatened all of their lives," he wrote, "that if they don't do what they are told, their brother or sister will die, their parents will die, their house will be burned, or they themselves will be killed. They have every reason to believe it since they have seen people killed."

Pace found that practically all of the victims he interviewed suffered from MPD, which he concluded was one of the objectives of the cultists, who need secrecy for such despicable acts. Pace admitted that the credibility of the victims is harmed by the fact that they are technically mentally ill, but added "when 60 witnesses testify to the same type of torture and murder, it becomes impossible for me, personally, not to believe them." He stressed that the 60 victims he spoke with, most of them in their 20s or 30s, are but a small sampling of the true number, which he said must be "expanding geometrically."

Pace avoided asking the victims to name the perpetrators, but the state of Utah investigated the claims in his memorandum for 30 months after it was leaked to the press in 1991. Predictably, the Mormon-dominated officialdom concluded there was no evidence to substantiate the testimony of the victims, which would be devastating to the Mormon Church.

The concept of amnesia as a programmable tool is not far-fetched. There is voluminous psychiatric evidence of the human mind's ability to avoid traumatic memories through amnesia and dissociation. For instance, the 20-year study conducted by Dr. Linda Williams of the University of Massachusetts Lowell on children who required emergency room treatment for medically confirmed sexual abuse revealed that only one-third of them remembered being abused when they reached adulthood. All others had repressed or dissociated their painful experiences.

In the systematic programming approach to using this phenomenon, "screen memories" are created through audio tapes, video tapes and movies shown to the subject while in drug-induced altered states, to hide what really happened to them.

Sex has been a highly successful aspect to mind control, according to victims, who say it has great use in blackmailing and controlling powerful politicians, military leaders and business leaders, especially when it involves children. As will be shown in detail later in this book, this device has been used on the very top levels of our government for decades, and whenever threatened by disclosure, these leaders have used various government agencies to squelch the story, sometimes opting for murder.

The suicide program is another form of murder. The victim is programmed to commit suicide when he or she begins to recall episodes of training and of deeds performed by alternate personalities. Many mind control victims have reported urges to kill themselves during periods of recall or during deprogramming by therapists.

Several have verified their childhood memories of being used on mind control missions by checking school records for absenteeism. Victims have been shocked to learn that they've missed as much as one-third of every school year and yet always received passing grades. Others have interviewed family members to learn there were periods when they were "away," or have checked family scrapbooks to learn they do not appear in many holiday photos.

These discoveries certainly implicate school administrators and family members as being complicit with those behind such operations. This is an indication of the power that the individuals behind this program must wield.

Victims who begin to discover their past also report harassment, including telephoned death threats, threatening mail or signs painted on their homes, being run off the road by another car while driving, and being accosted by strangers in the street or while shopping.

As will be demonstrated in subsequent chapters of this section, cults have provided what amounts to a lab setting for programming subjects, as well as providing the subjects themselves. Members of demonic cults (and even Masonic groups, according to some reports) have put their children into traumatic programming from infancy, often at their own hands as well as with trained personnel.

Satanic cults have succeeded for a long time in creating MPD through trauma from infancy. These cults are much more widespread than nearly everyone suspects, and include influential and powerful people on the community level as well as the national and international level.

For a long time, the majority of victims came from multi-generational satanic families, according to Ron Patton, each new generation being traumatized from infancy, shattered into alternate personalities and programmed by earlier generations. The intent is to create "bloodlines," supposedly with special rights and powers over the "expendable ones" to be sacrificed in rituals.

"There also appears to be a pattern of family members affiliated with government or military agencies," adds Patton.

Aside from MPD, men and women who claim to be mind control victims display a collection of other maladies, including Post Traumatic Stress Disorder (PTSD), multiple sclerosis or other muscular diseases, somatization disorder (complaints of physical symptoms that have no identifiable origin), cysts, brittle teeth, thyroid problems and tinnitus (constant high-pitched tone in the ear).

One odd physical attribute was reported by author Walter Bowart, whose 1978 book, *Operation Mind Control,* was a trailblazing journey into the topic. The Freedom of Thought Foundation asked Bowart to investigate the case of imprisoned murderer Robert Joe Moody, who was convicted of killing two women in 1993.

Bowart learned that Moody had a high security clearance in the US Marine Corps, so he hired a psychiatrist who specialized in MPD cases to interview the killer in prison.

"Within minutes," Bowart wrote, "this doctor had the killer manifesting four different personalities. When he first switched into the killer personality, the room filled with heat. The doctor told me that it was not unusual for a whole variety of physical changes to occur when a multiple switched….I'd like to see even the best trained actor do that on cue!"

In the police videotape of Moody being read his Miranda rights following his arrest, Bowart reported that the killer spoke in a halting voice while picking at a scab on his hand, having become a nine-year-old personality named "Bobby," discovered later by the psychiatrist.

"And as you might expect," Bowart wrote, "Bobby wasn't the killer. Nor was he even 'present' at the scene of the crime. The killer personality was named XE and was, by all present indications, created during Moody's service in the Marine Corps."

Organizations have appeared that offer help to victims of mind control and MPD, including the Advocacy Committee for Human Experimentation Survivors – Mind Control (ACHES-MC). It specifically formed to "assist survivors of un-consensual federally funded mind control experimentation as children or adults." Its goals are to declassify government documents pertaining to mind control experiments, to prosecute criminal conduct related to these operations, and to demand a presidential hearing into charges and remedies. These goals, of course, have not been met.

One of the foremost therapists treating mind control victims is

Valerie Wolf, whose clients literally have been "fired" by other therapists because they are so unruly, tend to cut themselves, attempt suicide and never seem to recover. Wolf, a clinical social worker, began treating victims of trauma and sexual abuse in 1973, but she wasn't exposed to mind control pathology until 1992 when a colleague referred a client who she said suffered from that syndrome. After learning more about mind control through this patient, Wolf realized that two of her own patients also had been mind control victims.

During her subsequent work in the field Wolf learned that "if you have someone who is a mind control survivor, and you try to use traditional methods, I don't care how good you are and what you do…if you don't have access to the information you can only go so far."

Wolf learned that opening the forgotten past to mind control victims can be dangerous. On one occasion, a patient showed up at her home during the night and said, "OK, you opened it up and unless you do something by midnight, I have to die."

After months, Wolf refined her technique to avoid such instances. Her therapy induced one client to write out recalled conversations during conditioning, which gave Wolf a clear notion of what was behind the experiments.

In an interview with Wayne Morris, Wolf said she one day realized that "I was dealing with programs as memories rather than getting lost in the complexity of numbers and codes. The numbers and codes were conditioned. People were taught to respond in certain ways if they heard certain sequences of numbers, tones, or whatever it is….It was done in a deep trance state, so you had post hypnotic suggestions that reinforced it…but it's still a memory."

The commonality of childhood abuse among MPD patients is striking, and Wolf believes the creation of alternate personalities in early life works like this:

"What happens is, 'This person who is abusing me, I also have to love them.' Little kids under the age of five can't handle ambivalence really well, so what they will do is actually create a part that has the ability to take the hurt and be hurt, and they will create a part that says, 'I love you,'…so they can hold these two mutually incompatible thoughts and feelings at the same time. There has to be amnesia between them, because the part that is being hurt would be too confused by having to love this person who is hurting them…As time goes on there is more abuse and it is prolonged. A child naturally creates more and more personalities and all of the personalities have a job...."

Through her patients, Wolf learned the basic systematic mechanics of conditioning with the purpose of gaining total control over an individual. She claims the experiments revealed that the best time to begin conditioning was in children between the ages of two and a half and three and a half, creating what survivors have called a "Matrix" inside their minds.

"Survivors talk about it as being like a Rubik's cube," Wolf said, "and they started with a simple nine-by-nine tic-tac-toe matrix and each little square was a cell or room, and every time an alter came out or was created through the pain, they would condition that alter to respond to a certain word, letter or whatever, and then they would have to go into their place in the matrix...."

Among Wolf's many patients, the name "Dr. Green" keeps coming up. Obviously a pseudonym, this Dr. Green apparently was a key figure in the government-sponsored mind control projects, MK-ULTRA and Monarch. You will recall that some victims claim Josef Mengele used this name.

"I think what happened was Dr. Green started screening kids," Wolf said. "Apparently there were several criteria for selecting kids for the project — one was that they already had to have been traumatized somewhat so they had the ability to dissociate; another was they had to have good memories; another was they had to be really intelligent....At some point you come across the fact that some of these kids were already being abused in sex rings....Dr. Green would order a trauma [to induce amnesia] and if [a kid] had a sex ring lurking in the background, he would just send them back to be ritually abused again...."

In Wolf's work with patients, she has come to the conclusion that an invisible government exists behind the façade of American democracy, among other things funding and implementing a broad system of creating mind-controlled humans.

"This is like a cancer," Wolf said. "I know I have talked to some reporters and they know about the shadow government that is really running things behind the scenes — that the elected public officials have no idea it exists, or if they do, they are powerless to do anything about it."

On March 15, 1995, Wolf and two of her clients, Claudia Mullen and Chris Denicola, testified before President Clinton's Advisory Committee on Human Radiation Experiments, revealing that many mind control victims also were used in government-run radiation experiments.

One might ask what all of this has to do with the subject matter of this book. Dr. Wolf's conclusions about an invisible government creating human robots is the tip of the iceberg, and you are about to learn more of what's beneath the surface. Human robots, after all, are a nifty item for use by a shadow government.

In the feudal system that globalist oligarchs plan, in which a caste of contented workers serves their agenda, mind control is a vital means to that end. And as its founding members often have repeated, the end always justifies the means.

Meet Commander Casbolt

James Michael Casbolt achieved the rank of commander in the British secret service branch, MI-6. Born in 1976, he is descended from a family that has served the British intelligence community for generations. His grandfather, also James Casbolt, was in British intelligence during World War II. His uncle, Brian Casbolt, was a logistics operative in MI-5. His father, Peter Casbolt, served with MI-6 and participated in a secret project that brought illegal drugs into Britain to collect "non-appropriated funds" for black operations.

The Casbolt family also had reached high positions inside the Illuminati Lodges of England. According to Casbolt, his grandfather was a ranking member of the Sindlesham Grand Masonic Lodge in Berkshire, which he claims was a hotbed of New World Order thought.

Because of his lineage, Casbolt believes he was tabbed even before his birth to participate in an NSA-sponsored mind control and genetic enhancement program called Project Mannequin. He tells this story in his 2008 autobiography, *Agent Buried Alive.*

Casbolt claims Project Mannequin was conducted in a six-level underground facility called AL/499, located about 200 feet beneath the town of Peasemore in Berkshire. The project got underway in 1972 and according to Casbolt, involved kidnapping targeted civilians, often young children, "to create programmed 'sleeper' agents using sophisticated hardware-based hypnosis." Among the pre-programmed tasks given to these agents is assassination, Casbolt claims.

"I was 'sold' into the project," he writes, adding that he only began recovering memories about Project Mannequin in 2006, and continues to gather more through therapy.

His training began when he was just five. He claims two men took him from Chalgrove primary school in Finchley, London, and drove him to the Greenham Common military base, where they escorted him to the underground AL/499 facility. He was among 16 children aged five to 10 who were tested there with puzzles for psychic abilities.

Following this, men roughly herded the children into the hall and strapped them into gurneys. The men wheeled them down a corridor to a "medical-type setting" where others in lab coats injected them with drugs. They moved again to a dark room filled with large cages housing fierce dogs and perhaps even wolves.

The children were unstrapped and stood huddled together, now sedated by the drugs into a compliant state. The woman who had administered the psychic puzzle test announced they would play a game to find "the first chosen one." Casbolt writes that this phrase struck him as Masonic terminology when he recovered these memories years later.

"I believe what happened next was a Masonic/Satanic ritual," he writes.

The woman hung colored ribbons on a wall and told the children to pick one apiece. They obeyed, and the woman asked, "Who has dark purple?" Casbolt claims that one of the children, a small girl, had this ribbon. A man grabbed the girl tossed her into a cage with an attack dog, which killed her while Casbolt and the other children watched. He also maintains the outrage was filmed and "probably passed around the intelligence community as a 'snuff' film," prompting him to write, "much of the secret service apparatus in the UK and US is an occult pedophile network run by corrupt factions of the 'Illuminted' degrees of Freemasonry (33rd degree and above)."

The organization is structured along the lines of the Jewish *kabala*, according to Casbolt, making use of numerology and advanced remote viewing. He describes the men who run AL/499 as a "hard line military regime that is ultimately a religious cult centered upon the corrupt Zionists and Rosicrucians." He describes the facility as resembling a religious center where black magic rites are performed, worshipping ancient deities and sacrificing children.

The program is generational, Casbolt claims, pointing out that his father had been programmed during his childhood at a Burnham facility code-named OMEGA, taken there by his own father. Casbolt's father took him to the same facility in 1984 when he was eight years old. They went to a wooded area, where hooded and robed men stood around Casbolt chanting in foreign tongues, although he claims to have heard once again the term "chosen one" in English.

A woman in a hood and robes carried a snake and forced it to bite the eight year old boy on the arm. Casbolt claims the venom quickly sent him into an altered state and he became ill. When he recovered, the boy noticed the people surrounding him had stripped naked, and once again the woman forced another snake to bite him.

"This time I almost died," Casbolt writes. "I was injected with a drug to revive me and I recovered."

Next he claims the adults buried him alive in a coffin filled with large snakes and left him there for what seemed like hours.

"There was no escape for me in the coffin," he says, "so I dissociated and went somewhere else in my mind."

By age 12, Casbolt had been taking martial arts courses for years. His proficiency was tested in front of a small audience at AL/499, where he fought and quickly defeated an older boy in a bare-knuckled fight. To reward him, his handler gave him a kitten, but then handed him a knife and ordered him to kill it. Casbolt refused despite repeated beatings and the handler himself killed the kitten.

"Because I failed this test," he writes, "I was deemed unsuitable for physical assassinations...." His handlers concentrated on training him instead for remote viewing.

The traumatic training left its mark on Casbolt, who was arrested at age 15 for attempted robbery of a local store. Although the pistol he used was only a replica, he served a 28-day jail sentence. He claims that his father, who recently had been released from prison on a drug trafficking conviction, was proud of him. During his short incarceration, Casbolt claims three boys attempted suicide, apparently due to sexual abuse at the hands of the guards.

The newly hardened 16-year-old inspired his handlers to try him again as an assassin. He received a nine-millimeter Smith & Wesson automatic pistol with verbal instructions.

He found his target sipping beer at an outdoor Brighton restaurant and emptied most of the clip into the man's head.

"When I started to shoot, everything went quiet in my mind," Casbolt writes. "I felt very pleased with myself, as if my superiors were going to be very happy. Maybe they wouldn't hurt me anymore, I thought."

He claims that post-hypnotic commands caused him to forget the murder for years.

Casbolt writes that he commanded a five-agent assassination unit consisting of four males and one female. He explains this was standard, and that three of these units would comprise a "Delta Team." He led his unit under the name, Commander Michael Prince, security code X4566-2.

By age 18, he writes that he was being used as a remote viewer in a

London-based underground facility.

"Intelligence-run mind control operations are usually a multi-generational thing," he claims, "with each generation more easily programmed...."

Casbolt maintains the NSA specifically targets individuals with aristocratic Celtic bloodlines because of their predisposition for psychic ability, owing to their rare Rh negative blood type. His grandmother, Vera deTilard, was a French aristocrat, and there were generations of high level Freemasons in the Tilard family.

During his remote viewing operations, Casbolt claims that he often heard comments like, "When it all goes down, people like you will run the planet for us."

One of the programs that Casbolt's handlers conditioned into him is called "Janus/End Times," which he claims is "a sleeping program that activates when major events happen, like 9/11 and the coming plan for martial law in America, which some researchers refer to as the New World Order."

He further maintains that private security firms run by programmed operatives and organized crime have been created to help police control the populace during chaotic times. Specifically mentioned in his book is the Noonan Security firm of Manchester, owned by crime boss Dominic Noonan. He also hints that some funding for these militia-type entities comes from Zionist sources in Israel.

Casbolt still fears that his "Janus/End Times" program could "kick in" if a national emergency occurred. He reveals this could be accomplished through telephoned "trigger" signals or by sending signals to implants located within the sleeper agents.

One of his most vivid memories involves being strapped into a dental-type chair in front of a screen and injected with Scopalamine, a drug that impairs human memory, and Dythenol C. Images began to appear on the screen before him, and after that he recalls nothing.

But Casbolt later tracked down a former security guard from AL/499 named Barry King who drew a diagram of the programming seat, referred to by the NSA (National Security Agency) as "trip seats," and he immediately recognized it. The guard also corroborated Casbolt's memory of small humanoid bio-robots, which he claims are part machine and part organic, called Programmable Life Forms or PLFs.

The similarity between the PLFs and descriptions of small gray aliens in human-UFO encounters is striking, and according to Casbolt there is a very definite extraterrestrial connection to the underground training of sleeper agents. He claims the Project Mannequin operatives have faced and sometimes come into conflict with "malevolent and terrifying extra-terrestrial and extra-dimensional life forms." His writings suggests an underground cooperation between certain human agencies and alien life forms which occasionally has become hostile.

Although such claims are difficult even for UFO researchers to accept, there is mountainous evidence for alien visitation and presence on Earth. Supporting Casbolt's claim that an uneasy balance of power exists between rival alien races (pro-human "grays" from the Pleiades system against hostile "reptilians" from the Draco system, according to Casbolt) is the September 1991 video shot by the space shuttle Discovery. It showed an object reversing course above Earth's atmosphere following an out-of-frame light flash and avoiding a subsequent beam of energy.

NASA explained the object as an ice particle close to the shuttle, but Dr. Jack Kasher of the Nebraska University physics department decided after studying the video for two years that the UFO cannot be explained as a natural phenomenon.

"It's clearly above the atmosphere and air glow of the Earth," he added. "It maneuvers. It changes direction. It accelerates, and so the only thing really left is [that it is a] space craft."

Kasher worked for nearly 10 years in research and development for the "Star Wars" defense system.

Casbolt writes that corroborating evidence for the presence of aliens in underground bases also came from Dean Warwick, who was a senior electrical engineer subcontracted by the NSA to the underground Los Alamos facility. Warwick, who Casbolt says worked for the NSA between the late 1980s and 1992, told him there were more than 4,000 underground bases worldwide and that many of them contain aliens working on caged human test subjects.

On October 7, 2006, Dean Warwick was delivering a lecture at a UFO conference called Probe International held in Blackpool, England, when he collapsed dead on stage. People who spoke to him immediately before he approached the stage claim that Warwick complained of feeling a "beam" or a "burning sensation" at the side of his head. He added, "I think I'm going to be bumped off."

According to Casbolt, a woman spied a man with dark hair leaving the hall immediately after Warwick fell. She followed him and said he whistled a tune as he went downstairs, then entered a car and talked to someone on his cell phone, laughing.

Casbolt believes Warwick was killed by an ELF (Extreme Low Frequency) weapon developed at the underground Dulce, New Mexico facility, which emits a "delta wave" capable of shutting down the human nervous system. Casbolt also believes Warwick was targeted for death due to an interview he gave journalist Dave Starbuck several weeks before. In it, Warwick maintained that the 1988 Lockerbie, Scotland, crash of Pan Am Fight 103 was not caused by a bomb, but by a missile, according to his sources.

Casbolt believes that much of the reasoning behind the use of children in the mind control programs comes from the discoveries made by Nazi doctors at the concentration camps during World War II.

"The German scientists developed a technique at the concentration camps known as trauma-based mind control," Casbolt writes. "They discovered that if you could systematically traumatize an individual, particularly before the age of five, their mind would shatter into different parts which the German doctors called 'alters.' When the torture or terror becomes so intolerable, a person's mind will dissociate itself from the pain and the alter will be created. These alters can then be programmed by the torturer to carry out almost any task. From my understanding, the limit is reached when operatives are ordered to kill their own children."

If the mind control victim is a 'sleeper' who lives an apparently normal life within a community, it is possible that even his or her family will not be aware of the alters, he maintains.

Casbolt says the Nazi scientists also discovered that trauma and torture can produce spectacular traits in an individual, namely incredibly high pain thresholds, photographic memories and psychic talents. It appears the German doctors took a page from Satanism in this respect, as its rituals involve the very same shattering of children into multiple personalities through applied trauma. The connection and cooperation between military and intelligence personnel and satanic cults is such a common feature in this bizarre topic as to be almost a standard attribute.

During the 1980s, Satanic Ritual Abuse (SRA) suddenly appeared in many parts of the US, resulting in court cases that featured lurid testimony by the alleged victims. Critics attempted to discredit the victims' testimonies as being extracted through improper therapy and questioning techniques, but there still remained the mystery of why so many people suddenly suffered from Multiple Personality Disorder

(MPD), a condition thought to be extremely rare.

Casbolt claims that in talking to other SRA survivors, he sees a common practice in the rituals of allowing poisonous snakes to bite victims "to transmute the poison and enhance the immune system." He adds that this ritual often goes to the point of near-death and revival.

Another SRA survivor, Cathy O'Brien, corroborates this in her book, *Trance Formation of America.* She describes various CIA facilities where she underwent such rituals as "near-death training."

There has been testimony claiming that victims are ritually "buried alive with their fear," locked in a coffin with a number of large snakes, and left in that state for hours. When the ordeal ends and the victim is removed from the coffin, he or she is considered to have "gone beyond fear."

Casbolt maintains that he freed himself from Project Mannequin with the help of renegade factions within the NSA and British intelligence who are opposed to such operations on moral grounds.

"There are both positive and negative factions in the NSA and British intelligence involved in an internal war with each other," he writes. "In fact, the whole global intelligence community has descended into chaos with much in-fighting going on between rival factions, often in the same organizations."

Casbolt says a "technology" developed in the 1960s by the NSA that opens neural pathways in the brain has helped him to regain memories that were programmed to be repressed. According to Casbolt, he employs highly classified methods of controlling his own brain waves, combining advanced meditation and biophysics technology, "to take control of myself instead of the project controlling me."

But deprogramming is a long and tedious procedure, because when one program is uncovered, another one usually exists beneath it, and more beneath that. Like peeling an onion, Casbolt says it takes years to eliminate the great number of programs given to him since he was a child. He, as many others like him, fears that treatment never will eliminate all of his alters and programs.

Memory suppression programming begins to deteriorate around the age of 30, he writes, which is why many "sleepers" are "thrown from the Freedom Train," a euphemism for elimination at around that age. Those who are not eliminated by murder often commit suicide or succumb to drug and alcohol addiction to cope with panic attacks that pepper the rest of their lives.

This certainly is the case in the incredible tale of a California woman.

The Susan Ford Saga

What you are about to read will be difficult to accept. Initially, this was the reaction of Professor Emeritus of Social Work, Dr. Mary R. Lewis, who treated Susan Ford in a long-running therapy program.

Dr. Lewis first came upon the "bizarre stories of Satanic Ritual Abuse" when she was the unit social worker at a mental hospital. Not knowing what to make of the stories at first, Lewis took notice of the surprisingly high number of these patients mutilating themselves, including one woman who infected her leg by driving a screw into it.

"Over a period of a year and a half," Lewis wrote, "I had three different clients draw pictures for me, talk to me and cry to me about the horrors of what happened to them while visiting Disney World....I began to hear such things that were so similar from people that did not know each other."

Lewis noticed the same similarities between her patients' stories and those included in Susan Ford's fictionalized account of her mind control experiences, *Starshine*. She contacted Ford, and after working with her, concluded that "the success of the programming depends on the triumph of the assault on the five senses. The programmers use sight, hearing, touch, smell, and taste to alter a child's perceptions. The method used works on the principal of operant conditioning."

While working with Ford, Lewis unearthed the now-familiar themes so prevalent in child programming: "The Disney Parks, the MGM Studios, Disney movies, Disney characters and Disney songs [that] have been used in conjunction with programming."

Other common traits included animals like dolphins. Birds often are used in keeping child victims silent about their experiences, because they are programmed to believe that birds hear what they say and will fly back to report on them.

Lewis noticed a special reaction to the ringing of a telephone among her patients, sometimes to the point of a panic attack. She also saw a common fear of jail with accompanying guilt. Obsession with their birthdays is yet another common aspect among her victim patients, according to Lewis.

"Once in recovery," Lewis wrote, "unless the suicide programs are disconnected, the desire to kill themselves as they remember their past is overwhelming, especially around the time of their birthday, and this has proven true with each individual I see."

Still, with all of her years of work with mind control victims, Lewis was challenged by the Susan Ford story, because it involved so many high-powered names — every US President from John Kennedy to William Clinton, male and female celebrities, foreign dignitaries — and the claim that her two controllers were Henry Kissinger and Bob Hope. However, having seen Susan Ford with Bob Hope during a Palm Desert, California, golf tournament, Lewis believes Ford is telling the truth to the best of her abilities.

"I know too much now," Lewis wrote. "I have seen too much now, and my only hope is that others of you that read [Ford's] book will believe her truth, and help stop this living nightmare."

What you are about to read are claims made by Susan Ford in her non-fiction account, *Thanks for the Memories,* which she wrote under the pseudonym of Brice Taylor.

"Much of the following information has been copied, often verbatim, from my private journals," Ford wrote. "Over the years, daily, I painstakingly documented my memories, in an attempt to deal with and sort out the often vivid, though confusing, memory flashbacks I had. What I remembered was so far from the reality I thought I had lived, that it was deeply disturbing."

Susan Ford was born in January, 1951, in Woodland Hills, California. She describes her father, Calvin Charles Eckhart, as being a ritually abused, programmed pedophile who began abusing her during infancy.

It was the opening stage of abuse that would last more than three decades "in many locations in and out of California, including hospitals, universities, and United States military and NASA bases, where I was subjected to 'high level' programming."

Regarding her father's programming, Ford recalls an incident when she was 16 in which her father underwent brain surgery at the UCLA Neuropsychiatric Institute. She claims that "suited men" monitored the operation, "and they gave him shots in his thighs and asked him questions over and over, and told him what to do with me."

After 16 years of paternal abuse, which will be detailed shortly, Ford learned from these men that her father "would no longer hold authority over me. Now he was totally under their control, and now they would be in total control of me….and all my progeny from then on."

During her torturous journey, Ford claims she was used as "a sex slave and human mind file computer" under the control of Henry Kissinger for a variety of purposes, not the least of which concerned having sex with Presidents John Kennedy, Lyndon Johnson, Richard Nixon, Gerald Ford, Ronald Reagan, and William Clinton. According to Ford, the purpose of her sexual escapades as "presidential model escort" was to both garner gratitude from the presidents and provide potential blackmail against them, all in the interest of keeping them under control of powerful men called "the Council," and their representative, Kissinger.

Her connection to Bob Hope, who she described as her "owner," served similar purposes with Hollywood celebrities, recording stars and influential California businessmen and politicians.

As we have seen in previous cases of inter-generational ritualized abuse, Susan's father began during her infancy with "the rigorous training and intentional torture required to shatter my base personality with the goal of creating many separate and individual personalities for training and use by others as I grew older."

He withheld food. He had the baby perform oral sex. He deliberately let her fall from the dining room table, a vivid memory she claims to retain despite being an infant.

Her older brothers, themselves abused, were part of her torment. At age one, Susan recalls an experience which we have seen in other mind control related programming cases. Her father placed her in a blanket suspended by a rope from the ceiling and spun her until she became disoriented, at which time he sexually traumatized her with a sharp object.

"He began…inserting objects into my vagina," she wrote, "gradually stretching it so that I would be able to accept a full grown man's penis by the time I was two. I was being groomed for early child prostitution, pornography, and a position in the 'inner circle' at church."

Certain members of the local church apparently were part of a cult that practiced pedophilia and ritual abuse, as Ford recalls being violated by them and even by the minister, who she identifies in her book. She remembers him taking her from a Sunday school class and forcing her to perform oral sex on him in a secluded area.

"When I was done, he wiped his mouth with a handkerchief and told me that I was going to hell for what I had just done," she wrote, "but that I would be forgiven if I never told anyone about it."

This mixture of guilt, low self-esteem and fear of confessing the truth are all elements of mind control programming seen in numerous cases.

The church secretary also partook in these degenerate episodes, according to Ford, who claims the woman also practiced sorcery and witchcraft in her home. She remembers the woman placing her on a table, chanting over her and burning her with candles, scaring her with spiders, and stabbing needles into her feet. The adults told her this ceremony was for her "training and preparation."

The church's "inner circle" clearly had satanic roots, as Ford recalls ceremonies in which they wore black robes, had sex orgies, killed both humans and animals and consumed their flesh.

"Their belief was that these cannibalistic and sexual acts would transfer the energy or life force from the victim to them in order to make them more powerful," she explained.

Ford claims she not only witnessed the killing of animals and babies, but was also "forced to eat their raw flesh and drink their blood or urine. Other children were involved in the rituals, and when we reached a certain age we were forced to participate in killing animals and babies."

Later, when she was used by more elite men like Kissinger, Hope and others, she learned that they considered the Satanist cults as a necessary evil.

"They looked at people who practiced Satanism as low level," she wrote, "but the job had to be done (trauma base for mind control), and they rationalized it by saying, 'Look how beautifully she turned out.'"

A female church member who ran choir practices at her home also used children in rituals. Here, Ford claims she was "forced to participate in child pornography films when a group of men entered her house and took over. Snuff pornography, where little children or babies were killed, was also filmed at her house."

Ford's father had an affair with one of the church members, and she recalls being included in their sexual encounters while she was a small child. She also was sleep-deprived, because "nighttime was…a time of training. My mother was the only one allowed and/or commanded to sleep."

Ford claims her mother also had been mind controlled, and could not do anything to stop the horrendous treatment her little daughter received. During her recovery in the 1980s, Susan asked her mother why she always cleaned the house instead of paying attention to her. Her mother responded blankly, "I felt like there was something really dirty about our home."

Her father actively created alternate personalities in Susan, one time using one of her dolls, saying, "You, Susie, will step aside as Doll fully enters your body." He triggered this by snapping his fingers three times, which programmed Ford to enter the "Doll" personality, later named "Sharon." This would be the sexualized personality, programmed to be sophisticated as well as licentious.

"Sharon" became "Susie's inner twin." This personality's training included torture with the intention of creating oblivion to pain. The tortures included burning by a hot poker and electric shocks, "so certain personalities within me took the pain and torture after which I would be switched back to Susie who had no knowledge of any of it."

At a very early age, Susan had her first experience at a US military base. Too young to know which base, she does remember men placing bands around her forehead, wrists and ankles, turning out the lights and applying electrical shocks while she had to watch messages on a screen.

When she was five, Ford remembers being taken to a separate military base, where a white-coated doctor examined and questioned her, "in order to check all my 'systems.'" If true, this indicates that the systematic nature of Ford's treatment went far beyond the ritual abuse for the twisted pleasures of a collection of cultists.

That same year, Ford remembers attending her first children's fashion show, which was really an auction for mind-controlled children. The "fashion show" degenerated into a strip tease by the children, who then were sponsored or sold.

Ford claims she was purchased by Bob Hope at one of these shows. She stresses that Hope did not have sex with her until she was well into adolescence, but used her for sex with others in a carrot-and-stick badger scheme to gain tight control over powerful individuals.

This also was the year when Ford met Henry Kissinger, introduced to him by her "Uncle Charlie" in a park-like area. After this, Kissinger occasionally phoned Ford at her home to test her programming.

When with her in person, Kissinger triggered the personality he desired by a variety of means, including tickling, according to Ford. It's important to note that Kissinger never had sex with her. At this point, she says he was most interested in developing in her a photographic memory so she could serve as a "mind file" for him in the future.

"I was taught to write backwards," Ford says, "because my programmers felt that I would be more intelligent if I was forced to use both sides of my brain."

As Dr. Lewis and other therapists treating mind control victims have pointed out, the Disney empire and films like *The Wizard of Oz* played important programming roles among child victims. Ford claims that during one Disneyland visit, her parents left her alone with Walt Disney, who handed her over to another man. He gave the little girl a View-master box that featured pictures of "Dead things — cut up bodies, dead cats skinned with big eyeballs and their tails cut off, people cut up, etc....Then the man took me to *Mr. Toad's Wild Ride* and sexually abused me....I was instructed to be extra sexy and wild and crazy in order to be 'good' and not get hurt."

Later, Ford met another man at the waterfall section of the Matterhorn ride, who told her that everything which happened was "washed away and gone forever." Following this, he returned Susan to her parents. She recalls her mother crying and her father smiling as the man told them, "She's now ready for the next level."

Ford maintains the Disneyland experience, in addition to programming, was intended to mask later trips she took to other locations, including overseas venues, to make her believe she'd only been to the theme park.

By the time she was five, Ford also had been "conditioned through torture and high-tech hypnotic techniques and electroshock, to hurt myself in many ways should I begin to remember the secretive activities I was part of....I would stub my big toe or burn myself on the stove, thereby removing my focus from the remembered secret experience, and re-routing my attention to my wound. I was instructed where to cut my wrist in order to take my own life, should I begin to remember or tell. There were also accident programs instilled to insure my death if I began to remember....My programmers also created within me reporting personalities that were instructed to tell on me in regard to anything I did that was stepping out of line."

Kissinger began programming her ability to become a "mind file" by conditioning a photographic memory at an early age. Ford remembers him marking her forehead with small x's to create what he called a "stellar map" of her systems. He instructed her to study the marks he'd made by looking into a mirror, and told the child that he and Bob Hope "rode on little space cycles all around inner space in my head in order to police everything and make sure everything was in perfect order..."

Other men participated in Ford's programming at top security places where she was taken as a child by her father. They called it "prep work" necessary to perform before she would meet again with Kissinger.

Ford repeatedly quotes Kissinger referring to her and other mind control subjects as "robots," adding that he seemed to spend more time perfecting her than the others.

"He said I was the perfect subject," Ford wrote, "and that my father had done such a great preliminary job that his work was a guaranteed success, where other robots fell short because they 'bled through' and so couldn't be relied upon."

As a child, it was impossible for Ford to understand the sophisticated programming techniques she underwent, which included time in isolation chambers, spinning devices to induce disorientation, powerful drugs, and being wired for electroshock. Decades later, during deprogramming and therapy, Ford had to force her way through multiple conditionings such as sleep, suicide, migraines and drug abuse to recapture these childhood memories.

"Often after I tenaciously battled my way through the journalizing of my memories," Ford wrote, "I would smile, having won, only to become immediately disoriented and look again the next moment to find that the information I had just spent one to two hours documenting had been erased by another part of my personality structure who was still following the ordered command of my controllers."

Games often served as tools for creating mind files. Kissinger played chess, checkers and other mind-oriented games with the child to create independent abilities to store information, house cryptic messages, and even know precisely what time it was in various places around the world. This latter program allowed Ford's controllers to know exactly what she did between certain times on certain dates, just by asking.

The game of bingo programmed Ford to successfully pull information from classified files in the Pentagon when she had reached adulthood. She claims Kissinger bribed a guard to shut down security cameras and escort her to a certain file room that contained important information, and left her there while she mentally photographed the targeted documents.

"Like a rat in a maze," she wrote, "I knew my way exactly to the desired destination….It took a few minutes to completely 'photograph' a multi-page document with my mind. There was not enough time to read it, but I photographed it quickly and then I returned to the guard."

Aside from prostituting her to certain top Pentagon officials, Ford is not clear what else Kissinger used to bribe or blackmail these men to where they would allow her entry to high security areas.

Even as a child, Ford was useful in a variety of ways as a message carrier, because, as Kissinger once said in her presence, "Who would suspect a kid?" On at least one occasion as a child, Ford was hidden inside a box that was delivered to a secure warehouse, with instructions to wait exactly two hours before getting out and unlocking the doors after breaking the security codes.

Behind Kissinger, Ford claims, was a group of globalist elites often called "the Council" by Kissinger and his associates. Ford heard conversations between Kissinger and Nelson Rockefeller that she was not supposed to remember, in which they discussed Council agendas that included a globalist New World Order that would eliminate nations, and a master plan to depopulate the world of humans on a vast, unprecedented scale.

Ford says that she heard them often talk about how more than 90 percent of humanity was stupid and genetically inferior to the elite, and would be eliminated through a variety of means, mainly by spreading pathogens.

"The Council contacted Henry and built a very strong relationship with him through lengthy discussions and information they sent to him through messages encoded in my mind file system," Ford wrote.

Ford's history of prostitution began during her childhood at home. She claims that her father sent her for sexual use by neighbors and business contacts in return for favors as petty as receiving free gas at the local gas station. Her father, who owned a welding business, also sold child pornography out of the shop. She remembers that he had a group of pedophile friends with daughters her age, who traded the girls sexually and filmed them pornographically, sometimes even with animals.

"There were times a personality within me was programmed and used to entice and kidnap other children off the street and into a big black car," Ford wrote, mirroring the testimony of many other victims. "The kidnapped children were initially kept in cages in back rooms and then used in pornography and usually killed, often in snuff films. We were all shocked with cattle prods and other electrical devices for lots of different offenses."

Ford reached her puberty around age 10, which heralded a new kind of abuse. In apparent satanic rituals, she was raped and impregnated. She claims this sometimes occurred twice a year.

"When the fetuses were two to three months old," she wrote, "they were aborted at rituals and ingested by members of the group in order to fulfill the beliefs of the group; that it made those participating 'more powerful.'"

While visiting her paternal grandfather, Ivan Charles Eckhart, a multi-millionaire and former mayor in Correctionville, Iowa, the still pre-teen Ford suffered through similar rituals including a forced abortion excruciatingly performed by a local doctor.

"My grandparents and my father performed a ritual behind their house in which they convinced me that I had killed my own baby," wrote Ford, "and they ate it and forced me to participate."

Susan Ford believes her strongest link to the global elitists was her uncle, Charles Lilley Horn, who was connected to the Federal Reserve Bank through his association with the US Mint in San Francisco and the F.W. Olin Foundation. During the 1970s, the Olin Corporation was associated with the Chase Manhattan Bank, chaired by David Rockefeller. It was this "Uncle Charlie" who introduced her to Kissinger.

"Uncle Charlie was a direct link with the Council through the money he was able to generate," Ford wrote. His generous donations to universities, including USC, had the hidden purpose of turning out thousands of "enhanced citizens" who would "function on behalf of the [globalist] cause," according to Ford.

She added, "These people were heavily into breeding and genetic bloodlines," and that she remembers one of these elitists saying, "It's time we quit wasting precious space on this planet supporting inferior human life."

When Ford reached age 11, Kissinger decided that she was ready for prime time. She learned of a presidential "escort" service, featuring "the CIA's latest human robot technology" in programmed sex and espionage. Presidents "were encouraged to use these escorts to satisfy their sexual and emotional needs instead of exposing themselves to outside individuals, because these escorts were guaranteed safe — had passed many tests to insure security, were able to provide guaranteed secrecy and were safe from venereal disease."

As part of Project Monarch's Beta training, Ford maintains these subjects were called "million dollar babies" due to the huge sums of money they could bring in from an early age.

"In the [']60s," Ford wrote, "the use of a Project Monarch Presidential Model sex slave cost around $1,200 for an evening. Henry called me his 'million dollar machine.'"

Aside from sexual favors and potential blackmail, the escorts could be programmed to subversively influence top government officials in matters that would benefit the men of "the Council."

John F. Kennedy was president when Ford entered the escort service at age 11. Although Ford was not privy to how the president would be introduced to the existence of these robotic child pleasure units, she claims the usual procedure was to give bits of information over time about the nature of mind control technology and its results. If the person seemed open to the idea and was willing to cooperate, more information drew him further in, until, after dozens of meetings in which he became deeply committed, he would be compromised if he backed out.

Before she met Kennedy, Ford received intense preparation from Kissinger. He programmed her to remember precisely everything the president said and did for later debriefing. Then Kissinger introduced her to the president and "just let me be with JFK so that he would get used to me, and Henry said, 'Then a plan will inevitably open up.'"

At first, Ford only delivered "high level council messages" to JFK, who she called in her child's voice, "John Feeee."

Soon afterward, "John Feeee" was having sex with the 11-year-old Ford, she claims. At first it took place in the back of a moving limousine on what was euphemistically known as "The Lincoln Memorial Tour."

"It was as common for foreign dignitaries, heads of state, senators, congressmen, governors, and other leaders to ride the Lincoln Memorial (Oral Sex) Tour, as it was for them to get their shoes shined," Ford recalled. "In fact, that was one of the jokes I was instructed to deliver to get a man loosened up. I was programmed to say, 'Want your shoes shined?' Then I would unzip him and begin."

JFK rode the Lincoln Memorial Tour with Ford often, she claims, adding that he would pat her back when she finished and say, "You're really going to amount to something when you grow up, kid." Ford also claims that Kennedy gave his Secret Service agents fits over this kind of recklessness regarding security. After that she says that he went so far as to ditch them just to be alone with her. One time, Ford maintains, Kennedy escaped his Secret Service escort and had sex with her in a public bathroom.

Eventually, the limo tours were replaced by "nooners," in which Kennedy arranged to sneak the girl into a White House bedroom at around lunch hour, sometimes along with another programmed sex slave.

"Jack said he was training me for the future," Ford wrote. "I didn't know what that meant. He said I was serving my country by meeting the needs of our leader...I was just out of braces."

During all of this, the 11- and 12-year-old Ford was taken from her home or from school by men in suits, or instructed to meet them at a certain place and time near her California home. They drove her to the local airport where she flew to Washington, and other suited men escorted her to Kissinger's limousine. From there, she would be driven to meet Kennedy while Kissinger set up specific programming parameters to make sure he could debrief her accurately later.

The information she provided no doubt was useful to the men behind Kissinger in several ways, including control through potential blackmail of a US president. After her JFK duties were completed and Kissinger debriefed her, men in suits reversed the process, flying to California and returning her to her home, school or rendezvous point.

Her teachers and school never questioned Ford's absenteeism and of course her parents were totally cooperative. Ford herself had no memory of her sojourns, because she was programmed to forget them and to ignore the "missing time" in her life.

When she was 12, Ford remembers Kissinger telling her that she won't be "servicing" JFK much longer, because "the higher ups" have other plans for him. "At the time I felt he meant death," Ford wrote.

Kennedy would be assassinated on November 22 of that year. When it was finished, Ford claimed she was told, "No one would ever miss you [if] you should step out of line. Then we would have to take care of you like your little boyfriend JFK."

Ford's "servicing" of the president continued with Kennedy's successor, Lyndon Johnson, who she claims often wore his cowboy hat and occasionally shocked her with an electrical device during their sessions. She also remembers that he usually wore an ankle-holstered or boot-holstered pistol, despite the heavy security at the White House and at his Texas ranch.

Ford would have been between the ages of 12 and 17 during Johnson's presidential tenure. A doctor had prescribed a continuous supply of the antibiotic Tetracycline for her, ostensibly to prevent acne.

Ford suspects now that it was a safeguard against contracting and infecting her high office sexual contacts with venereal diseases.

Kissinger's influence during the Nixon administration as national security advisor and later secretary of state insured a more direct path for passing Susan along to his boss. She recalls Nixon as being a business-first recipient of her talents, accessing her strategic messages and information "before, during and after a meeting, always leaving the sex for much later on." She claims to have accompanied Nixon on his diplomatic visits to China, the Soviet Union, the Far East and Vietnam.

At this time, Ford remembers that Nelson Rockefeller was her "corporate sponsor" who financed her "further education," a code phrase for more advanced programming. She now believes his request that she refer to him as "Uncle Rocky" was part of conditioning her to believe that he was part of her real family.

Today, Ford concludes that he, like Kissinger, represented an invisible government that dictated policy.

"In my experience," she wrote, "the Council and certain international individuals like the Rockefellers, was [at] a higher level, standing head and shoulders above the government and United States politicians."

Susan attended parties at the Rockefeller mansion as well as private meetings in which she witnessed the world's movers and shakers in action, "Men who decided when it was profitable and/or strategically timely to start a new war. They even had it planned who would begin the fighting and where. It always added up to big money, power, and control…."

"People in America think they elect their presidents, but from what I witnessed, they do not, as the process of putting them into office is a highly controlled and corrupt one. The media is so controlled that the American people never get the full and accurate story. The presidents are selected long before they are 'voted' into office."

Susan claims that the Rockefeller mansion in New York had a direct phone line to the White House that was known to only a few. "It was kept in a side closet behind a mirrored liquor cabinet," she wrote. "Nelson didn't even have to dial; he just picked it up and began talking."

The Rockefellers arranged for sexual interludes between Susan and Prince Charles of England, according to her account, because, "they wanted to know his dreams, desires, likes and dislikes…so that they could use that information in the future to control him, and ultimately, his country."

Along with the Rockefellers, Kissinger also absorbed this information, especially concerning Charles' shaky relationship with his wife, Diana. Kissinger and the Rockefellers used Ford to deliver messages that would drive a wedge between the couple, with an eye toward destabilizing the British crown, she wrote.

During Watergate, Ford believes that Nixon became dispensable to the invisible government power brokers, who did everything they could to protect Kissinger from the scandal because he was much more valuable to them. He was still secretary of state to President Gerald Ford following Nixon's resignation from office in 1974, and embarked on what he called his most difficult job in guiding an American chief of state. Gerald Ford kept going in his own direction, Kissinger told Susan, who also served as an escort to this president, and Kissinger added later he was happy that Ford's White House stay was so brief.

The next president, Jimmy Carter, did not have sex with her, according to Ford. Instead, Carter greedily accepted her messages and instructions, without realizing that Kissinger was on the other end of them. Ford claims that Carter believed the messages and instructions came only from "the Council," which pleased Kissinger because he was manipulating a Democrat who "didn't believe in adultery but would take top secret information from a whore and run the country from it."

Susan's relationship with Ronald Reagan began during his tenure as governor of California, while she was still a teenager in the late 1960s. Bob Hope arranged their initial meetings in a small theater on the grounds of the Motion Picture Country Hospital, close to Ford's Woodland Hills home.

At this early time, Ford claims that the invisible elite had already tabbed Reagan for high office.

"The Council had big plans for Ronald Reagan," she wrote, "and he fit the requirements for what they were looking for — someone who was pliable and could be directed....He was a 'good actor' and was willing to jump through their hoops without question. They always told him he was working for the 'good of the country' and he never seemed to question anything."

Ford went so far as to claim that Reagan actually practiced his speeches on the little theater stage, which she would memorize and repeat to "the Council," whose members made modifications and sent her back with the changes.

Kissinger held Reagan in the lowest regard, according to Ford, actually referring to him as a "bimbo" and a "stupid ignoramus" in a conversation she overheard. Nevertheless, "the Council" kept him on point, says Ford, who looks now upon this collection of power brokers with a stark warning.

"My experience was that the Council was publicly nameless and unknown," she wrote, "and this anonymity is what made it possible for them to wield power over the masses. From my perspective, these individuals acting in the shadows actually dictated in a subversive and inconspicuous manner the direction our government took at the time."

Ford claims that her use as a "presidential model" continued into the early portion of the Clinton administration, who she says had sex with her and her teenaged daughter, Kelly. By this time, Ford was several years into her "recovery" when she began remembering what had happened to her over the decades, and yet she still was unable to resist the programming instilled in her.

During the Reagan presidency, Ford claims that Vice President George H.W. Bush repeatedly used her then-underage daughter Kelly for sex. Kelly would have been between the ages of three and 11 during that administration, at which time, according to Ford, she "was created to be, as I later found out from a renegade CIA operative, what was called a 'Bush Baby.'"

Ford's accusations of pedophilia against Bush made her despise him more than any other man she mentions in her book, despite the fact that JFK allegedly used her sexually often when she was as young as 11.

"Bush was ruthless and brutal; the end justifies the means," Susan wrote. Late in her adolescence, Kelly Ford was hospitalized in a catatonic state following "many suicide attempts," which her mother insists was a direct result of the mind control conditioning and abuse she received to program her "to kill herself if she began to remember."

Susan Ford's experiences in Bob Hope's parties are no less bizarre. She maintains Hope specifically held these parties for influential people in order to tempt them to enjoy sexual favors with the young men, women and children he had on hand, in order to gain control over them through the threat of blackmail. Kelly was one of the children supplied by Hope to "known pedophiles," according to her mother.

Hope "would act like he really thought it was okay to have sex with a child, to men he knew were pedophiles," Ford remembers. "Without actually saying it in words, he portrayed that attitude, and then after the person had raped the child he would say something like, 'Do you know what news like this could do to your career?'...With people he really wanted to own or use, he would take pictures of the molestation with hidden cameras....Then afterwards he would show them the pictures of the rape of the child and say, 'We sure don't want these pictures or any others like them to get into the wrong hands and ruin your career, do we?'...He just knew how to control these men and they usually complied."

Susan remembers J. Edgar Hoover attending Hope's parties, one night showing up in a blue sequined dress. There are a number of reports from completely different sources, places and times corroborating Hoover's preference for dressing in drag. At this particular gathering, Hoover made some unwise admissions to Ford, who fully recorded them for her controllers.

"From then on the FBI was under Council control," she wrote, "and they even got Hoover to put in blocks and different rules, regulations and codes directly into the FBI operations."

Bob Hope also "sponsored" Michael Jackson, according to Ford. She met Jackson when he was only four or five as she accompanied Hope to a talent show. She is positive that Jackson, and a few other celebrities in the film, TV and recording industries, were and are mind control victims.

"They [the Jacksons] were made into a sensation and famous on purpose, so that they could be used in the future to influence large audiences," she wrote.

Among the other names that Ford believes were mind control victims are Elvis Presley and Barbra Streisand. She also claims that Bob Hope delivered her for sex to a variety of male and female celebrities, because, "stars had trouble getting 'secured' sex with people. They couldn't trust that people weren't coming on to them to manipulate or hurt them, and since they were famous, they couldn't risk losing their public reputation....They loved it [the sex slave service] just like the politicians did, since....many were told I was a robot that couldn't ever divulge their secrets."

There were times when Ford remembers being put on display to demonstrate her programmed abilities for scientists and government officials, for the purpose of getting "additional funding or permission to do more mind research into areas they wanted to explore." At times this took place in a circular amphitheater-style setting ringed by men sitting in chairs.

Kissinger informed her at another time that her "prototype" was not new, but was an expanded version, more versatile than the original "model." "He actually viewed me as a machine," Ford wrote.

On August 21, 1971, Susan married Craig Ford, who she met at age 13 and maintained the relationship throughout the intervening years. Upon introducing Craig to her mother after their first meeting, Susan remembers her saying, "That is the boy you will marry."

During the seven years of their friendship, she insists that her future husband had undergone programming with the intention of ensuring his cooperation in her future use.

"Craig and I were 'bonded' to each other through cross-programming and shared trauma," Ford wrote, "to insure that Craig was under sufficient mind control to later serve as my 'handler.'"

The conditioning, intended to force Craig to robotically surrender his wife to other men at specific times and places and to obey instructions, was immediately used after the wedding and the honeymoon. The newlyweds were forced to participate in a "black wedding" at night in a park, and on their Hawaii honeymoon, Craig had to allow his bride to have sex with other men, apparently to test the new programs.

The couple moved into a house in Agoura, California, not far from Ford's family home. She claims she was programmed not to lock the doors so that "men in suits" carrying guns could enter at will. After Ford gave birth to her first child, Kevin, she says these men, who came in a group of three, entered and tortured both her and the child. At times, they separated them by taking Kevin into another room, where Ford had to listen to the screams of her baby. The splitting of the next generation into multiple personalities had begun.

Ford gave birth to her daughter Kelly in 1978, and the infant immediately became the focus of traumatic conditioning. Even before Ford left the hospital with her baby, three men in suits arrived and held Kelly "faced downward and forced the wad of wet Kleenex into her mouth, interfering with her ability to breathe."

Over time, Ford claims she dutifully delivered Kelly to the Point Mugu Naval Weapons Base, where military men took the child away for unknown activities.

"Sometimes when they needed one of my children for programming," Ford remembers, "I was instructed to park my car on Las

Virgenes Road…and the men in suits picked us up and drove us the rest of the way to Point Mugu."

There were times when her young son Kevin was taken in a helicopter from Point Mugu, "and I never knew where they took him," Ford wrote.

Ford believes that she also was involved in genetic engineering procedures. One specific instance took place at Valley Presbyterian Hospital in Van Nuys, California, where she overheard a conversation between doctors.

"Her children by her husband are inferior compared to those created here," Ford claims to have heard. "These children will one day rule the world and we will be able to weed out the weaker genetic strains….These children will be raised in isolation, like the leaders in the shadows, and will be taught advanced skills from birth….The forms will be so advanced that the normal human species will not be able to compete, and so ours will be the elite — the ruling class — and the lower forms will be the so-called worker bees."

Ford maintains that these procedures are the result of decades of study on the human brain and experimentation that continue to this day.

"Over the years," she wrote, "the research has been tried and tested through the experimentation on children who were targeted before birth. The genetic engineering aspect is highly used and they take into consideration the inherent genetic talents and abilities coupled with just the right training at the right age to produce a 'highly advanced child.' But, in essence, what they truly have created is a highly advanced robot that has been dehumanized to the point of not being able to think or choose for themselves."

Today, Ford remembers Ronald Reagan explaining the US government's sale of guns, drugs and even children to foreign countries as being necessary to national security, because it brought in money to fund such black projects as mind control, through which foreign leaders could be manipulated. But attentive to Reagan's naïve nature, Ford believes he was manipulated himself by "the Council," which designed the program as "an international takeover…to insure the future for their own genetically advanced progeny."

Ford's recovery began with a 1985 head-on auto crash. The head injuries she sustained began to induce flashbacks. Believing her husband was under the control of the "men in suits," Ford took her children to the Hawaiian Islands where she attempted to go underground by moving from house to house.

However, after being discovered Ford had to send home the children under threat of a police intervention. She hired an attorney and a bodyguard, but still lost custody of her children by a court order. Broken, Ford returned to the islands and began her journal of recovered memories.

"In 1992 I purchased a light and sound machine of my own," she wrote, "and after mastering the fear associated with using some of the same technology my controllers had used on me, I began to more easily recover even deeper layers of memory."

To date, Ford has spent more than $300,000 on therapy. Most of the major physical ailments she suffered — migraine headaches, chronic sinus infections, sore throats, breathing problems, colitis, stomach aches, nausea and constant fatigue — have disappeared.

Harassment began immediately after she started writing her first book, with taps on her phones and strangers accosting her with threats, according to Ford.

"My car tires were slashed, my mail was tampered with, often held back for months, only to mysteriously arrive in bunches up to two years after the postmark date," she wrote. "Phone messages, powerfully, cryptically encoded and laced with programming intended to keep me under control were played over the phone or recorded on my answering machine....As I ran for my life from state to state, two separate individuals rear-ended my car on the same day, within hours of each other."

Ford suffered two more serious traffic accidents, oddly both occurring on April 12 two years apart.

Ford eventually moved to South Carolina, where she opened a healing center for other victims of mind control. She found through therapy that EEG Neurofeedback was helpful in preventing her from dissociating.

Like her daughter, she has been diagnosed by several therapists with Multiple Personality Disorder. Her attempts to use EEG to help Kelly resulted in such complete catatonia that the teen had to be hospitalized, unable to walk, talk or feed herself.

The harassment continued and on New Years Day, 1998, Ford's Holistic Health Care Clinic burned in a suspicious fire which destroyed the EEG Spectrum equipment she used to help victims. Despite the official report that the fire was due to faulty wiring, Ford decided it was deliberately caused when two bags of ashes mysteriously showed up at her home.

Ford has managed to stay alive by withholding important details from her book, *Thanks for the Memories,* with the threat that they will be revealed in the event of her death. Her book is more than a journal of horrors. It is a warning.

"If there is any one thing I could tell you about the inner workings of the New World Order," she wrote, "it's that it is subtle, organized and calculated. The plan has an agenda that spans generations with obvious long-term goals — as long-term as the intergenerational abuse pattern that was passed down through my family creating within our generational line Multiple Personality Disorder."

Based on what she remembers seeing and hearing, Ford believes the globalist elite can manipulate presidential elections, create celebrities, start wars, destroy nations, incite riots and "kill out a certain ethnic race" through bioweapons.

"These men don't just want to control the world," she wrote. "They already do that to a certain extent....The Council plans are to have a robotic working class that won't cause any problems, but will simply work to supply the needs of the Elite....They figure with the reduction of the population, there will be sufficient natural resources for the working class robots to support the genetically astute intellectuals who will be in power....They also have antibodies against the diseases they let loose [to] make sure they are protected."

Ford also issued a warning to those who join the Freemasons, allowing that they may do so for the best of reasons while remaining ignorant of the agenda dictated by those members at the top.

She maintains that the "secret knowledge" garnered by those at the 32nd and 33rd degree of Freemasonry includes "the ritualized abuse of young women who are raped on an altar as part of an initiation process. I know because I was there.

"I was taken to outdoor places in the '50s and '60s and subjected to satanic rituals performed by various men's fraternal societies, including the Masons and Shriners. I have also known and listened to other women who were healing from this mind control abuse, whose fathers were Masons and through that affiliation came to be young members of Job's Daughters or the Eastern Star, and were healing from the control abuse they suffered in secret."

The incredible story of Susan Ford received some verification from others who claim their Multiple Personality Disorder stems from systematic trauma-induced mind control. They share many details that are striking.

Ford's mother also corroborated some of her story in a special chapter of Susan's book, in which she admits her husband had been severely abused in his childhood and also suffered from Multiple Personality Disorder.

"Often I wanted to believe I was insane," Susan Ford wrote, "and at times I even wished I could choose to live out the rest of my days rocking back and forth in a drugged stupor in some sanitarium....I had moments when I contemplated suicide. But due to the ramifications that act would have had on my children, that was never a choice I could make."

Ford continues her struggle to heal, and to recall and neutralize the incredible memories of what she has suffered and what she has done — much like the woman whose story will provide punctuation to this tale.

"LIZ"

You will recall the woman who calls herself "Liz," featured in the opening chapter of this book. She claims to be a victim of government/military mind control that created a number of alternate personalities, at least several of them trained to kill.

Liz has been diagnosed as suffering from MPD. She refers to herself in the plural as "we," "our" and "us."

Born in Atlantic City, New Jersey, 48 years ago, she claims that her programming took place in Tennessee and in Florida. She continues to regain memories and says it appears from her recent recalls that she was born into an intergenerational program of mind control.

"I think both of my parents and my brothers are all multiples," she tells the author. "I broke off contact about a year and a half ago in deep deprogramming. I don't know about my grandparents, but I assume [they were programmed] because the bloodline is very Irish on my mother's side and my father's side had some Ashkenazi, which is an unusual combination....We have military on both sides of the family. My mother's brother was in the military and there was quite a bit [of military membership] on my father's side. As far as we know they had no official connections to any intelligence agencies, but at this point we're just guessing."

Liz is not absolutely sure when her traumatic programming began. "I've heard a lot of things in deprogramming about when it started," she tells the author. "We don't agree on a lot of ages that have been thrown around.

"I think there are certain ages [that are best for programming], but they started early, really early. My first conscious memory is I just can't breathe. I've relived this. It's called an abreaction and I totally dissociate. I wind up staring at the ceiling attempting to breathe and our mouth is stretched as wide as it can be. We're attempting to take in air and we just can't. It is there the dissociation starts, at the point of death."

Liz has a very clear memory of being among men dressed in "Navy denims" when she was three years old. "Whether they were officially Navy or not, who's to say?" she adds. "But this is when an animal personality was created by them. And there was someone else who had been beaten, a man who also wore denim Navy issue. He'd been tortured. They were coming back and the part we [recall] is that they were coming to finish him off. This took place in New Jersey, 1965."

At age five, when she was in Tennessee, Liz claims she has a conscious memory of an alien abduction.

"There was a lot going on there," she tells the author. "Sexual relationships were in full bloom with our father and our brother at that time. Then we go to Florida and there are more supposed alien abductions. I have very strong memories of this, yet what we think is that the words alien and some others can be interchanged.

"It's really hard to explain. What we suspect was happening in these abductions — I'm not just talking about encounters, but so-called alien abductions where we are taken somewhere — is that it was part of the ritual, because we have flashbacks of being in rituals where people are doing things to us and to other kids. We think that, over time from age five to 10 or 11, we were given alien abduction screens for rituals that were really happening."

Liz's use of the word "screens," mirrors the testimony of other alleged mind control victims who claim that false or screen memories deliberately were programmed into them to blot out true occurrences. The screen memory of an alien abduction would tend to destroy the victim's credibility as insurance against remembering these occurrences.

"Things were being done to us on a table," Liz continues, "and I don't know if we were actually undergoing experimentation by aliens. What I'm saying is that things are being done to us on a table by humans. But as an eight year old child, when you see a gray face come really close to your face, you believe it's an alien and as soon as he appears you immediately totally relax, body, mind, soul. We trust him and what we equate that to later, once the military abductions were evident to us in our teens, was that the alien abduction memories were red flags.

"This [alien] face was very two dimensional, very flat, but we weren't able to see that as a child. And the feeling we got from this was of somebody injecting a kid with valium. So it could have been drugs that made us relax, and the alien could have been on a virtual reality screen, or anything like that. As a child, you don't suspect that. By age eight, we'd already been abused enough that we were totally dissociated. We were very susceptible."

Liz has much more stark memories of her programming during her teenage years. "We started getting memories breaking into our conscious mind that something was wrong, that something else was going on," she adds. "About two and a half years ago we began to get a flooding of the whole history [of our programming], 24 hours a day, basically seven days a week. We wound up buying a tape recorder. It would happen all night. It would happen all day. It would happen consciously. It happened in a rest state. A flood of memories would come back. And what we see now is that some of the alien abductions were ritual. We remember being in a room, heavily drugged on a table, with a large number of men in the room.

"In one case we call it the Gold Bowl. There's a roughly hewn, pitted gold bowl. There are white pills in the gold bowl to which blood was being added to be drunk by these men.

"There was a lot of sexual activity going on. We were covered in semen at one point. It doesn't come back to us like a movie, where there's a beginning, a middle and an end. It doesn't come randomly at all.

"Once we began to see what our own alters were doing, [we saw] they were showing [memories] in sequence and on [time] dates. A date would arrive and we'd have the download. It took a while to see that it's not just randomly that they're showing us [memories]. There was some reason why they were showing us the information."

More than one of Liz's alters showed her at age 18, lying on a table and being tortured.

"You have to understand that at the time we had no conscious understanding of mind control," Liz says. "We didn't know what the hell that was. So through our alter we're re-experiencing this.

"We're on a table. We're naked. We're drugged. We're in a small, bright room. We know things are being put into our mind and taken out of our mind. There are two guys next to us. One wears a white coat. We're certain the guy in front of the door is military because he's wearing khakis. There are two or three men in the background and we're going through this scenario where all of a sudden, really close to our left eye, is what looks like a dinosaur. Its right eye is locked on to our left eye.

"Everything that's happening there is to invoke terror. Whatever this [thing] is would stay throughout our lives. We have encountered it as recently as during the last year. Many times in deep deprogramming it seems to start hitting us really hard. We have encountered not being able to move physically. We feel it crawling on top of us, but if somebody

387

walked into the room, I don't think they'd see it. To us, it seems to involve humans who at times don't seem human. It also involves humans who do seem human. Sometimes we see reptiles and sometimes felines. These are the two threats that are constantly stalking us. We have to admit that it's a real possibility these are planted visions, but they seem real to us. I can't say what it is."

Liz believes that military individuals created her numerous sex alters, including child sex alters. Many of the alters remain unnamed.

"We classify them as fragments," she tells the author. "Some people hold them for a special purpose. They basically have one act that they perform.

"When they're called up they don't have any consciousness of existing in the world. They don't even know it exists. When they take over, all they focus on is what they do. There's no reasoning capacity.

"There's a large group of those and they were some of the first ones to show up [in memory], meaning they began to push through. There is another group of adult alters like that, adult sex alters. They are more age advanced and they also have particular functions.

"The way we see it is that we have many uses, but there are predominant uses. It seems for us that the predominant uses were sexual and kill programming. So far we've discovered four alters that were programmed for killing. They're all adults, the youngest being a teenager around age 18, so she's [got an] adult body but is not quite emotionally mature.

"I recall being inside of places where we were trained, but I remember not so much the training as the doing. But the two [training] things that we know of so far are guns and crushing the windpipe.

"Before we knew who we are, a front alter showed us a spur-of-the-moment trip to a gun range with some people."

Years later, Liz accompanied a boyfriend to his father's shooting range, and with no memory of having ever fired a gun, she put on an extraordinary display of pistol marksmanship. She was so accurate that others at the range approached her and had her try their pistols.

Liz describes to the author what a programmed person experiences before an assassination.

"It's interesting about the combination of kill adrenaline and the sexual energy that comes up with it," she said. This is how she felt during the assassination described in the first chapter of this book.

"When [the memories] come to us," Liz continues, "we feel what the personality that was present experienced. We feel the same desires, and we feel the same feelings of the physical body, because it's our body that this happened in. It's like a dual consciousness. There's more than one of us watching, seeing and experiencing what that alter is showing us. And during that time, there is no reasoning capacity for the alters. The only reasoning capacity is in the programming. And at times it's almost as if the alter is attempting to go somewhere, and then it just shuts off. It's as if what I call the higher part of us is trying to figure out or is recognizing our own past and realizes that there is something wrong, and they're programmed not to. It just shuts right off."

Liz admits to having killed at least one child in what she calls a non-ritual situation.

"It was a father and son," she tells the author, explaining how the memory was retrieved. "We read something about Freemasonry explaining how they threaten and show other members [what could happen to them]. They would do a kill that is broadcast to many and without saying it, they show this is what will happen to you. When everybody sees it in, let's say, the papers, and they see how the body was found, all of those involved know who did it. So the message is sent broadly. And that is where the father and son were involved....We know we were responsible for the man and the boy. He [the boy] was adolescent."

She claims this dual murder was intended to be a message because of the way the bodies were left, dragged by ropes at a beach shoreline. The ropes were tied, one each, to the necks of the man and the boy, who lay in the shallows, discolored from days of exposure and putrefaction. The other ends of the ropes were fastened to separate small metal poles several feet inland of the bodies.

"When the download came, we didn't even believe it was real because it made no conscious sense," Liz explains. "Why would we do that, leaving the bodies near water? After they were killed, there was a rope around their necks and they were pulled near the water. It was only this year that we found a reference made in a book about how Freemasons will hang their murder victims by water. The book said it was a common practice for hundreds of years."

This recalls the death of Vatican financier Roberto Calvi, found hanging above water from the Blackfriars Bridge in London following the Masonic P2 scandal, which was mentioned earlier in this book.

One of the alters in Liz actually approached the wife-mother of the victims in the flashback and led her to the bodies.

"She lost it," Liz remembers. "She was trying to contain herself because we were reading that she was really afraid of us. We had no emotion about it. We believe that it was to warn this woman that her life would be taken as well. We don't know if we were responsible for her death, because there was also a man there that this alter knew as 'Consequences.' We remember that somebody was cleaning up the consequences."

Another of Liz's kill-programmed personalities is called "Alter 14." She says this one is highly focused, incredibly strong and has shown her a murder she apparently committed in a parking lot at night. Although the actual killing never is seen, Liz has watched through Alter 14's memory that she is moving toward a man, totally intent on grasping his windpipe and not just crushing it, but tearing it out.

The man backpedals, repeatedly hitting her arm away as she presses her attack, thinking "finish this quickly." Liz still marvels at the calm confidence of Alter 14, which focuses only on getting her fingers and thumb into a death grip on the man's throat.

Suddenly there is a blackout according to Liz, and her next picture memory is from a personality other than Alter 14, brought forth by the sound of a woman screaming. This new personality sees the screaming woman at the end of the parking lot, and then looks down at the blacktop in front of her to see the dead body of the man she had been attacking.

Liz doesn't know how many murders she allegedly committed. During one flashback, she claims one of her kill alters spent most of the night showing her some of the deeds in a matter-of-fact manner.

"She had a nine millimeter [pistol] at her side," Liz claims. "She showed us how she killed. Turn left. Boom. Turn right. Boom.

"I don't know if everything she showed us actually happened. But [the victims] were always males. She would shoot them in the forehead, just above the eyebrows. It went on for hours, and I think she was telling us that this was her life. There was nothing else to it except turn left, turn right, turn center.

"It appeared to be different men that she killed. It was her saying, 'This is all I know. This is what I do.'"

Remembering these scenes has an awesome effect on Liz, resulting in suicidal urges that she believes have been programmed into her when and if she begins to recall.

According to Liz, sexual programming is tied closely with kill programming. "A lot of times there was sex [with the victim] first, and then the kill came," she tells the author.

This was the pattern used in the killing described in the first chapter of this book. It may or may not have occurred in Las Vegas, although, according to Liz, "We know it was in a casino....When [the target] put his hand on my thigh, another alter takes over at that point.

"In deep deprogramming, it happened many times that one alter's memory of a situation just stops. We realized that in some cases the memories can be of a programming situation or the memory can be of an actual on-task situation.

"This memory was an on-task situation. When the next alter takes over, it's literally like someone throws a black veil [on everything]. You don't remember. You can't see anything after that, because that alter is downloading the memory only of what it's done. But we knew what happened afterward anyway, and we couldn't figure out why, if it stops, that we still know what happened. It took several months in deprogramming to realize that other alters held that information."

The pictures recalled during deprogramming or "downloading" are like video snippets from the point of view of the alter that saw them, according to Liz. There is no set chronology in which she sees herself, for instance, brushing her teeth on the morning of a given memory. The recollections come in brief scenes, jumbled in time.

What Liz has been able to discern from various alters about the killing described in the first chapter is this:

"The alter that was there was this person we call The Kill Alter. We also call her The Wild One, and the reason is that she's a loose cannon. She has this unbelievable sexual energy, but with innocence. She's a lot of guys' wet dream, but she's basically a psychopath when the trigger gets hit. It took us a while to realize that this is the alter that was there [in the casino-hotel], because she keeps coming up when we go back to this memory. She's the youngest alter that we have.

"You've really got to have a reason to kill, and her justification for killing was there in what she kept showing us repeatedly. She's got a snake in her hands. The snake is going to bite her in the face. If she doesn't kill the snake, it will kill her. The snake is a deathly terror.

"Obviously, the snake is phallic. I don't know how the kill part is triggered, but I know why she's doing it because I know what she's seeing. She's seeing a snake that's probably the man's penis near her face when she's performing oral sex. The erect penis that triggers the snake vision in her programming always is at face or eye level and she's got it in her hand. She's always got it in one hand as it comes toward her face. That's when her justification kicks in."

Liz did not recall the assassination itself until recently, when Alter 14 showed her the shocking scene.

"A monologue began of her talking to a man in an obviously sexual situation," Liz tells the author. "After telling him he would be brought to orgasm she tells him that she is going to kill him while he is having it....He thought he was getting kinky sex with some asphyxiation to reach a perverse, exaggerated level of orgasm. What she knew [and] he did not was that he would be killed by strangulation, as this alter has access to the 'right hand grip' that crushes the windpipe."

The man had been willingly tied down for the tryst and according to Liz, Alter 14 carried out her promise, accompanied by intense rage mixed with sexual release.

Who sent her on the mission and why this target was chosen is still a mystery. Liz admits that she was well into her programming by the military at this point.

"I have fragment [memories] of a different kill alter who is sitting in a small room with tables and chairs," she tells the author. "There are men in there, and she knows that they are CIA. Are they really CIA? I can't tell you. But in downloads she has shown us repeatedly that she knows they are CIA men."

Liz believes her long healing process began when she failed in her assignment to kill the family of Dr. A. True Ott, mentioned previously in this book as a radio talk show host who has revealed incendiary information about many government, intelligence and Mormon church activities relating to child trafficking, 9/11 and the JFK assassination. According to Liz, her controllers triggered "one of the most powerful ones [alters] that we're aware of. She is raw and hates humans. She doesn't consider herself human. She's called She-29th because of the date when she showed up."

"We took a big chance," Liz continues, describing what led up to the incident at Dr. Ott's home. "We showed up at a certain type of convention, because our memories were really bleeding through [at that time]. For the last dozen years we began realizing that there was something really bad going on, because we'd been running around the country hiding out. We couldn't keep things together and we were dealing with all kinds of symptoms and memories. So we were attempting to try to find a way to get help.

"The only place we knew we could go to and start talking about military abductions was in UFOlogy. We decided to go to [a UFO convention] in Laughlin, Nevada.

"I remember when I decided to go, getting all kinds of warnings saying do not do this. Do not go. You're outing us. I realized later what our alters were trying to tell us was that we were going to be tracked. They're going to know, because as soon as we walk into a room we're like a neon sign [saying], 'Reprogram me. My memories are coming back. You'd better get me now.' That's what high level slaves are walking into when they enter UFOlogy. They're making an announcement that they've reached the point of breakdown."

Liz actually worked for some pay during the long UFO conference in order to cut costs. Near the end of the gathering, a stranger approached her.

"There was this resonant thing that has happened so many times," she tells the author, "where we wonder, 'Why am I drawn to you?' Within about five minutes, what we call 'hooks' were dropped. He tossed out a few of these [triggers] that let us know he was an operative and that he has more information for us, but he's doing it in a nonchalant way, as if he's just a guy at the conference.

"You have to remember that we're seeking and we're about ready to die [at this time of life]. But we were awake enough to know that he was an operative and we wondered whether he knows what he's doing or does he not know, like us. We started talking about how we have to get together. It was an absolute obsession."

The man lived in Salt Lake City, Utah, at this time. Liz has since come to believe that this man is still under programming and so refused to reveal his name in order to protect him. For our purposes, we shall call him John.

True Ott told the author that he's "90 percent sure [John] is programmed." When Liz first began to see John, he invited her to stay at his large home. He was single, had money and never could explain where the money came from. The man owned a number of guns, according to Liz.

At this time, she had become "obsessed" with True Ott, perhaps due to his radio show and to the recommendations of her host/operative.

"As soon as he said Ott's name, I said I wanted to meet him," Liz tells the author. "In my mind I already felt that Ott knows me and I know him. This man [John] was trying to get us to meet other people, but I said, 'No, just get me to Ott.'

"I stayed five nights at this person's house and things started happening. On two occasions there were other people in the house. On one occasion there was another person and on second occasion there was a group.

"I realize now that this man [John] is a classic bloodline case of mind control. But back then I just wanted to see Ott…who invited us to come over. Before we left, [John] said to me, 'Now.' I remember today that when he said that, my body got this rush. I said, 'Now?' He repeated it, and after I thought for a second I said, 'OK.'"

Ott corroborates Liz's claim that John suddenly came into a lot of money.

"He bought a Hummer and was purchasing a lot of gold, and he was proud of it," Ott tells the author. "He came out [to the Ott home] and showed it to me. Before that he'd always been kind of indigent, living from paycheck to paycheck. I asked, 'Did somebody die?' and he said, 'I've got some relatives who gave me some money,' and that's all he would say about it.

"One day he called me and said, 'I've got something I have to show you. I'm right outside your office door.' I came out and he unwraps a nine millimeter stainless steel semi-automatic pistol, and says, 'This has got you and your family's name on it.' I thought he was offering it as a gift, so I told him I had no use for a handgun. He said, 'You don't understand. This has got your name on it.' Then he put it underneath the seat [of his vehicle]."

The bizarre episode ended abruptly when John hopped into his Hummer and drove away. Within days, he called Ott and said he had someone he wanted to introduce to him. This led to Ott's first meeting with Liz.

When she and John arrived at the Ott family home, the music of Led Zeppelin was playing loudly in their car. Liz claims this music was part of her programming, especially when played at almost ear-shattering levels.

"There was a nine millimeter [pistol] in the car under the seat," Liz tells the author. "We have no conscious memory of him telling us it was there. We just knew it. We went inside and started talking to Ott, but the whole while the same words kept repeating inside of us that, 'Time is of the essence.' Along with this we kept hearing, 'We don't want to do this.'"

Ott recalls their first meeting.

"She was dressed extremely provocatively," he told the author. "She exuded, 'I'm sexy, sexy.' [John] had told me she had a story to tell, but when she came into my house, she freaked out. She said, 'I gotta' go! I gotta' get out of here!' So they left.

"I have to explain that my home office is like a fortress. There's a lot of steel and bedrock in the walls and around the office I have some Hopi prayer wheels that were given to me by a Hopi friend, who said they would keep me spiritually safe.

"I think when she entered into that sanctum, she just kind of flashed back where she couldn't go through with what she was programmed to do. She went out of programming and broke down outside, sobbing. She finally said, 'I can't do what I've been assigned to do to your family.' She admitted that she was supposed to take that nine millimeter gun and kill my wife and daughters."

Ott told Liz that he was not surprised why she had come. He told her, "You're not the first one that was sent to do this." Ott recalls Liz then asking him, "How the hell do I get out of this? I don't want to do this anymore. I know I've done it more than once."

Liz and Ott met sporadically over a period of days as he attempted to help her, and at times they were alone. Ott admitted that he knew she was a mind control victim. Liz told him repeatedly that she was going to do something that she didn't want to.

"I remember being in his office and starting to cry, saying 'We don't want to do this,'" she adds.

After a handful of days, Ott disappeared. He took his family away without leaving word.

"I have a contact in DC that knows what's going on," Ott tells the author. "He simultaneously warned me that there was an assassin coming and that I should go. So we took a little vacation."

The contact, according to Ott, has sources within the CIA, and he has no doubts that the Agency was at least partially behind the assassination attempt.

"It's that Mormon rogue element," says Ott.

Liz continues: "At that time we moved out of the house in Salt Lake City because there was no doubt by then that the man [John] who lived there was a handler. We never were supposed to leave Salt Lake. We were to be in his home with him and be under reprogramming, and when we decided to drive away, we got hit on the road by a sleep program.

"It was in the middle of the day when we fell asleep at the wheel like a light switch going off. An 18-wheel truck coming the other way kept honking the horn and woke us in time. After that we rolled down the windows to keep awake."

Liz is positive today that the sleep program was intended to kill her for breaking away from her control in Salt Lake City and seeking treatment. However, she would have no contact with Ott for eight months, because he knew that Liz intended to murder his entire family in front of him. Liz claims her alter, She-29th, later revealed the truth to her.

"It was to shut him up," she says of the plan to kill Ott's family. "They didn't want to take him out at first. They would, but first they wanted him on his knees. Those were the words: 'Bring him to his knees.'

"We were to go in the house and whoever was there — he had a wife, a son and two daughters — would have a She-29th bloodbath. It was basically to destroy him internally by making him watch [the murders]. And if he didn't comply, he would go down as well.

"But they really wanted him on their side. They've always wanted him on their side. And to this day, I don't know who 'they' are. I could name some persons who were involved with me, but as far as naming the person who said, 'I want Ott on his knees,' I don't have a name. But our affiliation seems to flow into at least three branches of military — Army, Air Force and Navy — directly through individuals or locations, and the CIA. We also have Mormon church associations."

Ott corroborated Liz's story to the author.

"I felt they don't really want to kill me, but they want to get to my family," he said. "They admitted they didn't want to kill me and make me a martyr. They said they just wanted to ruin my support base. I told them when we first met that they fear me, but I don't fear them.

"There was not [a crucial moment] on my side, but I believe there was on her side. She's not the only one that has come to get us. There have been others, and they couldn't do it for whatever reason. I was told at the moment of crunch time, they couldn't do it. I think it was divine intervention."

There were at least two prior assassination attempts, according to Ott.

"They tracked and followed me," he told the author. "They sabotaged my vehicles. When I was out walking, I had bullets whiz close by me twice. According to my guy [contact] in Washington, it's amazing because these guys just don't miss."

Ott believes the globalist elites have made extraordinary use of mind control techniques in creating virtual human robots because, "The thing they fear the worst is that 'The barbarians will band together.' They do fear that people will waken and band together. I don't think the Tea Party movement was in their agenda. Everybody can have a change of heart. I don't believe anybody is too far gone."

Today, Liz continues her healing process in a rural portion of Utah. Having met her, one can see plainly that she's been emotionally shattered by her experiences since early childhood.

She cries easily and often. She is fearful much of the time. She continues to deal with alternate personalities that occasionally surface, often terrified that some untapped program for violence against others or against herself will emerge.

In short, she is precisely like all of the men and women featured previously in this section, and the uncounted others who have suffered systematic torture since early youth — all in the interest of creating utterly controllable human beings to be used by those few who consider themselves godlike, and the rest of humanity as livestock.

It is fitting to finally use a quote from the Bible:

"By their deeds ye shall know them."

We pray that the preceding has caused you to know them, while there is still time.

Epilogue - *Canto Firmo*

"All that is necessary for the triumph of evil is that good men do nothing."

—Edmund Burke

In 1773 Mayer Amschel Bauer (Rothschild) met with 12 wealthy and influential men in Frankfurt, Germany, and produced a set of 25 "instructions" for achieving a New World Order, which has been discussed in an earlier chapter. The revision of this plan by Adam Weishaupt some years later in his *Einige Original-Scripten* also has been covered. This latter document came into the hands of the Bavarian authorities and so horrified them that they expelled the members of Weishaupt's Illuminati from their region.

A condensed version of the 25 Illuminati instructions was published in the book, *Pawns in the Game,* by William Guy Carr. Based on what has been written in this book, *Battle Hymn,* it is frighteningly obvious how close those instructions of the 238-year-old master plan have come to fruition:

(1) Because the majority of men are inclined toward evil rather than good, the best means of governing them is through violence and terrorism. Law is force in disguise. By the laws of nature, right lies in force.

(2) Political freedom is an idea, not a fact. To usurp political power, liberalism must be preached to the electorate, convincing them to yield some of their power and prerogatives to us.

(3) The power of gold usurps the power of liberal rulers. Freedom has replaced faith, but the people do not know how to use it in moderation. Because of this, we may use the idea of freedom to foment class wars. It is immaterial to our plan whether established governments are destroyed by internal or external foes, because the victor will have need of the capital which is in our hands.

(4) The use of any and all means to reach our goal is justified. The

ruler who governs by a moral code is not a skilled politician. Those who wish to rule must be cunning and understand that frankness and honesty are vices in politics.

(5) Our right lies in force. The word right is an abstract. The new right is to attack by the right of the strong, and to destroy all existing forces of order and regulation. We must become the sovereign Lord of all those who gave us the rights to their powers by laying them down voluntarily in their liberalism.

(6) The power of our resources must remain invisible until the moment it has gained such strength that no cunning or force can undermine it. Deviation from this will bring to naught the labors of centuries.

(7) The might of the mob is blind, senseless, unreasoning and always at the mercy of suggestion from any side. Only a despotic ruler can control the mob efficiently because without absolute despotism, there can be no existence for civilization. The moment the mob seizes freedom, it turns to anarchy.

(8) We must corrupt the morals of the youth of the nations through alcoholic liquors, drugs, moral corruption and all forms of vice. Special *agenturs* should be trained as tutors, lackeys, governesses, clerks and women in places of dissipation frequented by the *goyim* [gentiles]. Among the women, count the so-called society ladies who follow others in corruption and luxury. We must not stop at bribery, deceit and treachery when they serve the attainment of our ends.

(9) We have the right to seize property by any means and without hesitation in order to secure submission and sovereignty. Our state has the right to replace the horrors of war by less noticeable and more satisfactory sentences of death necessary to maintain the kind of terror that produces blind submission.

(10) There is no place in nature for Equality, Liberty and Fraternity. These words are abstracts to be used by us to control the legions which bear our banners with enthusiasm. On the ruins of existing aristocracies we will set up an aristocracy of money. The qualification for this aristocracy is the wealth which is dependent upon us.

(11) It is our policy to foment wars and to direct the subsequent peace conferences so that neither of the combatants gains territory. Wars must be directed so that the nations engaged on both sides should be placed further in our debt and in the power of our *agenturs.*

(12) Our wealth must be used to choose candidates for public office

who are servile and obedient to our commands. They must be used as pawns by the learned and ingenious men we will appoint to operate behind the scenes of government as official advisors. The men we appoint as advisors will have been bred, reared and trained from childhood in accordance with our ideas to rule the affairs of the whole world.

(13) Our wealth should be used to control all outlets of public information while remaining in the shade, safe from blame regardless of the repercussions due to publication of libels, slanders and untruths.

(14) When social and economic conditions reach their lowest ebb and the masses are subjugated by want and terror, our *agentur* should appear on the scene. He will restore order in such a way that the victims will believe they have been the prey of criminals and irresponsibles. By executing the criminals and lunatics after they have carried out our preconceived reign of terror, we can make ourselves appear as the saviors of the oppressed and the champions of the workers.

(15) We must bring about industrial depressions and financial panics to serve our purposes. Enforced unemployment and hunger imposed on the masses because of the power we have to create shortages of food will create the right of capital to rule more surely than the aristocracy of kings. Once our *agentur* controls the mob, the mob can be used to wipe out all who stand in our way.

(16) We must take advantage of the facilities and secrecy that Freemasonry has to offer. We must organize our own Grand Orient Lodges within Freemasonry in order to carry out subversive activities under the cloak of philanthropy without revealing the true nature of our work. All members of our Grand Orient Lodges must be used to spread our atheistic-materialistic ideology.

(17) Our *agentur* must be trained to use high sounding phrases and popular slogans to assist in creating systematic deceptions. We should make lavish promises, for the opposite of what has been promised can always be done afterwards. By using such words as Freedom and Liberty, the people can be stirred up to such a pitch of patriotic fervor that they could be made to fight even against the laws of God and nature. For this reason, after we obtain control the very name of God will be erased from the lexicon of life.

(18) Every revolution must be accompanied by war, street fighting and a systematic reign of terror because this is the most economical way to bring the population to speedy subjection.

(19) We must insist upon secret diplomacy following all wars in order that our *agentur,* masquerading as political, financial and economic advisors, can carry out our mandates without fear of exposing who are the secret powers behind national and international affairs. By secret diplomacy, we must obtain such control that the nations cannot come to even an inconsiderable private agreement without our secret agents having a hand in it.

(20) Ultimate world government is our goal. To reach this goal, it will be necessary to establish huge monopolies, reservoirs of such colossal riches that even the largest fortunes of the wealthy will depend on us to such an extent that they will go to the bottom together with the credits of their governments on the day after the great political smash.

(21) A combination of high taxes and unfair competition must be implemented to bring about economic ruin of nations in their financial interests and investments. This can be achieved through careful control of raw materials, organized agitation among the workers for shorter hours and higher pay, and by subsidizing competitors. We must see to it that the increased worker wages will not benefit them in any way.

(22) Armaments should be supplied to the nations on a colossal scale for the purpose of making them destroy each other. In the end, there will be only the masses of the proletariat left in the world, with a few millionaires devoted to our cause, and police and soldiers sufficient to protect our interests.

(23) Members of the One World Government will be appointed by the Dictator, who will choose men from among the scientists, the economists, the financiers, the industrialists, and from the millionaires, because in substance, everything will be settled by the question of figures.

(24) It is vital to capture the interest of youth. Our *agenturs* should infiltrate into all classes and levels of society and government for the purpose of fooling, bemusing and corrupting the younger members of society by teaching them theories and principals we know to be false.

(25) National and international laws should not be changed, but should be used as they are to destroy existing civilization by twisting them into a contradiction of the interpretation, which first masks the law and then hides it altogether. Our ultimate aim is to substitute arbitration for law.

In more modern terms, Zbigniew Brzezinski, CFR member and former National Security advisor, warned his cohorts in the shadows:

"To put it in a terminology that harkens back to the more brutal age of ancient empires, the three grand imperatives of imperial geo-strategy are to prevent collusion and maintain security dependence among the vassals, to keep tributaries pliant and protected, and to keep the barbarians from coming together."

Regarding this fear of a popular uprising against their plans, the 18th century Illuminati wrote of creating an "underground" called "The Metropolitans," which would be established "in the capitals and the cities of all countries before that danger threatens."

Is it not time to create that danger?

Afterword
by Dane Phillips

"...et ne nos inducas in tentationem, sed libera nos a malo."

—The Lord's Prayer

"And Elijah came to all the people, and said, 'How long will you falter between two opinions? If the Lord is God, follow Him; but if Baal, follow him.' But the people answered him not a word."

—1 Kings 18 verse 21 (Old Testament of the Holy Bible)

I have written you seeking to impart vital information concerning the New World (Global) Order. What you have read might well have changed you and reset your priorities—for this is a story of global tragedy and hope that began with the origins of the Rothschild banking dynasty in mid 18th century Germany that revealed how members of this and other banking families financially influenced and cunningly manipulated nations for nearly 240 years of world history and what this means to all of us today.

You've been confronted with information your sensibilities probably wanted to resist. And well they should, for this is no ordinary Orwellian tale.

Initially, I too raised an arm of caution to shield myself from what I was reading. As compelling as this information is, my comfort level was at risk, my priorities were called into question and the life I knew was changing.

The truth hit hard.

Eventually, the barriers crumbled, falling from the weight of my personal discovery amidst the knowledge of what others learned long ago. What I discovered is not inaccessible or new. It's just beyond plain view. And who's been looking?

For many years, our government has kept vital information away from the American people. The hidden satanic forces behind Washington's political stage hold the illusion of choice while concealing the truth. Therefore, transparency, always the companion of truth, suffers from our elected representatives' neglect.

The very foundation of our Constitution was planted in the soil of this transparency. Where, then, is it written in our Constitution that truth be hidden behind drawn curtains of privacy and privilege for reasons of "national security?" There is no such seed of secrecy planted into our Constitution.

The responsibilities of daily living make us all easy prey for deception. We simply lack the time to think about anything that is hidden from us—until there's an awakening.

Author, James Perloff warned that a monumental battle is shaping up between the Kingdom of Christ and the Antichrist: *"An evil, one-world government—the kingdom of the Antichrist. Many notables of the American Establishment have given themselves over to one side in this conflict, and it is not the side that ancient scriptures recommend. Whether or not they are conspirators, whether they are conscious or not of the ultimate consequences of their actions, their powerful influence has helped move the world toward apocalyptic events."*

Consequently, gale force winds are rising throughout Washington for one reason: to confiscate all of our Constitutional liberties by way of martial law for the sole purpose of establishing a New World Order. This global cartel serves a dark spirit hidden just beneath the surface. Cartel members labor tirelessly in building a massive stage worthy of their coming world leader.

The construction materials used by them come from our academic, agricultural, diplomatic, economic, media, military, pharmaceutical, political, religious and scientific communities. Workmen with names like Aldrich, Aquino, Astor, Bernanke, Brzezinski, Buffett, Bush, Carter, Casey, Cheney, Clinton, Coy, Disney, Drucker, Du Pont, Fromm, Gates, Geithner, Graham, Greenspan, Hamilton, Heitzig, Helms, Hitler, Hoover, Hybels, Kissinger, Kolvenbach, Laurie, McLaren, Morgan, Murdock, Nixon, Obama, Paulson, Ratzinger, Reagan, Reid, Rockefeller, Roosevelt, Rothschild, Rumsfeld, Silverstein, Smith, Sweet, Truman, Turner, Vanderbilt, Warburg, Warren, Wilson and Windsor have worked side by side to enslave all of us — including Pastor Chuck, who led me to Christ.

They use tools labeled Bilderberg, Billy Graham Evangelical Association, Bohemian Grove, *Christianity Today*, CIA, CNP, Committee of 300, Council on Foreign Relations, DARPA, Emergent Church, FBI, Federal Reserve System, FEMA, Freemasons, HAARP, Harvest Crusade, IRS, JDL, Illuminati, Jesuits, Knights of the Garter/Malta, LDS, NBA, NFL, Operation Paperclip, Opus Dei, Project MK-ULTRA/Monarch, Purpose Driven, Quantum Spirituality, Round

Table Group, Skull and Bones, SRA, Tavistock Institute, Trilateral Commission, Trinity Broadcasting Network, Watchtower Society and *Worship Leader* Magazine to fasten the evil of Fascism and Zionism into a one-world collective Luciferian/totalitarian state. The leader that ascends to this sinister stage will command absolute subordination from every single human being on this planet — including you..

"He causes all, both small and great, rich and poor, free and slave, to receive a mark on their right hand or on their foreheads, and that no one may buy or sell except one who has the mark or the name of the beast or the number of his name. Here is wisdom. Let him who has understanding calculate the number of the beast, for it is the number of a man."

—Revelation 13: verses 16-18 (New Testament of the Holy Bible)

The seed of this world ruler was planted long ago in soil absent of any vigilance — born, raised and nourished on a diet poisoned rich in consistent neglect and prepared by our elected representatives. A standard, absent of any care, grew the seed into a man. The dark spirit beneath the surface, the primary architect and stage maker is Satan. The man is the Antichrist, *"His number is 666."*—Revelation 13: verse 18 (New Testament of the Holy Bible)

This is a story of what our world truly is, how it got there and most importantly, where we go from here. This book was not written to put you at ease. Its purpose was twofold: to warn you of the present and rising storm while calling your attention to the eternal hope for those carrying the faith of our Founding Fathers. However, before you can receive the blessing, you'll be called upon to deal with the evil thorns.

At the website, www.BattleHymn.com, you will find the original *Battle Hymn* document. This document contains over 3,522 quotes, 93 vital informational videos, links to 30 websites, 18 music videos, 13 core documents and seven search phrases. The companion site, BBNWorldNews.com, provides vital breaking news, films, videos and documents. The information in these sites is the key to this work.

My personal discovery started on March 17, 2010. By simply typing "Federal Reserve," followed by "Rothschild," then the key phrase "Federal Reserve System and the Rothschild family," into Google Search, I was impressed by the variety of information available. I recall thinking, "Let's have a look." It didn't take long to realize that a group of powerful men came together many years ago for the express purpose of destroying our Constitution.

I began to write as I read and watched videos well into the morning of the next day. I was completely shaken by my discovery and instinctively knew I needed to speak to my family and friends. The first night provided the inspiration for what was to become *Battle Hymn,* simply because we all need to know the truth.

Though the Luciferian/Zionist Rothschild and Rockefeller families are cast at center stage, this tragic story runs much deeper than the moral breakdown of any one particular family. This story is not at all anti-Semitic—God loves the Jewish people and so do I.

However, politically, Zionism seeks to separate the Jewish people from their God, render the Divine Covenant null and void and substitute a modern statehood and fraudulent sovereignty in place of the principles taught in the Torah and Talmud. The Jewish people were chosen by God to set an example of moral behavior and spiritual purity. Zionism rose from the depths of hell. Its followers claim they are Jews. They are not.

Our one and only hope lies in the answer to these four eternal questions: Does God exist? Does He know me? Does He care? Is He willing to pay the price for what I have done? The answers lie in the bedrock at the foot of the Cross. By the Power of the Holy Spirit, may He impart to you the necessity and reason for having paid the cost.

To all of you: Remember, *the battle is truly all His.* It is not the American people, or those who follow Christ, who Satan and his minions of evil men have cursed and defiled with their deceitful, arrogant and evil crimes. The treachery and treason I speak of has been spit into the face of the one true living God—our eternal Father, Jesus Christ and the Holy Spirit.

The judgment day of the Lord is coming and is even at the door. **A true New World Order will be established at the second coming of Jesus Christ,** replacing the counterfeit world order spoken of in *Battle Hymn.*

"I tremble for my country when I reflect that God is just, that His justice cannot sleep forever."

—President Thomas Jefferson

President Andrew Jackson's Final Words to you.
*"**Providence has showered on this favored land blessings without number**, and has chosen you as the guardians of freedom to preserve it*

*for the benefit of the human race. May He who holds in His hands the destinies of nations make you worthy of the favors He has bestowed and enable you, with **pure hearts** and **pure hands** and sleepless vigilance, **to guard and defend to the end of time** the great charge He has committed to your keeping. My own race is nearly run; advanced age and failing health warn me that before long I must pass beyond the reach of human events and cease to feel the vicissitudes of human affairs. I thank God that my life has been spent in a land of liberty and that He has given me a heart to love my country with the affection of a son. And filled with gratitude, for your constant and unwavering kindness, **I bid you a last and affectionate farewell.***"

—The final words of President Andrew Jackson's Farewell Address spoken to you, 174 years ago on March 4, 1837.

Dane Phillips
Summerlin, Nevada
2011

BIBLIOGRAPHY

Allen, Gary, *The Rockefeller File* ('76 Press, 1976)

Anderson, Paul, "The Aspen Institute: A 'Private University' Running the World from High in the Rockies?" (*Aspen Times Weekly*, July 25-26, 1998)

Baigent, Michael and Leigh, Richard, *The Temple and the Lodge* (Arcade Publishing, 1989)

Bain, Donald, *The Control of Candy Jones* (Playboy Press, 1976)

Batten, Samuel Zane, *The New World Order* (General Books, LLC, 2010)

Bowart, Walter, *Operation Mind Control* (Dell Publishing, 1978)

Brzezinski, Zbigniew, *Between Two Ages: America's Role in the Technocratic Era* (Greenwood Press, 1982)

Cantril, Hadley, *The Human Dimension: Experiences in Policy Research* (Rutgers University Press, 1967)

Carr, William Guy, *Pawns in the Game* (Noontide Press, 2007)

Churchill, Winston, *The World Crisis* (Scribner's Sons, 1949)

Coleman, Dr. John, *Conspirators' Hierarchy: The Story of the Committee of 300* (America West Publishers, 1992)

Congressional Record, Volume 54 (February 9, 1917)

DeCamp, John W., *The Franklin Cover-Up* (AWT Inc., 1992)

"Doe, John," *Report from Iron Mountain on the Possibility and Desirability of Peace* (The Dial Press, 1967)

Domhoff, William, *The Bohemian Grove and Other Retreats: A Study in Ruling-Class Cohesiveness* (Harper-Collins College Division, 1975)

Epperson, A. Ralph, *The Unseen Hand: An Introduction to the Conspiratorial View of History* (Publius Press, 1985)

Epperson, A. Ralph, *Masonry, Conspiracy Against Christianity* (Publius Press, 1997)

Epperson, A. Ralph, *The New World Order* (Publius Press, 1990)

Eringer, Robert, *The Global Manipulators* (Pentacle Books, 1980)

Estulin, Daniel, *The True Story of the Bilderberg Group* (TrineDay, LLC, 2009)

Ferguson, Niall, *The House of Rothschild* (Viking, 1998)

Finney, Ross Lee, *A Sociological Philosophy of Education* (The

MacMillan Co., 1929)

Fuller, R. Buckminster, *Critical Path* (St. Martin's Press, 1981)

Gibson, Donald, *Battling Wall Street: The Kennedy Presidency* (Sheridan Square Press, 1994)

Goldwater, Barry, *With No Apologies* (William Morrow Co., 1979)

Grant, Madison, and Osborn, Henry Fairfield, *The Passing of the Great Race: Or, the Racial Basis of European History* (Nabu Press, 2010)

Greider, William, *Secrets of the Temple: How the Federal Reserve Runs the Country* (Simon & Schuster, 1987)

Greider, William, *One World, Ready or Not* (Simon & Schuster, 1997)

Griffin, G. Edward, *The Fearful Master* (Western Islands, 1964)

Halberstam, David, *The Best and the Brightest* (Random House, 1972)

Hall, Manly P., *The Secret Teachings of All Ages* (The Philosophical Research Society, 1988)

Hammer, Richard, *The Vatican Connection* (Charter Books, 1982)

Haslam, Edward T., *Mary, Ferrie & the Monkey Virus: The Story of an Underground Medical Laboratory* (Wordsworth Communications, 1997)

Henry, William, *One Foot in Atlantis* (Earthpulse Press, 1998)

Higham, Charles, *Trading with the Enemy: An Expose of the Nazi-American Money Plot* (Delacorte Press, 1983)

Hougan, Jim, *Secret Agenda: Watergate, Deep Throat and the CIA* (Random House, 1984)

Isaacson, Walter and Thomas, Evan, *The Wise Men* (Simon & Schuster, 1986)

Katz, Howard S., *The Warmongers* (Books in Focus, Inc., 1979)

Katz, Jacob, *Jews and Freemasonry in Europe* (Harvard Press, 1970)

Levenda, Peter, *Unholy Alliance* (Avon Books, 1995)

Loftus, John, and Aarons, Mark, *The Secret War Against the Jews: How Western Espionage Betrayed the Jewish People* (St. Martins, Griffin, 1997)

Lynes, Barry, *The Cancer Cure That Nearly Worked* (Marcus Books, 1981)

Mackey, Albert Gallatin, *The History of Freemasonry* (Gramercy Books, 1996)

Marrs, Jim, *Rule by Secrecy* (Harper Collins, 2000)

Marrs, Jim, *Above Top Secret* (The Disinformation Co., Ltd., 2008)

Marrs, Jim, *The Rise of the Fourth Reich* (Harper Collins, 2008)

Marrs, Jim, *Inside Job: Unmasking the 9/11 Conspiracies* (Origin Press, 2004)

Martin, James Stewart, *All Honorable Men* (Little Brown, 1950)

McMaster, H.R., *Dereliction of Duty* (Harper Perennial, 1997)

Morton, Frederic, *The Rothschilds: A Family Portrait* (Atheneum, 1962)

Moscow, Alvin, *The Rockefeller Inheritance* (Doubleday & Company, Inc., 1977)

Mullins, Eustace, *The Secrets of the Federal Reserve* (Bankers Research Institute, 1983)

Ollinger, Crenshaw, "The Knights of the Golden Circle," *The American Historical Review* (Volume XLVII, No.1, October, 1941)

Parenti, Michael, *Inventing Reality: The Politics of the Mass Media* (St. Martin's Press, 1986)

Perloff, James, *The Shadows of Power: The Council on Foreign Relations and the American Decline* (Western Islands, 1988)

Perry, Roland, *The Fifth Man* (Sidgwick & Jackson, 1994)

Pool, James, *Who Financed Hitler: The Secret Funding of Hitler's Rise to Power* (Pocket Books, 1997)

Prouty, L. Fletcher, *The Secret Team: The CIA and Its Allies in Control of the United States and the World* (Prentice-Hall, Inc., 1973)

Quigley, Carroll, *Tragedy and Hope: A History of the World in Our Time* (MacMillan, 1966)

Quigley, Carroll, *The World Since 1939: A History* (Collier Books, 1968)

Ravenscroft, Trevor, *The Spear of Destiny* (Samuel Weiser, Inc., 1973)

Rostow, Walt, *The United States in the World Arena: An Essay in Recent History* (Harper and Brothers, 1960)

Russell, Bertrand, *The Impact of Science on Society* (Unwin Hyman Co., 1988)

Sanger, Margaret, *The Pivot of Civilization* (Echo Library, 2006)

Schlafly, Phyllis and Ward, Chester, *Kissinger on the Couch* (Arlington House, 1975)

Schmidt, Helmut, *Men and Power: A Political Retrospective* (Jonathan Cape, Ltd. 1990)

Simpson, Colin, *The Lusitania* (Little, Brown & Company, 1972)

Speer, Albert, *Inside the Third Reich* (The MacMillan Company, 1970)

Still, William T., *New World Order: The Ancient Plan of Secret Societies* (Huntington House Publishers, 1990)

Sutton, Anthony C. and Wood, Patrick M., *Trilaterals over*

Washington (The August Corp., 1979)

Sutton, Anthony C., *America's Secret Establishment: An Introduction to the Order of Skull & Bones,* (TrineDay Publishing, 2004)

Tarpley, Webster Griffin and Chaitkin, Anton, *George Bush: The Unauthorized Biography* (Executive Intelligence Review, 1992)

Taylor, Brice (Ford, Susan), *Thanks for the Memories* (Brice Taylor Trust, 1999)

Toland, John, *Adolf Hitler* (Doubleday & Company, Inc., 1976)

Vanderlip, Frank, *From Farmboy to Financier* (D. Appleton Century, Inc., 1935)

Vankin, Jonathan and Whalen, John, *The Fifty Greatest Conspiracies of All Time: History's Biggest Mysteries, Cover-Ups and Cabals* (Citadel Press, 1994)

Vierek, George Sylvester, *The Strangest Friendship in History: Woodrow Wilson and Colonel House* (Liveright Publishers, 1932)

Wells, H.G., *The New World Order* (Hesperides Press, 2006)

Wilson, Derek, *Rothschild: The Wealth and Power of a Dynasty* (Charles Scribner's Sons, 1988)

Wilson, Robert Anton, *The Illuminati Papers* (Ronin Publishing, 1997)

Wise, David and Ross, Thomas B., *The Invisible Government* (Vintage Books, 1974)

CPSIA information can be obtained at www.ICGtesting.com
Printed in the USA
BVOW021144300911

272216BV00002B/3/P